lonely planet

Venice & the Veneto

"All you've got to do is decide to go
and the hardest part is over.

So go!"

TONY WHEELER, COFOUNDER – LONELY PLANET

D0311460

PETER DRAGICEVICH, PAULA HARDY

Feb 2020

Contents

Plan Your Trip   4

Explore Venice & the Veneto   46

Understand Venice & the Veneto   203

Survival Guide   243

Venice Maps   272

i

(left) **Basilica di San Marco p52** Aerial view of the basilica and square

....

(above) **Verona p176** View from the Adige river

....

(right) **Carnevale p20** Elaborate festive masks

....

Murano, Burano & the Northern Islands p148

Cannaregio p107

San Polo & Santa Croce p90

Dorsoduro p73

San Marco p50

Castello p121

Giudecca, Lido & the Southern Islands p138

Welcome to Venice & the Veneto

Imagine the audacity of building a city of marble palaces on a lagoon – and that was only the start.

Epic Grandeur

Never was a thoroughfare so aptly named as the Grand Canal, reflecting the glories of centuries of Venetian architecture in the 50 palazzi and six churches lining its banks. At the end of Venice's signature S-shaped waterway, the Palazzo Ducale and Basilica di San Marco add double exclamation points. But wait until you see what's hiding in the narrow backstreets: neighbourhood churches lined with Veroneses and priceless marbles, convents graced with ethereal Bellinis, Tiepolo's glimpses of heaven on homeless-shelter ceilings, and a Titian painting that mysteriously lights up an entire basilica.

Venetian Feasts

Garden islands and lagoon aquaculture yield speciality produce and seafood you won't find elsewhere – all highlighted in inventive Venetian cuisine. The city knows how to put on a royal spread, as France's King Henry III once found out when faced with 1200 dishes and 200 bonbons. Today such feasts are available in miniature at happy hour, when bars mount lavish spreads of *cicheti* (Venetian tapas). Save room and time for a proper sit-down Venetian meal, with lagoon seafood to match views at canalside bistros and toasts with Veneto's signature bubbly, prosecco.

An Artful Lifestyle

The Piazza San Marco is Venice's showstopper, but you need time to see what else Venice is hiding. Stay longer in this fairy-tale city and you'll discover the pleasures of *la bea vita* (the beautiful life) that only locals know: the wake-up call of the gondoliers' 'Ooooeeeee!', a morning *spritz* in a sunny *campo* (square), lunch in a crowded *bacaro* (bar) with friends and fuschia-pink sunsets that have sent centuries of artists mad.

Defying Convention

Eyeglasses, platform shoes and uncorseted dresses were all outlandish Venetian fashions that critics sniffed would never be worn by respectable Europeans. Venetians are used to setting trends, whether it be with controversial artwork in the Punta della Dogana, racy operas at La Fenice or radical new tech start-ups. On a smaller scale, this unconventional creative streak finds vibrant expression in the showrooms of local artisans where you can find custom-made red-carpet shoes, purses fashioned from silk-screened velvet, and glass jewels brighter than semiprecious stones. In a world of cookie-cutter culture, Venice's originality still stands out.

Why I Love Venice

By Paula Hardy, Writer

My love of Venice begins with the lagoon in which it stands. Although often overlooked, this 550-sq-km shallow bowl is as great a marvel of engineering as San Marco's golden domes. Every palace and every person is reflected in its teal-coloured waters, creating the mirage-like double image that lends the city its magical quality. Not only has it inspired the extraordinary physical fabric of the city and countless creative and technological inventions, but it also shapes the unconventional and creative spirit of all who reside here. Therein lie possibilities barely imagined in other cities.

For more about our writers, see p296.

Top: Basilica di Santa Maria della Salute (p78)

Venice & the Veneto's
Top 10

Basilica di San Marco (p52)

1 Early risers urge you to arrive when morning sunlight bathes millions of *tesserae* (mosaic tiles) with an other-worldly glow, and jaws drop to semiprecious-stone floors. Sunset romantics lobby you to linger in Piazza San Marco until fading sunlight shatters portal mosaics into golden shards, and the Caffè Florian house band strikes up the tango. Yet no matter how you look at it, the basilica is a marvel. Two eyes may seem insufficient to absorb 800 years of architecture and 8500 sq metres of mosaics – Basilica di San Marco will stretch your sense of wonder.

👁

Palazzo Ducale (p55)

2 Other cities have government buildings; Venice has the Palazzo Ducale, a monumental propaganda campaign. To reach the halls of power, you must pass the Scala dei Censori (Stairs of the Censors) and Sansovino's staircase lined with 24-carat gold, then wait in a Palladio-designed hall facing Tiepolo's *Venice Receiving Gifts of the Sea from Neptune*. Veronese's *Juno Bestowing her Gifts on Venice* graces the trial chambers of the Consiglio dei Dieci (Council of Ten), Venice's CIA. Upstairs is the Piombi attic-prison, where Casanova was confined in 1756 until his escape.

👁

Tintoretto's Heaven on Earth (p92)

3 During Venice's darkest days of the Black Death, flashes of genius appeared. Tintoretto's loaded paintbrush streaks across 50 dramatic ceiling scenes inside the Scuola Grande di San Rocco like a lightning bolt, revealing glimmers of hope in the long shadow of the plague that reduced Venice's population by a third. Downstairs scenes from the story of the Virgin Mary adorn the vast assembly hall, starting with the *Annunciation* and culminating in a brooding *Assumption* where angels lift Mary heavenwards amid a turbulent, stormy sky.

Opera at Teatro La Fenice (p63)

4 Before the curtain rises, the drama has already begun at La Fenice. Wraps shed in lower-tier boxes reveal jewels, while in top *loggie* (balconies), *loggione* (opera critics) predict which singers will be in good voice, and which understudies may merit promotions. Meanwhile, architecture aficionados debate whether the theatre's faithful reconstruction after its 1996 arson attack was worth €90 million. But when the overture begins, all voices hush. No one wants to miss a note of performances that could match premieres here by Stravinsky, Rossini, Prokofiev and Britten.

Gallerie dell'Accademia (p75)

5 They've been censored and stolen, raised eyebrows and inspired generosity: all the fuss over Venetian paintings becomes clear at the Accademia. The Inquisition did not appreciate Venetian versions of biblical stories – especially Veronese's *Last Supper,* a wild dinner party of drunkards, dwarves, dogs, Turks and Germans alongside apostles. But Napoleon quite enjoyed Venetian paintings, warehousing them here as booty. Wars and floods took their toll, but international donations have restored Sala dell'Albergo's crowning glory: Titian's *Presentation of the Virgin in the Temple,* where a young Madonna inspires Venetian merchants to help the needy.

La Biennale di Venezia *(p41)*

6 When Venice dared the world to show off its modern masterpieces, delegations from Australia to Venezuela accepted the challenge. Today La Biennale di Venezia is the world's most prestigious creative showcase, featuring art and architecture and hosting the Venice Film Festival and performing-arts extravaganzas annually. Friendly competition among nationals is obvious in the Giardini Pubblici's pavilions, which showcase architectural sensibilities ranging from magical thinking (Austro-Hungary) to repurposed industrial cool (Korea). ITALIAN PAVILION, GIARDINI PUBBLICI (P124)

☆

Basilica di Santa Maria Assunta *(p150)*

7 Nowhere is Venice's wild and woolly past more evident than on the island of Torcello, once Ernest Hemingway's favourite bolthole and the former capital of the Byzantine city. The island is still charmingly overgrown and harbours at its centre the mesmerising medieval basilica of Santa Maria Assunta, covered in golden mosaics. Climb the attached bell tower and you'll be rewarded by stunning views over the swampy landscape, a rare snapshot of what Venice must have looked like to those early escapees from the mainland.

👁

DALUV/SHUTTERSTOCK ©

7

EDEN BREITZ/ALAMY STOCK PHOTO ©

8

Venetian Artisans *(p43)*

8 In Venice, you're not just in good hands – you're in highly skilled ones. As has been done for centuries, artisans here ply esoteric trades, those that don't involve a computer mouse, such as glass-blowing, paper-marbling and oarlock-carving. Yet while other craft traditions have fossilised into relics of bygone eras, Venetian artisans have kept their creations current. A modern Murano-glass chandelier morphs into an intergalactic octopus, marbled paper turns into must-have handbags, and oarlocks custom-made for rock-and-roll legends are mantelpiece sculptures that upstage any marble bust.

Padua's Scrovegni Chapel (p163)

9 Squint a little at Giotto's 1303–05 Cappella degli Scrovegni frescoes, and you can see the Renaissance coming. Instead of bug-eyed Byzantine saints, Giotto's biblical characters evoke people you'd recognise today: a middle-aged mother (Anne) with a miracle baby (Mary), a new father (Joseph) nodding off while watching his baby boy (Jesus), a slippery schemer (Judas) breezily air-kissing a trusting friend (Jesus). Giotto captures human nature in all its flawed and complex beauty, making a detour to elegant, erudite Padua well worth the effort.

PHOTOBEGINNER/SHUTTERSTOCK ©

OLENA Z/SHUTTERSTOCK ©

Verona (p176)

10 Verona, Shakespeare's city of star-crossed lovers, is one of Italy's most romantic destinations, its tight knit of medieval streets set beside the sparkling River Adige. Although the city is synonymous with summer operas held in the Roman amphitheatre beneath the stars, there is so much more to enjoy. Frescoed churches, Renaissance gardens, smart museums and galleries, jazz bands and wine concerts, and dozens of excellent *osterie* (casual eateries). And in summer, when the heat settles on the historic centre, take to a raft and paddle down that handsome river.

What's New

Ocean Space

Derelict for nearly a century, the Benedictine church of San Lorenzo has been restored to house the ground-breaking Ocean Space gallery dedicated to exploring climate change through art. (p128)

Palazzo Grimani

This frescoed palazzo was constructed around Cardinal Grimani's exceptional Graeco-Roman collection, which has returned to the palace for display after a 430-year absence. (p127)

Venezia Autentica

Want to connect with locals and support local businesses? Then explore this ethical website, which features Venetian-run restaurants, shops and tours and offers a useful discount pass to signed-up 'Friends'. (p26)

Classic Boats Venice

Passionate about preserving Venice's traditional flat-bottomed boats, the young crew at CBV have restored a vintage fleet and equipped them with electric motors. (p249)

V-A-C Foundation

This Grand Canal culture house hosts avant-garde exhibitions and offers beautiful shared workspace and interesting Levantine cuisine in their on-site restaurant. (p81)

Salone Nautico

A new boat show attracting big nautical names and and businesses aims to revive Venice's historic dockyard, while showcasing the city's long seafaring history and traditions. (p21)

Giudecca Art District

The preferred island-home to many of Venice's contemporary artists, the newly launched Giudecca Art District is the city's first permanent art quarter. (p141)

Fairbnb Venice

A new ethical, home-sharing platform combating the flight of residents from the city. Book with them and 50% of the booking fee goes to vital local projects, which you can visit or participate in while you're in the city. (p196)

Music in Venice

A one-stop online shop for the purchase of tickets to all the musical events in the city. The platform provides information about performances and useful location maps. (p40)

Feelin' Venice

A fabulous new design shop selling super-cool Venetian souvenirs designed by graduates from Ca' Foscari University. (p119)

Lagoon Vineyard Tours

Launch off into the lagoon for full-day wine tasting tours on some of the city's lesser-known islands with the sommeliers of Venetian Vine. (p37)

Emerging Food Trends

With Venice's trade-route history, the city's lack of culinary diversity is surprising. But things are beginning to change with the opening of some exciting new international eateries.

For more recommendations and reviews, see **lonelyplanet. com/venice**

Need to Know

For more information, see Survival Guide (p243).

Currency
euro (€)

Language
Italian, Venetian (dialect)

Visas
Not required for EU citizens. Nationals of Australia, Brazil, Canada, Japan, New Zealand and the USA do not need visas for visits of up to 90 days.

Money
ATMs are widely available and credit cards accepted at most hotels, B&Bs and shops. To change money you'll need to present your ID.

Mobile Phones
GSM and tri-band phones can be used in Italy with a local SIM card.

Time
Central European Time (GMT/UTC plus one hour)

Tourist Information
Vènezia Unica (☑041 24 24; www.veneziaunica.it) runs tourist information services in Venice.

Daily Costs
Budget: Less than €120
➡ Dorm bed: €35–60
➡ Basilica di San Marco entry: free
➡ *Cicheti* at All'Arco: €5–15
➡ Chorus Pass: €12
➡ *Spritz:* €2.50–4

Midrange: €140–250
➡ Double room in a B&B: €70–180
➡ Civic Museum Pass: €24
➡ Happy hour in Piazza San Marco: €10–16
➡ Concert ticket: €21–28
➡ Dinner at an *osteria:* €40–50

Top end: More than €250
➡ Double room in a boutique hotel: €200 plus
➡ Gondola ride: €80
➡ Palazzo Grassi and Punta della Dogana ticket: €18
➡ Dinner at Antiche Carampane: €55–65
➡ La Fenice theatre ticket: €80 plus

Advance Planning
Two months before Book high-season accommodation, 'Skip the Line' tickets for the Basilica and Campanile, and tickets to La Fenice operas, Venice Film Festival premieres and Biennale openings.

Three weeks before Check special-event calendars at www.unospitedivenezia.it and www.veneziadavivere.com, and re-serve boat trips and tour guides.

One week before Make classy-restaurant reservations; skip queues by booking tickets to major attractions, exhibitions and events online at www.veneziaunica.it.

Useful Websites
Lonely Planet (www.lonelyplanet.com/venice) Expert travel advice.

Vènezia Unica (www.veneziaunica.it) The main tourism portal with information on museums, churches and special events, as well as online ticketing for public transport and tourist cards.

Venezia da Vivere (www.veneziadavivere.com) Music performances, art openings, nightlife and child-friendly events.

Venice Comune (www.comune.venezia.it) City of Venice official site with essential info, including high-water alerts.

WHEN TO GO

Spring is damp. Summer is hot, crowded and expensive. Autumn offers warm days and thinning crowds. Winter has chilly days and fewer visitors.

Venice

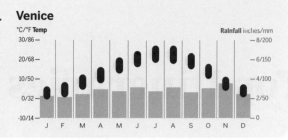

Arriving in Venice

Marco Polo Airport Water shuttles (€15) and water taxis (from €110, or from €25 per person for shared taxis) depart from the airport ferry dock. Buses (one-way €8) run every 30 minutes (5.20am to 12.50am) to Piazzale Roma. A taxi costs €40.

Treviso Airport Buses run to Piazzale Roma (one-way €12, one hour) or Tronchetto (for the monorail to Piazzale Roma). Buses run to Treviso train station for trains to Santa Lucia station. Taxis cost €80.

Piazzale Roma (car parks and bus station) *Vaporetti* (small passenger ferries) to city destinations depart Piazzale Roma docks.

Venezia Santa Lucia train station *Vaporetti* depart from Ferrovia (Station) docks.

Venezia Mestre train station Transfer by train to Venezia Santa Lucia.

Venezia Terminal Passeggeri Docking cruise liners usually shuttle passengers into Venice; otherwise, taxis and *vaporetti* leave from the waterfront.

For much more on **arrival** see p244.

Getting Around

➡ **Vaporetto** These small passenger ferries are Venice's main public transport. Single rides cost €7.50; for frequent use, get a timed pass for unlimited travel within a set period (1-/2-/3-/7-day passes cost €20/30/40/60). Tickets and passes are available dockside from ACTV ticket booths and ticket vending machines, or from tobacconists.

➡ **Gondola** Daytime rates run to €80 for 40 minutes (six passengers maximum) or €100 for 40 minutes from 7pm to 8am, not including songs (negotiated separately) or tips.

➡ **Traghetto** Locals use this daytime public gondola service (€2) to cross the Grand Canal between bridges.

➡ **Water taxi** Sleek teak boats offer taxi services for €15 plus €2 per minute, plus €5 for prebooked services and extra for night-time, luggage and large groups. Ensure the meter is working when boarding.

For much more on **getting around** see p247.

Sleeping

With many Venetians opening their homes to visitors, you can become a local overnight here. In peak seasons quality hotels fill up fast. In summer, many people decamp to the Lido where prices are more reasonable and swimming is an option after hot days in the Rialto.

Useful Websites

➡ **Fairbnb Venice** (https://fairbnb.coop/venice) Home-sharing platform where 50% of booking fees support local projects.

➡ **Lonely Planet** (lonelyplanet.com/italy/venice/hotels) Expert author reviews, user feedback, booking engine.

➡ **Luxrest Venice** (www.luxrest-venice.com) Selection of apartments.

➡ **Venice Prestige** (www.veniceprestige.com) Apartments to rent in aristocratic palaces.

➡ **Views on Venice** (www.viewsonvenice.com) Apartments picked for their personality, character and view.

For much more on **sleeping** see p188.

Top Itineraries

Day One

San Marco (p50)

 Begin your day with the Secret Itineraries tour of the **Palazzo Ducale**, then break for espresso at the baroque counter of **Grancaffè Quadri** before the blitz of golden mosaics inside **Basilica di San Marco**. Don't miss the museum upstairs which gives you close-up views of the dome and the four original bronze horses that were plundered from Constantinople.

> ✖ **Lunch** Come down to earth with deli fare at Rosa Salva (p65).

San Marco & Dorsoduro (p50 & p73)

☼ In the afternoon, go small or large at **Museo Fortuny** or the epic **Gallerie dell'Accademia**. If you choose the latter, pause atop the **Ponte dell'Accademia** on your way for **Grand Canal** photo ops. Afterwards, wander past **Squero di San Trovaso** to glimpse gondolas under construction before enjoying priceless views of Palladio's **Chiesa del Santissimo Redentore** along the **Zattere**. Stop at **Chiesa di San Sebastiano** to view the Veroneses, then boutique-hop along Calle Lunga San Barnaba to catch cocktail hour in **Campo Santa Margherita**.

> ✖ **Dinner** Swoon over lagoon seafood at Zanze XVI (p101).

Dorsoduro (p73)

☽ Leap back into the 1700s at nearby **Scuola Grande dei Carmini**, the evocative setting for classical concerts by **Musica in Maschera**. Alternatively, end the night on a saxy note at the **Venice Jazz Club**.

Day Two

San Polo & Santa Croce (p90)

 Kick off day two with a crash course in lagoon delicacies at the produce-packed **Rialto Market**, side-stepping it to **Drogheria Mascari** for gourmet pantry fillers and regional wines, and to **All'Arco** for a cheeky morning prosecco. Boutiques and artisan studios punctuate your way to Campo San Rocco, home to Gothic show-off **I Frari** and its sunny Titian altarpiece. Once admired, slip into **Scuola Grande di San Rocco** for prime-time-drama Tintorettos.

> ✖ **Lunch** Market-fresh bites and impeccable wines at Estro (p82).

Dorsoduro (p73)

☼ Explore the modern art that caused uproars and defined the 20th century at the **Peggy Guggenheim Collection**, and contrast it with works that push contemporary buttons at **Punta della Dogana**. Duck into Baldassare Longhena's domed **Basilica di Santa Maria della Salute** for blushing Titians and legendary curative powers.

> ✖ **Dinner** Superlative Venetian cuisine at Riviera (p83).

San Marco & Dorsoduro (p50 & p73)

☽ The hottest ticket in town during opera season is at **La Fenice**, but classical-music fans shouldn't miss the fascinating concerts of historic musical scores rescued from obscurity by the **Venice Music Project** and staged in St George's Anglican Church.

Mosaic at the Basilica di Santa Maria Assunta (p150)

Day Three

Castello (p121)

 Start with a stroll down **Riva degli Schiavoni** for views across the lagoon to Palladio's **San Giorgio Maggiore**. Then seek out Carpaccio's sprightly saints at the **Scuola Dalmata di San Giorgio degli Schiavoni** and Bellini's glowing *Madonna and Saints* in the **Chiesa di San Francesco della Vigna**. Then studio-hop down Barbaria delle Tole on your way to Gothic **Zanipolo**, where you'll find the tombs of 25 doges.

 Lunch Join the locals for excellent *cicheti* at Ossi di Seppia (p132).

Cannaregio (p107)

 Dip into pretty, Renaissance **Chiesa di Santa Maria dei Miracoli**, a polychrome marble miracle made from Basilica di San Marco's leftovers, before visiting Baron Franchetti's stunning art collection at **Ca' d'Oro**. Then head north to **Chiesa della Madonna dell'Orto**, the Gothic church Tintoretto pimped with masterpieces.

Dinner Inventive Venetian cuisine at Anice Stellato (p114).

Cannaregio (p107)

Venice's happiest hours beckon along the broad canal banks of Fondamenta Ormesini and Fondamenta Misericordia. Or cast off on a romantic **gondola** ride through Cannaregio's long canals, seemingly purpose-built to maximise moonlight.

Day Four

Murano, Burano & the Northern Islands (p148)

 Make your lagoon getaway on a *vaporetto* (small passenger ferry) bound for green-and-gold **Torcello**. Follow the sheep trail to Torcello's Byzantine **Basilica di Santa Maria Assunta**, where the apse's golden Madonna calmly stares down the blue devils opposite. Catch the boat back to **Burano** to admire extreme home-design colour schemes and handmade lace at **Museo del Merletto**.

 Lunch Try hearty lagoon cuisine at Trattoria al Gatto Nero (p158).

Murano & Giudecca (p148 & p138)

Take in the fiery passions of glass artisans at Murano's legendary *fornaci* (furnaces), and see their finest moments showcased in the beautifully curated **Museo del Vetro** (Glass Museum). When showrooms close, head to **Giudecca** for some spa-loving at the **Palladio Spa** and unbeatable views of San Marco glittering across glassy waters.

Dinner Wine and dine with artists at Trattoria Altanella (p145).

San Marco (p50)

Celebrate your triumphant tour of the lagoon with a prosecco toast and tango across Piazza San Marco at time-warped **Caffè Florian**; repeat these last steps as necessary.

If You Like...

Curiosities

Museo del Manicomio 'Museum of Madness' is as creepy as it sounds, featuring 'cures' happily no longer in use. (p143)

Museo di Storia Naturale di Venezia Dinosaurs, monstrous Japanese spider crabs and other bizarre specimens brought home by intrepid Venetian explorers. (p98)

Museo d'Arte Orientale The attic of Ca' Pesaro hides Japanese samurai treasures, thanks to a prince's shopping binge. (p97)

Fondazione Vedova Robots designed by Renzo Piano display Emilio Vedova's abstract canvases, then whisk them back into storage. (p81)

Fashion

Museo Fortuny Glimpse inside the palatial, radical fashion house that freed women from corsets and innovated bohemian chic. (p59)

Palazzo Mocenigo Find inspiration in a palace packed with Venetian glamour, from bustles and knee breeches to dashing waistcoats. (p97)

Pied à Terre Stock up on candy-coloured velvet and damask gondolier slippers fit for a doge. (p105)

Nicolao Atelier One-of-a-kind period costumes in luxe fabrics with jewelled detailing make you stand out in Carnevale crowds. (p120)

Bottega d'Arte Giuliana Longo Dive into this historic milliner for

SERGEY NOVIKOV/SHUTTERSTOCK ©

Museo di Storia Naturale di Venezia (p98)

handcrafted pieces, from Louise Brooks cloches to authentic gondolier hats. (p72)

Arnoldo & Battois Handmade handbags in bold colours, butter-soft leather and cool shapes. (p72)

Boats

Salone Nautico This June Boat Show brings Venice's legendary Arsenale shipyards back to life. (p21)

Squero di San Trovaso Watch gondolas being shaped by hand and custom-sized to match the gondolier's weight and height. (p81)

CBV Captain your very own (electric) vintage boat and glide soundlessly across the teal-coloured lagoon. (p249)

Le Fórcole di Saverio Pastor Take home Venice's most memorable souvenir: a sculptural walnut oarlock. (p87)

Gilberto Penzo Scale-model gondolas for your bathtub and build-your-own-boat kits from a master artisan. (p106)

Row Venice Learn to row across lagoon waters standing like a gondolier. (p153)

Hidden Gems

Chiesa di Santa Maria dei Miracoli The little neighbourhood church with big Renaissance ideas and priceless marble. (p112)

Ocean Space A pioneering gallery and lab using artistic and scientific collaborations to tackle global warming. (p128)

Palazzo Grimani A frescoed Renaissance palace designed to showcase Cardinal Grimani's first-class sculpture collection. (p127)

Ghetto synagogues Climb to rooftop synagogues on tours run by Museo Ebraico. (p109)

Scala Contarini del Bovolo A secret spiral staircase in an ancient courtyard sets the scene for a clandestine smooch. (p62)

Chiesa di San Francesco della Vigna All-star Venetian art showcase and Palladio's first commission. (p129)

Sweet Treats

VizioVirtù From edible plague-doctor masks to vino-infused pralines, this artisan chocolate maker is terrific-calorific. (p137)

Suso Creamy seasonal gelato, homemade cones and addictive pistachio cream make this Venice's best gelateria. (p65)

Panificio Volpe Giovanni A kosher bakery peddling heavenly pastries with the rabbi's blessing. (p114)

Pasticceria Tonolo Flaky apple strudel and mini-profiteroles bursting with hazelnut-chocolate mousse. (p82)

Magiche Voglie Take a beach break and order a cajá (Brazilian fruit) ice cream from the Lido's best gelateria. (p145)

Backstreet Bars

All'Arco Bargain-priced, lip-smacking cicheti (Venetian tapas) invented daily with Rialto Market's freshest finds, plus perfect wine pairings. (p99)

Vino Vero Venice's only bacaro (bar-eatery) dedicated to biodynamic wines paired with gourmet bar bites. (p115)

Cantine del Vino già Schiavi A legendary local bacaro serving up memorable cicheti beside the Grand Canal. (p81)

For more top Venice spots, see the following:

➡ Eating (p29)

➡ Drinking & Nightlife (p35)

➡ Entertainment (p39)

➡ Shopping (p43)

Salvmeria A gourmet cichetteria with a devoted local following set on the sunny side of Via Garibaldi. (p131)

Cantina Aziende Agricole A tried-and-tested local bacaro serving well-priced ombre (half-glasses of wine) and generous cicheti. (p114)

Local Hangouts

Lido Beaches When temperatures nudge past 29°C, Venice races to the Lido-bound vaporetto to claim sandy beachfront. (p144)

Campo San Giacomo da l'Orio bars Kids tear through the campo (square), while parents watch through glasses of natural-process prosecco. (p104)

Rialto Market Whet your appetite as grandmothers and Michelin chefs drive hard bargains with witty grocers. (p95)

Via Garibaldi Venetian workers heading home make time for one last spritz in Via Garibaldi bars. (p134)

Giudecca Escape to this one-time industrial island to hang out with budding young artists at Giudecca Art District. (p141)

Murano Linger after the day trippers disperse for soothing glasses of Lugana and Venice's best pizza. (p158)

Month by Month

February

Snow does occasionally fall in Venice, blanketing gondolas and the domes of St Mark's. Velvet costumes and wine fountains warm February nights, when revellers party like it's 1699 at masked balls.

Carnevale

Masqueraders party in the streets for just over two weeks preceding Shrove Tuesday. Tickets to nightly balls cost up to about €800, but there's no shortage of less expensive diversions at Carnevale, from costume competitions in Piazza San Marco to Cannaregio Canal flotillas.

March

A blissfully quiet period between Carnevale and Easter, March is ideal for sightseeing. Sunny skies and cold nights mean you should pack for every eventuality.

Arte Laguna Prize

Aimed at promoting contemporary art, this increasingly prestigious two-week art competition (p124) showcases over a hundred large-scale international works in the restored warehouses of the Arsenale.

April

The winning springtime combination of optimal walking weather and reasonable room rates lasts until Easter, when art-history classes and school children on holiday briefly flood the city.

Festa di San Marco

Join the celebration of Venice's patron saint on 25 April, when Venetian men carry a *bocolo* (rosebud) in processions through Piazza San Marco, then bestow them on the women they love.

May

As summer edges closer, it's time for headline-grabbing contemporary art and a regatta that sees swarms of boats fill the lagoon. This is also the most scenic month in Venice, when the blossom is out.

La Biennale di Venezia

Running between May and November, La Biennale di Venezia (p41) is Venice's largest event, showcasing contemporary art in odd years and architecture in even years. Alongside it there are a host of avant-garde dance, theatre and musical performances.

Festa della Sensa

Vows have been professed annually since AD 1000 in the Sposalito del Mar (Wedding to the Sea), with celebrations including regattas, outdoor markets and Mass on the Lido. The event takes place on the Feast of the Ascension.

🏃 Vogalonga

Not a race so much as a show of endurance (p153), this 32km 'long row' starts with over 1500 boats in front of the Palazzo Ducale, loops past Burano and Murano, and ends with cheers and prosecco at Punta della Dogana. Held in May or June.

June

As the weather warms further, gardens bloom and Venice enjoys its most temperate climate. In Castello, the festive vibe kicks on as the city's former cathedral turns into a party backdrop.

🏃 Salone Nautico

This boat show is staged in the world's most historic dockyards, showcasing some of the most advanced seafaring vessels, alongside traditional crafts and skills. Expect boat races, exhibits and demonstrations of Venetian rowing and sailing.

🎆 Festa de San Piero de Casteo

The Festival of St Peter of Castello takes place in the last week of June at the steps of the church that was once the city's cathedral, with Mass, games, puppetry, hearty rustic fare and rock tribute bands.

July

Fireworks over Giudecca and occasional lightning illuminate balmy summer nights on the lagoon, and performances by jazz greats end sunny days on a sultry note.

☆ Venice Jazz Festival

International legends from Wynton Marsalis to Buena Vista Social Club bring down the house at La Fenice, while crowd-favourite acts play venues as diverse as the Peggy Guggenheim Collection and Punta della Dogana. Check the calendar for shows in Vicenza, Verona and Treviso year-round.

🎆 Festa del Redentore

Walk on water across the Giudecca Canal to Il Redentore via a wobbly pontoon bridge during this celebration on the third Saturday and Sunday in July. Join the massive floating picnic along the Zattere, and don't miss the fireworks.

September

Movie stars bask in flattering autumnal light along Venice Film Festival red carpets, and regattas make the most of optimal weather on the lagoon.

🏃 Regata Storica

Never mind who's winning, check out the gear: Regata Storica (www.regattastoricavenezia.it) sees 16th-century costumes and eight-oared gondolas re-enact the Venice arrival of the Queen of Cyprus. A floating parade is followed by four races, where kids and adult rowers compete for boating bragging rights.

🏃 Burano Regata

Fishing island Burano angles for attention the third Sunday in September with Venice's only mixed men's and women's rowing regatta (www.isoladiburano.it). It's the last regatta of the rowing season, so victors are celebrated with an after-party on the island.

☆ Venice International Film Festival

The only thing hotter than Lido beaches this time of year is the red carpet at this star-studded event, running for 11 days from late August or early September.

October

High season ends, festival crowds disperse and hotel rates come back down to earth.

🍷 Festa del Mosto

A genuine country fair on 'garden isle' Sant'Erasmo (www.veneziaunica.it), held on the first Sunday in October. The wine-grape harvest is celebrated with a parade, gourmet food stalls, live music and free-flowing vino.

November

Venice gives thanks for its miraculous survival before kicking off another year of revelry on 1 January.

🎆 Festa della Madonna della Salute

If you'd survived plague and an Austrian invasion, you'd throw a party, too. Every 21 November since the 17th century, Venetians have crossed a Grand Canal pontoon bridge to light a candle in thanks at Santa Maria della Salute and splurge on sweets.

With Kids

Adults think Venice is for them; kids know better. This is where fairy tales come to life, prisoners escape through the roof of a palace, Murano glassblowers breathe life into pocket-sized sea dragons, and spellbound Pescaria fish balance on their tails.

Museo Storico Navale (p131)

Attractions

Make an early-morning run down the Grand Canal for cheeky hot chocolates at Caffè Florian (p68); the cafe's fairy-tale interiors are plucked straight out of a giant storybook. Slip into Palazzo Mocenigo (p97) to explore the Cinderella fashions of the past, roam the secret attic-prisons of the Palazzo Ducale (p55) and sign up for art workshops at the Peggy Guggenheim Collection (p77).

For something more off-beat seek out the giant samurai swords at the Museo d'Arte Orientale in Ca' Pesaro (p97) and the massive sea monsters and dinosaurs at the Museo di Storia Naturale (p98). Or, grab your sailor hat and shout out 'Ship Ahoy!' at the Museo Storico Navale (p131), jam-packed with golden barges, model warships and enough cannons to make any pirate nervous.

Stunning city and swampy lagoon views never fail to elicit gasps of amazement. Take a peek from the Campanile (p59), the campaniles of Chiesa di San Giorgio Maggiore (p140) and Basilica di Santa Maria Assunta (p150) on Torcello, and the top-floor viewing platform at the Fondaco dei Tedeschi (p72).

Activities

Beaches & Picnics

Lido beaches and lagoon picnics on Torcello, La Certosa and Le Vignole give the whole family some reinvigorating downtime.

Boating & Kayaking

Glide across teal-blue waters in your own boat from CBV (p249) or kayak across the lagoon with Venice Kayak (p155).

Photography Walks & Painting

Teens will love Venice Photo Tour (p26) with Marco Secchi, especially when his professional tips make their Instagram shots the envy of all their social-media peers. Alternatively, budding artists will enjoy outdoor art classes with Painting Venice (p120).

Island Biking

Team up on tandem bikes for leisurely Lido itineraries, or strike out on two-wheeled nature excursions on the garden island of Le Vignole.

Hands-On Learning

Rowing & Sailing

Kids who are tall and strong enough to hold an oar can learn to row like *gondolieri* with Row Venice (p153). Alternatively, sign up for a week of lagoon sailing with Vento di Venezia (p155), which has courses for budding sailors aged seven to 13 as well as for older teens.

Arts & Crafts

Kids inspired by watching Venetian artists and artisans at work can make their own Carnevale masks at Ca' Macana (p86) and La Bauta (p105), build their own gondolas with scale-model kits from Gilberto Penzo (p106), and try their hand at printing and etching at Fallani Venezia (p120) and Plum Plum Creations (p120).

Pasta Making

Spend the morning eyeing up sci-fi-like lagoon creatures at the Rialto Market (p95), then head to the Acquolina Cooking School (p147) to learn the art of making pasta and, more importantly, tiramisu. Suitable for teens.

Learning the Lingo

Ordering gelato is an essential skill, so give your kids a head start with a fun, engaging morning language session at the Venice Italian School (p106). For kids aged five and up.

Food

When feet and spirits begin to drag, there's pizza and pasta galore to pick them back up. For an impromptu tea party, settle in with freshly baked brownies and other sweet treats at Rosa Salva (p136) and Serra dei Giardini (p126). Unless your kids are superadventurous, navigating *cicheti* (Venetian tapas) may be hard, although Basegò (p99) tempts budding gourmets

inside with a desk set up with drawing material.

The best compromise is to opt for restaurants that serve full menus as well as *cicheti*. The Lido is the land of pizza lovers and ice-cream shops. Other popular takeaway options good for a cheap, quick feed include Antico Forno (p99), Toletta Snack-Bar (p82), Cip Ciap (p132), Didovich (p131), Pizzeria alla Strega (p131) and Osteria al Duomo (p158). That done, challenge your budding gastronomes to try fig-and-walnut ice cream at Gelato di Natura (p101) or Suso (p65).

Given the expense of eating out, many families find that opting for a self-catering apartment is a lifesaver. Not only does it offer the flexibility of having your own kitchen, but the experience of shopping at the Rialto or the city's floating produce barges is a memorable cultural experience. Views on Venice (p196) has a good selection of family-friendly apartments to choose from.

Admission Prices

Most attractions in Venice offer reduced admission for children. City-run museums (www.visitmuve.it) generally give a 60% to 70% discount to visitors aged from six to 14, and free entry to those aged five and under. State-owned museums are free for those under 18. Free entry at privately owned institutions is often restricted to children under 12 years, with reduced fees applied to those between 12 and 18 years.

NEED TO KNOW

Change facilities Available on the public restrooms list on www.venezia unica.it.

Emergency care Venice's main hospital (p253) offers emergency care.

Babysitting High-end hotels and some B&Bs can organise babysitters.

Strollers & baby carriers Stroller use is challenging. A better substitute is an ergonomic baby carrier. Venice Rental Services (p249) hires out both, along with travel cots and other products.

For Free

Despite its centuries-old reputation as a playground for Europe's elite, some of Venice's finest moments are freebies, from glittering glimpses of heaven in Basilica di San Marco to soothing vespers at the healing Basilica di Santa Maria della Salute.

Historical Sites

Some of the most pivotal sites in Venetian history have free entry: Rialto Market (p95), where an empire sprang up around fishmongers; Basilica di Santa Maria della Salute (p78), the domed church built as thanks for Venice's salvation from plague; and Basilica di San Marco (p52), the apotheosis of Venice's millennium of brilliant self-invention.

The Basilica di Santa Maria della Salute also offers free afternoon organ vespers.

Arts & Architecture

While entry to the main Biennale art and architecture shows and Venice Film Festival premieres isn't free, many citywide dance, music, cinema and ancillary arts programs are. Art lovers will appreciate the superb (and often free) shows at Palazzo Franchetti (p64) and Ocean Space (p128), a new gallery dedicated to raising awareness of climate change through art activism.

Commercial art galleries and Murano glass showrooms are yours to enjoy at no cost, and state-run museums such as the Gallerie dell'Accademia (p75) and Ca' d'Oro (p111) are gratis during Museum Week in March. Then there is Venice's spectacular architecture. Take in Grand Canal *palazzi* (mansions) for the price of a *vaporetto* (ferry) ticket, or discover hidden gems like the Scala Contarini del Bovolo (p62) on a San Marco walking tour (p67).

Island Getaways

The Lido (p143) offers six free-access beaches, a miniature version of Venice at Malamocco, a thriving Tuesday produce market (p147) and free summer concerts. Giudecca comes with mesmerising views, galleries, a 14th-century church and the Fortuny showroom (p147). Visit the haunting cemetery isle of San Michele (p151) on your way to Murano, where you can glimpse glassmakers at work and spot dragon's bones among the Byzantine mosaics of San Donato (p151). Take a photography expedition to technicolour Burano and, while you're there, spot masterpieces inside Chiesa di San Martino (p152). For welcome stretches of green, hop off at Torcello, Mazzorbo, La Certosa, Sant'Erasmo and Le Vignole.

Cutting Costs

Access some of Venice's finest masterpieces in 16 churches with a Chorus Pass (p252). It includes such spectacular sights as I Frari, Chiesa di Santa Maria dei Miracoli, Chiesa di San Sebastiano and Chiesa della Madonna dell'Orto.

For €28.90 the San Marco City Pass covers the Palazzo Ducale, Museo Correr, Museo Archeologico Nazionale and Biblioteca Nazionale Marciana. Or for €24, buy the Civic Museum Pass, which grants access to 11 civic museums.

Ditch those €80 gondola rides for the cheap thrill of standing on the *traghetto* (public gondola) as you cross the Grand Canal (€2 per ride). Or ride the length of the Grand Canal on *vaporetto* 1 in the early morning or evening for a spectacular architectural tour for just €7.50.

Tours

To get to know Venice from the inside out, you first have to see the lagoon city as Venetians have for a millennium – by water – then dive into the calli (lanes) and ascend secret staircases for glimpses of Venetian life behind the scenes and above the fray.

Tours on Water

The following outings offer maritime adventures down canals and out on the lagoon. Reserve ahead, bring sunscreen and check weather forecasts, as trips are subject to climatic conditions.

Rowing

Find your footing on the lagoon with champion regatta rowers at Row Venice (p153), who will show you how to propel a handcrafted Venetian *batellina coda di gambero* (shrimp-tailed boat) standing up. The outfit also offers evening lessons on the Grand Canal and a combined rowing and *cicheti* (Venetian tapas) bar-hop.

Kayaking & Paddling

Venice Kayak (p155) offers a highly unique way to experience the lagoon and its quieter islands. Group and private tours are offered, including half- and full days.

Swimming skills and some prior paddling experience are required. Beginners are able to join a more-experienced paddler in a two-person kayak.

Also open to confident paddlers over the age of 14 are stand-up paddleboard tours with SUP in Venice (p155). There's a two-hour tour through the quieter canals of Castello and Cannaregio, or an island-to-island tour of the lagoon.

Sailing

Eolo Cruises (☏349 7431551; www.cruis ingvenice.com; full-day cruise for 4-6 people per person €350-450) sails the lagoon on a double-masted 1946 *bragozzo* (flat-bottomed fishing boat) for one- to eight-day trips (€350 to €450 per person up to six people), including on-board cooking workshops.

Boating

Ecofriendly Terra e Acqua (p155) offers wild rides to the outer edges of the lagoon. Itineraries can cover abandoned islands, fishing and birdwatching hot spots, and the monastic retreat of San Francesco del Deserto. Lunch is served on board its motorised bragozzo or at a local trattoria.

More confident seafarers can fashion their own DIY tour of the lagoon in a restored flat-bottomed boat from CBV (p249). Before being let loose, you'll be given a short training session and will be fitted with a tracking device so you can't get lost. A more luxurious alternative is a day out with lagoon expert Francesco Calzolaio on the luxurious Linseen yacht of **Lagunalonga** (☏380 305 30 78; www. lagunalonga.com; 6-person cruises from €2430; ☉mid-Mar–Oct).

Tours on Land

Many major sights offer guided tours, especially the 10 civic museums (www. visitmuve.it), which include the Doge's Palace, Museo Correr, Ca' Rezzonico, Ca' Pesaro, Museo del Vetro, Museo del Merletto, Palazzo Mocenigo, Palazzo Fortuny, Casa di Carlo Goldoni and Museo di Storia Naturale di Venezia. They can be arranged for groups of between four and 25 people and need to be booked in advance online.

The only way to visit the Torre dell'Orologio (p59) and the Fondazione Giorgio Cini (p142) is by pre-arranged tour. Tours of the Basilica di San Marco (p53) are offered by the diocese but need to be prebooked by sending an email to turismo@patriarcatovenezia.it. Alternatively, **Walks of Italy** (☎069 480 4888; www.walksofitaly.com/venice-tours; tours per person €69-150) offers excellent tours of the basilica, including an after-hours evening tour (from €89). Expert guided tours of La Fenice (p63) (€150) are also possible for groups.

Tourist offices can set you up with authorised tour guides and can book various tours through accredited providers. Otherwise consult the **Best Venice Guides** (http://bestveniceguides.it; per hr €65-85) website, which lists the city's best tour guides.

Cultural Tours

International franchise **Context Travel** (☎800 691 60 36; www.contexttravel.com; group tours from €300; ⛟) offers a fantastic range of Venetian 'seminars' with knowledgeable docents and specialists. Groups are no larger than six people, and subjects range from politics to art, history and ecology. Other insightful cultural tours are offered by Venetian native Luisella Romeo at **See Venice** (☎349 084 8303; www.seevenice.it; tours per hr €75). She covers all the grand-slam sights as well as off-the-beaten path itineraries and detailed arts and crafts tours that expand visitors experience of the city.

For those with an artful eye, consider Getty-photographer Marco Secchi's snap-

happy **Venice Photo Tour** (☎041 852 02 62; www.venicephototour.com; 2/3/5hr walking tours for up to 4 people €220/300/500), which takes you around hidden corners of the city and offers instruction in the finer points of Venetian light and photography. Also excellent are the tours and experiences offered by **Venezia Autentica** (https://veneziaautentica.com), which run from night walks with locals to accompanied jogs and bar crawls.

Walking Tours

Venicescapes (☎041 850 57 42; www.venicescapes.org; 4-6hr tour for 2 adults US$280-320, additional adult US$60, under 18yr US$30), a nonprofit historical society, runs intriguing walking tours with themes such as 'A City of Nations', exploring multiethnic Venice through the ages. Proceeds support ongoing Venetian historical research.

Walks of Italy offers a select number of top-quality tours of the Doge's Palace, St Mark's basilica and the Rialto market. Likewise, **Walks Inside Venice** (☎041 524 17 06; www.walksinsidevenice.com; 3-4hr tours €170-420, lagoon tour €420-830; ⛟) has a spirited team that helps you explore the city's major monuments and backstreets. Similarly good tours, and well-priced, are those run by **L'Altra Venezia** (www.laltravenezia.it; walking tours per hour €70, thematic tours from €200, boat tours from €400), which focus on music, theatre and food.

Food Tours

Venice Urban Adventures (☎348 980 85 66; www.veniceurbanadventures.com; group tours €90-94; ⏱tours 11.30am & 5.30pm Mon-Sat) and **Monica Cesarato** (www.monicacesarato.com; 3hr tours €40; ⛟) offer year-round *cicheti* (bar snacks) tours, covering five or six backstreet *bacari* (hole-in-the-wall bars) on a local-guided Venetian bar crawl. For guided wine tastings with trained sommeliers join a Venetian Vine (p37) tasting evening or join them on a full-day tour of the lagoon vineyards, which include a fabulous island lunch.

Escaping the Crowds

Recently, Venice has made headlines for its crowded calli, congested canals and oversized cruise ships. In high season the throng along the Riva degli Schiavoni and in Piazza San Marco can be overwhelming, but further afield you'll find areas undisturbed by mass tourism.

Ca' Pesaro (p97) from a narrow canal

Best Time to Visit

March, May, October, November and December are all good months to visit Venice, avoiding major religious and school holidays. If you can, avoid the peak season of June through August, when global holidaymakers descend and prices rocket. The summer months also bring stifling heat and pesky mosquitos. If you're in town at this time, base yourself on the breezy, outer islands of Murano, Burano, Lido or Giudecca.

Other busy (and expensive) periods to be aware of are the two weeks of Carnevale (January or February), the Easter and Christmas holidays, the first week of La Biennale (May), and the days of the Venice Film Festival in early September. Weekends are particularly crowded during these periods as thousands of day trippers converge on the city.

Crowd-Free Attractions

Although the media focus on the queues snaking around the basilica, the Campanile and Palazzo Ducale, Venice is a city full of world-class museums and many of them are surprisingly undervisited.

Museo Fortuny

The museum of choice for many locals, Museo Fortuny (p59) hosts superbly curated, creative exhibitions in the atmospheric salons of art nouveau designer Mariano Fortuny.

Galleria Giorgio Franchetti alla Ca' d'Oro

A stunning gallery (p111) stuffed with masterpieces, housed in one of the most beautiful buildings on the Grand Canal. Don't miss the views from the 1st-floor galleries.

Ca' Pesaro

Venice's Modern Art Museum (p97) includes works by Matisse, Rodin, Chagall, Kandinsky, Lichtenstein and Wildt and outshines the vastly-more-popular Peggy Guggenheim Collection.

NEED TO KNOW

➔ Getting your bearings Good planning helps avoid queues and crowds. Comprehensive information can be found at Vènezia Unica (p250).

➔ Skip the line Prebook tickets to avoid queues at the Basilica di San Marco, the Campanile, Palazzo Ducale, the Accademia and the Peggy Guggenheim Collection.

➔ Getting around Avoid getting held up on public transport by downloading the useful transport app daAaB (www.daaab.it).

Scuola Grande di San Giovanni Evangelista

Established by a sect of flagellants, this gorgeous confraternity (p95) for the brothers of St John the Evangelist is extravagantly decorated with major artworks and a stunning marble floor in the hall of St John.

Ocean Space

A new academy (p128) combining art and science, with cross-disciplinary shows tackling the subject of climate change in the fantastic restored shell of Chiesa di San Lorenzo.

Palazzo Grimani

Discover Cardinal Grimani's impressive Graeco-Roman statuary collection, in this frescoed palace (p127) hidden down an easy-to-miss alley.

Casa dei Tre Oci

A fascinating photography museum (p141) showcasing the work of modernist Venetian photographer Mario de Maria, alongside temporary contemporary-photo exhibitions, in his beautifully renovated neo-Gothic house.

The Ghetto

A living, breathing monument, Venice's Ghetto (p109) is still home to the city's Jewish community who keep their history alive in their ancient synagogues, a number of which are visitable on a tour.

Chiesa di San Sebastiano

A seemingly modest neighbourhood church (p79) decked out in floor-to-ceiling masterpieces by Paolo Veronese.

Monastero di San Lazzaro degli Armeni

A historic island monastery (p143), still home to a community of Armenian monks who allow a daily tour of their home, including the valuable library where Byron spent six months preparing an English-Armenian dictionary.

The Lagoon

Venice is surrounded by a watery garden, where the city-centre crowds seem far away. Get out there in a vintage vessel from CBV (p249).

Local Know-How

Best Tour Guides

Visiting popular tourist sites or areas with a Best Venice Guide (p26) is a great way to avoid crowds. They know exactly what to visit and when.

Stay Local

New start-up Fairbnb (p196) is a community-powered, home-sharing platform. Book a stay with them and donate to local projects that you can participate in while you're in town.

Authentic Experiences

Get away from the tourist throngs and meet Venetians passionate about their city through Venezia Autentica (p26).

Event Planning

Music in Venice (p40) is a one-stop shop for all musical performances in Venice. Information is up to date and bookings can be made in real time.

Best Day Trips

If you still feel the urge to get away for the day, consider one or more of our recommended day trips.

Cicheti

Eating

The visual blitz that is Venice tends to leave visitors weak-kneed and grasping for the nearest panino *(sandwich). But there's more to La Serenissima than simple carb-loading. For centuries Venice has gone beyond the call of dietary duty, and lavished visitors with inventive feasts. Now it's your turn to devour addictive* cicheti *(Venetian tapas) and a lagoon's worth of succulent seafood.*

Venetian Cuisine

'Local food' is the latest foodie credo, but it's nothing new in Venice. Surrounded by garden islands and a seafood-rich lagoon, Venice dishes up local specialities that never make it to the mainland, because they're served fresh the same day in Venetian *bacari* (hole-in-the-wall bars) and *osterie* (casual eateries). A strong sea breeze wafts over the kitchens of the lagoon city, with the occasional meaty dish from the Veneto mainland and traditional, local options of rice and polenta in addition to classic Italian pastas and gnocchi. But side dishes of Veneto vegetables often steal the show, and early risers will notice Venetians risking faceplants in canals to grab *violetti di Sant'Erasmo* (tender purple baby artichokes), *radicchio trevisano* (ruffled red bitter chicory) and prized Bassano del Grappa white asparagus from produce-laden barges.

Cross-cultural fusion fare is old news here, dating back to Marco Polo's heyday. Thirteenth-century Venetian cookbooks include recipes for fish with galangal, saffron and ginger; a tradition that still inspires dishes at nosh spots like Zanze XVI (p101), Bistrot de Venise (p66), Anice Stellato (p114) and

NEED TO KNOW

Opening Hours

Cafe-bars generally open from 7am to 8pm, although some stay open later and morph into drinking hang-outs. Restaurant kitchens are generally open from noon to 2.30pm or 3pm at lunch and from 7pm to 10pm or 11pm at dinner.

Price Ranges

With some notable exceptions in Venice – *cicheti*, sandwiches, pizza and gelato – a meal typically consists of two courses, a glass of house wine, and *pane e coperto* (bread and cover charge). Meal prices are defined as follows:

€ less than €25

€€ €25 to €45

€€€ more than €45

Reservations

Call ahead to book at restaurants and *osterie* whenever possible, especially in high season. You may get a table when you walk in off the street, but some restaurants buy ingredients according to how many bookings they've got – and when the food runs low, they stop seating. *Cicheti* are a handy alternative.

Pane e Coperto

'Bread and cover' charges range from €1.50 to €6 for sit-down meals at most restaurants.

Service Charges

Service may be included in *pane e coperto* (especially at basic *osterie*) or added onto the bill (at upscale bistros and for large parties). Read the fine print before you leave an additional tip.

Osteria Trefanti (p101). Don't be surprised if some Venetian dishes taste vaguely Turkish or Greek rather than strictly Italian, reflecting Venice's preferred trading partners for over a millennium. Spice-route flavours from the Mediterranean and beyond can be savoured in signature Venetian recipes such as *sarde in saor,* traditionally made with sardines in a tangy onion marinade with pine nuts and sultanas.

Exceptional ingredients from other parts of Italy sneak into Venetian cuisine, such as Tuscan steaks, white truffles from Alba, aromatic Amalfi lemons, and Sicilian pistachios and blood oranges. Just don't ask for pesto: the garlicky basil spread hails from Genoa, Venice's chief trade-route rival for 300 years, and some Venetians still hold culinary grudges.

Cicheti

Cicheti are some of the best culinary finds in Italy, served at lunch and from around 6pm to 8pm with sensational Veneto wines by the glass. *Cicheti* range from basic bar snacks (spicy meatballs, fresh tomato and basil bruschetta) to highly inventive small plates: think white Bassano asparagus and plump lagoon shrimp wrapped in pancetta at All'Arco (p99); Fassone beef and peppers at Salvmeria (p131); creamy cheeses from Monte Veronese at Malvasia all'Adriatico Mar (p84); wild boar salami at Vino Vero (p115); mixed plates of garden greens and steamed mussels at Ossi di Seppia (p132); or fragrant, bite-sized bread rolls crammed with tuna, chicory and horseradish at Al Mercà (p102).

Prices start at €1 for tasty meatballs and range from €3 to €6 for gourmet fantasies with fancy ingredients, typically devoured standing up or perched atop stools at the bar. Filling *cicheti* such as *crostini, panini* and *tramezzini* (sandwiches on soft bread, often with mayo-based condiments) cost €1.50 to €6. Nightly *cicheti* spreads could easily pass as dinner.

Peckish? Venice's *cicheti* hotspots include the following:

Cannaregio Along Fondamenta dei Ormesini and off Strada Nova.

San Polo & Santa Croce Around the Rialto Market and Ruga Ravano.

Castello Via Garibaldi and Calle Lunga Santa Maria Formosa.

San Marco Around Campo San Bartolomeo, Campo Santo Stefano and Campo della Guerra.

The Menu

Even in unpretentious Venetian *osterie* and *bacari,* most dishes cost a couple of euros more than they might elsewhere in Italy – not a bad mark-up, considering all that fresh seafood and produce brought in by boat. *Cicheti* are fresh alternatives to fast food worth planning your day around, but you'll also want to treat yourself to a leisurely sit-down meal while you're in town. If you stick to tourist menus you're bound to be disappointed, but adventurous diners who order seasonal specialities are richly rewarded, and often spend less, too.

PIATTI

No one expects you to soldier through multiple courses plus antipasti and dessert, but we wouldn't blame you for trying either, given the many tempting *piatti* (courses) on the local menu. Consider your à la carte options:

➡ **Antipasti** (appetisers) vary from lightly fried *moeche* (tiny soft-shell crabs) and lagoon-fresh *crudi* (Venetian sushi) such as sweet mantis prawns, to old-school *baccalà mantecato* (whipped salted cod with olive oil) and traditional platters of cheeses and rustic cured meats.

➡ **Primi** (first courses) usually include the classic Italian pasta or risotto; one Venetian speciality pasta you might try is *bigoli*, a thick wholewheat pasta, often served *in salsa* (with salted anchovies, Chioggia onions and black pepper). Equally loved are *pasta e fagioli*, a soupy concoction of pasta and borlotti beans, and *risi e bisi*, a risotto-like classic made with peas, pancetta and parmesan. Many Venetian restaurants have adopted a hearty Verona speciality: gnocchi. Another regional option is polenta, white or yellow cornmeal formed into a cake and grilled, or served semisoft and steaming hot. As the Venetian saying goes, '*Xe non xe pan, xe poenta*' (If there's no bread, there's still polenta).

➡ **Secondi** (second or main courses) are usually seafood or meat dishes. Adventurous eaters will appreciate a traditional Venetian *secondo* of *trippa* (tripe) or *fegato alla veneziana* (calf's liver lightly pan-roasted in strips with browned onion and a splash of red wine). If you're not an offal fan, you can find standard cuts of *manzo* (beef), *agnello* (lamb) and *vitello* (veal) on most menus. Committed carnivores might also try carpaccio, a dish of finely sliced raw beef served with a sauce of crushed tomato, cream, mustard and Worcestershire sauce dreamed up by Harry's Bar (p68) and named for the Venetian painter Vittore Carpaccio, famous for his liberal use of blood-red paint. Popular surf options include *fritto misto*, a golden mix of fried fish and seafood, sometimes accompanied by tempura-style seasonal vegetables.

➡ **Contorni** (vegetable dishes) are more substantial offerings of *verdure* (vegetables). For vegetarians, this may be the first place to look

on a menu – and meat-eaters may want to check them out too, since *secondi* don't always come with a vegetable side dish. Go with whatever's fresh and seasonal.

➡ **Dolci** (desserts) are often house-made in Venice, especially Veneto-invented tiramisu, Vienna-influenced *bigne* (cream puffs) and strudel, and saffron-scented Burano *esse* (S-shaped biscuits). Otherwise, gelaterie (ice-cream shops) offer tempting options for €1.50 to €5.

DAILY SPECIALS

Here's one foolproof way to distinguish a serious Venetian *osteria* from an imposter: lasagne, spaghetti Bolognese and pizza are not Venetian specialities, and when all three appear on a menu, avoid what is essentially a tourist trap. Look instead for places where there's no menu at all, or one hastily scrawled on a chalkboard or laser-printed in Italian only, preferably with typos. This is a sign that your chef reinvents the menu daily, according to what looked best that morning at the market.

Although fish and seafood are increasingly imported, many Venetian restaurant owners pride themselves on using only fresh, local ingredients, even if that means getting up at the crack of dawn to get to the Pescaria (Fish Market). Lagoon tides and changing seasons on the nearby garden island of Sant'Erasmo bring a year-round bounty to Venetian tables at the Rialto Market.

Beware any menu dotted with asterisks, indicating that several items are *surgelati* (frozen) – seafood flown in from afar is likely to be unsustainable, and indigestible besides.

DRINKS

No Venetian feast would be complete without at least one *ombra* (glass of wine) – and that includes lunch. Fishmongers at the Pescaria get a head start on landlubbers, celebrating the day's haul at 9am by popping a cork on some prosecco (sparkling white wine), the Veneto's beloved bubbly. By noon, you already have some catching up to do: start working your way methodically through the extensive seafood menu of tender octopus salad, black squid-ink risotto, and *granseola* (spider crab), paired with appropriate *ombre*.

Many Venetian dishes are designed with local wines specifically in mind to round out the flavours – especially delicate lagoon seafood, whose texture may be changed by the powerful acidity of lemon juice. Some *enoteche* (wine bars) and *osterie* have wine selections that run into the hundreds of labels, so don't be shy about soliciting suggestions from your server. Or sign up for a tasting class with Venetian Vine (p37).

Of course, no meal is complete without a glass of the Veneto's own firewater – grappa. Far from the rocket fuel you may be accustomed to, respected distilleries such as Bassano del Grappa's Poli (p71) produce sophisticated versions that are equally smooth and nuanced.

Vegetarians & Vegans

Even in a city known for seafood, vegetarians need not despair: with a little advance savvy, vegetarian visitors in Venice can enjoy an even wider range of food choices than they might at home. Island-grown produce is a point of pride for many Venetian restaurants, and *primi* such as polenta, pasta and risotto *contorni* (vegetable dishes) make the most of such local specialities as asparagus, artichokes, radicchio and *bruscandoli* (wild hops). Venetian *contorni* include grilled local vegetables and salads, and *cicheti* showcase marinated vegetables and Veneto cheeses.

La Tecia Vegana (p82) is Venice's only organic vegan restaurant, while Le Spighe (p132) and Sullaluna (p114) serve vegetarian and vegan food. Otherwise there are eateries that serve a good range of meat-free dishes at all price points. Meat-free and cheese-free pizza is widely available, and gelaterie offer milk-free *sorbetto* (sorbet) and gelato with *latte di soia* (soy milk). Self-catering is always an option for vegans and others with restricted diets, but if you call ahead, specific dietary restrictions can usually be accommodated at restaurants and *osterie*.

Self-Catering

Picnicking isn't allowed in most *campi* (squares) – Venice tries to keep a lid on its clean-up duties, since all refuse needs to be taken out by barge – but you can assemble quite a feast to enjoy at your B&B, rental apartment or hotel. For lunch with sweeping lagoon views, pack a picnic and head to the Lido beaches, the Biennale gardens or the northern lagoon islands of Mazzorbo, Torcello, Le Vignole and Sant'Erasmo.

FARMERS MARKETS

The Rialto Market (p95) offers superb local produce and lagoon seafood at the centuries-old Pescaria (p95). Second only to it is the Lido's Tuesday food market, Mercato Setti-manale del Lido (p147), while on Thursday morning on Giudecca you can pick up organic produce at the Mercato della Prigione Femminile (p147), straight from the women's prison organic garden. For produce that floats, make a beeline for the produce barge on the Rio di Sant'Anna at the end of Via Garibaldi in Castello, or the one pulled up alongside Campo San Barnaba in Dorsoduro, near Ponte dei Pugni.

GROCERIES

The area around the Rialto Market has gourmet delis and speciality shops. I Tre Mercanti (p137) also stocks an excellent range of speciality regional products and wine. Close to Piazzale Roma is **Coop** (Map p281; ☑041 296 06 21; Fondamenta di Santa Chiara 507b; ☺8.30am-9pm; ⛴Piazzale Roma), an agricultural cooperative grocery with a good deli section. You'll find other branches throughout the city, including at Campo San Giacomo da l'Orio. The small supermarket chain **Rizzo** (Map p282; ☑041 528 99 08; www.rizzovenezia.it; Strada Nova 3832a; ☺7am-10pm; ⛴Ca' d'Oro) stocks sandwiches at its deli counters; Rosa Salva (p65) and Didovich (p131) offer takeaway deli dishes, and Rosticceria Gislon (p66) dishes up roast chickens to take away.

Cooking Courses

If all that produce and tradition inspires the chef within, consider signing up for a Venetian cooking course. Acquolina Cooking School (p147) runs four- and eight-hour courses, the latter option including a morning trip to the Rialto Market. It also offers multiday courses, including accommodation. Local market trawls are also on the menu at **Cook in Venice** (www.cookinvenice. com; tours €40-60, courses €150-350), whose one- and three-day cooking courses include gluten- and lactose-free nosh on request.

Mealtimes

Restaurants and bars are generally closed one day each week, usually Sunday or Monday. If your stomach growls between official mealtimes, cafes and bars generally open from 7am to 8pm and serve snacks all day.

Prima colazione (breakfast) is eaten between 7am and 10am. Venetians rarely eat a sit-down breakfast, but instead bolt down a cappuccino with a *brioche* (sweet bread) or other type of *pastine* (pastry) at a coffee bar before heading to work.

Pranzo (lunch) is served from noon to 2.30pm. Traditionally, lunch is the main meal of the day, and some shops and businesses close for two or three hours to accommodate it. Relax and enjoy a proper sit-down lunch, and you may be satisfied with *cicheti* for dinner.

Cena (dinner) is served between 7pm and 10.30pm. Opening hours vary, but many places begin filling up by 7.30pm and few take orders after 10.30pm.

Dining Etiquette

With thousands of visitors trooping though Venice daily demanding to be fed, service can be slow, harried or indifferent. By showing an interest in what Venice brings to the table, you'll get more attentive service, better advice and a more memorable meal. You'll win over your server and the chef with these four gestures that prove your mettle as *una buona forchetta* ('a good fork', or good eater):

Ignore the menu. Solicit your server's advice about seasonal treats and house specials, pick two options that sound interesting, and ask your server to recommend one over the other. When that's done, snap the menu shut and say, '*Allora, facciamo cosi, per favore!*' (Well then, let's do that, please!) You have just won over your server, and flattered the chef – promising omens for a memorable meal to come.

Drink well. Bottled water is entirely optional; *acqua del rubinetto* (tap water) is perfectly potable and highly recommended as an environment-saving measure. But fine meals call for wine, often available by the glass or half-bottle. Never mind that you don't recognise the label: the best small-production local wineries don't advertise or export (even to other parts of Italy), because their yield is snapped up by Venetian *osterie* and *enoteche*.

Try primi without condiments. Your server's relief and delight will be obvious. Venetian seafood risotto and pasta are rich and flavourful enough without being smothered in Parmesan or hot sauce.

Enjoy lagoon seafood. No one expects you to order an appetiser or *secondo*, but if you do, the tests of any Venetian chef are seasonal seafood antipasti and *frittura* (seafood fry). Try yours *senza limone* (without lemon) first: Venetians believe the subtle flavours of lagoon seafood are best complemented by salt, pepper and subtle trade-route spices like star anise. Instead, try washing down seafood with citrusy Veneto white wines that highlight rather than overwhelm briny flavours.

Gourmet Hotspots

Bad advice has circulated for decades about how it's impossible to eat well and economically in Venice, which has misinformed day trippers clinging defensively to congealed, reheated pizza slices in San Marco. Little do they realise that for the same price a bridge away, they could be dining on *crostini* (open-face sandwiches) topped with scampi and grilled baby artichoke, or tuna tartare with wild strawberries and balsamic reduction. Luckily for you, there's still room at the bar to score the best *cicheti*, and reservations are almost always available at phenomenal eateries – especially at dinner, after the day trippers depart.

To find the best Venetian food, dodge restaurants immediately around San Marco, near the train station and along main thoroughfares. Instead, aim your fork at these gourmet trails:

Cannaregio Along Fondamenta Savorgnan, Fondamenta della Sensa and Calle Larga Doge Priulli.

San Polo & Santa Croce Around the Rialto Market.

Castello Along Via Garibaldi, around Campo Bandiera e Moro and Zanipolo.

San Marco Along Calle delle Botteghe, Calle Spezier and Frezzeria.

Dorsoduro Along Calle Lunga San Barnaba, Calle della Toletta and Calle Crosera.

Giudecca Along Fondamenta delle Zitelle.

Eating by Neighbourhood

➜ San Marco (p65) *Panini, cicheti* and high-end, traditional restaurants.

➜ Dorsoduro (p81) Snug bistros, *campo*-side bar bites and cheap-and-easy pizza by the slice.

➜ San Polo & Santa Croce (p99) Market-inspired cuisine, creative *cicheti*, pizza and vegetarian fare.

➜ Cannaregio (p113) Traditional *cicheti*, authentic *osterie* and canalside dining.

➜ Castello (p131) Daring, creative cuisine, pizza, and bargain *cicheti*.

➜ Giudecca, Lido & the Southern Islands (p145) Traditional seafood and waterfront dining.

➜ Murano, Burano & the Northern Islands (p155) Just-caught lagoon seafood and garden dining.

Lonely Planet's Top Choices

Ristorante Quadri (p66) Michelin-starred cuisine in opulent surroundings overlooking San Marco.

Zanze XVI (p101) Inventive Venetian tasting menus courtesy of a Michelin-starred chef.

Riviera (p83) The finest Venetian seafood enjoyed with picture-perfect sunsets.

Trattoria Corte Sconta (p133) Superlative surf antipasti, inspired pasta dishes, and subtle modern subversion.

Best by Budget

€

Cantine del Vino già Schiavi (p81) Flavour-packed *panini* and delicious *cicheti*.

Salvmeria (p131) Gourmet *cicheti* and sophisticated plates of sesame tuna.

Al Theatro (p65) Mini *panini* filled fit for famished opera-goers.

€€

Osteria Bakán (p82) Home-made pasta in a cosy tavern.

CoVino (p132) Inventive dishes based on Slow Food–accredited produce.

Osteria Trefanti (p101) Intimate, pared-back elegance meets blue-ribbon produce, textures and arresting wines.

€€€

Ristorante Quadri (p66) Complex cooking by the Michelin-starred Alajmos.

Zanze XVI (p101) Refined, inventive cuisine in a contemporary bistro.

Riviera (p83) Seafood is the star of the show at this stylish waterside restaurant.

Best by Cuisine

Classic Venetian

Trattoria Altanella (p145) Fresh, succulent seafood on the island of Giudecca.

Trattoria al Gatto Nero (p158) The best seafood restaurant on an island of fisherfolk.

Da Codroma (p82) Thoroughly authentic Venetian dishes accredited by Slow Food.

Osteria da Pampo (p132) Superb *fritto* (fried fish) in a vintage setting.

Trattoria da Bepi Già '54' (p114) A popular neighbourhood trattoria serving well-executed classics.

Inventive Venetian

Zanze XVI (p101) Culinary magic courtesy of an ex-Noma chef.

Venissa Osteria (p158) Graze on the island landscape in lagoon-inspired dishes.

Glam (p102) A modern take on Venetian classics from a Michelin-starred chef.

Anice Stellato (p114) Venice redefines the neighbourhood bistro with this inventive menu.

CoVino (p132) A pocket-sized showcase for Slow Food produce cooked with modern soul.

Cicheti

Cantine del Vino già Schiavi (p81) Thoughtful flavour combinations and excellent wine pairings.

All'Arco (p99) Market-fresh morsels and zingy prosecco close to the Rialto Market.

Vino Vero (p115) Inventive *cicheti* accompanied by natural-process wines.

Salvmeria (p131) Unexpected quality concoctions and sunny outdoor seating.

Ossi di Seppia (p132) A tiny bar, top-quality *cicheti* and good over-the-counter banter.

International

Gibran (p132) Top-notch Middle Eastern fare in Venetian-inspired surroundings.

Africa Experience (p82) Venice's first African restaurant staffed by new migrants.

Best for Waterfront Dining

Trattoria Altanella (p145) Wine, dine and sigh on a balcony that hovers right over the water.

Riviera (p83) Perfectly positioned on the Zattere for hot-pink sunsets and romance.

La Palanca (p145) Panoramic waterfront dining at mere-mortal prices.

Trattoria al Gatto Nero (p158) Canalside seafood with crayon-coloured Burano backdrop.

Mirai (p115) An elegant Japanese restaurant with a terrace on the Grand Canal.

Best for Vegetarians

Bistrot de Venise (p66) Fine-dining establishment with an excellent vegetarian menu.

Osteria La Zucca (p101) Market-driven menus in a snug, canalside bolt-hole.

Ossi di Seppia (p132) A cute *bacaro* with an excellent choice of vegetarian *cicheti*.

La Tecia Vegana (p82) Organic vegan dishes, including a top selection of desserts.

Frary's (p100) Pan-Mediterranean and Middle Eastern flavours in the shadow of a Gothic giant.

Bar Terrazza Danieli (p134)

🍷 Drinking & Nightlife

When the siren sounds for acqua alta *(high tide), Venetians close up shop and head home to put up their flood barriers – then pull on their boots and head right back out again. Why let floods disrupt a toast? It's not just a turn of phrase: come hell or high water, Venetians will find a way to have a good time.*

Happy Hour(s)

The happiest hour (or two) in Venice begins around 6pm with booze and *cicheti* (Venetian tapas) at *bacari* (hole-in-the-wall bars). If you're prompt, you might beat the crowds to the bar for *un'ombra* (a 'shade'; a small glass of wine), which can go for as little as €0.70 at cupboard-sized Bacareto da Lele (p104). Heading in early also means grabbing *cicheti* while they're fresh. *Osterie* (taverns) and *enoteche* (wine bars) are also renowned for their vino-friendly bites.

Giro d'Ombra

An authentic Venetian *giro d'ombra* (pub crawl) begins around the Pescaria by 9am, drinking prosecco (sparkling white wine) with fisherfolk toasting a hard day's work that began at 3am. For layabouts, Venice offers a second-chance *giro* with *cicheti* at *bacari* that ring the Rialto Market around noon. Afterwards, it's a long four-hour dry spell until the next *giro d'ombra* begins in buzzing spots around Campo Santa Margherita in Dorsoduro, Fondamenta dei Ormesini in Cannaregio, Campo Santa Maria Formosa

NEED TO KNOW

Opening Hours

Cafe-bars generally open from 7am to 8pm, although some stay open later and morph into drinking hang-outs. Pubs and wine bars are mostly shut by 1am or 2am.

Noise Regulations

Keep it down to a dull roar after 10pm: sound travels in Venice, and worse than a police bust for noise infractions is a scolding from a Venetian *nonna* (grandmother).

and Via Garibaldi in Castello, and the warren of *calli* (lanes) around Campo San Bartolomeo and Campo Manin in San Marco.

What to Order

No rules seem to apply to drinking in Venice. No mixing spirits and wine? Venice's classic cocktails suggest otherwise; try a *spritz*, made with prosecco, soda water and bittersweet Aperol, bitter Campari or herbaceous Cynar. Price is not an indicator of quality – you can pay €2.50 for a respectable *spritz*, or live to regret that €16 Bellini tomorrow (ouch). If you're not pleased with your drink, leave it and move on to the next *bacaro*. Don't be shy about asking fellow drinkers what they recommend; happy hour is a highly sociable affair.

LOCAL FAVOURITES

Prosecco The crisp, sparkling white that's the life of any Venetian party, from nonvintage to DOCG Conegliano Prosecco Superiore. Persistent bubbles and straw-yellow hues.

Spritz A stiff drink at an easy price, this prosecco cocktail is a cross-generational hit with students and pensioners at bars across Venice – except at *enoteche*.

Soave A well-balanced white wine made with Veneto Garganega grapes, ideal with seafood in refreshing young versions or as a conversation piece in complex Classico versions.

Amarone The Titian of wines: a profound, voluptuous red blended from Valpolicella Corvina grapes. Complex and costly (€6 to €18 per glass), but utterly captivating while it lasts.

Ribolla Gialla A weighty white with all the right curves from Friuli-Venezia Giulia, this wine gets more voluptuous with age; irresistible with buttery fish, gnocchi and cheese.

Valpolicella A versatile grape that's come into its own with a bright young DOC namesake red wine more food-friendly than Amarone; a structured, aged version called DOG Valpolicella Ripasso; and DOCG sweet late-harvest Recioto della Valpolicella.

Lugana A mineral-rich, well-structured white from Trebbiano grapes grown at the border of Veneto and Lombardy; a favourite with gastronomes.

Refosco dal Peduncolo Rosso Intense and brooding, a Goth rocker that hits the right notes. This order is guaranteed to raise your sommelier's eyebrow, and probably your bill.

Raboso One of Italy's top reds at full maturity, rich in tannins, packed with flavour and with a bouquet of spicy cherries. Perfect with aged cheeses, game and grilled red meats.

Cafes

To line your stomach with coffee and pastry before your next *giro d'ombra,* check out Venice's legendary cafe-bars, and skip milky cappuccino for a stronger *macchiatone* (espresso with a 'big stain' of hot milk). For local flavour, try the Torrefazione Cannaregio (p117) *noxea:* coffee beans roasted with hazelnuts. House-roasted speciality blends are also the order of the day at Caffè del Doge (p102).

Historic baroque cafes around Piazza San Marco, such as Caffè Florian (p68) and Grancaffè Quadri (p68), serve coffee and hot chocolate with live orchestras – though your heart might beat a different rhythm once you get the bill. Hint: Caffè Lavena (p69) offers a €1.50 espresso at the counter.

Enoteche

Request *qualcosa di particolare* (something interesting), and your sommelier will accept the challenge to reach behind the bar for one of Veneto's obscure varietals or innovative wines. Even ordinary varietals take on extraordinary characteristics in growing areas that range from marshy to mountainous.

Speciality *enoteche* like Vino Vero (p115), Estro (p82), Malvasia all'Adriatico Mar (p84), Salvmeria (p131), Ossi di Seppia (p132), Al Prosecco (p104), El Sbarlefo (p84) and La Cantina (p118) uphold Venice's time-honoured tradition of selling good stuff by the glass, so you can discover new favourites without committing to a bottle.

ADVENTURES IN WINE & CICHETI

Prosecco, Soave and Amarone aren't the only wines in town. Expand your happy-hour options with an immersion experience in Veneto wines at local *bacari* (bars) led by an English-speaking sommelier from **Venetian Vine** (https://venetianvine.org; tastings per person €75); tastings cost €75 per person. Tastings host Nan is also a dab hand at *voga* (the distinctive Venetian style of rowing) and is one of the tutors at Row Venice (p153). The brave (or foolhardy) may be tempted to try her **Cichetto Row**, a gentle 2½-hour row between canalside bars (€240/280 for two/four people).

For those who fancy greater immersion, Venetian Vine also creates bespoke, small-group **tours of lagoon vineyards** (€600 for four people) in a traditional San Pierota boat. Along the way you'll be introduced to Laguna nel Bicchiere (www.lagunanelbicchiere.it), an organisation dedicated to recovering lost vines. Wine tastings take place in monastic cloisters littered with old wine barrels, and are followed by a vinous lunch on Sant'Erasmo.

Landlubbers in search of a good backstreet *bacaro* crawl, should opt for fun and informed *cicheti* (Venetian tapas) tours with Venetian home cook Monica Cesarato from Cook in Venice (p32). She'll ply you with more wine, *cicheti* and anecdotes than is seemly for one night; you'll no doubt end the evening toasting Venice with grappa-soaked grapes and chocolate 'salami'.

Venice Urban Adventures (p26) offers 2½-hour tours of hotspots led by knowledgeable, enthusiastic, English-speaking local foodies. Tours cost €90 per person (with up to 12 participants), covering *ombre* (wine by the glass) and *cicheti* in four *bacari* and a tipsy Rialto gondola crossing (weather permitting). Departure points vary seasonally; consult the website.

DOC Versus IGT

In Italy, the official DOC *(denominazione di origine controllata)* and elite DOCG (DOC *garantita* guaranteed) designations are usually assurances of top-notch vino. Taste the DOCG wines that put the Veneto on the world wine-tasting map at select wineries in Valdobbiadene and Conegliano (prosecco), Soave (Soave Superiore and Recioto di Soave) and Valpolicella (Amarone and Valpolicella).

Yet, successful as its wines are, the Veneto also bucks the DOC/DOCG system. Many of the region's small-production wineries can't be bothered with such external validation as they may already sell out to Venetian *osterie* and *enoteche*. As a result, some top producers prefer the IGT *(indicazione geografica tipica)* designation, which guarantees grapes typical of the region but leaves winemakers room to experiment with nontraditional blends and methods, such as natural-yeast fermentation.

Drinking & Nightlife by Neighbourhood

➡ San Marco (p66) High-end cocktails and DOC wines with DJs.

➡ Dorsoduro (p84) Bargain booze, buzzing *osterie* and rivers of *spritz*.

➡ San Polo & Santa Croce (p102) Inspired *ombre* and *cicheti* at historic *bacari*.

➡ Cannaregio (p115) Happy-hour sun spots on southern-facing canal banks.

➡ Castello (p134) Drink like a sailor at local *bacari*, or join *artistes* for pre-Biennale cocktails.

➡ Giudecca, Lido & the Southern Islands (p146) Fall film festivals, summer beach clubs and year-round happy hours.

Lonely Planet's Top Choices

Vino Vero (p115) Superlative wines from small and biodynamic producers, top-notch *cicheti* and an effortlessly cool vibe.

Bar Longhi (p68) The most beautiful cocktail bar in town, with drinks and a view to match.

Malvasia all'Adriatico Mar (p84) Veneto's finest natural-process wines accompanied by convivial toasts with fellow drinkers.

Marciano Pub (p117) Homebrews, craft beers, serious spirits and sustainably sourced burgers.

Cantine del Vino già Schiavi (p81) Tiny bottles of beer and outsized neighbourhood personalities keep this historic canalside joint hopping.

Al Timon (p115) Canalside tables, *crostini* (open-face sandwiches), carafes of good house wine and the occasional live gig.

Best Happy-Hour Hangouts

Al Mercà (p102) Delectable DOC vino, bargain bar bites and al fresco conviviality beside Venice's best-loved market.

Al Timon (p115) Swill and swoon on a moored vessel with savvy local dreamers.

Cantine del Vino già Schiavi (p81) Appetite-piquing *cicheti* and a mixed local crowd by a Dorsoduro canal.

Cantina Aziende Agricole (p114) Cannaregio's neighbourhood clubhouse.

Bacareto da Lele (p104) Filthy-cheap *ombre*, petite *panini* (sandwiches) and crowds of loyal locals.

Best for Wine

Vino Vero (p115) Natural, biodynamic and boutique drops in a standout Cannaregio wine bar.

Malvasia all'Adriatico Mar (p84) Natural Veneto wines accompanied by superb cheese and charcuterie platters.

Estro (p82) Has 500 personally chosen wines, plus handpicked cheeses, *salumi* (cured meats) and produce-driven menus.

Salvmeria (p131) Sophisticated regional-wine selection and unusual, gourmet *cicheti* in a vintage deli.

Al Prosecco (p104) Organic grapes, wild-yeast fermentation and biodynamic methods worthy of a toast.

Best for Beer

Marciano Pub (p117) Serious global craft beers served at a shining wood bar with brass taps.

Birreria Zanon (p117) Popular pints on tap and amber ales beside a sunny canal.

Il Santo Bevitore (p118) Trappist ales, seasonal stouts and chat-igniting football matches on the TV.

Best Signature Cocktails

Harry's Bar (p68) The driest classic in town is Harry's gin-heavy martini (no olive).

Londra Bar (p134) Perfectly balanced Manhattans in a bar as sleek as a million-dollar yacht.

Bar Longhi (p68) Drink top-class cocktails (like the orange martini) in a jewel-like interior.

Locanda Cipriani (p158) Harry's famous white-peach

Bellini tastes even better at the Ciprianis' island retreat.

Bar Terrazza Danieli (p134) Apricot and orange moonlight with gin and grenadine in the Danieli.

Best for Coffee

Caffè Florian (p68) An 18th-century time warp in show-off Piazza San Marco.

Torrefazione Cannaregio (p117) A veteran coffee roaster famed for its hazelnut-laced espresso.

Caffè del Doge (p102) A serious selection of world coffees, including the rare kopi luwak.

Best Wine-Tasting Destinations

La Strada del Prosecco (p172) The Veneto's revered epicentre of prosecco production.

Soave (p182) Medieval walls and crisp, vibrant whites await east of Verona.

Valpolicella (p184) Northwest of Verona, the celebrated home of coveted red Amarone.

Best for Drinks with a View

Bar Longhi (p68) Exquisitely crafted cocktails and a first-class view of La Salute.

Bar Terrazza Danieli (p134) Late-afternoon cocktail sessions with sweeping canal and Palladio views.

L'Ombra del Leoni (p69) The Biennale's bargain bar on the Grand Canal.

Performance at Verona Opera Festival

⭐ Entertainment

After the fall of Venice's shipping empire, the curtain rose on the city's music scene. A magnet for classical music fans for four centuries, Venice continues to fill its palaces with the sounds of arias, cantatas and freestyle sax. The annual Biennale also brings a host of contemporary music, theatre and dance to the city.

Opera

Venice is the home of modern opera and the legendary, incendiary La Fenice (p63), one of the world's top opera houses since its founding in 1792, and the place where Giuseppe Verdi premiered *Rigoletto* and *La Traviata*. But the music doesn't stop when La Fenice takes its summer break: opera divas from around the world perform under the stars from June to early September at Verona's Roman Arena (p177), Italy's top summer opera festival.

Today you can see opera as Venetians did centuries ago, inside a whimsical pleasure-palace music room at Palazzetto Bru Zane (p104), in Grand Canal palace salons with Musica a Palazzo (p69), among heavenly frescoes at Scuola Grande di San Giovanni Evangelista (p95) and in period costume at Scuola Grande dei Carmini (p81). In Vicenza, you can see classical concerts and opera at the unique Teatro Olimpico (p169), designed by Palladio.

VERONA'S OPERA FESTIVAL

On balmy summer nights, when 14,000 music lovers fill the Roman Arena during the opera festival and light their candles at

NEED TO KNOW

Opening Hours

Event start times vary, with doors at evening concerts typically opening from 7pm to 8.30pm. Due to noise regulations in this small city with big echoes, live-music venues are limited, and shows typically end by 11pm.

Advance Tickets

Shows regularly sell out in summer, so purchase tickets online at the venue website, www.veneziaunica.it or www.musicinvenice.com. Tickets may also be available at the venue box office, or from Vènezia Unica information offices, located off San Marco, at the train station and on Piazzale Roma.

Events Calendar

For schedules of upcoming performances, Venetian discographies and online ticket sales, see www.musicinvenice.com. For upcoming openings, concerts, performances and other cultural events, check listings at www.veneziadavivere.com (mostly in Italian), and www.venezianews.it and look online at www.veneziaunica.it and www.musicinvenice.com.

Cover Charge

Entry is often free at bars, but the cover runs from €10 to €25 for shows in established venues; pay in advance or at the door.

Free Shows

In summer, don't miss Venice Jazz Festival outdoor events, plus free beach concerts on the Lido and on Lido di Jesolo. Year-round in good weather, you might luck into outdoor happy-hour shows around Campo San Giacomo da l'Orio and Fondamenta dei Ormesini.

sunset, expect goosebumps even before the performance starts. The **festival** (☑045 800 51 51; www.arena.it; Via Dietro Anfiteatro 6; ⊘late Jun-late Aug) was started in 1913 and is now the biggest open-air lyrical music event in the world. It draws international stars and the staging is legendary – highlights have included Franco Zeffirelli's lavish productions of *Carmen* and *Aida*.

Prices rise at weekends, ranging from €25 on unreserved stone steps to €208 for the central gold seats. Performances usually start at 8.45pm or 9pm with locals booking their dinner table for after the show. Tucking into a preshow picnic on the unreserved stone steps is fine, so decant that wine into a plastic bottle (glass and knives aren't allowed), arrive early, rent a cushion and prepare for an utterly unforgettable evening.

Classical Music

Venice is the place to hear baroque music in its original and intended venues, with notes soaring to Sebastiano Ricci-frescoed ceilings at Palazzetto Bru Zane (p104), sweeping through the salons at Palazzo Querini Stampalia, and reverberating through La Pietà (p130), the original Vivaldi venue. Between opera seasons, summer symphonies are performed by La Fenice's Philharmonic Orchestra at the opera house or affiliated Teatro Malibran (p118).

Ever-changing classical and jazz concerts are hosted by a variety of orchestras and bands in *palazzi* and churches around the city. Check out **Music in Venice** (☑348 190 8939; www.musicinvenice.com) for performances and to book tickets online.

Music becomes a religious experience surrounded by Venetian art masterpieces during organ vespers at Basilica di Santa Maria della Salute (p78) and when the Venice Music Project (p85) performs long-lost 17th- and 18th-century scores in St George's Anglican Church.

Jazz, Rock & Pop

July's Venice Jazz Festival showcases international stars like Keith Jarrett, Cassandra Wilson and Jack Savoretti in iconic venues throughout the city, including La Fenice and the Peggy Guggenheim Collection. Its organising body, VenetoJazz (www.venetojazz.com), delivers year-round concerts in numerous towns across the Veneto, including Padua and Bassano del Grappa, while Vicenza hosts its own jazz festival (p169) in May.

Year-round tributes to Miles Davis, Chet Baker and Charles Mingus await at Venice's only dedicated jazz venue, Venice Jazz Club (p85). Otherwise, a handful of bars sporadically host live music acts, usually rock, reggae, folk and *leggera* (pop). For all-ages alt-rock and punk, check events at Laboratorio Occupato Morion (p136). Bars with

LA BIENNALE DI VENEZIA

Europe's premier arts showcase since 1907 is something of a misnomer: **La Biennale di Venezia** (www.labiennale.org; Giardini della Biennale; ⊘mid-May–Nov; ⊛Giardini Biennale) is actually held every year, but the spotlight alternates between art (odd-numbered years) and architecture (even-numbered years). The summer art biennial is the biggest draw, with some 300,000 visitors viewing contemporary-art showcases in 30 national pavilions in the Giardini, with additional exhibitions in venues across town. The architecture biennial fills the vast boat sheds of the Arsenale with avant-garde conceptual structures and is a great opportunity to see the usually closed complex.

But the Biennale doesn't stop there. The city-backed organisation also organises an International Festival of Contemporary Dance, not to mention the iconic Venice International Film Festival. Running parallel to the Biennale is a growing number of fringe arts events, offering opportunities to see hidden corners of the city usually not accessible to the public. Of particular note is the new **Design.Ve** (www.designve.org; ⊘May-Jun), which is a curation of design-focused itineraries around the city. Check the Biennale website for upcoming event listings, venues and tickets.

regular musical interludes include Paradiso Perduto (p118), Al Timon (p115), El Sbarlefo (p84), Bacarando (p68) and Il Santo Bevitore (p118). But don't expect to roll in late and still catch the show: according to local noise regulations, bars are expected to end concerts at 11pm.

Summer concerts are held on beaches on the Lido and on Lido di Jesolo – check the local press in July and August.

Theatre & Dance

Although dance performances are staged year-round in Venice, they are especially prolific during the Biennale's International Festival of Contemporary Dance, usually held the first two weeks in June. Ballet performances are usually staged at Teatro Goldoni (p69), which also delivers contemporary theatre and Shakespeare, usually in Italian.

Cinema

International star power and Italian fashion storm Lido red carpets during the Venice Film Festival, where films are shown in their original language. Year-round, catch films (sometimes subtitled) and blockbusters (usually dubbed) at Multisala Rossini (p70), a three-screen venue with digital sound in the heart of San Marco. La Casa del Cinema (p104) in Santa Croce is where the film archive is located and where you'll often find art-house and independent films being screened (some of them in the original language).

Entertainment by Neighbourhood

➡ **San Marco** Opera, classical music, dance, theatre and cinema.

➡ **Dorsoduro** Jazz.

➡ **San Polo & Santa Croce** Cinema and live-music nights.

➡ **Cannaregio** Concerts, live-music nights, cinema and the casino.

➡ **Castello** Classical music and alternative live-music nights.

➡ **Giudecca, Lido & the Southern Islands** Cinema and DJ-fuelled beach parties on the Lido.

Lonely Planet's Top Choices

La Biennale di Venezia (p41) Europe's signature art and architecture biennials draw international crowds, with musicians and dancers in summer showcases.

Teatro La Fenice (p69) Divas hit new highs in this sumptuous, legendary theatre for less than 1000 lucky ticket-holders.

Palazzetto Bru Zane (p104) World-class classical music amid heavenly frescoes.

Venice International Film Festival (p21) A paparazzi-packed spectacle of silver-screen royalty and international premieres.

Verona's Roman Arena (p177) Larger-than-life tenors rock the Roman amphitheatre June to early September, rousing choruses of '*Bravo!*'.

Best Modern Music Events

Venice Jazz Festival (p169) A-list names play theatres, palaces and galleries.

La Biennale di Venezia (p41) A jam-packed program of new works, including numerous world premieres.

Laboratorio Occupato Morion (p136) A radical backdrop for rocking regional bands.

Teatrino di Palazzo Grassi (p64) Cutting-edge contemporary musical performances.

Best for Opera

Teatro La Fenice (p69) Top-tier productions in one of Italy's grandest theatres.

Verona's Roman Arena (p177) Summertime arias in an ancient Roman stadium.

Musica a Palazzo (p69) Historic compositions sung in sumptuous palace surrounds.

Scuola Grande di San Giovanni Evangelista (p95) Sopranos belt out baroque where flagellants once flogged.

Scuola Grande dei Carmini (p81) Costumed opera in a jewel-box former hostel.

Teatro Olimpico (p169) Intimate opera performances in Palladio's miniature opera house in Vicenza.

Best for Classical Music

Palazzetto Bru Zane (p104) Renowned musicians and lesser-played compositions in the presence of cheeky cherubs.

Teatro La Fenice (p69) A robust program of grand symphonies and choral concerts.

Teatro Malibran (p118) Intimate chamber-music concerts in a 17th-century theatre.

Venice Music Project (p85) Musical archaeology resurrects lost scores, which are played on historic instruments.

Best for Theatre & Dance

La Biennale di Venezia (p41) Envelope-pushing moves at an international dance fest.

Teatro Goldoni (p69) Mighty classics in the city's starring theatre.

Teatrino di Palazzo Grassi (p64) Unusual contemporary dance and theatre performances in a beautiful venue.

Best for Cinema

Venice International Film Festival (p21) Red-carpet premieres and Hollywood royalty on the Lido.

Multisala Rossini (p70) Venice's largest cinema screens the odd original-language film.

Circuito Cinema Giorgione Movie d'Essai (p118) Two screens playing film-fest favourites, classics and kid-friendly animations.

Best Live Music Nights

Laboratorio Occupato Morion (p136) World music, hip hop and folk-rock orchestras shake up Venice.

Paradiso Perduto (p118) Jazz, salsa and the odd legend in an arty, old-school tavern.

Venice Jazz Club (p85) Jazz great tributes and sultry Latin rhythms.

Il Santo Bevitore (p118) Occasional pop, blues and funk in a beer-lover's paradise.

🛍 Shopping

Beyond the world-famous museums and architecture is Venice's best-kept secret: the shopping. No illustrious shopping career is complete without trolling Venice for one-of-a-kind, artisan-made finds. All those souvenir tees and kitschy masks are nothing more than decoys for the amateurs. Dig deeper and you'll stumble across the prized stuff – genuine, local and nothing short of inspiring.

Artisan Specialities

Your Venice souvenirs may be hard to describe back home without sounding like you're bragging. 'It's an original', you'll say, 'and I met the artisan.' Venice has kept its artisan traditions alive and vital for centuries, especially glass, paper, textiles and woodworking.

STUDIO VISITS

For your travelling companions who aren't sold on shopping, here's a convincing argument: in Venice, it really is an educational experience. In backstreet artisan studios, you can watch ancient techniques used to make strikingly modern *carta memorizzata* (marbled-paper) travel journals and Murano glass waterfalls worn as necklaces. Studios cluster together, so to find unique pieces, just wander key artisan areas: San Polo around Calle Seconda dei Saoneri; Santa Croce around Campo Santa Maria Mater Domini; San Marco along Frezzeria and Calle de la Botteghe; Castello along Barbaria de le Tole; Cannaregio along Fondamenta dei Ormesini; Dorsoduro around the Peggy Guggenheim Collection; and Murano.

Glass showrooms and shelves of fragile handicrafts may be labelled *non toccare* (don't touch) – instead of chancing breakage, just ask to see any piece. The person who shows it to you may be the artisan who made it, so don't be shy about saying *'Complimenti!'* (my compliments!).

Venetian Shopping Highlights

Italian style earns its international reputation for impeccable proportions, eye-catching details, luxe textures and vibrant colours – but Venice goes one step further, with eclectic fashion statements, highly creative artisanal accessories, limited-edition sunglasses and no shortage of prized and intriguing antiques.

CLOTHING

Venice has the standard Italian designer brands you can find back home, from Armani to Zegna, along Larga XXII Marzo and Marzaria in San Marco – but for original fashion and better value, venture into Venice's backstreets. The chances of a colleague back home showing up to the office party in the same Venetia Studium (p72) goddess dress, rock 'n' roll silk jacket from SV Lab (p71) or Arnoldo & Battois (p72) sculpted frock are infinitesimal. Finish off your outfit with a dashing woollen *tabarro* (Venetian cloak) from Barena (p70).

ACCESSORIES

Don't call Venetian artisans designers: their highly skilled handicrafts can't be mass produced, and stand out in a globalised fashion crowd. Paris' latest 'it' bags seem uninspired compared to the hand-crafted leather satchels from Il Grifone (p86), or 'beaded' necklaces made from hand-painted, quilled paper at Paperoowl (p106).

Indeed, the choice of Venetian-made objects are as eclectic as they are irresistible: hand-beaten copper and silver bracelets that look like lagoon ripples from Bottega Orafa

NEED TO KNOW

Opening Hours

Shops open 10am to 1pm and 3.30pm to 7pm Monday to Saturday. Shops in tourist areas stay open 10am to 7pm daily, while smaller shops may remain closed on Monday morning, and Murano showrooms close at 6pm. Many shops close for major Italian holidays and part of August and January.

Shipping

Never mind arbitrary airline luggage limits: most home decor and Murano glass showrooms offer shipping services at reasonable costs, especially within Europe. On new merchandise, customs duties may apply in your home country – check before you buy.

Taxes

Visitors from outside the EU may be entitled to VAT sales tax refunds on major purchases (p254).

ABC (p106), hand-sewn velvet Venetian slippers at Pied à Terre (p105), vibrant vegetable-dyed boots from Kalimala (p137) and Japanese-inspired tube scarves at Anatema (p106). Add cascading, hand-blown glass-bead necklaces from Marina e Susanna Sent (p160) or earrings made from Murano glass and semiprecious stones from Designs 188 (p87), and there really is no point of comparison.

EYEWEAR

Centuries before geek chic, the first eyeglasses known to Europe were worn in the Veneto c 1348, and Venetian opticians have been hand-grinding lenses and stylish frames ever since. Bring your prescription to San Marco's Ottica Carraro (p70) or San Polo's Ottica Vascellari (p106), or snap up a replica of Peggy Guggenheim's outrageous frames at the Peggy Guggenheim Museum Shop (p77) in Dorsoduro.

ANTIQUES

Venice's penchant for conjuring up the past goes beyond Byzantine domes and baroque salons. The city is a giant attic of rare, well-worn trinkets and treasures, from 19th-century postcards and lithographs to centuries-old leather-bound books. Dorsoduro is a good place to start your antiques hunt, whether you're looking for vintage lighting at L'Angolo del Passato (p86), turn-of-the-century Venetian prints, erotic literature or baroque card games at Segni nel Tempo (p87), or fin-de-siècle miniatures and repurposed earrings at Claudia Canestrelli (p87). Bibliophiles lust after rare prints and antiquarian books from Libreria Linea d'Acqua (p70) and La Stamperia del Ghetto (p119), whose inventory includes Emanuele 'Lele' Luzzati's highly collectible Chagall-style illustrations.

Vintage jewels and homewares await at Cannaregio's Antichità al Ghetto (p120), whose beautifully curated collection includes Jewish liturgical objects, damask and 18th-century cameos. Across in Castello lies Ballarin (p136), its eclectic, well-priced booty spanning everything from long-forgotten toys to elegant prints and hand-painted glassware. Last but not least is San Marco's Mercatino dell'Antiquariato (p72), a much-loved antiques flea market held several weekends a year in Campo San Maurizio. Head in early for the best finds, among them vintage Campari posters, Venetian postcards, Murano glassware and delicate Burano lace.

Shopping by Neighbourhood

➡ San Marco (p70) Art galleries, international designers and high-end artisan showcases.

➡ Dorsoduro (p85) Antique shops and fashion-forward boutiques.

➡ San Polo & Santa Croce (p105) Artisan studios: glass, paper, fashion, gondolas.

➡ Cannaregio (p119) High-street retail and artisan bargains.

➡ Castello (p136) Cutting-edge artisans and quirky curios.

➡ Giudecca, Lido & the Southern Islands (p147) Heritage textiles, paper-made design and sculptural knits.

➡ Murano, Burano & the Northern Islands (p158) Handmade lace and the world's finest art glass.

Lonely Planet's Top Choices

Chiarastella Cattana (p70) Locally loomed linens in history-inspired modern designs and Venetian colours.

Paolo Olbi (p86) Ordinary travel journals just can't compare with Mr Olbi's beautifully handbound books.

ElleElle (p158) Murano art glass balancing modernity and tradition.

Ca' Macana (p86) Elaborate carnival masks made by a master artisan.

Oh My Blue (p105) Striking contemporary jewellery and accessories curated with a Venetian eye.

Artisti Artigiani del Chiostro (p147) A collective of different artisan studios in the repurposed cloisters of an old convent.

Best Venetian Souvenirs

Ca' Macana (p86) Masks made by masters.

Il Pavone di Paolo Pelosin (p105) Rippled blue sketchbooks.

Fonderie Valese (p71) Miniature St Mark's lions forged in copper and brass.

Paolo Brandolisio (p137) Miniature *forcole* (carved gondola oarlocks).

Best for Home Decor

Bevilacqua Fabrics (p71) Purveyors of the world's finest brocades and tassles, as seen in a palace near you.

Chiarastella Cattana (p70) Sophisticated linens to restyle every corner of your *palazzo*.

Atelier Alessandro Merlin (p136) Talking-point ceramics for a provocative cup of coffee.

Giobagnara (p71) Murano glass and leather desk accessories galore.

Best for Fashion

Venetia Studium (p72) Delphos tunic dresses and handstamped silk-velvet purses.

Venetian Dreams (p72) Lagoon-inspired necklaces made with antique seed beads.

SV Lab (p71) Cutting-edge fashion with a Venetian twist.

Fiorella Gallery (p72) Head-turning couture for style rebels.

Barena (p70) Purveyors of the finest wool coats in the lagoon.

L'Armadio di Coco Luxury Vintage (p72) Couture fashions of yesteryear at affordable prices.

Best for Antiques

Ballarin (p136) A treasure chest packed with period furniture, lamps, glass and more.

Claudia Canestrelli (p87) A walk-in curiosity cabinet of prints, miniatures and repurposed antique earrings.

Antichità al Ghetto (p120) A nostalgic mix of Venetian maps, art and jewellery.

Libreria Linea d'Acqua (p70) The finest antiquarian book dealer in the city, with some beautiful contemporary books.

Segni nel Tempo (p87) A burst of rare books, prints and historic oddities.

Best for Jewellery

Marina e Susanna Sent (p160) Striking, contemporary wearables good enough for MoMA.

Sigfrido Cipolato (p71) Arresting pieces bursting with imagination and intrigue.

Oh My Blue (p105) Cutting-edge creations from local and foreign designers.

Materialmente (p72) Delicate contemporary jewellery fashioned on-site.

Best for Leather Goods

Atelier Segalin di Daniela Ghezzo (p71) Custom-made shoes created with rare leather and seasoned style.

Arnoldo & Battois (p72) Hand-crafted bags with historically inspired details.

Balducci Borse (p120) Shoes and bags from a master leather craftsman.

Il Grifone (p86) Colourful satchels and belts handcrafted from Tuscan leather.

Best for Paper Products

Paolo Olbi (p86) One of the last remaining masters of paper, printing and bookbinding.

Gianni Basso (p119) Get letterpressed business cards from an artisan who supplies the stars.

Paperoowl (p106) Ingenious paper jewellery and delicate paper chimes.

La Stamperia del Ghetto (p119) A treasure trove of copperplate prints and Lele Luzzati illustrations.

Plum Plum Creations (p120) Handmade etchings, linocuts and watercolours that make perfect souvenirs.

Explore Venice & the Veneto

VENICE'S
TOP SIGHTS

Neighbourhoods at a Glance

❶ San Marco p50

San Marco is packed with so many world-class attractions that some visitors never leave – and others are loath to visit, fearing the crowds. But why deny yourself the pleasures of two of the most famous buildings in the world, Basilica di San Marco and Palazzo Ducale, not to mention the wonderful Museo Correr and Venice's famous jewel-box opera house La

Fenice? Judge for yourself whether they earn their reputations – and don't stop there: San Marco's backstreets are packed with galleries, boutiques and *bacari* (wine bars).

❷ Dorsoduro p73

Dorsoduro covers prime Grand Canal waterfront with Ca' Rezzonico's golden-age splendour, the Peggy Guggenheim Collection's

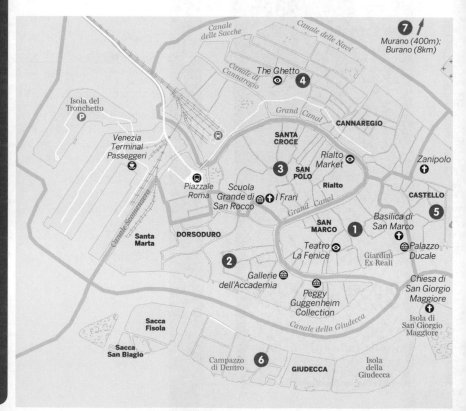

modern edge, Gallerie dell'Accademia's Renaissance beauties and Punta della Dogana's ambitious installation art. The neighbourhood lazes days away on the sun-drenched Zattere, and convenes in Campo Santa Margherita for *spritz* (prosecco cocktail) and flirtation.

❸ San Polo & Santa Croce p90

Heavenly devotion and earthly delights co-exist in San Polo and Santa Croce, where divine art rubs up against the ancient red-light district, now home to artisan workshops and *osterie* (taverns). Don't miss fraternal-twin masterpieces: Titian's glowing *Madonna* at I Frari and turbulent Tintorettos at Scuola Grande di San Rocco. Quirky museums fill Grand Canal *palazzi* (mansions) with fashion and natural history oddities, while island grown produce crams the stalls of the Rialto Market.

❹ Cannaregio p107

Between the art-filled Chiesa della Madonna dell'Orto, the Renaissance miracle of Chiesa di Santa Maria dei Miracoli and the tiny island Ghetto, a living monument to the outsized contributions of Venice's Jewish community, are some of Venice's top casual eateries and *cicheti* (Venetian tapas) bars.

❺ Castello p121

The crenellated walls of the Arsenale still dominate Venice's largest *sestiere* (district), but where it was once the secret preserve of highly skilled artisans serving Venice's naval war machine, it is now thrown open annually to alternating throngs of art and architecture lovers during the Biennale. The Riva degli Schiavoni is Venice's prime waterfront promenade, but step back into the maze of lanes and you'll find little neighbourhood cafes on sunny squares.

❻ Giudecca, Lido & the Southern Islands p138

The most evocative of Venice's southern islands are tiny specks capped with monasteries such as San Giorgio Maggiore, its gracious Palladio church forming the essential backdrop for dreamy lagoon views. The much larger crescent of Giudecca has its own Palladian masterpieces and is a fascinating mash-up of luxury hotels, workaday apartments, the remnants of industry and a still-functioning women's prison. Lido is Venice's 12km beach escape, its A-list film festival a hangover from its days as one of Europe's most glamorous resorts.

❼ Murano, Burano & the Northern Islands p148

Venetian life had its origins in the northern reaches of the lagoon, and when things get too frantic in the city proper, these ancient island settlements remain the best escape. Serious shoppers head to Murano for one-of-a-kind glass art. Others prefer to head to the islands of Burano and Mazzorbo for extended seafood feasts, or to Torcello for glimpses of heaven in the golden mosaics.

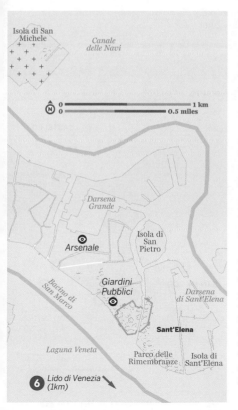

San Marco

Neighbourhood Top Five

1 **Basilica di San Marco** (p52) Joining the chorus of gasps rippling through the crowd as you enter Venice's magnificent cathedral, looking up to discover angels dancing across 8500 sq metres of glittering golden mosaics.

2 **Palazzo Ducale** (p55) Discovering over-the-top

state rooms, dark secrets, dingy prisons and blockbuster exhibitions behind the rosy facade.

3 **La Fenice** (p63) Shouting *'Brava!'* from one of the boxes at Venice's jewel-box opera house for an encore performance.

4 **Museo Correr** (p62) Adopting a philosopher

painted by Veronese or Tintoretto as your personal mentor at the Biblioteca Nazionale Marciana.

5 **Caffè Florian** (p68) Tangoing across Piazza San Marco at sunset to the tune of the orchestra.

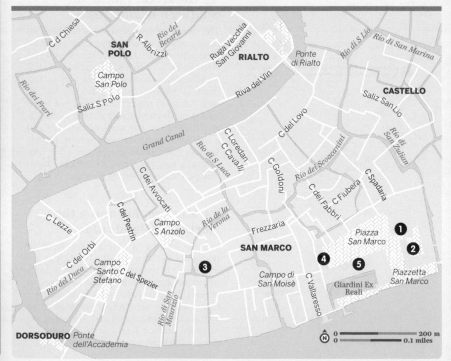

For more detail of this area see Map p274. ➡

Explore San Marco

The neighbourhood of San Marco is Venice's oldest and most famous. Everything started here in the 9th century when Doge Partecipazio founded the modern settlement of Venice in the vicinity of the Rialto Bridge (Ponte di Rialto). Venice's fairy-tale golden basilica followed shortly after, built to house the bones of St Mark the Evangelist.

With the palace, prisons, government offices, mint and library crowding around the basilica, Piazza San Marco was the fulcrum of Venetian power and it attracts the majority of visitors today. You could spend days here, so start early and choose one big sight before striking out west towards Ponte dell'Accademia (p64). Just as in the past, your path from Campo San Moisè to Campo Santo Stefano is lined with purveyors of dazzling luxury goods and window browsers. The throngs only thin out when narrow *calli* (lanes) disgorge them, blinking, into sunny *campi* (squares) faced by the lavishly decorated churches of Santa Maria del Giglio (p63), San Maurizio and Santo Stefano (p59). The latter is ringed with cafes and is a perfect pit stop.

In the evening, the red carpets and gilt boxes of La Fenice (p63) and Teatro Goldoni (p69) beckon music and theatre enthusiasts for high-brow operas, intimate classical music concerts, ballet and low-brow *opera buffa*. Alternatively, take a pew on the terrace of Gritti Palace for sunset views over Salute or dive down canyon-like *calli* near the Rialto for cheap eats, welcoming trattorias and endless glasses of *vino* (wine).

Local Life

➡ **Attend church** Venice's famous art-filled churches are far from museum pieces; attend Sunday Mass at any of the parish churches and you'll see locals keeping their age-old traditions alive.

➡ **Cultural highs** Join local culture vultures at brilliantly curated shows at Museo Fortuny (p59) and Teatrino di Palazzo Grassi (p64) .

Getting There & Away

➡ **Vaporetto** San Marco has six stops of its own (Rialto, Sant'Angelo, San Samuele, Giglio, San Marco Vallaresso and San Marco Giardinetti) – seven if you count Accademia, which is just across the bridge. Line 1 chugs slowly past most stops. The much faster line 2 stops at Rialto, San Samuele and San Marco Giardinetti. Line 10 stops at San Marco Giardinetti.

➡ **Traghetto** A gondola ferry service shunts back and forwards across the Grand Canal from **Santa Maria del Giglio**.

Lonely Planet's Top Tip

Palazzo Ducale and Museo Correr are combined on one ticket, but if you upgrade to a Museums Pass you gain access to another seven civic museums (including Murano's Glass Museum, Burano's Lace Museum and the wonderful Ca' Rezzonico *palazzo*) for only €5 extra.

SAN MARCO

✖ Best Places to Eat

➡ Ristorante Quadri (p66)
➡ Taverna La Fenice (p66)
➡ Bistrot de Venise (p66)
➡ Trattoria da Fiore (p66)
➡ Rosa Salva (p65)
➡ Suso (p65)

For reviews, see p65. ➡

🍷 Best Places to Drink

➡ Caffè Florian (p68)
➡ Bar Longhi (p68)
➡ Grancaffè Quadri (p68)
➡ Osteria All'Alba (p68)
➡ Le Café (p68)

For reviews, see p66. ➡

◉ Best Interior Decor

➡ Museo Correr (p62)
➡ Palazzo Ducale (p55)
➡ Museo Fortuny (p59)
➡ Negozio Olivetti (p62)
➡ Palazzo Grassi (p63)

For reviews, see p52. ➡

CLAUDIO STOCCO/SHUTTERSTOCK ©

TOP SIGHT
BASILICA DI SAN MARCO

In a city packed with architectural wonders, nothing beats Basilica di San Marco for sheer spectacle and bombastic exuberance. In AD 828, wily Venetian merchants allegedly smuggled St Mark's corpse out of Egypt in a barrel of pork fat to avoid inspection by Muslim authorities. Venice built a basilica around its stolen saint in keeping with the city's own sense of supreme self-importance.

Construction

Church authorities in Rome took a dim view of Venice's tendency to glorify itself and God in the same breath, but the city defiantly created a private chapel for their doge that outshone Venice's official cathedral (the Basilica di San Pietro in Castello) in every conceivable way. After the original St Mark's was burned down during an uprising, Venice rebuilt the basilica twice (mislaying and rediscovering the saint's body along the way). The current incarnation was completed in 1094, reflecting the city's cosmopolitan image, with Byzantine domes, a Greek cross layout and walls clad in marbles looted from Syria, Egypt and Palestine. Unbelievably, Basilica di San Marco only replaced San Pietro as Venice's cathedral in 1807, after the fall of the Republic.

Facade

The front of the basilica ripples and crests like a wave, its five niched portals capped with shimmering mosaics and frothy stonework arches. It's especially resplendent just before sunset, when the sun's dying rays set the golden mosaics ablaze. Grand entrances are made through the central portal, under an ornate triple arch featuring Egyptian purple porphyry columns and intricate 13th- to 14th-century stone re-

DON'T MISS

➡ Pala d'Oro
➡ Dome of Genesis
➡ Loggia dei Cavalli
➡ Ascension Cupola
➡ St Mark's sarcophagus

PRACTICALITIES

➡ St Mark's Basilica
➡ Map p48
➡ ☑041 270 83 11
➡ www.basilicasan marco.it
➡ Piazza San Marco
➡ admission free
➡ ⏱9.30am-5pm Mon-Sat, 2-5pm Sun summer, to 4.30pm Sun winter
➡ 🚤San Marco

liefs. The oldest mosaic on the facade, dating from 1270, is in the lunette above the far-left portal, depicting St Mark's stolen body arriving at the basilica. The theme is echoed in three of the other lunettes, including the 1660 mosaics above the second portal from the right, showing turbaned officials recoiling from the hamper of pork fat containing the sainted corpse.

Set into a corner of the church's southern wall, near the entrance to the Palazzo Ducale, is a highly significant ancient Roman statue looted from Constantinople. Carved out of purple porphyry, it depicts Diocletian (ironically, a great persecutor of the Christians) and his three co-emperors of the short-lived Tetrachy (AD 293–313).

Ceiling Mosaics

Blinking is natural upon your first glimpse of the basilica's 8500 sq metres of glittering mosaics, many made with 24-carat gold leaf fused onto the back of the glass to represent divine light. Just inside the narthex (vestibule) glitter the basilica's oldest mosaics, **Apostles with the Madonna**, standing sentry by the main door for more than 950 years. The atrium's medieval **Dome of Genesis** depicts the separation of sky and water with surprisingly abstract motifs, anticipating modern art by 650 years.

Inside the church proper, three golden domes vie for your attention. The images are intended to be read from the altar end to the entry, so the **Cupola of the Prophets** shimmers above the main altar, while the **Last Judgment** is depicted in the vault above the entrance (and best seen from the museum). The dome nearest the door is the **Pentecost Cupola**, showing the Holy Spirit represented by a dove shooting tongues of flame onto the heads of the surrounding saints. In the central 13th-century **Ascension Cupola**, angels swirl around the central figure of Christ hovering among the stars. Scenes from St Mark's life unfold around the main altar, which houses the saint's simple stone **sarcophagus**.

Treasury

Holy bones and booty from the Crusades fill the **Tesoro** (admission €3), including a 4th-century rock-crystal lamp, a 10th-century rock-crystal ewer with winged feet made for Fatimid Caliph al-'Aziz-bi-llah, and an exquisite enamelled 10th-century Byzantine chalice. Don't miss the bejewelled 12th-century Archangel Michael icon, featuring tiny, feisty enamelled saints. In a separate room, velvet-padded boxes preserve the remains of sainted doges alongside the usual assortment of credulity-challenging relics: St Roch's femur, the arm St George used to slay the dragon and even a lock of the Madonna's hair.

SERVICES

Those simply wishing to pray or attend Mass can enter from the Porta dei Fiori, on the north side of the church. If attending evening vespers, a sung service held before the main evening Mass, you can enter the basilica after hours. Everyone is welcome, as long as you sit quietly and behave respectfully.

TOP TIPS

➡ It's free to enter the church and wander around the roped-off central circuit.

➡ Dress modestly (ie knees and shoulders covered) and leave large bags at the **Ateneo San Basso Left Luggage Office** (Piazza San Marco; max 1hr free; ⊘9.30am-5pm; 🚊San Marco).

➡ Between April and October, reserve 'Skip the Line' access through the website (€3 per person; children under five free) and head directly into the central portal. Present your voucher at the entrance.

➡ Beat the crowds by getting here early before the doors open.

➡ Free official **tours** (☑041 241 38 17; ⊘11.30am Mon-Sat mid-Sep–Oct; 🚊San Marco) explain the theological messages in the mosaics.

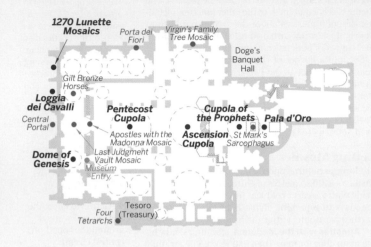

1270 Lunette Mosaics
Porta dei Fiori
Virgin's Family Tree Mosaic
Doge's Banquet Hall
Gilt Bronze Horses
Loggia dei Cavalli
Pentecost Cupola
Cupola of the Prophets
Central Portal
Apostles with the Madonna Mosaic
Ascension Cupola
St Mark's Sarcophagus
Pala d'Oro
Dome of Genesis
Last Judgment Vault Mosaic
Museum Entry
Four Tetrarchs
Tesoro (Treasury)

Pala d'Oro

Tucked behind the main **altar** (admission €2), this stupendous golden screen is studded with 2000 emeralds, amethysts, sapphires, rubies, pearls and other gemstones. But the most priceless treasures here are biblical figures in vibrant cloisonné, begun in Constantinople in AD 976 and elaborated by Venetian goldsmiths in 1209. The enamelled saints have wild, unkempt beards and wide eyes fixed on Jesus, who glances sideways at a studious St Mark as Mary throws up her hands in wonder – an understandable reaction to such a captivating scene. Look closely to spot touches of Venetian whimsy: falcon-hunting scenes in medallions along the bottom, and the by-now-familiar scene of St Mark's body smuggled out of Egypt on the right.

Museum

Accessed by a narrow staircase leading up from the basilica's atrium, the **Museo di San Marco** (Map p274; ☑041 2730 8311; www.basilicasanmarco.it; Basilica di San Marco; adult/reduced €5/2.50; ☺9.45am-4.45pm; ⑤San Marco) transports visitors to the level of the church's rear mosaics and out onto the **Loggia dei Cavalli**, the terrace above the main facade. The four magnificent bronze horses positioned here are actually reproductions of the precious 2nd-century originals, plundered from Constantinople's hippodrome, displayed inside.

Architecture buffs will revel in the beautifully rendered drawings and scale models of the basilica. In the displays of 13th- to 16th-century mosaic fragments, the Prophet Abraham is all ears and raised eyebrows, as though scandalised by Venetian gossip. Positioned above an interior balcony, Salviati's restored 1542–52 mosaic of the **Virgin's family tree** shows Mary's ancestors perched on branches, alternately chatting and ignoring one another, as families do. A corridor leads into a section of the Palazzo Ducale containing the **doge's banquet hall**, where dignitaries would wine and dine among lithe stucco figures of *Music, Poetry* and *Peace*.

TOP SIGHT
PALAZZO DUCALE

Don't be fooled by its genteel Gothic elegance: behind that lacy pink-and-white patterned facade, the doge's palace shows serious muscle and a steely will to survive. The seat of Venice's government for more than seven centuries, this powerhouse stood the test of storms, crashes and conspiracies – only to be outwitted by Casanova, the notorious seducer who escaped from the attic prison.

Exterior

The doge's official residence probably moved to this site in the 10th century, although the current complex only began to take shape around 1340. In 1424 the wing facing Piazzetta San Marco was added and the palace assumed its final form. The 1st-floor **loggia** fronting the square served a solemn purpose: death sentences were read between the darker coloured ninth and 10th columns from the left. Abutting Basilica di San Marco, Zane and Bartolomeo Bon's 1443 **Porta della Carta** (Paper Door) was an elegant point of entry for dignitaries, and served as a public bulletin board for government decrees.

Courtyard

Entering through the colonnaded courtyard you'll spot Sansovino's brawny statues of *Apollo* and *Neptune* flanking Antonio Rizzo's **Scala dei Giganti** (Giants' Staircase). Recent restorations have preserved charming cherubim propping up the pillars, though slippery incised-marble steps remain off-limits. Just off the courtyard in the wing facing the square is the **Museo dell'Opera**, displaying a collection of stone columns and capitals from previous incarnations of the building.

DON'T MISS

➔ Sala del Maggior Consiglio (Grand Council Chamber)
➔ Sala dello Scudo (Shield Room)
➔ Scala d'Oro (Golden Staircase)
➔ Anticollegio (Council Antechamber)
➔ Scala dei Giganti (Giants' Staircase)

PRACTICALITIES

➔ Ducal Palace
➔ Map p48
➔ ☎041 271 59 11
➔ www.palazzoducale. visitmuve.it
➔ Piazzetta San Marco 1
➔ adult/reduced incl Museo Correr €20/13, with Museum Pass free
➔ ⊙8.30am-7pm summer, to 5.30pm winter
➔ ⛴San Zaccaria

THE MISSING DOGE

A frieze along the top of the Sala del Maggior Consiglio depicts the first 76 doges of Venice, but note the black space: Doge Marin Falier would have appeared here had he not lost his head for treason in 1355.

TOP TIPS

➡ Book tickets online in advance to avoid queues.

➡ Tickets (valid for three months) include Museo Correr (p62) but it's worth paying an extra €5 for a Museum Pass, which gives access to several other high-profile civic museums.

➡ Last admission is one hour prior to closing.

➡ Don't leave your run until too late in the day, as some parts of the palace, such as the prisons, may close early.

➡ Get here when the doors open to avoid groups, which start arriving at around 9.30am to 10am.

The Main Circuit

A standard entry ticket takes you on a circuit through main state and institutional rooms of the palace as well as the armoury and prisons.

Level 2

From the loggia level, head to the top of Sansovino's 24-carat gilt stucco-work **Scala d'Oro** (Golden Staircase) and emerge into rooms covered with gorgeous propaganda. In Palladio-designed **Sala delle Quattro Porte** (Hall of the Four Doors), ambassadors awaited ducal audiences under a lavish display of Venice's virtues by Giovanni Cambi, whose over-the-top stucco work earned him the nickname Bombarda.

Delegations waited in the **Anticollegio** (Council Antechamber), where Tintoretto drew parallels between Roman gods and Venetian government.

Few were granted an audience in the Palladio-designed **Collegio** (Council Chamber), where Veronese's 1575–78 *Virtues of the Republic* ceiling shows Venice again as a blonde figure waving her sceptre like a wand over Justice and Peace. Father-son team Jacopo and Domenico Tintoretto attempt similar flattery, showing Venice keeping company with Apollo, Mars and Mercury in their *Triumph of Venice* ceiling for the **Sala del Senato** (Senate Chamber), but frolicking lagoon sea monsters steal the scene.

Government cover-ups were never so appealing as in the **Sala Consiglio dei Dieci** (Chamber of the Council of Ten), where Venice's star chamber plotted under Veronese's *Juno Bestowing her Gifts on Venice,* depicting a glowing goddess strewing gold ducats. Above the slot where anonymous treason accusations were slipped into the **Sala della Bussola** (Compass Room) is Veronese's *St Mark in Glory* ceiling. The route then finishes in the weapon-laden **Armoury**.

Level 1

Outside the Armoury, stairs lead down to the chambers of the **Quarantia Civil Vecchia** (Council of Forty), a kind of court, split into sections dealing with criminal matters, civil disputes concerning Venetians and civil disputes pertaining to Venice's other territories. This last room is now used by restorers; peer through the windows to see them at work.

Beyond is the cavernous 1419 **Sala del Maggior Consiglio** (Grand Council Chamber), where the doge's throne once stood in front of the staggering 22m-by-7m *Paradise* backdrop (by Tintoretto's son, Domenico) that's more politically correct than pretty: heaven is crammed with 500 prominent Venetians, including several Tintoretto patrons.

This room opens out onto the only slightly less vast **Sala dello Scrutinio** (Ballot Room), a former library that was subsequently used for elections of

PALAZZO DUCALE

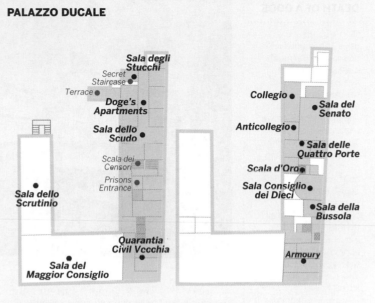

Level 1   Level 2

the doge and the various councils of state. From here the route backtracks and passes through more rooms relating to the Quarantia Civil Vecchia, before entering the prisons.

Prisons & Loggia Level
Follow the path of condemned prisoners across the Ponte dei Sospiri (p65) to Venice's 16th-century **Priggione Nove** (New Prisons). Dank cells covered with graffitied protestations of innocence are spread over three floors, with a central courtyard. One room has a small display of archaeological finds. After crossing back over the bridge, the route descends to the loggia level and through the rooms of the **censors**, **state advocates** and **naval captains**.

Doge's Apartments
The doge's suite of private rooms takes up a large chunk of the 1st floor above the loggia. The 18 roaring lions decorating the **Sala degli Stucchi** are a reminder that Venice's most powerful figurehead lived like a caged lion in his gilded suite, which he could not leave without permission. Still, consider the real estate: a terrace garden with private entry to Basilica di San Marco, and a dozen salons with splendidly restored marble fireplaces carved by Tullio and Antonio Lombardo.

The most intriguing room is the **Sala dello Scudo** (Shield Room), which is covered with world maps that reveal the extent of Venetian power (and the limits of its cartographers) c 1483 and 1762. The New World map places California near *Terra Incognita d'Antropofagi* (Unknown Land of the Maneaters), aka Canada, where Cuzco is apparently located.

This space is now used for high-profile temporary art exhibitions, which are ticketed separately (around €10 extra). These include diverse shows such

Palazzo Ducale

DEATH OF A DOGE

On the death of the doge, the Council announced: 'With much displeasure we have heard of the death of the most serene prince, a man of such goodness and piety; however, we shall make another.' The signet ring, symbol of his power, was then slipped from his finger and broken in half. The doge's family had three days to vacate the palace and remove all their furniture. Three Inquisitors were also appointed to scrutinise the doge's past office and, if necessary, punish his heirs for any fraud or wrongdoing.

THE LION'S MOUTH

On the terrace of the loggia level look for the face of a grimacing man with his mouth agape. This *bocca di leoni* (lion's mouth) was a postbox for secret accusations. These slanders reported any number of unholy acts, from cursing and tax avoidance (forgivable) to Freemasonry (punishable by death). The notes, which had to be signed by two accusers, were then investigated by Venice's dreaded security service, led by the Council of Ten.

as 'Venice, the Jews & Europe', 'Treasures of the Mughals & the Maharajas' and, most recently, 'Canaletto & Venice'.

Secret Itineraries Tour

Further rooms, too small for the masses, can be visited on a fascinating 75-minute guided **tour** (Map p274; ☑041 4273 0892; adult/reduced €20/14; ☺tours in English 9.55am, 10.45am & 11.35am). It takes in the damp ground-floor cells known as **Pozzi** (wells) and then heads up through a hidden passageway into the cramped, unadorned **Council of Ten Secret Headquarters**. Beyond this ominous office suite, the vast **Chancellery** is lined with drawers of top-secret files, including reports by Venice's far-reaching spy network, accusations by Venetians against their neighbours, and judgements copied in triplicate by clerks. The accused might be led to the windowless **Torture Chamber**, where until 1660 confessions were sometimes extracted from prisoners dangling from a rope. Upstairs lie the **Piombi** (Leads), the attic prison cells where Casanova was condemned to five years' confinement in 1756 for corrupting nuns and the more serious charge of spreading Freemasonry. As described in his memoirs, Casanova made an ingenious escape through the roof, then convinced a guard he was an official locked into the palace overnight. He would later return to Venice, enlisted as a spy for the Consiglio dei Dieci (Council of Ten).

⊙ SIGHTS

Venice's most famous sights are gathered around Piazza San Marco, including Palazzo Ducale, Basilica di San Marco and its freestanding *campanile* (bell tower), and Museo Correr. The rest of the tongue-shaped district spreads west from here, with La Fenice opera house at its centre. Interesting churches are scattered all around, along with a handful of smaller museums.

BASILICA DI SAN MARCO   CATHEDRAL
See p52.

PALAZZO DUCALE   MUSEUM
See p55.

CHIESA DI SANTO STEFANO   CHURCH
Map p274 (🖉041 522 50 61; www.chorusvenezia. org; Campo Santo Stefano; museum €3, with Chorus Pass free; ☉10.30am-4.30pm Mon-Sat, to 7pm Sun; 🛥Sant'Angelo) **FREE** The freestanding bell tower, visible from the square behind, leans disconcertingly, but this brick Gothic church has stood tall since the 13th century. Credit for shipshape splendour goes to Bartolomeo Bon for the marble entry portal and to Venetian shipbuilders, who constructed the vast wooden *carena di nave* (ship's keel) ceiling that resembles an upturned Noah's ark.

It's well worth visiting the sacristy museum to see three extraordinary and brooding 1575–80 Tintorettos: *The Last Supper,* with a ghostly dog begging for bread; the gathering gloom of *The Agony in the Garden;* and the mostly black, surprisingly modern, *Washing of the Feet.* There's also a small cloister.

MUSEO FORTUNY   MUSEUM
Map p274 (🖉041 520 09 95; www.fortuny.visit muve.it; Campo San Beneto 3958; adult/reduced €10/8; ☉10am-6pm Wed-Mon; 🛥Sant'Angelo) Find design inspiration at the palatial home studio of art nouveau designer Mariano Fortuny y Madrazo (1871–1949), whose uncorseted Delphi-goddess frocks set the standard for bohemian chic. The 1st-floor salon walls are eclectic mood boards: Fortuny fashions and Isfahan tapestries, family portraits and artfully peeling plaster. Interesting temporary exhibitions spread from the basement to the attic, the best of which use the general ambience of grand decay to great effect.

If these salons inspire, visit Fortuny Tessuti Artistici (p147) in Giudecca, where textiles are still hand-printed according to Fortuny's top-secret methods.

★CAMPANILE   TOWER
Map p274 (www.basilicasanmarco.it; Piazza San Marco; adult/reduced €8/4; ☉8.30am-9pm summer, 9.30am-5.30pm winter, last entry 45min before closing; 🛥San Marco) Basilica di San Marco's 99m-tall bell tower has been rebuilt twice since its initial construction in AD 888. Galileo Galilei tested his telescope here in 1609 but modern-day visitors head to the top for 360-degree lagoon views and close encounters with the **Marangona**, the booming bronze bell that originally signalled the start and end of the working day for the *marangoni* (artisans) at the Arsenale shipyards. Today it rings twice a day, at noon and midnight.

The tower's distinctive profile was the brainchild of Bartolomeo Bon, whose 16th-century design was initially criticised for being ungainly. However, when the tower suddenly collapsed in 1902, the Venetians painstakingly rebuilt it exactly as it was, brick by brick. Sansovino's classical marble loggia at the base of the campanile is decidedly mythical, showcasing bronzes of pagan deities Minerva, Apollo and Mercury, as well as Peace.

The campanile attracts long queues in high season due to the limited capacity of the small lift that whisks you up to the top. Between April and October for a surcharge of €5 you can book 'Skip the Line' access via the basilica's website. There are only 12 places available for each hourly time slot, so book well in advance.

TORRE DELL'OROLOGIO   LANDMARK
Map p274 (Clock Tower; 🖉041 4273 0892; www. museiciviveneziani.it; Piazza San Marco; adult/ reduced €12/7; ☉tours in English 11am & noon Mon-Wed, 2pm & 3pm Thu-Sun; 🛥San Marco) The two hardest-working men in Venice stand duty on a rooftop around the clock, and wear no pants. The 'Do Mori' (Two Moors) exposed to the elements atop the Torre dell'Orologio are made of bronze, and their bell-hammering mechanism runs like, well, clockwork. Below the Moors, Venice's gold-leafed 15th-century timepiece tracks lunar phases. Visits are by guided tour; bookings essential.

The clockworks required constant upkeep by a live-in clockwatcher and his

Grand Canal

A WATER TOUR

The 3.5km route of vaporetto (passenger ferry) No 1, which passes some 50 palazzi (mansions), six churches and scene-stealing backdrops featured in four James Bond films, is public transport at its most glamorous.

The Grand Canal starts with controversy: **❶ Ponte di Calatrava** a luminous glass-and-steel bridge that cost triple the original €4 million estimate. Ahead are castle-like **❷ Fondaco dei Turchi**, the historic Turkish trading-house; Renaissance **❸ Palazzo Vendramin**, housing the city's casino; and double-arcaded **❹ Ca' Pesaro**. Don't miss **❺ Ca' d'Oro**, a 1430 filigree Gothic marvel.

Points of Venetian pride include the **❻ Pescaria**, built in 1907 on the site where fishmongers have been slinging lagoon crab for 600 years, and neighbouring **❼ Rialto Market** stalls, overflowing with island-grown produce. Cost overruns for 1592 **❽ Ponte di Rialto** rival Calatrava's, but its marble splendour stands the test of time.

The next two canal bends could cause architectural whiplash, with Sanmicheli-designed Renaissance **❾ Palazzo Grimani** and Mauro Codussi's **❿ Palazzo Corner-Spinelli** followed by Giorgio Masari-designed **⓫ Palazzo Grassi** and Baldassare Longhena's baroque jewel box, **⓬ Ca' Rezzonico**.

Wooden **⓭ Ponte dell'Accademia** was built in 1930 as a temporary bridge, but the beloved landmark remains. Stone lions flank the **⓮ Peggy Guggenheim Collection**, where the American heiress collected ideas, lovers and art. You can't miss the dramatic dome of Longhena's **⓯ Chiesa di Santa Maria della Salute** or **⓰ Punta della Dogana**, Venice's triangular customs warehouse reinvented as a contemporary art showcase. The Grand Canal's grand finale is pink Gothic **⓱ Palazzo Ducale** and its adjoining **⓲ Ponte dei Sospiri**.

PHOTOGOLFER / SHUTTERSTOCK ©

Palazzo Grassi
French magnate François Pinault scandalised Paris when he relocated his contemporary art collection here, to be displayed in galleries designed by Gae Aulenti and Tadao Ando.

Ca' Rezzonico
See how Venice lived in baroque splendour at this 18th-century art museum with Tiepolo ceilings, silk-swagged boudoirs and even an in-house pharmacy.

⓭ Ponte dell'Accademia

Peggy Guggenheim Collection

Chiesa di Santa Maria delle Salute

Punta della Dogana
Minimalist architect Tadao Ando creatively repurposed abandoned warehouses as galleries, which now host contemporary art installations from François Pinault's collection.

MUSICIAN_IZ/SHUTTERSTOCK ©

Ponte di Calatrava
With its starkly streamlined fish-fin shape, the 2008 bridge was the first to be built over the Grand Canal in 75 years.

Fondaco dei Turchi
Recognisable by its double colonnade, watchtowers, and dugout canoe parked at the Museo di Storia Naturale's ground-floor loggia.

Ca' d'Oro
Behind the triple Gothic arcades are priceless masterpieces: Titians looted by Napoleon, a rare Mantegna and semiprecious stone mosaic floors.

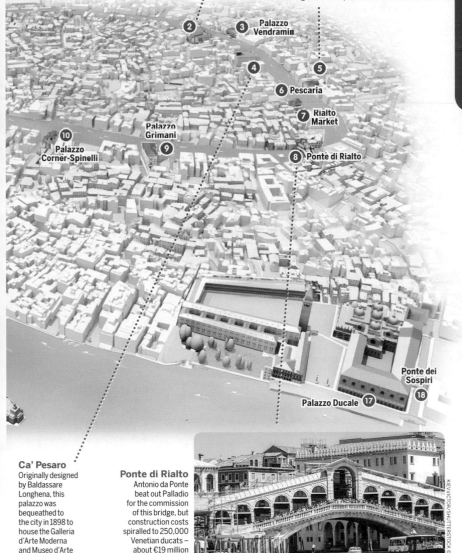

②

③ Palazzo Vendramin

④

⑤

⑥ Pescaria

⑦ Rialto Market

Palazzo Grimani

⑩

⑨

Palazzo Corner-Spinelli

⑧ Ponte di Rialto

Palazzo Ducale **⑰**

Ponte dei Sospiri

⑱

Ca' Pesaro
Originally designed by Baldassare Longhena, this palazzo was bequeathed to the city in 1898 to house the Galleria d'Arte Moderna and Museo d'Arte Orientale.

Ponte di Rialto
Antonio da Ponte beat out Palladio for the commission of this bridge, but construction costs spiralled to 250,000 Venetian ducats – about €19 million today.

family until 1998. After a nine-year renovation, they are now in independent working order – 132-stroke chimes keep time in tune; moving barrels indicate minutes and hours on the world's first digital clock face (c 1753); and wooden statues of the three kings and angel emerge from side panels annually on Epiphany and the Feast of the Ascension. Tours climb four-storeys of steep spiral staircases past the clockworks to the roof terrace, for giddy, close-up views of the Moors in action.

Children must be over six years of age to climb the tower, and the steep climb is not recommended for pregnant women and those suffering from vertigo or claustrophobia.

NEGOZIO OLIVETTI ARCHITECTURE

Map p274 (Olivetti Store; ☑041 522 83 87; www.negoziolivetti.it; Piazza San Marco 101; adult/reduced €8/5; ☉10am-6.30pm Tue-Sun Feb-Dec; ⓢSan Marco) Like a revolver pulled from a petticoat, ultramodern Negozio Olivetti was an outright provocation when it first appeared under the frilly arcades of the Procuratie Vecchie in 1958. High-tech pioneer Olivetti commissioned Venetian architect Carlo Scarpa to transform a narrow, dim souvenir shop into a showcase for its sleek typewriters and 'computing machines' (several 1948–54 models are displayed).

Instead of fighting the elements, Scarpa invited them indoors. He sliced away walls to let light flood in, included a huge planter for tall grasses and added a black slab-marble fountain as a wink at *acque alte* (high tide). Semicircular porthole windows resemble eyes open wide to the historic piazza and the Architecture Biennale's modernist horizons.

GALLERIA CATERINA TOGNON GALLERY

Map p274 (☑041 520 15 66; www.caterinatognon.com; Corte Barozzi 2158; ☉10am-7pm Tue-Sat; ⓢSan Marco Vallaresso) Hidden behind busy Via XXII Marzo, this gallery is worth seeking out for its interesting shows by internationally renowned artists, who mainly work in glass. Exhibits take place regularly throughout the year. Check the website.

SCALA CONTARINI DEL BOVOLO NOTABLE BUILDING

Map p274 (☑041 309 66 05; www.gioiellinascos tidivenezia.com; Calle Contarini del Bovolo 4299; adult/reduced €7/6; ☉10am-6pm; ⓢSant'Angelo) Under the Republic, only the Church and state were permitted to erect towers, as the

---

◉ TOP SIGHT
MUSEO CORRER

Napoleon built and filled his Piazza San Marco palace with the doges' riches, and took Venice's finest heirlooms back to France. Less than a year later, however, he lost Venice to Austrian emperor Franz Joseph. The Habsburgs loved luxury, and **Empress Sissi's suite** showcases her 19th-century penchant for brocade-swagged curtains, silk-swathed walls and frescoed ceilings – shocking, considering the abject poverty of Venice's citizenry at the time.

Napoleon's wing links the 16th-century **Procuratie Vecchie** on the northern side of the square to the **Procuratie Nuove** on the south. The latter, described by Palladio as the most sumptuous palace ever built, is incorporated into the museum. It includes the magnificent **Biblioteca Nazionale Marciana**, arguably Europe's first public library, designed by Jacopo Sansovino in the 16th century and covered with frescoes of philosophers painted by Veronese, Titian and Tintoretto. Adjoining it, the **Museo Archeologico Nazionale** showcases an extraordinary array of ancient sculpture and cameos, which Venice successfully reclaimed from France. Upstairs, the **Pinacoteca** has a large collection of mainly religious masterpieces spanning four centuries.

TOP TIPS

➔ Admission ceases an hour before closing.

➔ It pays not to visit too late in the day, as some sections close early.

PRACTICALITIES

➔ Map p274, F5

➔ ☑041 240 52 11

➔ www.correr.visit muve.it

➔ Piazza San Marco 52

➔ adult/reduced incl Palazzo Ducale €20/13, with Museum Pass free

➔ ☉10am-7pm Apr-Oct, to 5pm Nov-Mar

➔ ⓢSan Marco

structures could conceivably be used for military purposes. In around 1400 the Contarini family, eager to show off their wealth and power, cheekily built this non-tower instead. Combining Venetian Gothic, Byzantine and Renaissance elements, this romantic 'staircase' looks even higher than its 26m due to the simple trick of decreasing the height of the arches as it rises.

There's a wonderful view from the **belvedere** at the top, gazing over the rooftops to San Marco. Admission includes entry to the **Tintoretto Room** gallery on the second landing.

CHIESA DI SANTA MARIA DEL GIGLIO
CHURCH

Map p274 (Santa Maria Zobenigo; www.chorus venezia.org; Campo di Santa Maria del Giglio; €3, with Chorus Pass free; ⊙10.30am-4.30pm Mon-Sat; 🚤Giglio) Founded in the 9th century but almost completely rebuilt in the late 17th century, this church is distinguished by a series of six relief maps on its facade featuring Rome and five cities that were Venetian possessions at the time: Padua, the Croatian cities of Zadar and Split, and the Greek cities of Heraklion and Corfu. Inside are some intriguing masterpieces.

Two canvases by Tintoretto, each featuring two of the four evangelists, flank the organ. There's a small treasury in the Molin Chapel, although the real gem is Peter Paul Rubens' bare-breasted *Madonna & Child with St John,* featuring a characteristically chubby baby Jesus.

Admiral Antonio Barbaro commissioned Giuseppe Sardi to undertake the reconstruction of the church for the glory of the Virgin, Venice, and of course himself – his statue gets prime facade placement and the cities featured are all places where he served. This self-glorifying architectural audacity enraged 19th-century architectural critic John Ruskin, who called it a 'manifestation of insolent atheism'.

PALAZZO GRASSI
GALLERY

Map p274 (📞041 200 10 57; www.palazzograssi. it; Campo San Samuele 3231; adult/reduced incl Punta della Dogana €18/15; ⊙10am-7pm Wed-Mon mid-Mar–Nov; 🚤San Samuele) Grand Canal gondola riders gasp at their first glimpse of the massive sculptures by contemporary artists docked in front of Giorgio Masari's neoclassical palace (built 1748–72). The provocative art collection of French billionaire François Pinault overflows Palazzo Grassi,

---

⊙ TOP SIGHT
TEATRO LA FENICE

Once its dominion over the high seas ended, Venice discovered the power of high Cs, hiring San Marco choirmaster Claudio Monteverdi, the father of modern opera, and opening La Fenice (The Phoenix) in 1792. Rossini, Donizetti and Bellini staged operas here, making La Fenice the envy of Europe – until it went up in flames in 1836.

Venice without opera was unthinkable, and within a year the opera house was rebuilt. Verdi premiered *Rigoletto* and *La Traviata*, and international greats Stravinsky, Prokofiev and Britten composed for the house. But La Fenice was again reduced to ashes in 1996; two electricians, found guilty of arson, were apparently behind on repairs. A €90-million replica of the 19th-century opera house reopened in late 2003 (though some critics had lobbied for Gae Aulenti's avant-garde design), and a reprise performance of *La Traviata* was a sensation.

Opera season is in full swing from January to July and September to October. Attending a **performance** (p69) is highly recommended, but it's possible to explore the theatre with an audio guide. Check also for chamber-music concerts staged at La Fenice's sister venue, **Teatro Malibran** (p118).

TOP TIPS

→ Come during Carnevale to see the audience dressed in masks and capes.

→ Dress smartly; dinner suits aren't necessary, but neither are they out of place.

PRACTICALITIES

→ Map p274, D5
→ 📞041 78 66 75
→ www.teatrolafenice.it
→ Campo San Fantin 1977
→ ⊙9.30am-6pm
→ 🚤Giglio

while clever curation and shameless art-star name-dropping are the hallmarks of rotating temporary exhibits. Despite all this artistic glamour, it's Tadao Ando's creatively repurposed interior architecture that steals the show.

Postmodern architect Gae Aulenti peeled back rococo decor to highlight Masari's muscular classicism in 1985–86, and minimalist master Ando added stage-set drama in 2003–05 with ethereal backlit scrims and strategic spotlighting. Ando's design directs attention to the contemporary art, without detracting from baroque ceiling frescoes. Don't miss the cafe overlooking the Grand Canal, the interior of which is redesigned by contemporary artists with each new show.

Next door, the **Teatrino di Palazzo Grassi** (Map p274; ☏041 240 13 08; www.palazzograssi.it; Salizzada San Samuele 3260; ⧉San Samuele) occupies a space that once served as the palace's garden before it was converted into a theatre. Here, once again, Ando has worked his magic, transforming the interior into a curvaceous 220-seat concrete auditorium that now hosts concerts, conferences and film projections.

PALAZZO FRANCHETTI
PALACE

Map p274 (Istituto Veneto di Scienze Lettere ed Arti; ☏041 240 77 11; www.palazzofranchetti.it; Campo Santo Stefano 2842; ◷10am-6pm Mon-Fri; ⧉Accademia) This 16th-century *palazzo* (mansion) passed through the hands of various Venetian families before Archduke Frederik of Austria snapped it up and set about modernising it. The Comte de Chambord (aka King Henry V of France in exile) continued the work, while the Franchetti family, who lived here after independence, restored its Gothic fairy-tale look and introduced a fantastical art nouveau staircase dripping with dragons. It's now used for art exhibitions, although the works have to compete with showstopping Murano chandeliers.

PONTE DELL'ACCADEMIA
BRIDGE

Map p274 (btwn Campo di San Vidal & Campo della Carità; ⧉Accademia) The wooden Ponte dell'Accademia was built in 1933 as a temporary replacement for an 1854 iron bridge, but this span, arched like a cat's back, remains a beloved landmark. Engineer Eugenio Miozzi's notable works include the Lido Casino, but none has lasted like this elegant little footbridge – and more recent structural improvements will preserve it for decades to come.

CHIESA DI SAN VIDAL
CHURCH

Map p274 (www.interpretiveneziani.com; Campo di San Vidal 2862; ◷9am-6pm; ⧉Accademia) **FREE** Built by Doge Vitale Falier in the 11th century, Chiesa di San Vidal got a 1706–14 Palladian facelift to commemorate Doge Francesco Morosoni's victory over Turkish foes. Inside is *St Vitale on Horseback and Saints* by Vittore Carpaccio, featuring his signature traffic-light red and miniaturist's attention to detail. The deconsecrated church now houses a collection of historic musical instruments and serves as a concert venue for Interpreti Veneziani (p70).

MUSEO DELLA MUSICA
MUSEUM

Map p274 (☏041 241 18 40; www.museodellamusica.com; Campo San Maurizio 2603; ◷9.30am-7pm; ⧉Giglio) **FREE** Housed in the restored neoclassical Chiesa di San Maurizio, this collection of rare 17th- to 20th-century instruments is accompanied by informative panels on the life and times of Venice's Antonio Vivaldi. To hear the instruments in action, check out the kiosk with CDs and concert tickets for Interpreti Veneziani (p70), which runs the museum.

CHIESA DI SAN MOISÈ
CHURCH

Map p274 (☏041 528 58 40; Campo di San Moisè; ◷9.30am-12.30pm & 3.30-7pm Mon-Sat, 9.30-11am & 2.30-7pm Sun; ⧉San Marco) **FREE** Flourishes of carved stone like icing across the 1660s facade of this church, dedicated to Moses, make it appear positively lickable, although 19th-century architecture critic John Ruskin found its wedding-cake appearance indigestible. From an engineering perspective, Ruskin had a point: several statues had to be removed in the 19th century to prevent the facade from collapsing under their combined weight.

The remaining statuary by Flemish sculptor Heinrich Meyring (aka Merengo in Italian) includes scant devotional works but a sycophantic number of tributes to church patrons. Among the scene-stealing works inside are Tintoretto's *Washing of the Feet,* in the chapel to the left of the altar, and Palma il Giovane's *The Supper,* facing it.

COLUMN OF ST THEODORE
MONUMENT

Map p274 (Piazzetta di San Marco; ⧉San Marco) One of two twin granite columns in the Piazzetta di San Marco, bearing the two patron saints of Venice. This column bears the image of warrior-saint Theodore, who was the patron of the city before St Mark. He holds a spear and stands above a crocodile, which is meant to represent a slain dragon.

LION OF ST MARK COLUMN
MONUMENT

Map p274 (Piazzetta di San Marco; ⛴San Marco) One of a pair of granite columns bearing the two patron saints of Venice in Piazzetta di San Marco, this eastern column bears a statue representing a winged lion – a symbol of both St Mark and Venice itself.

PONTE DEI SOSPIRI
BRIDGE

Map p274 (Bridge of Sighs; ⛴San Zaccaria) One of Venice's most photographed sights, the Bridge of Sighs connects Palazzo Ducale to the 16th-century Priggione Nove (New Prisons). Its improbable popularity is due to British libertine Lord Byron (1788–1824), who mentioned it in one of his long narrative poems *Childe Harold's Pilgrimage.* Condemned prisoners were said to sigh as they passed through the enclosed bridge and glimpsed the beauty of the lagoon. Now the sighs are mainly from people trying to dodge the picture-snapping masses.

CHIESA DI SAN ZULIAN
CHURCH

Map p274 (⛴041 523 53 83; Campo San Zulian 604; ⛴8.30am-7pm; ⛴Rialto) FREE Founded in 829, San Zulian got a Sansovino makeover funded by physician Tomasso Rangone, who made his fortune by selling syphilis cures and secrets to living past 100 (he died at 84). The doctor is immortalised in bronze over the portal, holding sarsaparilla – his 'miracle cure' for venereal disease. Inside, beneath a painted ceiling, are works by Palma il Giovane and Veronese's *Dead Christ and Saints.*

CHIESA DI SAN SALVADOR
CHURCH

Map p274 (⛴041 523 67 17; www.chiesasansalvador.it; Campo San Salvador 4835; ⛴9am-noon & 4-6pm Mon-Sat, 3-7pm Sun; ⛴Rialto) FREE A dream made real, San Salvador was conceived in the 7th century when Jesus appeared to a sleeping Bishop Magnus and pointed out on a lagoon map the exact spot to build a church. There was, however, a minor technical glitch: the city of Venice didn't exist yet, and the area was mostly mud banks. But Bishop Magnus had faith that once the church was built the parishioners would follow – and today this church perched on a bustling *campo* (square) proves his point.

Built on a plan of three Greek crosses laid end to end, San Salvador has been embellished many times over the centuries, with the present facade erected in 1663. Among the noteworthy works inside are two Titians: the *Transfiguration* behind the main altar, and at Sansovino's altar (third on the right as you approach the main altar), his spectacular *Annunciation,* with a radiant dove overseeing the blushing young angel eagerly delivering the news to a startled Mary.

✖ EATING

San Marco has Venice's priciest restaurants and while some of them, such as Michelin-starred Quadri, are well worth the indulgence, many are simply overpriced. Seek out places off the main thoroughfares and with short menus focused on local produce. Alternatively, there are also some great bakeries and *cicheti* (Venetian tapas) bars to fall back on if you're just after a snack.

★SUSO
GELATO €

Map p274 (⛴348 5646545; www.gelatovenezia.it; Calle de la Bissa 5453; scoops €1.60; ⛴10am-midnight; ⛴Rialto) 🍴 Suso's gelati are locally made and free of artificial colours. Indulge in rich, original seasonal flavours such as marscapone cream with fig sauce and walnuts. Gluten-free cones are available.

★ROSA SALVA
BAKERY €

Map p274 (⛴041 521 05 44; www.rosasalva.it; Calle Fiubera 951; items €1.30-7.50; ⛴8am-8pm; ⛴Rialto) With just-baked strudel and reliable cappuccino, Rosa Salva has provided Venetians with fresh reasons to roll out of bed for more than a century. Cheerfully efficient women working the spotless counter supply gale-force espresso and turbo-loaded pistachio profiteroles to power you across 30 more bridges. Come lunchtime, the sweet pastries are replaced by plump sandwiches and hot deli plates.

AL THEATRO
CAFE €

Map p274 (⛴041 522 10 52; www.altheatro.it; Campo San Fantin 1917; snacks €6-16; ⛴8am-10.30pm; 🛜; ⛴) Hiding in the plain-looking site next to La Fenice, this very good cafe and restaurant serves famished opera-goers. Don't overlook it: Al Theatro's deli counter is filled with delicious *tramezzini* (small triangular, stacked sandwiches) filled with ham and eggs, smoked salmon and pesto, and prawns and paprika. There's also a selection of salads, crostini and *pizzette* (mini pizzas), and sunny seats outside.

ROSTICCERIA GISLON
DELI €

Map p274 (📞041 522 35 69; Calle de la Bissa 5424; meals €15-25; ⏰9am-9.30pm Tue-Sun, to 3.30pm Mon; 🚤Rialto) Serving San Marco workers since the 1930s, this no-frills *rosticceria* (roast-meat specialist) has an ultramarine canteen counter downstairs and a small eat-in restaurant upstairs. For a quick bite you'll find *arancini* (rice balls), deep-fried mozzarella balls, croquettes and fish fry-ups. No one said it was going to be healthy!

AI MERCANTI
ITALIAN €€

Map p274 (📞041 523 82 69; www.aimercanti.it; Calle Fuseri 4346a; meals €35-40; ⏰11.30am-3pm & 7-10pm Tue-Sat, 7-11pm Mon; 🚤Rialto) With its pumpkin-coloured walls, gleaming golden fixtures and jet-black tables and chairs, Ai Mercanti effortlessly conjures up a romantic mood. No wonder diners whisper over glasses of wine selected from the vast list before tucking into modern bistro-style dishes. Although there's a focus on seafood and secondary cuts of meat, there are some wonderful vegetarian options as well.

OSTERIA DA CARLA
VENETIAN €€

Map p274 (📞041 523 78 55; www.osteriadacarla.it; Corte Contarina 1535a; meals €40-45; ⏰9am-10.30pm Mon-Sat; 🚤San Marco) Diners in the know duck into this hidden courtyard, less than 100m from Piazza San Marco, to snack on *cicheti* at the counter or to sit down to a romantic meal. The surroundings are at once modern and ancient, with exposed brick and interesting art.

OSTERIA AL BACARETO
VENETIAN €€

Map p274 (📞041 528 93 36; https://bacareto.it; Crosera de le Boteghe; meals €35-40; ⏰8am-4pm & 6.30-10.30pm; 🚤San Samuele) This traditional tavern remains untouched by fashion fads and fussy menus and instead remains rooted in Venetian food traditions. Expect bowls of buckwheat *bigoli* (Venetian fresh pasta) with salted sardines and turnip greens; cuttlefish with polenta; and a wide array of lagoon fish. There's also an array of *cicheti* at the bar if you don't want a sit-down meal.

⭐RISTORANTE QUADRI
ITALIAN €€€

Map p274 (📞041 522 21 05; www.alajmo.it; Piazza San Marco 121; meals €140-225; ⏰12.30-2.30pm & 7.30-10.30pm Tue-Sun; 🚤San Marco) When it comes to Venetian glamour, nothing beats this historic Michelin-starred restaurant overlooking Piazza San Marco. A small swarm of servers greets you as you're shown to your table in a room decked out with silk damask, gilt, painted beams and Murano chandeliers. Dishes are precise and delicious, deftly incorporating Venetian touches into an inventive modern Italian menu.

⭐TAVERNA LA FENICE
ITALIAN €€€

Map p274 (📞041 522 38 56; www.ristorantelafenice.it; Campiello de la Fenice 1939; meals €45-60, menu du jour €25-30; ⏰noon-midnight; ❄; 🚤Santa Maria del Giglio) 🌿 Step back in time at this historic dining room with a coffered wooden ceiling, gleaming terrazzo floors and red-and-gold wallpaper. The official caterers for La Fenice banquets, Taverna La Fenice serves a refined menu with the likes of beef fillet in Barolo wine, truffle ravioli and intense little bowls of hazelnut icecream. Just like a night at the opera, it's one to remember.

⭐BISTROT DE VENISE
VENETIAN €€€

Map p274 (📞041 523 66 51; www.bistrotdevenise.com; Calle dei Fabbri 4685; meals €47-78; ⏰noon-3pm & 5pm-1am; ✏; 🚤Rialto) Indulge in some culinary time travel in the red-and-gilt dining room at this fine-dining bistro reviving the recipes of Renaissance chef Bartolomeo Scappi. Dine like a doge on braised duck with wild apple and onion pudding, or enjoy the Jewish recipe of goose, raisin and pine-nut pasta. Even the desserts are beguilingly exotic.

TRATTORIA DA FIORE
VENETIAN €€€

Map p274 (📞041 523 53 10; www.dafiore.it; Calle de le Botteghe 3461; meals €45-60; ⏰12.30-2.30pm & 7.30-10.30pm; 🚤San Samuele) Rustic-chic decor sets the scene for excellent Venetian dishes composed of carefully selected seasonal ingredients from small Veneto producers. The restaurant is justly famous for its seafood dishes. Next door, the bar's *cicheti* counter serves tasty snacks at more democratic prices.

🍷 DRINKING & NIGHTLIFE

Nowhere does old-world glamour better than Venice, and San Marco has some of the most famous and glitzy cafes

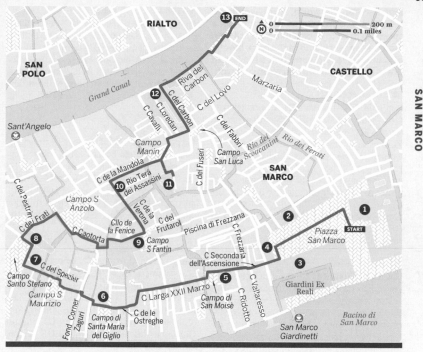

Neighbourhood Walk
San Marco Highlights

START PIAZZA SAN MARCO
END RIALTO BRIDGE
LENGTH 2KM; TWO HOURS

Arrive in Piazza San Marco at 7am to catch sight of the **1 Basilica di San Marco** (p52) free of crowds and souvenir stalls. You'll also have a clear view of Mauro Codussi's 16th-century **2 Procuratie Vecchie** and Scamozzi-designed and Longhena-completed **3 Procuratie Nuove**, which flank either side of the piazza. Today the Museo Correr occupies the Procuratie Nuove and **4 Ala Napoleonica**, the palace Napoleon brazenly razed San Geminiano church to build. Cut through the arcade and follow Venice's ritziest shopping strip past **5 Chiesa di San Moisè** (p64) and **6 Chiesa di Santa Maria del Giglio** (p63). Bridge-hop over three more canals until you land in sunny Campo Santo Stefano. Here you can refuel at **7 Le Café** (p68). Set off again down Calle dei Frati beside **8 Chiesa di Santo Stefano** (p59).

In Campo San Anzolo turn right down Calle Caotorta, skip over the canal, then immediately left over Rio de le Ostreghe to appear in front of **9 La Fenice** (p63). Take canyon-like Calle de la Verona into the shadows and continue on to **10 Calle dei Assassini**. Corpses were so frequently found here that in 1128 Venice banned the full beards that assassins wore as disguises. Turn right when you arrive on Calle de la Mandola to arrive in Campo Manin. From here detour down Calle de Vida o de le Locande to see romantic **11 Scala Contarini del Bovolo** (p62). Return to Campo Manin and pick up Salizada San Luca at the northern corner of the square. Just before you reach Campo San Luca turn left down Calle del Carbon. It runs down the side of **12 Ca' Loredan**, Venice's city hall; George Clooney and Amal Alamuddin were married here in 2014. On the side facing Calle del Carbon look for a plaque honouring Elena Cornaro Piscopia, the first woman to earn a PhD, in 1678. Follow Riva del Carbon to the **13 Rialto Bridge**.

and bars in the world. Sure, you'll be paying up to five times as much for a *spritz* (prosecco cocktail) on Piazza San Marco than you would in the back blocks of Cannaregio, but sometimes it's fun to dress up and pretend you're an oligarch.

★ CAFFÈ FLORIAN   CAFE

Map p274 (☏041 520 56 41; www.caffeflorian. com; Piazza San Marco 57; ☺9am-11pm; ☻San Marco) The oldest still-operating cafe in Europe and one of the first to welcome women, Florian maintains rituals (if not prices) established in 1720: besuited waiters serve cappuccino on silver trays; lovers get cosy on plush banquettes; and the orchestra strikes up as the sunset illuminates San Marco's mosaics. Piazza seating during concerts costs €6 extra, but dreamy-eyed romantics will hardly notice.

★ BAR LONGHI   COCKTAIL BAR

Map p274 (☏041 79 47 81; www.hotelgrittipalace venice.com; Campo di Santa Maria del Giglio 2467; ☺11am-1am; ☻Giglio) Gritti Palace's beautiful Bar Longhi may be pricey, but if you consider your surrounds – Fortuny fabrics, an intarsia marble bar, 18th-century mirrors and million-dollar Piero Longhi paintings – the price of a signature orange martini starts to seem reasonable. In summer you'll have to choose between the twinkling interior and a spectacular Grand Canal terrace.

★ GRANCAFFÈ QUADRI   CAFE

Map p274 (☏041 522 21 05; www.alajmo.it; Piazza San Marco 121; ☺9am-midnight; ☻San Marco) Powdered wigs seem appropriate inside this baroque bar-cafe that's been serving happy hours since 1638. During Carnevale, costumed Quadri revellers party like it's 1699 – despite prices shooting up to €15 for a *spritz*. Grab a seat on the piazza to watch the best show in town: the basilica's golden mosaics ablaze in the sunset.

★ VINERIA DAI DO CANCARI   WINE BAR

Map p274 (☏041 241 06 34; www.daidocancari. it; Calle de le Botteghe 3455; ☺10.45am-1.15pm & 2.30-11pm; ☻San Samuele) Marco Nordio has filled his jam-packed wine store in characterful Calle de le Botteghe with a stash of unusual Veneto and Italian wines, as well as some very good and reasonably priced *vini sfuso* (tap wine). Join him at the counter over tasty plates of cheese for a guided tasting before you buy. He's deeply knowledgeable and speaks English and French.

OSTERIA ALL'ALBA   WINE BAR

Map p274 (Ramo del Fontego dei Tedeschi 5370; ☺4pm-midnight; ☻Rialto) That roar behind the Rialto means the DJ's funk set is kicking in at All'Alba. Squeeze inside to order salami sandwiches and DOC Veneto wines, and check out walls festooned with vintage LPs and effusive thanks scrawled in 12 languages.

LE CAFÉ   CAFE

Map p274 (☏041 523 00 02; www.lecafevenezia. com; Campo Santo Stefano 2797; ☺8am-11pm summer, to 8.30pm winter; ☻San Samuele) So much more than a cafe, Le Café serves everything from croissants to pasta to cocktails – but the real reason to come here is to enjoy a drink at the outdoor tables and watch the world go by.

HARRY'S BAR   BAR

Map p274 (☏041 528 57 77; www.cipriani.com; Calle Vallaresso 1323; ☺10.30am-11pm; ☻San Marco) Aspiring auteurs hold court at tables well scuffed by Ernest Hemingway, Charlie Chaplin, Truman Capote and Orson Welles, enjoying the signature €21 Bellini (Giuseppe Cipriani's original 1948 recipe: white peach juice and prosecco) with a side of reflected glory.

CAFFÈ BRASILIA   WINE BAR

Map p274 (☏041 523 99 18; Calle dei Assassini 3658; ☺7am-2am Mon-Sat, from 11am Sun; ☻Sant'Angelo) There's a pub-like quality to this friendly little back-lane bar – a rarity in ritzy San Marco. It's the main haunt of a local football team comprising off-duty lawyers, hence the trophy cabinet.

BLACK-JACK   WINE BAR

Map p274 (Campo San Luca 4267b; ☺7.30am-9pm; ☻Rialto) Charming staff dispense delicious *cicheti* from a central horseshoe-shaped bar in this upmarket little place in the main shopping precinct. It's a great place for a snack and a tipple on your way to La Fenice or Teatro Goldoni; you could easily make a meal of it.

BACARANDO   BAR

Map p274 (☏041 523 82 80; www.bacarando. com; Corte dell'Orso 5495; ☺10.30am-midnight; ☻Rialto) If you've managed to find this wood-panelled bar in the warren of streets off San Bartolomeo, toast yourself with a cocktail and order a plate of heaped *cicheti*. Thanks to its divey vibe and a lively program of cultural events and live music, it's popular with a hip young crowd.

L'OMBRA DEL LEONI
BAR

Map p274 (☑041 521 87 11; Calle Ridotto 1364a; ☺9am-9pm; ᠍San Marco) Enjoy Palazzo Ca' Giustinian's peerless waterside Grand Canal position in this cafe-restaurant. Try to nab a seat on the outdoor terrace – it's the perfect spot to watch the gondolas come and go against a backdrop of basilicas.

CAFFÈ LAVENA
CAFE

Map p274 (☑041 522 40 70; www.lavena.it; Piazza San Marco 133/134; ☺9.30am-11pm; ᠍San Marco) Opera composer Richard Wagner had the right idea: when Venice leaves you weak at the knees, get a pick-me-up at Lavena. An espresso at the mirrored bar is a baroque bargain – never mind the questionable antique 'Moor's head' chandeliers. Spring for piazza seating to savor *caffe corretto* (coffee 'corrected' with liquor) accompanied by Lavena's nimble violinists.

ENOTECA AL VOLTO
WINE BAR

Map p274 (☑041 522 89 45; http://enotecaalvolto.com; Calle Cavalli 4081; ☺10am-4pm & 6-10pm; ᠍Rialto) Join the crowd working its way through the vast selection of *cicheti* in this historic wood-panelled bar that feels like the inside of a ship's hold. Lining the ceiling above the golden glow of the brass bar lanterns are hundreds of wine labels from just some of the bottles of regional wines that are cracked open every night.

TEAMO
WINE BAR

Map p274 (☑041 528 37 87; www.teamowinebar.com; Rio Terà de la Mandola 3795; ☺8.30am-10.30pm Fri-Wed; ᠍Sant'Angelo) By day this is more of a cafe, but in the evening its little tables fill up with a mixed crowd, drinking wine and snacking on massive platters of *salumi* (cured meats) and cheese.

CAFFÈ CENTRALE
COCKTAIL BAR

Map p274 (☑041 887 66 42; www.caffecentralevenezia.com; Piscina de Frezzaria 1659b; ☺7pm-1am; ᠍San Marco) You might spot a celebrity or two lurking on the black-leather sofas under Centrale's moody Murano chandeliers. Meals are pricey and canalside VIP tables chilly, but this slick modern bar draws La Fenice post-opera crowds with signature *spritz* cocktails, midnight snacks, chill-out DJ sets and occasional live jazz.

BÀCARO JAZZ
BAR

Map p274 (Salizada del Fontego dei Tedeschi 5546; ☺noon-2am; ᠍Rialto) A bar with a ceiling completely covered with bras could hardly be accused of being classy, but if you're after a change from sedate *cicheti* bars, this loud and unashamedly trashy place is usually packed to its quirkily decorated rafters on the weekends.

☆ ENTERTAINMENT

★TEATRO LA FENICE
OPERA

Map p274 (☑041 78 66 54; www.teatrolafenice.it; Campo San Fantin 1977; tickets €25-250; ᠍Giglio) One of Italy's top opera houses, La Fenice stages a rich roster of opera, ballet and classical music. The main opera season runs from January to July and September to October. The cheapest seats (€25) are in the boxes at the top: the view is extremely restricted, but you will get to hear the music, watch the orchestra, soak up the atmosphere and people watch.

TEATRO GOLDONI
THEATRE

Map p274 (☑041 240 20 14; www.teatrostabileveneto.it; Calle del Teatro 4650b; ᠍Rialto) Named after the city's great playwright, Carlo Goldoni, Venice's main theatre has an impressive dramatic range that runs from Goldoni's comedy to Shakespearean tragedy (mostly in Italian), plus ballets and concerts. Don't be fooled by the huge 20th-century bronze doors: this venerable theatre dates from 1622, and the jewel-box interior seats just 800.

MUSICA A PALAZZO
OPERA

Map p274 (☑340 9717272; www.musicapalazzo.com; Palazzo Barbarigo Minotto, Fondamenta Duodo o Barbarigo 2504; tickets incl beverage €85; ☺from 8pm; ᠍Giglio) Hang onto your prosecco and brace for impact: in historic salons the soprano's high notes imperil glassware, and thundering baritones reverberate through inlaid floors. During performances of opera from Verdi or Rossini, the drama progresses from receiving-room overtures to parlour duets overlooking the Grand Canal, followed by second acts in the Tiepolo-ceilinged dining room and bedroom grand finales.

WAGNER SAYS 'SHHHH!'

By the 19th century, Venice's great families were largely ruined and could not afford to heat their enormous *palazzi* (mansions). Instead, aristocrats would spend much of the day at La Fenice, which served as a members-only club, where they could gamble, gossip and provide running commentary during performances. When he first performed at La Fenice, German composer Richard Wagner miffed the notoriously chatty Venetian opera crowd by insisting on total silence during performances.

INTERPRETI VENEZIANI CLASSICAL MUSIC
Map p274 (☎041 277 05 61; www.interpretiven eziani.com; Chiesa San Vidal, Campo di San Vidal 2862; adult/reduced €30/25; ☉performances 8.30pm; ☒Accademia) Hard-core classical fans might baulk at the idea of Vivaldi being played night after night for decades, but it truly is a fitting soundtrack to this city of intrigue. You'll never listen to *The Four Seasons* again without hearing summer storms erupting over the lagoon, or snow-muffled footsteps hurrying over footbridges in winter's-night intrigues.

MULTISALA ROSSINI CINEMA
Map p274 (☎041 241 72 74; Salizada de la Chiesa o del Teatro 3997a; adult/reduced €7.50/7; ☉shows Tue-Sun; ☒; ☒Sant'Angelo) Award-winning films and blockbusters screen year-round at the city's main cinema. Films are screened in their original language on Fridays and Mondays, otherwise they are dubbed in Italian.

🛍 **SHOPPING**

San Marco is Venice's main shopping district and is crammed full of high-end stores. The main strips are the network of lanes radiating out from the Rialto Bridge towards Campo San Anzolo and Piazza San Marco, and west from the piazza towards Campo di Santa Maria del Giglio.

★**CHIARASTELLA CATTANA** HOMEWARES
Map p274 (☎041 522 43 69; www.chiarastel lacattana.com; Salizada San Samuele 3216;

☉11am-1pm & 3-7pm Mon-Sat; ☒San Samuele) Transform any home with these locally woven, strikingly original Venetian linens. Whimsical cushions feature chubby purple rhinoceroses and grumpy scarlet elephants straight out of Pietro Longhi paintings, and hand-tasselled jacquard hand towels will dry your guests in style. Decorators and design aficionados should save an afternoon to consider dizzying woven-to-order napkin and curtain options.

★**LIBRERIA LINEA D'ACQUA** BOOKS
Map p274 (☎041 522 40 30; https://lineadacqua. it; Calle de la Mandola 3717d; ☉9am-1pm & 3-7pm Mon-Fri, 10am-1pm Sat; ☒Rialto) This beautiful store selling antiquarian books, first editions, maps, sculptures and engravings is much more than a shop: it's a guardian of Venice's soul. Owner Luca Zentilini is a scholar and artist, preserving books and publishing a line of beautifully illustrated and affordable titles on Venetian history, culture, art and food. Check out its online magazine, In Time (https://intimemaga zine.com).

★**BARENA** CLOTHING
Map p274 (☎041 523 84 57; www.barenavenezia. com; Rio Terà San Paternian 4260b; ☉10am-1pm & 4-7.30pm Mon, Tue & Thu-Sat, 4-7.30pm Wed; ☒Rialto) This internationally recognised Venetian brand has been turning out timelessly classic clothes and coats since 1961. Named after the sandbanks that dot the lagoon, it specialises in comfortable leisurewear in a range of earthy tones made from the finest yarns produced in the Veneto. This is also *the* place to pick up a *tabarro,* the Venetian cloak worn by kings and brigands.

L'OTTICO FABBRICATORE CLOTHING
Map p274 (L'O.FT; ☎041 522 52 63; Calle del Lovo 4773; ☉10am-1pm & 3.30-7.30pm Mon-Sat, 11am-5pm Sun; ☒Rialto) Husband-and-wife team Francesco and Marianna run this classy store that stocks some of the most brilliant names in Italian fashion. Delicate silks and cashmere are trademark fabrics, while sublime sunglasses accessorise the look – it's no surprise to learn that Francesco is an optician and that the store was one of the oldest optician's in Venice.

OTTICA CARRARO FASHION & ACCESSORIES
Map p274 (☎041 520 42 58; www.otticacarraro. it; Calle de la Mandola 3706; ☉9.30am-1pm &

3-7.30pm Mon-Sat; ⬛Sant'Angelo) Lost your sunglasses on the Lido? Never fear: Ottica Carraro can make you a custom pair within 24 hours, including the eye exam. The store has its own limited-edition 'Venice' line, ranging from cat-eye shades perfect for facing paparazzi to chunky wood-grain frames that could get you mistaken for an art critic at the Biennale.

GIOBAGNARA
GLASS

Map p274 (Il Prato Venezia; ☑041 523 11 48; www. ilpratovenezia.com; Calle delle Ostreghe 2456/9; ⏱10am 7pm; ⬛Santa Maria del Giglio) This elegant store sells predominantly glass, most notably beautiful pieces by Nason e Moretti, but also has innovative items in wood, metal and even silicone.

FONDERIE VALESE
ARTS & CRAFTS

Map p274 (☑041 522 72 82; http://valese.it; Calle Fiubera 793; ⏱10.30am-6.30pm Mon-Fri, 11am-6pm Sat & Sun) For a meaningful memento of Venice, hunt down Fonderie Valese, the last remaining bronze and brass sand-casting foundry in the city. Here you'll find an Aladdin's cave full of gleaming gondola accessories, miniature models of the bronze Horses of Saint Mark, golden Venetian lions, Carnival masks, door knockers and paperweights. They're unique, affordable artworks.

MARINA E SUSANNA SENT
GLASS

Map p274 (☑041 521 04 14; www.marinaesusannasent.com; Ponte San Moisè 2090; ⏱10am-6.30pm Mon-Sat; ⬛San Marco Vallaresso) This postage-stamp-sized shop on the bridge of San Moisé sells fabulous jewellery by Muranese sisters Marina and Susanna Sent, whose designs can also be found in New York's MoMA. Though predominantly glass, the jewellery occasionally features other materials, such as silver.

POLI DISTILLERIE
ALCOHOL

Map p274 (☑041 866 01 04; www.grappa.com; Campiello Feltrina 2511b; ⏱10am-7pm; ⬛Santa Maria del Giglio) This grappa store positively gleams, thanks to its copper-chrome fittings. The Poli family has been distilling grappa since 1898, and the friendly sales team can guide you through the variety on offer.

SIGFRIDO CIPOLATO
JEWELLERY

Map p274 (☑041 522 84 37; www.sigfridocipolato.com; Calle de la Mandola 3717a; ⏱11am-

8pm Mon-Sat; ⬛Sant'Angelo) Booty worthy of pirates is displayed in the fishbowl-sized window display: a ring with a constellation of diamonds in star settings, a tiny enamelled green snake sinking its fangs into a pearl, and diamond drop earrings that end in enamelled gold skulls. Though they look like heirlooms, these small wonders were made on the premises by master jeweller Sigfrido.

BEVILACQUA FABRICS
DESIGN

Map p274 (☑041 241 06 62; www.bevilacquatessuti.com; Campo di Santa Maria del Giglio 2520; ⏱10am-7pm; ⬛Giglio) Turn your TV den into a grand salon at Bevilacqua, purveyor of fine *soprarizzo* silk-velvet brocades, damasks and tassels to Europe's grandest palaces and Italy's swankiest modern apartments. Master artisans still weave the fabrics in Venice on 18th-century wooden looms, and the front-room display here is just a sample of their artistry; ask about custom cushions and upholstery.

ATELIER SEGALIN DI DANIELA GHEZZO
SHOES

Map p274 (☑041 522 21 15; www.danielaghezzo.it; Calle dei Fuseri 4365; ⏱10am-1pm & 3-7pm Mon-Fri, 10am-1pm Sat; ⬛San Marco) A gold chain pulled across this historic atelier doorway means Daniela is already consulting with a client, discussing rare leathers while taking foot measurements. Each pair of shoes is custom-made, so you'll never see your emerald ostrich-leather boots on another diva, or your dimpled manta-ray brogues on a rival mogul. Expect to pay around €1000 and wait six weeks for delivery.

CAIGO DA MAR
HOMEWARES

Map p274 (☑041 243 32 38; www.caigodamar.com; Salizzada San Samuele 3157/A; ⏱10am-1pm & 4-7pm Mon-Sat; ⬛San Samuele) Venetian pirates once headed to Constantinople for all their interior-decoration needs, but today they'd need look no further than Caigo da Mar. This tiny treasure trove brims with dramatic black Murano glass candelabras and a designer booty of Fornasetti cushions, plus enough octopus-shaped lamps and nautilus-shell dishes to make any living room look like the lost city of Atlantis.

SV LAB
FASHION & ACCESSORIES

Map p274 (☑041 522 05 95; www.svlab.it; Campo San Maurizio 2663; ⏱10am-7.30pm Mon-Sat, 11am-6pm Sun; ⬛Giglio) SV Lab sells deadly cool men's and women's apparel with a rock-and-roll sensibility but a patrician's eye to quality. The silk and cashmere jackets are particularly beautiful, but you might need access to a patrician's wallet as well.

FONDACO DEI TEDESCHI   DEPARTMENT STORE
Map p274 (www.dfs.com; Calle del Fontego dei Tedeschi 5350; ⊙10am-8pm; 🚢Rialto) Occupying one of the Grand Canal's most imposing buildings, a 16th-century German trading house, this branch of the DFS chain is worth visiting whether you're in the market for a handbag with a four-digit price tag or not. Four floors of colonnaded galleries rise up to line the vast central void, leading to sublime views from the rooftop.

L'ARMADIO DI COCO LUXURY VINTAGE   VINTAGE
Map p274 (📞041 241 32 14; www.larmadiodi coco.it; Campo di Santa Maria del Giglio 2516a; ⊙10.30am-7pm; 🚢Giglio) Jam-packed with pre-loved designer treasures from yesteryear, this tiny shop is the place to come for classic Chanel dresses, exquisite cashmere coats and limited-edition Gucci shoulder bags.

VENETIAN DREAMS   FASHION & ACCESSORIES
Map p274 (📞041 523 02 92; www.marisaconven to.it; Calle de la Mandola 3805a; ⊙10.30am-7pm Mon-Sat; 🚢Sant'Angelo) High fashion meets *acqua alta* (high water) in Marisa Convento's aquatic accessories. La Fenice divas demand her freshwater-pearl-encrusted velvet handbags, while Biennale artistes snap up octopus-tentacle glass-bead necklaces. Between customers, Marisa can be glimpsed at her desk, painstakingly weaving coral-branch collars from antique Murano *conterie* (seed beads). To wow Carnevale crowds, ask about ordering a custom-made costume.

ARNOLDO & BATTOIS   FASHION & ACCESSORIES
Map p274 (📞041 528 59 44; www.arnoldoebat tois.com; Calle dei Fuseri 4271; ⊙10.30am-1pm & 3.30-7pm Mon-Sat; 🚢Rialto) Handbags become heirlooms in the hands of Venetian designers Massimiliano Battois and Silvano Arnoldo, whose handcrafted clutches come in bold turquoise and magenta leather with baroque closures in laser-cut wood. Artfully draped emerald and graphite silk dresses complete the look for Biennale openings.

VENETIA STUDIUM   FASHION & ACCESSORIES
Map p274 (📞041 523 69 53; www.venetiastudium. com; Calle de le Ostreghe 2427; ⊙10.30am-7pm Mon-Sat, from 11am Sun; 🚢Giglio) Get that 'just got in from Monaco for my art opening' look beloved of cashed-up bohemians. The high-drama Delphos tunic dresses make anyone look like a high-maintenance modern dancer or heiress (Isadora Duncan and Peggy Guggenheim were both fans), and the hand-stamped silk-velvet bags are more arty than ostentatious.

MATERIALMENTE   DESIGN
Map p274 (📞041 528 68 81; www.material mentevenezia.com; Mercerie San Salvador 4850; ⊙10.30am-7pm Mon-Sat; 🚢Rialto) Prolific sibling artisans Maddelena Venier and Alessandro Salvadori pack their tiny boutique with whimsical creations such as wire fish-skeleton chandeliers, whale mobiles and interesting jewellery.

BOTTEGA D'ARTE GIULIANA LONGO   HATS
Map p274 (📞041 522 64 54; www.giulianalongo. com; Calle del Lovo 4813; ⊙10am-7pm Mon-Sat; 🚢Rialto) Giuliana's shop is the dream hat-cupboard of any true sartorialist. Styles range from hand-woven Montecristi panama hats to a fuchsia felt number made for Peggy Guggenheim that looks like a doge's cap. Giuliana is here most days, polishing leather aviator hats or affixing a broad band to a *baretero,* the wide-brimmed gondolier's hat best worn with a rakish tilt (from €65).

FIORELLA GALLERY   FASHION & ACCESSORIES
Map p274 (📞335 8200873; www.fiorellagallery. com; Campo Santo Stefano 2806a; ⊙hours vary; 🚢Accademia) Fiorella has been pioneering rebel couture since 1968 but you'll need a rock-star budget to afford one of her silk-velvet smoking jackets in louche lavender and oxblood, printed by hand with skulls, peacocks or a Fiorella signature: wide-eyed rats. Hours vary; as the sign says, 'open some time'.

MERCATINO DELL'ANTIQUARIATO   MARKET
Map p274 (www.mercatinocamposanmaurizio. it; Campo San Maurizio; 🚢Giglio) A much-loved antiques flea market held several weekends a year; check the website for dates. Head in early for the best finds, among them vintage Campari posters, Venetian postcards, Murano glassware and delicate Burano lace.

Dorsoduro

Neighbourhood Top Five

❶ Gallerie dell'Accademia (p75) Getting a crash course in Venetian painting at a former convent, now positively blushing with masterpieces of glowing colours, censored subjects and breathless elegance.

❷ Basilica di Santa Maria della Salute (p78) Testing the curative powers of Baldassare Longhena's mystical architecture and finding hidden Titian wonders.

❸ Ca' Rezzonico (p79) Waltzing through baroque palace ballrooms, salons and boudoirs surrounded by sublime Venetian art.

❹ Peggy Guggenheim Collection (p77) Schmoozing with Picasso, Pollock and Giacometti at the former Grand Canal pad of an American heiress.

❺ Punta della Dogana (p80) Comparing, contrasting and debating fearless contemporary art amid boldly repurposed architecture.

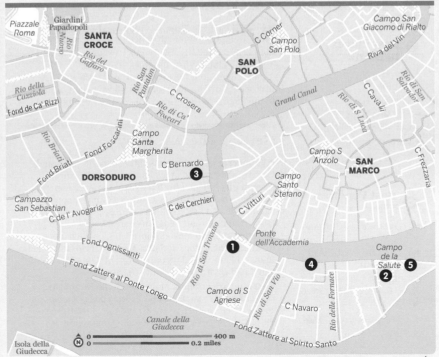

For more detail of this area see Map p284.

Lonely Planet's Top Tip

If you're mad about modern art, consider signing up for the Peggy Guggenheim's annual Open Pass (€45), which gives you free access to the collection, reduced admission for guests, a discount on the audio guide and in the museum cafe and shops, and free entrance to 10 other major modern-art museums in Italy. The Young Pass (€25) offers the same benefits for those under the age of 26.

✖ Best Places to Eat

➜ Riviera (p83)

➜ Cantine del Vino già Schiavi (p81)

➜ Osteria Bakán (p82)

➜ Enoteca ai Artisti (p83)

➜ Da Codroma (p82)

For reviews, see p81.➜

☕ Best Places to Drink

➜ Malvasia all'Adriatico Mar (p84)

➜ Chet Bar (p84)

➜ El Sbarlefo (p84)

➜ Osteria ai Pugni (p84)

➜ Caffè Rosso (p84)

For reviews, see p84.➜

◉ Best Venetian Views

➜ Terrace, Peggy Guggenheim Collection (p77)

➜ Water-gate, Punta della Dogana (p80)

➜ Canaletto's *View of the Grand Canal*, Ca' Rezzonico (p79)

For reviews, see p75.➜

Explore Dorsoduro

Dorsoduro is home to some of Venice's most high-profile galleries along with some fascinating art-filled churches. If you're an art aficionado, you'll need two or three days to do it justice; fair-weather fans could cram a lot into a day.

Sights in Dorsoduro are spread out: museums flank the Grand Canal on the eastern side, while bars and upbeat eateries rustle around Campo Santa Margherita and Campo San Barnaba to the northwest. Start east with masterpieces at Gallerie dell'Accademia (p75), then recover with canalside prosecco and *cicheti* (Venetian tapas) at Cantine del Vino già Schiavi (p81). Revived, see how Pollock splatter-paintings and Marini sculptures make an impact at the Peggy Guggenheim Collection (p77).

Steal a glance of haunted Ca' Dario on your way to 17th-century Basilica di Santa Maria della Salute (p78) and cutting-edge art space Punta della Dogana (p80). Alternatively, head northwest from the Guggenheim to mingle with Venetian socialites of yore at Ca' Rezzonico (p79). Either way, refocus with a post-museum stroll and *spritz* (prosecco cocktail) along the Zattere as the sun sets over the lagoon.

Local Life

➜ **Cicheti bars** For wine accompanied by slices of fresh bread weighed down with delicious toppings, the best options are along the Rio di San Trovaso.

➜ **Spritz o'clock** When the clock strikes *spritz* o'clock (around 6pm), join the neighbourhood's eclectic cast of students, artists and stock-standard hedonists in Campo Santa Margherita, Venice's nightlife hub.

Getting There & Away

➜ **Vaporetto** Dorsoduro has three stops on the Grand Canal (Ca' Rezzonico, Accademia and Salute); line 1 stops at all of them. Line 2 only stops at Accademia, but it also heads along the Giudecca Canal, stopping at San Basilio and Zattere. Route 5.1/5.2, which loops from Lido around the outer edge of central Venice, stops at Zattere and Santa Marta. Route 4.1/4.2, which loops to Murano, also stops at Santa Marta. Line 6 (Piazzale Roma to Lido, weekdays only) stops at Santa Marta, San Basilio, Zattere and Santo Spirito.

➜ **Traghetto** The Santa Maria del Giglio **traghetto** (Map p284; Calle Lanza; 1-way €2; ☺9am-5pm) is a stand-up gondola that zips across the Grand Canal from outside the Gritti Palace to the end of Calle Lanza (west of Salute).

TOP SIGHT
GALLERIE DELL'ACCADEMIA

Hardly academic, these galleries contain more murderous intrigue, forbidden romance and shameless politicking than the most outrageous Venetian parties. The former Scuola della Carità complex maintained its serene composure for centuries, but ever since Napoleon installed his haul of Venetian art trophies here in 1807 – mainly looted from various religious institutions – there's been nonstop visual drama inside these walls.

DON'T MISS

➡ Bellini's *Miracle of the Reliquary of the Cross at San Lorenzo Bridge*

➡ Titian's *Presentation of the Virgin*

➡ Tintoretto's *Creation of the Animals*

➡ Giorgione's *The Storm*

PRACTICALITIES

➡ Map p284, E5

➡ ☏041 522 22 47

➡ www.gallerieaccadem ia.it

➡ Campo de la Carità 1050

➡ adult/reduced €12/2

➡ ⏰8.15am-2pm Mon, to 7.15pm Tue-Sun

➡ 🚤Accademia

Layout & Gallery Restoration

The bulk of the collection's treasures are on the 1st floor, and this is the best place to start your visit. Ordinarily you can trace a circular route through the numbered rooms (each floor is numbered separately). However, at the time of writing, the gallery was in the midst of a lengthy restoration and several rooms were closed. An attempt has been made to move some of the most famous works into spaces usually used for temporary exhibitions, but don't be surprised if some of the masterpieces that we've described are not on view or are not where we've said they'll be.

The ground floor houses major exhibitions, sculpture and a less showstopping collection of paintings from 1600 to 1880. These rooms may also be affected by the restoration. At the time of writing, the ground floor's Rooms 1 to 3 could be accessed from behind the ticket desk, while Rooms 7 to 13 could only be approached from the central staircase on the 1st floor.

First Floor

Take the stairs up from the grand entry hall and prepare to be overwhelmed by the sensory overload of **Room 1**, where a swarm of angels flutter their golden wings from the carved ceiling, gazing down upon a swirling polychrome marble floor. Competing valiantly for your attention are a collection of vivid 14th- and 15th-century religious works that show Venice's precocious flair for colour and drama. Case in point: Jacobello Alberegno's late-14th-century *Apocalypse polyptych* shows the Whore of Babylon riding a hydra, babbling rivers of blood from her mouth.

UFO arrivals seem imminent in the eerie, glowing skies of Carpaccio's lively *Crucifixion and Glorification of the Ten Thousand Martyrs of Mount Ararat* in **Room 2**. But Giovanni Bellini's *San Giobbe altarpiece* shows hope on the horizon, in the form of a sweet-faced Madonna and Child enthroned beneath golden mosaics as angels play their instruments. The saints surrounding them include Roch and Sebastian, suggesting that this luminous, uplifting work dates from the dark days of Venice's second plague in 1478.

Lock eyes with fascinating strangers across **Room 4**. Hans Memling captures youthful stubble and angst with exacting detail in *Portrait of a Young Man*. The highlight, however, is Giovanni Bellini's sublimely elegant *Madonna and Child between Saints Catherine and Mary Magdalene*.

Venice's Renaissance awaits in **Room 6**, where you'll find Titian and Tintoretto. The latter's *Creation of the Animals* is a fantastic bestiary suggesting God put forth his best efforts inventing Venetian seafood (no argument here).

ACCADEMIA ARCHITECTURE

The Accademia inhabits three conjoined buildings. The **Scuola della Carità** (founded 1260) was the oldest of Venice's six *scuole grandi* (religious confraternities); the current building dates to 1343. Bartolomeo Bon completed the spare, Gothic-edged facade of the **Chiesa di Santa Maria della Carità** (Church of Our Lady of Charity) in 1448. A century later, Palladio took a classical approach to the **Convento dei Canonici Lateranensi**. From 1949 to 1954, Carlo Scarpa chose a minimalist approach to restorations; his restrained style is most apparent in the central staircase.

TOP TIPS

➡ There's free admission to the gallery on the first Sunday of each month.

➡ To avoid high-season queues, arrive at opening time or towards the end of the day. Last entry is 45 minutes before closing, but a proper visit takes at least 1½ hours.

➡ To skip ahead of the queues, book timed tickets in advance online (booking fee €1.50).

➡ The audio guide (€6) is largely unnecessary.

Room 20 is full of large canvases taken from the Scuola Grande di San Giovanni Evangelista (p95). Among them is Gentile Bellini's *Miracle of the Reliquary of the Cross at San Lorenzo Bridge*, thronged with cosmopolitan crowds. The artist's *Procession in Piazza San Marco* offers an intriguing view of Venice's most famous square before its 16th-century makeover, while the former wooden version of the city's most famous bridge appears in Vittore Carpaccio's *Miracle of the Reliquary of the Cross at Rialto Bridge*.

The former church (**Room 23**) is a serene show-stopper fronted by a Bellini altarpiece. Sharing the space is Giorgione's highly charged *The Storm*. Art historians still debate the meaning of the mysterious nursing mother and passing soldier, with a bolt of summer lightning: is this an expulsion from Eden, an allegory for alchemy, or a reference to Venice conquering Padua in the War of Cambria? The rear of the church displays massive canvases looted from the Scuola Grande di San Marco (p128).

The final room, **Room 24**, has been left untouched from when it was the Scuola della Carità's boardroom, the Sala dell'Albergo. Board meetings would not have been boring here, under a lavishly carved ceiling and facing Antonio Vivarini's *Madonna Enthroned with Child in the Heavenly Garden*, filled with fluffy-bearded saints. Titian closes the 1st-floor circuit with his touching *Presentation of the Virgin*. Here, a young, tiny Madonna trudges up an intimidating staircase while a distinctly Venetian crowd of onlookers point at her.

Moving Masterpieces

At the time of writing, Room 15 was being used to display gallery highlights that were usually displayed in Room 10 (under restoration), including Tintoretto's action-packed *St Mark Rescues a Saracen* (1562) and Titian's *Pietà* (1576).

Ground Floor

The highlight of the ground-floor collection is Room 2, which is devoted to 18th-century Venice's go-to ceiling guy Giambattista Tiepolo. The focal point is a large fresco *The Exaltation of the Cross & St Helen*, which originally adorned the ceiling of a church in Castello.

Rooms 7, 10 and 13 feature the work of the city's most famous sculptor, Antonio Canova, including funeral steles, classical figures and sycophantic effigies of Venice's new French overlords, the Bonapartes. There's a Canaletto tucked away in Room 9 – one of only a couple of works by the artist on public display in his home town.

TOP SIGHT
PEGGY GUGGENHEIM COLLECTION

After tragically losing her father on the *Titanic*, heiress Peggy Guggenheim befriended Dadaists, dodged Nazis and changed art history at her palatial home on the Grand Canal. Peggy's Palazzo Venier dei Leoni is a showcase for surrealism, futurism and abstract expressionism by some 200 breakthrough modern artists, including Peggy's ex-husband Max Ernst and Jackson Pollock (among her many rumoured lovers).

Collection

Peggy collected according to her own convictions rather than for prestige or style, so her collection includes inspired folk art and lesser-known artists alongside Kandinsky, Picasso, Magritte, Man Ray, Rothko, Mondrian, Chagall, Miró and Dalí. Major modernists also contributed custom interior decor, including the Alexander Calder silver bedstead hanging in the former bedroom. In the corners of the main galleries, you'll find photos of the rooms as they appeared when Peggy lived here, in fabulously eccentric style.

For this champion of modern art who'd witnessed the dangers of censorship and party-line dictates, serious artwork deserved to be seen and judged on its merits. The Jewish American collector narrowly escaped Paris two days before the Nazis marched into the city, and arrived in Venice in 1948 to find the city's historically buoyant spirits broken by war.

More than a mere taste-maker, Peggy became a spirited advocate for contemporary Italian art, which had largely gone out of favour in the aftermath of WWII. She resurrected the reputation of key Italian futurists, whose dynamic style had been co-opted to make Fascism more visually palatable. Her support led to reappraisals of Umberto Boccioni, Giacomo Balla and Giorgio de Chirico, and aided Venice's own Emilio Vedova and Giuseppe Santomaso.

Never afraid to make a splash, Peggy gave passing gondoliers an eyeful on her Grand Canal quay: Marino Marini's *The Angel of the City* (1948), a bronze male nude on horseback, is visibly excited by the possibilities on the horizon.

Garden & Pavilion

The Palazzo Venier dei Leoni was never finished, but that didn't stop Peggy from filling every available space indoors and out with art. Wander past bronzes by Henry Moore and Alberto Giacometti, and intriguing granite creations by Anish Kapoor and Isamu Noguchi in the **Nasher Sculpture Garden**. The city of Venice granted Peggy an honorary dispensation to be buried in the garden, alongside her dearly departed lapdogs in 1979.

The museum has also acquired the buildings behind the garden, which house a sunny cafe, a bookshop, bathrooms and a temporary exhibition space. Around the corner from the museum, on Fondamenta Venier dei Leoni, is a larger **museum shop** (Map p284; ☑041 240 54 22; www.guggenheim-venice.it; Fondamente Venier dei Leoni 710; ⊙10am-6pm Wed-Mon; ⎒Accademia), selling art books in several languages and gifts inspired by various artworks.

TOP TIPS

➡ There are excellent audio guides (€7) in Italian, English, German, French and Spanish.

➡ Free daily presentations in Italian and English are given on the life of Peggy Guggenheim (noon and 4pm) and individual works in the collection (11am and 5pm).

➡ Bags must be stored in the free lockers near the ticket office.

PRACTICALITIES

➡ Map p284, G5

➡ ☑041 240 54 11

➡ www.guggenheim-venice.it

➡ Calle San Cristoforo 701

➡ adult/reduced €15/9

➡ ⊙10am-6pm Wed-Mon

➡ ⎒Accademia

◉ SIGHTS

Minds blown by the sight of San Marco might require a bracing espresso before taking on artistically inclined Dorsoduro, which pivots around the show-stopping Accademia gallery. Nearby is Peggy Guggenheim's stylish Grand Canal villa full of modern masters. Beyond these blockbusters, Veronese lavished his parish church of San Sebastian with masterpieces; Tiepolo and Baldassare Longhena worked wonders on the Grand Canal palace of Ca' Rezzonico, the Scuola Grande dei Carmini and La Salute; and minimalist maestro Tadao Ando transformed Punta della Dogana from a warehouse customs dock to a world-class contemporary show space.

GALLERIE DELL'ACCADEMIA   GALLERY
See p75.

PEGGY GUGGENHEIM
COLLECTION   MUSEUM
See p77.

★BASILICA DI SANTA
MARIA DELLA SALUTE   BASILICA
Map p284 (Our Lady of Health Basilica; www.
basilicasalutevenezia.it; Campo de la Salute 1;
sacristy adult/reduced €4/2; ⊙9.30am-noon &
3-5.30pm; ⛴Salute) FREE Baldassare Longhena's magnificent basilica is prominently
positioned near the entrance to the Grand
Canal, its white stones, exuberant statuary
and high domes gleaming spectacularly
under the sun. The church makes good on
an official appeal by the Venetian Senate directly to the Madonna in 1630, after 80,000
Venetians had been killed by plague. The
Senate promised the Madonna a church in
exchange for her intervention on behalf of
Venice – no expense or effort spared.

Before 'La Salute' could be started, at least
100,000 pylons had to be driven deep into the
barene (mudbanks) to shore up the tip of Dorsoduro. The Madonna provided inspiration,
but La Salute draws its structural strength
from a range of architectural and spiritual
traditions. Architectural scholars note striking similarities between Longhena's unusual
domed octagonal structure and both Greco-
Roman goddess temples and Jewish Kab-
balah diagrams. The lines of the building
converge beneath the dome to form a vortex
on the inlaid marble floors; some believe the
central black dot radiates healing energy.

The basilica's interior is flooded with
light filtered through disks of pale-tinted
glass encircling the implausibly high dome.
The main focus of devotion is the elaborately carved baroque high altar, with a
12th-century Cretan icon of the *Madonna
of Good Health* set into it. A side altar near
the entrance to the sacristy showcases *The
Descent of the Holy Spirit* (1546) by Titian.

Entry to the church is free, but there is a
charge to visit the art-slung sacristy (closed
on Sunday mornings). The sacristy is a wonder within a wonder, its glorious collection
of Titian masterpieces including moody
ceiling frescoes, a vivid self-portrait in the
guise of St Matthew, and his earliest known
work, *Saint Mark Enthroned with Sts Cosmas, Damian, Roch & Sebastian* (1510). Salute's most charming allegory for Venice's
miraculous survival of the plague is Palma il
Giovane's painting of Jonah emerging from
the mouth of the whale, where the survivor
stomps down the creature's tongue like an
action hero walking the red carpet. Life in
a time of plague is a miracle worth celebrating in Tintoretto's upbeat *Wedding Feast of
Cana* (1561), featuring a Venetian throng of
multicultural musicians, busy wine pourers
and Tintoretto himself, depicted with a long
beard near the bottom left of the canvas.

CHIESA DI SANTA
MARIA DEL ROSARIO   CHURCH
Map p284 (Our-Lady-of-the-Rosary Church; www.
chorusvenezia.org; Fondamenta Zattere ai Gesuati
918; adult/reduced €3/1.50, with Chorus Pass
free; ⊙7.30am-7pm Mon-Sat, 9am-1pm & 5-7.30pm
Sun; ⛴Zattere) Venetians have long memories, which is why this church is still called
I Gesuati by locals despite the namesake
religious order having been replaced by the
Dominicans in 1668. The Dominican friars
commissioned Giorgio Massari to design
a completely new church a couple of doors
down from the old one, which still remains.
Unsurprisingly, St Dominic plays a leading
role in Tiepolo's acclaimed ceiling frescoes
(1738–39) in the new church, which was
completed in 1735.

Overwhelming grief grips the Madonna
in Tintoretto's sombre 1565 *Crucifixion*,
positioned on the altar to the left of the
main altar. Altogether lighter is Sebastiano
Ricci's *Saints Peter and Thomas with Pope
Pius V* (1730–33), complete with comical
cherubim performing celestial tumbling
routines.

CHIESA DI SAN PANTALON   CHURCH

Map p284 (St Pantaleon's Church; Campo San Pantalon 3703; ⊘10am-noon & 3.30-6pm; 🚤San Tomà) **FREE** It's not the prettiest from the outside, but the bald brick facade of this 17th-century church (rent by a concerning crack), doesn't give any indication of the drama contained within. The entire ceiling is engulfed in a vast, overwhelming *trompe l'oeil* fresco by Gianantonio Fumiani, featuring a dark cacophony of saints and angels seemingly bursting through the roof. This extraordinary 1704 fresco may have been the artist's last: he's said to have fallen to his death while working on it.

Once you've uncrinked your neck, look for the magnificent gilded 14th-century crucifix to the right and, behind it, Veronese's last known work – a 1587 altarpiece of St Pantalon.

More treasures are to be found in the side chapels hidden to the left of the main altar (admission €1). The Holy Nail Chapel houses an extraordinarily vivid icon of the *Coronation of the Virgin* (1444) by Antonio Vivarini, with a bearded Heavenly Father sternly overlooking the ecstatic scene, backed by assembled ranks of day-glow angels and a swarm of naked cherubs. Behind it, the Loreto Chapel has the remains of 18th-century frescoes of the Madonna and Child by Pietro Longhi.

CHIESA DI SAN SEBASTIANO   CHURCH

Map p284 (St Sebastian's Church; www.chorus venezia.org; Campo San Sebastian 1687; adult/reduced €3/1.50, free with Chorus Pass; ⊘10.30am-4.30pm Mon-Sat; 🚤San Basilio) Antonio Scarpignano's relatively austere 1508-48 facade creates a sense of false modesty at this neighbourhood church. The interior is adorned with floor-to-ceiling masterpieces by Paolo Veronese, executed over three decades. According to popular local legend, Veronese found sanctuary at San Sebastiano in 1555 after fleeing murder charges in Verona, and his works in this church deliver lavish thanks to the parish and an especially brilliant poke in the eye to his accusers.

Veronese chose to be buried here, underneath his masterpieces – his memorial bust is to the right of the organ. The artist's virtuosity is displayed all around, from the horses rearing on the coffered ceiling to the organ doors covered with his *Presentation*

◉ TOP SIGHT
CA' REZZONICO

Baroque dreams come true at this Baldassare Longhena–designed Grand Canal *palazzo*, where a marble staircase leads to a vast gilded **ballroom** and sumptuous salons filled with period furniture, paintings, porcelain and mesmerising ceiling frescoes, four of which were painted by Giambattista Tiepolo. The building was largely stripped of its finery when the Rezzonico family departed in 1810, but this was put right after the city acquired it in 1935, and refurnished it with pieces salvaged from other decaying palaces.

The 2nd floor opens with the showstopping **Picture Gallery Portego**, featuring an amazingly detailed *View of the Grand Canal* by Canaletto – one of only two works by the artist on public display in Venice.

The top floor is given over to the **Egidio Martini Pictures Gallery** (showcasing Venetian artists from the 15th to the 20th century) and the interiors of a **historic pharmacy**, which once stood on Campo San Stin, complete with 183 majolica ceramic jars of 18th-century remedies. Apparently pharmaceutical-grade scorpions don't cure everything: the poet Robert Browning died at Ca' Rezzonico in 1889.

TOP TIPS

➜ Tickets can be booked online.

➜ Ticket office closes an hour before the museum.

PRACTICALITIES

➜ Museum of 18th-Century Venice

➜ Map p284, E3

➜ ☑041 241 01 00

➜ www.visitmuve.it

➜ Fondamenta Rezzonico 3136

➜ adult/reduced €10/7.50, or with Museum Pass

➜ ⊘10am-5pm Wed-Mon

➜ 🚤Ca' Rezzonico

in the Temple. In the *Martyrdom of Saint Sebastian* near the altar, the bound saint defiantly stares down his tormentors amid a Venetian crowd of socialites, turbaned traders and Veronese's signature frisky spaniel. St Sebastian was a fearless patron of Venice's plague victims, and Veronese suggests that, although sticks and stones may break his bones, Venetian gossip couldn't kill him. Peek into the sacristy to glimpse Veronese's glowing *Coronation of the Virgin* (1555) on the ceiling.

However, there's more than one master at work here; don't miss Titian's *St Nicholas* (1563) to the right of the entry.

CHIESA DI SAN NICOLÒ
DEI MENDICOLI   CHURCH

Map p284 (St Nicholas of the Beggars Church; ☑041 528 45 65; Campo San Nicolò dei Mendicoli 1907; ⊙10am-noon & 3-5.30pm Mon-Sat, 9am-noon Sun; ☒Santa Marta) **FREE** Other churches might be grander, but none is more quintessentially Venetian than this 12th-century church with a history of service to the poor. Its cloisters once functioned as a women's refuge and its portico sheltered the *mendicoli* (beggars) to whom it owes its name. The tiny, picturesque *campo* (square) out front is Venice in miniature, surrounded on three sides by canals and featuring a pillar bearing the lion of St Mark.

Dim interiors are illuminated by an 18th-century golden arcade and a profusion of clerestory paintings, including Palma il Giovane's masterpiece *Resurrection* (c 1610) at the rear, to the left of the organ. In the painting, onlookers cower in terror and awe as Jesus leaps from his tomb in a blaze of golden light. The front right-hand chapel is a typically Venetian response to persistent orders from Rome to limit music in Venetian churches: the Madonna in glory, thoroughly enjoying a concert by angels on flutes, lutes and violins. The parish's seafaring livelihood is honoured in Leonardo Corona's 16th-century ceiling panel *St Nicholas Guiding Sailors Through a Storm*.

Film buffs might recognise the interiors from the 1973 Nicolas Roeg thriller *Don't Look Now* as the church Donald Sutherland was assigned to restore. Although the movie cast Venice in a spooky light, the publicity apparently helped San Nicolò: the British Venice in Peril Fund underwrote extensive renovations, completed in 1977.

◉ TOP SIGHT
PUNTA DELLA DOGANA

Fortuna, the weather vane atop Punta della Dogana, swung Venice's way in 2005, when bureaucratic hassles in Paris convinced art collector François Pinault to showcase his works in Venice's long-abandoned customs warehouses.

Built by Giuseppe Benoni in 1677 to ensure that no ship entered the Grand Canal without paying duties, the warehouses re-opened in 2009 after a striking reinvention by Tadao Ando. Inside, the Japanese architect stripped back centuries of alterations, returning the interior to its pure form of red brick and wooden beams. Within this pared-back space, Ando added his own contemporary vision, cutting windows in Benoni's ancient water gates to reveal views of passing ships, adding floating concrete staircases in honour of innovative Venetian modernist Carlo Scarpa, and erecting his own trademark polished concrete panels.

The end result is a conscious and dramatic juxtaposition of the old and the new, one that simultaneously pays due regard to the city's seafaring history and its changing architecture, and provides a suitable scale and mood for Pinault's rotating exhibitions of ambitious, large-scale contemporary artworks.

TOP TIPS

➔ Book tickets online to avoid queuing for popular exhibitions.

➔ Get a combined ticket including Palazzo Grassi.

PRACTICALITIES

➔ Map p284, H5

➔ ☑041 200 10 57

➔ www.palazzograssi.it

➔ Fondamenta Salute 2

➔ adult/reduced €15/10, incl Palazzo Grassi €18/15

➔ ⊙10am-7pm Wed-Mon Apr-Nov

➔ ☒Salute

CHIESA DI SAN RAFFAELE ARCANGELO
CHURCH

Map p284 (Church of the Archangel Raphael; ☑041 522 85 48; Campo de l'Anzolo Rafael 1721; ☉10am-noon & 3-5pm Mon-Sat, 9am-noon Sun; ⚓San Basilio) **FREE** The neighbours called, and they want their grime back: when centuries of accumulated dirt were removed from the stone angels above the portals of Francesco Contino's 17th-century facade, it caused a local uproar. Had Venice lost its respect for the patina of age? They needn't have worried: the soot has already started to return. No similar argument was raised about the restoration of the baptistery, where Francesco Fontebasso's baroque frescoes glow in shades of pink, gold and pale green.

SCUOLA GRANDE DEI CARMINI
HISTORIC BUILDING

Map p284 (☑041 528 94 20; www.scuolagrande carmini.it; Campo Santa Margherita 2617; adult/reduced €7/5; ☉11am-5pm; ⚓Ca' Rezzonico) Seventeenth-century backpackers must have thought they'd died and gone to heaven at this magnificent confraternity clubhouse, dedicated to Our Lady of Mt Carmel, with its lavish interiors by Giambattista Tiepolo and Baldassare Longhena. The gold-leafed, Longhena-designed stucco stairway heads up towards Tiepolo's nine-panel ceiling of a rosy *Virgin in Glory*. The adjoining hostel room is bedecked in marble and *boiserie* (wood carving).

This *scuola* (religious confraternity) was the only one of the six *scuole grandi* to admit women – a nod to the women who founded its predecessor in the 13th-century. The Carmini continued to extend hospitality to destitute and wayward travellers right through to the time of Napoleon's occupation of Venice. Sadly, cots are no longer available in this jewel-box building, but evening **Musica in Maschera** (Map p284; ☑041 528 76 67; www.musicainmaschera.it; Scuola Grande dei Carmini 2617; tickets €25-52; ⚓Ca' Rezzonico) concerts are held here, and members of the Carmini continue to organise charitable works to this day.

V-A-C FOUNDATION
ARTS CENTRE

Map p284 (www.v-a-c.ru; Fondamenta Zattere al Ponte Longo 1401; ☉11am-5pm Sat-Tue & Thu, to 9pm Fri; ⚓Zattere) **FREE** Occupying a large *palazzo* with views over the Giudecca Canal, this beautiful new space for contem-

porary art was lovingly restored by the Russian V A C Foundation. Exhibitions run regularly throughout the year, along with film screenings and performances. Even if there's nothing on, it's a great place to escape to if you need quiet desk space with free wi-fi.

SQUERO DI SAN TROVASO
HISTORIC SITE

Map p284 (Campo San Trovaso 1097; ⚓Zattere) This wooden cabin on the Rio di San Trovaso looks like a stray ski chalet, but it's one of Venice's few working *squeri* (shipyards), with refinished gondolas drying in the yard. It's best viewed from across the canal, but if the door's open you might be able to peek inside.

FONDAZIONE VEDOVA
GALLERY

Map p284 (Magazzini del Sale; ☑041 522 66 26; www.fondazionevedova.org; Fondamenta Zattere ai Saloni 266; adult/reduced €8/4; ☉10.30am-6pm Wed-Sun during exhibitions; ⚓Spirito Santo) A retrofit designed by Pritzker Prize–winning architect Renzo Piano transformed Venice's historic salt warehouses into art galleries. Although the facade is from the 1830s, the warehouses were established in the 14th century, when the all-important salt monopoly secured Venice's fortune. The repurposing of the buildings is only fitting, now that the city's most precious commodity is art. They're only open for exhibitions staged by the foundation formed in honour of Venetian painter Emilio Vedova; check the website for details.

EATING

Still a popular residential neighbourhood, Dorsoduro abounds with canalside *cicheti* (Venetian tapas) joints, affordable *osterie* (taverns serving food) and a few very good restaurants. It's also a favoured hangout for students, which means you'll find plenty of cheap eats in all-day cafes, bars and fast-food outlets selling pizza by the slice around Campo Santa Margherita.

★CANTINE DEL VINO GIÀ SCHIAVI
VENETIAN €

Map p284 (☑041 523 00 34; www.cantinaschi avi.com; Fondamenta Priuli 992; cicheti €1.50; ☉8.30am-8.30pm Mon-Sat; ⚓Zattere) It may look like a wine shop and function as a bar, but this legendary canalside spot also serves the best *cicheti* on this side of the Grand Canal. Choose from the impressive counter selection or ask for a filled-to-order roll. Chaos cheerfully prevails, with an eclectic cast of locals propping up the bar.

BACARO VINTIDÒ 22
VENETIAN €

Map p284 (☑348 2603456; www.bacaro-vintido.it; Calle de la Dona Onesta; meals €15-20; ☺6-11pm Tue-Thu, noon-11pm Fri-Sun; 🐾; ⚓San Tomà) Daniela and Ruggero really make this little tavern feel like a home, with worn carpets, a ramshackle bookshelf and an exceedingly warm welcome offered to all. A limited blackboard menu of classic Venetian pasta and risotto dishes is chalked up daily and shunted between the tiny tables. If you're lucky, a regular might drop by to play the piano.

PASTICCERIA TONOLO
PASTRIES €

Map p284 (☑041 523 72 09; http:/pasticceria-tonolo-venezia.business.site; Calle San Pantalon 3764; pastries €1-4; ☺7.30am-8pm Tue-Sat, to 1pm Sun; ⚓Ca' Rezzonico) Long, skinny Tonolo is the stuff of local legend, a fact confirmed by the never-ending queue of customers. Ditch packaged B&B croissants for flaky apple strudel, velvety *bignè al zabaione* (marsala cream pastry) and oozing chocolate croissants. Devour one at the bar with a bracing espresso, then bag another for the road.

TOLETTA SNACK-BAR
SANDWICHES €

Map p284 (☑041 520 01 96; Sacca de la Toletta 1191; sandwiches €1.60-5; ☺7am-8pm; 🐾; ⚓Ca' Rezzonico) Midway through museum crawls from Accademia to Ca' Rezzonico, Toletta satisfies starving artists with lip-smacking, grilled-to-order *panini* (sandwiches), including *prosciutto crudo* (dry-cured ham), rocket and mozzarella, and daily vegetarian options. *Tramezzini* (triangular stacked sandwiches) are tasty too. Get yours to go, or grab a seat for around €1 more.

LA TECIA VEGANA
VEGAN €

(☑041 524 62 44; www.lateciavegana.com; Calle dei Sechi 2104; meals €20-26; ☺noon-3pm & 7-11pm Tue-Sat, noon-3pm Sun; 🐾; ⚓Santa Marta) Venice's only organic vegan restaurant serves delectable dishes such as Thai rice noodles, *seitan* lasagne and tempeh *mafè* (peanut butter sauce) with rice. There is a great dessert selection and many gluten-free dishes.

AFRICA EXPERIENCE
AFRICAN €

Map p284 (☑041 476 78 65; www.facebook.com/africaexperiencevenezia; Calle Lunga San Barnaba 2722; meals €15-27; ☺noon-3pm & 6pm-midnight Tue-Sun; 🐾; ⚓Ca' Rezzonico) Staffed by refugees and migrants from all over Africa, the menu at this attractive restaurant reflects that diversity, with dishes from Egypt, Morocco, Senegal, Guinea, Ivory Coast, Congo, Ethiopia, Eritrea and Somalia. The dishes are heavy on the rice and might not be the finest African cuisine, but the atmosphere and social engagement is what this place is all about.

★OSTERIA BAKÁN
ITALIAN €€

Map p284 (☑041 564 76 58; Corte Maggiore 2314a; meals €36-44; ☺8am-3pm & 6-10pm Wed-Mon; ⚓Santa Marta) A strange mix of local drinking den and surprisingly adventurous restaurant, Bakán has bucketloads of atmosphere – with old beams and soft jazz inside, and tables on a tucked-away courtyard. The homemade pasta is excellent, or you could opt for the likes of *guance di vitello* (veal cheeks) or ginger prawns with pilaf rice.

DA CODROMA
VENETIAN €€

Map p284 (☑041 524 67 89; www.facebook.com/dacodroma; Fondamenta Briati 2540; meals €34-42; ☺10am-4pm & 6-11pm Tue-Sat; 🐾; ⚓San Basilio) In a city plagued by high prices and indifferent eating experiences, the shared wooden tables at Da Codroma are the antidote. Chef Nicola faithfully maintains Venetian traditions here, serving up *il saor* (cured sardines and prawns), *bigoli in salsa* (buckwheat pasta with anchovy and onions) and delicious semifreddo to locals and savvy tourists alike.

ESTRO
INTERNATIONAL €€

Map p284 (☑041 476 49 14; www.estrovenezia.com; Calle Crosera 3778; meals €32-47; ☺noon-11pm Wed-Mon; ✳; ⚓San Tomà) Estro can be a wine bar, *aperitivo* pit stop or sit-down degustation restaurant. The vast selection of wine was chosen by young-gun owners Alberto and Dario, whose passion for quality extends to the food – from *baccalà mantecato* (creamed cod) on polenta crisps, to guinea-fowl lasagne or a succulent burger dripping with Asiago cheese.

DO FARAI
VENETIAN €€

Map p284 (☑041 277 03 69; Calle del Capeler 3278; meals €32-47; ☺noon-2.30pm & 7-10.30pm Mon-Sat; ⚓Ca' Rezzonico) Venetian

Interior of Ca' Rezzonico (p79)

regulars pack this crimson wood-panelled room, decorated with Regata Storica victory pendants and Murano glass decanters. The mixed antipasto is a succulent prologue to classic Venetian dishes like pasta with shellfish, grilled *orata* (bream), *fegato alla veneziana* (veal liver with onions on polenta) and *sarde in suor* (sardines in a tangy onion marinade).

LA BITTA   VENETIAN €€

Map p284 (☎041 523 05 31; Calle Lunga San Barnaba 2753a; meals €34-37; ☺7-10.30pm Mon-Sat; ☌; ☙Ca' Rezzonico) Venice is known for its seafood but this cosy, woody bistro tapo into the other side of the cuisine, serving a concise menu focused on meat and seasonal veggies. It's one of the best places in town to try the classic *fegato alla veneziana* (veal liver with onions). Reservations recommended; cash only.

OSTERIA AI 4 FERI   VENETIAN €€

Map p284 (☎041 520 69 78; Calle Lunga San Barnaba 2754a; meals €27-34; ☺12.30-2.30pm & 7-10.30pm Mon-Sat; ☙Ca' Rezzonico) Adorned with artworks by some well-known creative fans, this honest, good-humoured *osteria* (casual tavern) is well known for its simple, classic seafood dishes like *spaghetti con seppie* (with cuttlefish), grilled *orata* (sea bream) and tender calamari. Post-meal coffees are made using a traditional Italian percolator for that homely, old-school feeling. No credit cards.

★RIVIERA   ITALIAN €€€

Map p284 (☎041 522 76 21; www.ristoranteriviera.it; Fondamenta Zattere al Ponte Lungo 1473; meals €67-157; ☺12.30-3pm & 7-10.30pm Fri-Tue; ☙Zattere) A former rock musician, GP Cremonini now focuses his considerable talents on ensuring his top-end restaurant – Dorsoduro's finest – delivers exemplary service and perfectly cooked seafood: think homemade pasta with scallops or sea-bass poached with prawns. The setting, overlooking the Giudecca Canal, is similarly spectacular. For serious gourmands, the 11-course tasting menu (€150) with wine pairings (€55) is an unmissable experience.

ENOTECA AI ARTISTI   ITALIAN €€€

Map p284 (☎041 523 89 44; www.enotecaartisti.com; Fondamenta de la Toletta 1169a; meals €48-55; ☺12.45-2.30pm & 7-10pm Mon-Sat; ☙Ca' Rezzonico) Dishes might include a lightly curried rabbit *maltagliati* (cut pasta) or beef cheeks with polenta chips at this elegant *enoteca* (wine-orientated bistro), paired with exceptional wines by the glass. Sidewalk tables make for great people-watching, but book ahead as space is limited inside and out. Note: only turf (no surf) dishes on Mondays, as the fish market is closed.

ANTINOO'S   MEDITERRANEAN €€€

Map p284 (☎041 3 42 81; www.sinahotels.com; Calle del Bastion 173; meals €78-117; ☺12.30-2.30pm & 7.30-10.30pm; ☙Salute) Be the envy of the passing Grand Canal traffic by nabbing one of the few tables on the deck of the Sina Centurion Hotel, or hide away inside the dazzling designer White Room. Dress up and be pampered with faultless service and the ambitious contemporary cuisine of chef Massimo Livan.

🍷 DRINKING & NIGHTLIFE

Residents of Dorsoduro convene nightly in Campo Santa Margherita or along the Zattere boardwalk for mandatory happy-hour *spritzes* and pretty pink sunsets. Other areas that attract a drinking crowd include Fondamenta Nani, which overlooks the San Trovaso boat shed, dinky Campo San Barnaba and Calle Crosera, where the party regularly spills out into the street.

★MALVASIA ALL'ADRIATICO MAR
WINE BAR

Map p284 (☑041 476 43 22; www.facebook.com/MalvasiaAdriaticoMar; Calle Crosera 3771; ⊗5-10pm Mon, 10am-10pm Tue-Sun; ☻San Tomà) Wine lovers should stake out a place in this small, upmarket and extremely welcoming bar and let owner Francesco guide them through the range of naturally produced regional wines. Bar snacks include delicious cheeses and meats on tasty bread. Squeeze onto the tiny deck in the warmer months and watch the gondolas go by.

CHET BAR
COCKTAIL BAR

Map p284 (www.facebook.com/chetcocktailbar; Calle de la Chiesa 3684; ⊗5pm-2am; 🛜; ☻San Tomà) With its chequerboard floor tiles and Prohibition-era ephemera on the walls, this little cocktail bar is a hip extension to the *spritz*-swilling Campo Santa Margherita scene. Look out for DJ sets, silent discos and promotional nights from leading spirit brands.

EL SBARLEFO
BAR

Map p284 (☑041 524 66 50; www.elsbarlefo.it; Calle San Pantalon 3757; ⊗10am-11pm; 🛜; ☻San Tomà) If you're looking to escape the raucous student scene on Campo Santa Margherita, head to this chic bar with its sophisticated soundtrack, high-quality *cicheti* and live music on the weekends. Aside from the long list of regional wines, there's a serious selection of spirits here.

OSTERIA AI PUGNI
BAR

Map p284 (☑346 9607785; www.osteriaaipugni.com; Fondamenta Gherardini 2856; ⊗8am-11pm Mon-Sat, 10am-11pm Sun; ☻Ca' Rezzonico) Centuries ago, brawls on the bridge out the front inevitably ended in the canal, but now Venetians settle differences with one of over 50 wines by the glass at this ever-packed bar, pimped with recycled Magnum-bottle lamps and wine-crate tables. The latest drops are listed on the blackboard, with *aperitivo*-friendly nibbles including *polpette* (meatballs) and cured local meats on bread.

CAFFÈ ROSSO
CAFE

Map p284 (☑041 528 79 98; www.cafferosso.it; Campo Santa Margherita 2963; ⊗7am-1am Mon-Sat; 🛜; ☻Ca' Rezzonico) Affectionately known as *Il Rosso*, this red-fronted cafe has been at the centre of the bar scene on Campo Santa Margherita since the late 1800s. It's at its best in the early evening, when locals snap up the sunny piazza seating to sip on inexpensive *spritzes*. The espresso machine looks like a prop from a steam-punk fantasy.

OSTERIA AL SQUERO
BAR

Map p284 (☑041 296 04 79; http://osteriaalsquero.wordpress.com; Fondamenta Nani 944; ⊗11am-8.30pm Thu-Tue; 🛜; ☻Zattere) After a stroll along the Zattere, retreat to this snug local drinking hole, right opposite the city's oldest functioning gondola workshop. Wines are well priced and the *cicheti* varied and delicious. It does get seriously crowded, though, and regulars spill out onto the canal even in winter. Load up a paper plate and join them.

AI ARTISTI
BAR

Map p284 (☑393 9680135; Campo San Barnaba 2771; ⊗8am-midnight; ☻Ca' Rezzonico) True to its name, artsy student types pack out this cafe-bar on the weekends and spill out onto the street outside. It's been serving drinks and snacks since 1897, and retains a local feel despite the city's shifting demographics.

BAKARÒ DO DRAGHI
BAR

Map p284 (☑041 241 27 58; www.bakaro.it; Campo Santa Margherita 3665; ⊗10am-1am; ☻Ca' Rezzonico) Not to be confused with it's large sister bar-restaurant Bakarò on the corner, this trendy, pocket-sized bar is so small that the crowd inevitably spills onto the

A HEALTHY STROLL: THE ZATTERE

On sunny days, the leisurely stretch of Dorsoduro's **Giudecca Canal** waterfront known as the Zattere becomes an idyllic waterfront promenade, the perfect spot for a lazy stroll – but a few centuries back, the Zattere was the absolute last resort for many Venetians. The imposing building at Zattere 423 was once better known as **Ospedale degli Incurabili** (Hospital of the Incurables), built in the 16th century to address a problem spreading rapidly through Europe's nether regions. Euphemistically called the 'French sickness', syphilis quickly became a Venetian problem, passing from the ranks of its 12,000 registered prostitutes to the general populace.

With no known cure for syphilis at the time, and blindness and insanity its common side effects, Venetians petitioned the state to create a hospice for the afflicted and the orphans they left behind. Venetian women were outspoken lobbyists for this forward-thinking effort, and funds were pledged early on by prostitutes and madams with a particular interest in the problem. Venice was ahead of its time in dedicating public funds to this public health crisis, though at times even this large building was sometimes overcrowded. When penicillin provided a cure, the facility was happily rendered obsolete, and since 2003 the building has housed the **Accademia delle Belle Arti** (Fine Arts School), formerly located in the Gallerie dell'Accademia building.

Nearby you'll spot a plaque dedicated to Nobel Prize–winning Russian American poet **Joseph Brodsky**, a sometime local resident who named his 1989 book *Fondamenta degli Incurabili* after this infamous canalbank. He is fondly remembered internationally for his book *Watermark*, which captures Venice's ebbs and flows, its murky tragedies and crystalline graces. As the plaque says in Russian and Italian: 'He loved and sang this place'. Brodsky died in New York in 1996, but by his request and the city's exceptional permission, his body was buried in Venice's cemetery at Isola di San Michele.

sidewalk, trying not to spill drinks in the process. Below a tangle of filament bulbs is the tiny wooden bar, peddling respectable *cicheti* and around 45 wines by the glass.

CAFÉ NOIR COCKTAIL BAR
Map p284 (☎041 200 78 93; Calle Crosera 3805; ⏰11am-2am Sun Fri, 6.30pm-2am Sat, 🛜, 🚤San Tomà) Just gritty enough to be bohemian without being divey, this dark-beamed drinking den offers a long list of cocktails, Guinness on tap and cheap wine by the glass. Accompanying the beverages is an extensive list of jaw-busting *panini* and *piadine* (flatbreads). No wonder it's a solid favourite with the university crowd.

⭐ ENTERTAINMENT

VENICE JAZZ CLUB JAZZ
Map p284 (☎041 523 20 56; www.venicejazzclub. com; Fondamenta del Squero 3102; admission incl 1st drink €20; ⏰7-11pm Mon-Wed, Fri & Sat; 🛜; 🚤Ca' Rezzonico) Jazz is alive and swinging in Dorsoduro, where the resident VJC Jazz Quartet takes to the stage on Mondays, Wednesday and Saturdays, while the VJC

Latin Jazz & Bossa Nova Quartet takes over on Tuesdays and Thursdays; shows start at 9pm. The venue closes for August, December and January, and much of February.

VENICE MUSIC PROJECT CLASSICAL MUSIC
Map p284 (☎345 791 1948; www.venicemusic project.it; St George's Anglican Church, Campo San Vio; adult/reduced €30/25; ⏰Mar-Jun & Sep-Nov; 🚤Accademia) Classical music fans shouldn't miss these unusual concerts staged in the pretty Anglican church of St George. Historic baroque musical scores rescued from obscurity in the Marciana library are brought back to life by a group of nine musicians, accompanied by soprano Liesl Odenweller, who has performed not only at La Fenice but the Carnegie Hall.

🛍 SHOPPING

Venice's arts precinct is also one of its most tourist focused. Hence, you won't get many bargains, but you will find some extraordinary artisans basing themselves here, producing high-end

GRAND CANAL BLING & BOGEYMEN

As magnificent as the Grand Canal remains, it was once even more colourful – with Giorgione and Titian frescoes gracing the facade of the Fondaco dei Tedeschi (p72), and gold leaf glistening from the Ca' d'Oro (p111). Yet that didn't stop aristocratic noses being put out of joint when a pair of Murano glass companies decided to pimp their Grand Canal headquarters with golden mosaics in the late 19th and early 20th centuries. **Palazzo Barbarigo** dates to the 16th century but gained its glitzy wrapping in 1886, featuring images of glass blowers displaying their work to architects and the doge himself. **Palazzo Salviati** followed suit in 1924, with a large central mosaic of a blonde effigy of Venice enthroned in splendour. You can easily spot them as you cruise along the canal between the Guggenheim and La Salute.

Close by is **Ca' Dario** (Map p284; Ramo Ca' Dario 352; Salute), a 15th-century palazzo with three levels of arched windows abutted by three oculi surrounded by disks of coloured marble. Its mesmerising reflection was once painted by Claude Monet, but it's famous for a more nefarious reason: starting with the daughter of its original owner, Giovanni Dario, an unusual number of its occupants have met untimely deaths. Gossips claim this effectively dissuaded Woody Allen from buying the house in the late 1990s. The former manager of The Who, Kit Lambert, moved out after complaining of being hounded by the palace's ghosts, and was found dead shortly after in 1981. One week after renting the place for a holiday in 2002, The Who's bass player, John Entwhistle, died of a heart attack. Look for it just past the first small canal to the left of the Guggenheim.

handmade products. **Shopping hotspots include the area around the Accademia, Calle de le Botteghe and Calle Lunga San Barnaba.**

⭐ **IL GRIFONE**   FASHION & ACCESSORIES
Map p284 (041 522 94 52; www.ilgrifonevenezia.it; Fondamenta del Gafaro 3516; 10am-6pm Tue, Wed & Fri, 10am-1pm & 4-7pm Thu & Sat; Piazzale Roma) All of the Griffin's brightly coloured leather belts, bags and wallets are proudly made right here, using only traditionally tanned leather from Tuscany. Call in for a satchel or handbag to last a lifetime.

L'ANGOLO DEL PASSATO   GLASS
Map p284 (041 528 78 96; Campiello dei Squelini 3276; 3.30-7pm Mon, 9.30am-12.30pm & 3.30-7pm Tue-Sat; Ca' Rezzonico) The 19th century bumps into the 21st in this hidden corner showcase of rare Murano glass, ranging from spun-gold chandeliers beloved by royal decorators to sultry smoked-glass sconces that serve Hollywood stars better than Botox. Contemporary creations line the shelves, from geometric-patterned vases to bold drinking glasses.

PAOLO OLBI   ARTS & CRAFTS
Map p284 (041 523 76 55; www.olbi.atspace. com; Calle Foscari 3253; 10.30am-12.40pm & 3.30-7.30pm Mar-Dec, 3.30-7.30pm Jan & Feb; San Tomà) Thoughts worth committing to

paper deserve Paolo Olbi's keepsake books, albums and stationery, whose fans include Hollywood actors and NYC mayors (ask to see the guestbook). Ordinary journals can't compare to Olbi originals, handmade with heavyweight paper and bound with exquisite leather bindings. The watercolour postcards of Venice make for beautiful, bargain souvenirs.

SIGNOR BLUM   TOYS
Map p284 (041 522 63 67; www.signorblum. com; Campo San Barnaba 2840; 10am-1.30pm & 2.30-7.30pm Mon-Sat; Ca' Rezzonico) Kids may have to drag adults away from these 2D wooden puzzles of the Rialto Bridge and grinning wooden duckies before these clever handmade toys induce acute cases of nostalgia. Mobiles made of colourful carved gondola prows would seem equally at home in an arty foyer and a nursery. And did we mention the Venice-themed clocks?

CA' MACANA   ARTS & CRAFTS
Map p284 (041 520 32 29; www.camacana.com; Calle de le Botteghe 3172; 10am-8pm summer, to 6.30pm winter; Ca' Rezzonico) Glimpse the talents behind the Venetian Carnevale masks that impressed Stanley Kubrick so much he ordered several for his final film *Eyes Wide Shut*. Choose your papier-mâché persona from the selection of coquettish courtesan's eye-shades, chequered Casano-

Ceiling artwork, Gallerie dell'Accademia (p75)

va disguises and long-nosed plague doctor masks – or decorate your own at Ca' Macana's mask-painting workshops (from €39).

SEGNI NEL TEMPO
BOOKS

Map p284 (☑041 72 29 09; www.facebook.com/segnineltempolibriantichivenezia; Calle Lunga San Barnaba 2856; ☺9.30am-1.30pm & 2-7.30pm; ☕Ca' Rezzonico) Not so much a bookshop as a tiny time machine, Segni's cramped shelves might reveal a 16th-century edition of Giovanni Pontano's *De Prudentia* or a *History of Oxford* dating from 1676. Most titles are in Italian, with a good selection of Venetian history books. Bound beauties aside, you'll also find vintage prints of the city and the odd curiosity.

CLAUDIA CANESTRELLI
ANTIQUES

Map p284 (☑340 5776089; Campiello Barbaro 364a; ☺11am-1pm & 3-5pm Mon-Sat; ☕Salute) Hand-coloured lithographs of fanciful lagoon fish, 19th-century miniatures of cats dressed as generals, and vintage cufflinks make for charming souvenirs of Venice's past in this walk-in curio cabinet. Collector-artisan Claudia Canestrelli brings back bygone elegance with her repurposed antique earrings, including free-form baroque pearls dangling from gilded bronze elephants.

DESIGNS 188
JEWELLERY

Map p284 (☑041 523 94 26; Calle del Bastion 188; ☺11am-7pm Mon-Sat; ☕Salute) American transplant Trina Tygrett studied glassmaking at the Academy of Fine Arts and subsequently married into a Murano-glass family. She now works alongside Giorgio Nason and Debora Biolo, creating original jewellery that mixes semi-precious stones, gold, fabric and glasswork in a refreshing contemporary style.

LE FÓRCOLE DI
SAVERIO PASTOR
ARTS & CRAFTS

Map p284 (☑041 522 56 99; www.forcole.com; Fondamenta Soranzo detta de la Fornace 341; ☺8.30am-6pm Mon-Fri; ☕Salute) Only one thing actually moves like Jagger: Mick Jagger's bespoke *fórcola,* hand-carved by Saverio Pastor. Each forked wooden gondola oarlock is individually designed to match a gondolier's height, weight and movement, so the gondola doesn't rock too hard when the gondolier hits a groove. Pastor's miniature *fórcole* twist elegantly, striking an easy balance on gondolas and mantelpieces alike.

K. SAMURKAS/SHUTTERSTOCK ©

1. I Frari (p94) **2.** Rialto Market (p95) **3.** Scuola Grande di San Marco (p128) **4.** Canal in The Ghetto (p109)

FCOTTOO/SHUTTERSTOCK ©

Secrets of the Calli

Yellow signs point the way to major sights, but that *calle* (backstreet) behind the thoroughfare leads to a world of artisan studios, backstreet *bacari* (bars) and hidden *campi* (squares).

Campo San Polo to San Giacomo dall'Orio

Take Calle del Scalater past a couple of artisan studios to hidden Campiello Sant'Agostin for draught beer and dramatic glass jewellery; cross the bridge to join happy hour and tag games alongside medieval San Giacomo dall'Orio.

Campo Bandiera e Moro to Campo San Giovanni e Paolo

Head north of Riva degli Schiavoni through neighbourly Campo Bandiera and along studio-lined Salizada San Antonin. Then zigzag up narrow *fondamente* and *calli* to emerge on Barbaria de le Tole for sundowners in the shadow of Zanipolo.

Rialto Market to Museo di Storia Naturale

Gather picnic supplies at Rialto Market, then *campo*-hop from Campo delle Beccarie through Campo San Cassian to artisan studio dotted Campo Santa Maria Domini; then follow narrow *calli* to Museo di Storia Naturale for your garden picnic.

Chiesa della Madonna dell'Orto to the Ghetto

Calm restores overloaded senses as you pass sculptures flanking Campo dei Mori, stroll the sunny Fondamente de la Misericordia and Ormesini, and reach bridges leading into the historic Ghetto.

Chiesa di San Sebastiano to I Frari

Follow bargain *osterie* (taverns) along Calle Lunga San Barnaba to its bustling namesake *campo*, where Calle delle Botteghe leads past antiques, vintage photography, jewellery and contemporary glassware to Titian's masterpiece.

San Polo & Santa Croce

SAN POLO | SANTA CROCE

Neighbourhood Top Five

❶ Scuola Grande di San Rocco (p92) Seeing lightning strike indoors at this lavish confraternity clubhouse, where Tintoretto's streaky brushwork illuminated hope in a time of plague, death and despair.

❷ I Frari (p94) Watching Titian's red-hot Madonna light up this cavernous friary church, lined with fanciful memorials to the city's politicians and artists.

❸ Rialto Market (p95) Working up a serious appetite over lagoon surf and turf at this gut-rumbling, produce-bursting market.

❹ Ca' Pesaro (p97) Ping-ponging between modern masterpieces and Japanese antiques in a particularly ostentatious Grand Canal palace.

❺ Scuola Grande di San Giovanni Evangelista (p95) Taking over-the-top interior-design cues from some of Venice's top architects and artists.

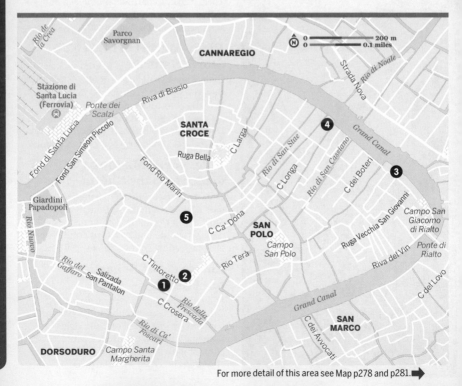

For more detail of this area see Map p278 and p281. ➡

Explore San Polo & Santa Croce

So this is how Venice lives when it's not busy entertaining. These twin *sestieri* are a warren of winding lanes in which you can easily lose yourself for hours browsing artisan studios and neighbourhood churches, before emerging in sunny *campi* (squares) where kids tear round on tricycles and adults sip wine at ring-side bars.

Start the morning among masterpieces at Scuola Grande di San Rocco (p92), then bask in the glow of Titian's Madonna at I Frari (p94). Shop backstreet galleries and artisan studios all the way to the Rialto Market (p95), where glistening purple octopus and feathery red *radicchio treviso* (chicory) present technicolor photo ops.

Stop at All'Arco (p99) for *cicheti* (Venetian tapas) before breezing through elegant salons of fashion, art and scents at vainglorious Palazzo Mocenigo (p97). Alternatively, zip through millennia of natural history at the epic Museo di Storia Naturale di Venezia (p98).

Next, head to Campo San Giacomo da l'Orio for happy hour at Al Prosecco (p104). Appetite piqued, wander the maze of Venice's former red-light district to Antiche Carampane (p100) for dinner.

Local Life

→ **Market mornings** Gently elbow fastidious chefs and *nonne* (grandmothers) on your quest for the morning's finest produce at Rialto Market (p95).

→ **Bacaro-hopping** Ringing the Rialto are authentic, pocket-sized *bacari* (bars) offering inventive Venetian bites, best devoured standing with top-notch *ombre* (half-glasses of wine).

Getting There & Away

→ **Bus** All services from the mainland terminate at Piazzale Roma, including airport shuttles.

→ **Vaporetto** Most water-bus routes terminate at Piazzale Roma, which is a major hub. The neighbourhood has six Grand Canal stops (Piazzale Roma, Riva di Biasio, San Stae, Rialto Mercato, San Silvestro and San Tomà); line 1 stops at all of them. The much faster line 2 only stops at Piazzale Roma and San Tomà. Route 5.1/5.2, which loops from Lido around the edge of central Venice, stops at Piazzale Roma and Riva di Biasio before cutting through Cannaregio.

→ **Traghetto** Gondola ferries nip across the Grand Canal at two crossing points: **Rialto Mercato** (Map p278; Pescaria; 1-way €2; ⊗7.30am-6.30pm Mon-Sat, 9am-6.30pm Sun) and near **San Tomà** (Map p278; Calle del Traghetto; 1-way €2; ⊗9am-5pm).

Lonely Planet's Top Tip

Many of Venice's best restaurants, artisan studios and *bacari* (bars) are in the backstreets of San Polo and Santa Croce – if you can find them. This is the easiest area in which to get lost, so allow extra time if you have dinner reservations or a powerful thirst. If totally lost, follow the flow of foot traffic towards yellow Rialto or Ferrovia signs, or red-and-white Scuola Grande di San Rocco signs.

Best Places to Eat

→ Zanze XVI (p101)
→ Osteria Trefanti (p101)
→ Glam (p102)
→ All'Arco (p99)
→ Osteria La Zucca (p101)

For reviews, see p99.→

Best Places to Drink

→ Il Mercante (p102)
→ Cantina Do Spade (p102)
→ Osteria da Filo (p104)
→ Al Prosecco (p104)
→ Bacareto da Lele (p104)

For reviews, see p102.→

Best Places to Shop

→ Process Collettivo (p105)
→ Il Pavone di Paolo Pelosin (p105)
→ Paperoowl (p106)
→ Damocle Edizioni (p105)

For reviews, see p105.→

SAN POLO & SANTA CROCE

TOP SIGHT
SCUOLA GRANDE DI SAN ROCCO

You'll swear the paint is still fresh on the 50 action-packed Tintorettos completed between 1575 and 1587 for this confraternity meeting house, dedicated to St Roch, the patron of the plague-stricken. While the 1575–77 plague claimed one-third of Venice's residents, Tintoretto painted nail-biting scenes of looming despair and last-minute redemption, illuminating a survivor's struggle with breathtaking urgency.

Ground-floor Hall

Downstairs in the Sala Terrena, Tintoretto illustrates key scenes from the life of the Virgin Mary, starting on the left wall with the *Annunciation,* where the angel Gabriel sneaks up on the saint at her sewing table. *The Massacre of the Innocents* is particularly harrowing, infusing this gruesome subject with all the horror of the plague years. Tintoretto's Madonna cycle ends with the *Assumption*; it's a dark and cataclysmic work, especially compared with Titian's glowing version at I Frari.

When Tintoretto painted these works, Venice's outlook was grim indeed: the bubonic plague had just taken the lives of 50,000 Venetians, including the great Titian, and the cause of and cure for the plague would not be discovered for centuries. By focusing his talents on dynamic lines instead of Titianesque colour, Tintoretto created a shockingly modern, moving parable for epidemics through the ages. Titian's work is also on show here; you will pass his framed *Annunciation* as you head up the stairs.

TOP TIPS

➡ From spring to late autumn the artworks provide a backdrop to top-notch classical-music concerts.

➡ Grab a mirror to avoid neck strain when viewing Tintoretto's ceiling panels.

➡ The feast of St Roch (16 August) is celebrated with a solemn Mass and procession around the Campo San Rocco.

PRACTICALITIES

➡ Map p278, A6

➡ ☎041 523 48 64

➡ www.scuolagrandesanrocco.org

➡ Campo San Rocco 3052

➡ adult/reduced €10/8

➡ ⊙9.30am-5.30pm

➡ 🚊San Tomà

Chapter Room

Take the grand **Scarpagnino staircase** to the Sala Capitolare, where you may be seized with a powerful instinct to duck, given all the action in the **Old Testament ceiling scenes** – you can almost hear the swoop overhead as a winged angel dives to nourish the ailing prophet in *Elijah Fed by an Angel*. Mercy from above is a recurring theme, with Daniel's salvation by angels, the miraculous fall of manna in the desert, and Elisha distributing bread to the hungry.

The vast hall is quite overwhelming, with acres of shiny inlaid marble underfoot and ornate gilt plasterwork edging the ceiling panels. It's little wonder that it's been called Venice's Sistine Chapel. An image of Tintoretto with his paintbrushes is captured in Francesco Pianta's 17th-century carved wooden **sculpture**, third from the right beneath the artist's New Testament masterpieces.

Tintoretto's **New Testament wall scenes** read like a modern graphic novel, with eerie lightning-bolt illumination striking his protagonists against the backdrop of the Black Death. Scenes from Christ's life aren't in chronological order: birth and baptism are followed by resurrection. The drama builds as background characters disappear into increasingly dark canvases, until an X-shaped black void looms at the centre of *The Agony in the Garden*.

Sala dell'Albergo

Everyone wanted the commission to paint this building, so Tintoretto cheated: instead of producing sketches like rival Veronese, he gifted a splendid ceiling panel of the saint, knowing it couldn't be refused, or matched by other artists. Tintoretto's restored *St Roch in Glory* crowns the Sala dell'Albergo, where the *scuola*'s governors once met. The saint is surrounded by representations of the four seasons and the saving graces of Felicity, Generosity, Faith and Hope. Feeble Hope is propped up on one elbow – still reeling from the tragedy of the Black Death, but miraculously alive.

This uplifting scene rises above the turmoil of the wall panels that illustrate Christ's Passion, culminating in a vast painting of the *Crucifixion* on the rear wall.

Treasury

Through a side door in the Sala Capitolare, head past the framed Tiepolo paintings and climb the stairs to the Tesoro. Its treasures include reliquaries, liturgical vessels and an enchanting candlestick made from a branch of coral.

ARCHITECTURE

Scarpagnino's uplifting, proto-baroque facade includes windows and doors with veined-marble frames, figures leaning out from atop the capitals, and flowering garlands adorning pillars as welcome signs of life post-plague. Bartolomeo Bon began the *scuola* in 1517, and at least three other architects were called in to finish the work by 1588.

AN INTERFAITH EFFORT AGAINST THE PLAGUE

As the Black Death ravaged Europe, Venice mounted an interfaith effort against the disease. While attending to citizen's spiritual needs through the likes of this confraternity and its associated church, the city also consulted resident Jewish and Muslim doctors about preventative measures. Crucially, it established the world's first quarantine, with inspections and 40-day waiting periods for incoming ships at the Lazzaretto Nuovo. Venice's forward-thinking, holistic approach created artistic masterpieces that provided comfort to the afflicted and bereaved, and set a public-health standard that has saved countless lives down the centuries.

TOP SIGHT
I FRARI

As you've no doubt heard, there's a Titian – make that *the* Titian – altarpiece at the Friary. But the 14th-century Gothic basilica is itself a towering achievement, with a heaven-scraping ceiling, intricate marquetry choir stalls and a succession of grandiose monuments lining its high brick walls.

Architecture

Built of modest brick rather than stone for the Franciscans in the 14th and 15th centuries, I Frari has none of the flying buttresses, pinnacles and gargoyles typical of international Gothic – but its vaulted ceilings and broad, triple-nave, Latin-cross floor plan give this basilica a grandeur befitting the masterpieces it contains.

The facade facing the canal has delicate scalloping under the roofline, contrasting red-and-white mouldings around windows and arches, and a repeating motif of *oculi* (porthole windows) around a high rosette window. The tall bell tower has managed to remain upright since 1386 – a rare feat, given the shifting *barene* (shoals) of Venice.

Titian Treasures

Visitors are inexorably drawn to the front of this cavernous Gothic church by a 6.7m by 3.4m altarpiece that seems to glow from within. This is Titian's 1518 *Assunta* (Assumption), capturing the split second the radiant Madonna reaches heavenward, finds her footing on a cloud, and escapes this mortal coil in a dramatic swirl of red and blue robes. Both inside and outside the painting, onlookers gasp and point at the glorious, glowing sight. Titian outdid himself here, upstaging even his own 1526 Pesaro altarpiece – a dreamlike composite family portrait of the Madonna and Child with the Venetian Pesaro family. You'll find it on the fourth altar on the left nave.

Other Masterpieces

As though this weren't quite enough artistic achievement for one church, there's Giovanni Bellini's achingly sweet *Madonna with Child* triptych (1488) in the **sacristy**, and Bartolomeo Vivarini's *St Mark Enthroned* (1474), showing the fluffy-bearded saint serenaded by an angelic orchestra in the **Capella Corner**. The gilt-edged wooden **choir stalls** are just as extraordinary, each with its own carved saint and marquetry street scene.

On the left hand side of the nave, Baldassare Longhena's **Doge Giovanni Pesaro funereal monument** (1669) is hoisted by four burly, black-marble figures while creepy skeletons unfurl their memorial scrolls. Mourners ascend the stairs past a disconsolate winged lion on the striking pyramid-shaped **Canova monument** (1827), erected in honour of Venice's most famous sculptor but originally designed by Canova as a monument to Titian. The great painter was lost to the plague at the age of 90 in 1576, but legend has it that, in light of his contributions here, Venice's strict rules of quarantine were bent to allow Titian's burial near his masterpiece. In 1838, Austrian emperor Ferdinand I commissioned the **Titian monument** (positioned opposite Canova's), featuring bas reliefs of some of his most famous works, including the *Assunta*.

TOP TIPS

➡ Photography is discouraged and appropriate dress is required.

➡ Grab a map at the ticket desk for a DIY tour of the incredible range of artworks.

➡ An audio guide (€2) is available in six languages.

PRACTICALITIES

➡ Basilica di Santa Maria Gloriosa dei Frari

➡ Map p278, B6

➡ 041 272 86 18

➡ www.basilicadeifrari.it

➡ Campo dei Frari 3072, San Polo

➡ adult/reduced €3/1.50, with Chorus Pass free

➡ 9am-6pm Mon-Sat, 1-6pm Sun

➡ San Tomà

◉ SIGHTS

Side-by-side *sestiere* **San Polo and Santa Croce are graced with a few charmingly quirky museum collections in historic Grand Canal** *palazzi:* **standout modern art and Japanese antiques at Ca' Pesaro, original baroque fashion and perfumes at Palazzo Mocenigo, and, yes, dinosaurs at the Fondaco dei Turchi. Other than that you can kick back and relax in sunny** *campi* **with the locals.**

◉ San Polo

SCUOLA GRANDE DI SAN ROCCO   HISTORIC BUILDING
See p92.

I FRARI   BASILICA
See p94.

SCUOLA GRANDE DI SAN GIOVANNI EVANGELISTA   HISTORIC BUILDING
Map p278 (☑041 71 82 34; www.scuolasangiovanni.it; Campiello de la Scuola 2454; adult/reduced €10/8; ⊗9.30am-5.15pm; ☷San Tomà) One of

Venice's five main religious confraternities, the lay brothers of St John the Evangelist performed works of charity but also supported the arts by lavishing their clubrooms with treasures by the city's most famous painters and architects. Highlights include Pietro Lombardo's elaborately carved Renaissance **entry gate** (1481), topped with the eagle of St John; a Mauro Codussi-designed **staircase** (1498); and Giorgio Massari's spectacularly ostentatious **St John's Hall** (1727-62).

Bellini and Titian turned out world-class works for the *scuola* that Napoleon looted and moved to the Gallerie dell'Accademia – but Palma il Giovane's works still illuminate the Sala d'Albergo, and Pietro Longhi's wriggling baby Jesus is magnetic in the *Adoration of the Magi* in St John's Hall. Across the courtyard (and included in the entry price), the deconsecrated **Chiesa di San Giovanni Evangelista**, erected in 970 as a private chapel for the Badoer family, houses a Domenico Tintoretto *Crucifixion* and Pietro Liberi's painting of St John the Evangelist holding a pen, eagerly awaiting inspiration from God.

The confraternity was originally founded in 1261 by a group of flagellants, a sect who

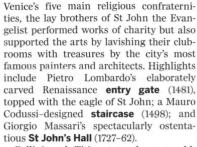

◉ TOP SIGHT
RIALTO MARKET

Restaurants worldwide are catching on to a secret that this market has loudly touted for 700 years: food tastes better when it's seasonal and local. Before there was a bridge at the Rialto or palaces along the Grand Canal, there was a **Pescaria** (Fish Market; Map p278; Campo de la Pescaria; ⊗7am-2pm Tue-Sun; ☷Rialto Mercato) and a produce market here. So loyal are locals to their market that talk of opening a larger mainland fish market was swiftly crushed. To see it at its best, arrive early in the morning along with the trolley-pushing shoppers.

Fishmongers call out today's catch in two open-sided Venetian Gothic buildings. Look out for the sea creatures and fishermen carved into the capitals of the columns. Sustainable fishing practices are not a new idea here; marble plaques show regulations set centuries ago for the minimum allowable sizes for fish.

In the open-air section, Veneto *verdure* (vegetables) intrigue with their otherworldly forms, among them Sant'Erasmo *castraure* (baby artichokes), white Bassano asparagus, *radicchio trevisano* and, in winter, the prized *rosa di Gorizia*, a rose-shaped type of chicory. The shops surrounding the market sell everything from cheese and wine to horsemeat.

TOP TIPS

➡ Tuesday and Friday are the best market days; the Pescaria is closed on Monday.

➡ The fish stalls are all packed up by 2pm, but a few stalls usually linger on into the afternoon, selling produce, nuts, dried fruit and cooking oils.

PRACTICALITIES

➡ Rialto Mercato
➡ Map p278, G3
➡ ☑041 296 06 58
➡ Campo de la Pescaria
➡ ⊗7am-2pm
➡ ☷Rialto Mercato

processed through the city publicly whipping themselves as a form of penance; the practice was banned by the Pope later that year, and the organisation morphed into a less bloody brotherhood. The Scuola Grande was suppressed by Napoleon in 1806 but subsequently revived as a Mutual Aid Society. Today it hosts conferences and concerts, opening to the public when not in use for events.

PONTE DI RIALTO   BRIDGE

Map p278 (🚣Rialto) A superb feat of engineering, Antonio da Ponte's 1592 Istrian stone span took three years and 250,000 gold ducats to construct. Adorned with stone reliefs depicting St Mark and St Theodore on the north side and the Annunciation on the other, the bridge crosses the Grand Canal at its narrowest point, connecting the neighbourhoods of San Polo and San Marco.

Interestingly, it was da Ponte's own nephew, Antonio Contino, who designed the city's other famous bridge, the Ponte dei Sospiri (p65).

CHIESA DI SAN GIACOMO
DI RIALTO   CHURCH

Map p278 (📞348 2815492; www.chorusvenezia. org; Campo San Giacomo di Rialto 1; ⊘9am-5pm Mon-Sat; 🚣Rialto Mercato) FREE Steps away from the Rialto Bridge, the most distinctive feature of 12th-century St James' Church is the 15th-century clock set into the facade facing the square. It's now home to a collection of antique musical instruments, and sells tickets to concerts by Interpreti Veneziani (p70).

IL GOBBO   STATUE

Map p278 (Campo San Giacomo di Rialto; 🚣Rialto Mercato) Rubbed for luck for centuries, this 1541 statue is now protected by an iron railing. Il Gobbo (The Hunchback) served as a podium for official proclamations and punishments: those guilty of misdemeanours were forced to run a gauntlet of jeering citizens from Piazza San Marco to the Rialto. The minute they touched the statue their punishment was complete.

CHIESA DI SAN GIOVANNI
ELEMOSINARIO   CHURCH

Map p278 (St John the Almsgiver's Church; www. chorusvenezia.org; Ruga Vecchia San Giovanni 478; €3, with Chorus Pass free; ⊘10.30am-1.15pm Mon-Sat; 🚣Rialto Mercato) Hunkering modestly behind T-shirt kiosks is this soaring brick church, built by Scarpagnino after

a disastrous fire in 1514 destroyed much of the Rialto area. Cross the threshold to witness flashes of Renaissance genius: Titian's tender *St John the Almsgiver* (1545) altarpiece and gloriously restored dome frescoes of frolicking angels by Pordenone.

CHIESA DI SAN POLO   CHURCH

Map p278 (www.chorusvenezia.org; Campo San Polo 2118; adult/reduced €3/1.50, with Chorus Pass free; ⊘10.30am-4.30pm Mon-Sat; 🚣San Tomà) Travellers pass modest St Paul's Church (founded in the 9th century) without guessing that major dramas unfold inside. Under the *carena di nave* (ship's keel) ceiling, Tintoretto's *Last Supper* (1569) shows apostles alarmed by Jesus' announcement that one of them will betray him. Giandomenico Tiepolo's *Way of the Cross* cycle in the Oratorio del Crocifisso (accessed from the rear of the church) shows onlookers tormenting an athletic Jesus, who leaps triumphantly from his tomb in the ceiling panel.

The main church also features works by Giandomenico's more famous father, Giambattista Tiepolo, along with Paolo Veronese and Palma il Giovane.

CASA DI CARLO GOLDONI   MUSEUM

Map p278 (📞041 275 93 25; www.carlogoldoni.vis itmuve.it; Calle dei Nomboli 2794; adult/reduced €5/3.50, with Museum Pass free; ⊘10am-4pm Thu-Tue; 🚣San Tomà) Venetian playwright Carlo Goldoni (1707–93) mastered second and third acts: he was a doctor's apprentice before switching to law, which proved handy when an *opera buffa* (comic opera) didn't sell. But as the 1st-floor display at his birthplace explains, Goldoni had the last laugh with his social satires. There's not really much to see here; the highlight is an 18th-century puppet theatre.

CHIESA DI SAN ROCCO   CHURCH

Map p278 (📞041 523 48 64; www.scuolagrande sanrocco.org; Campo San Rocco 3053; adult/reduced €2/free; ⊘9.30am-5.30pm; 🚣San Tomà) FREE Built by Bartolomeo Bon between 1489 and 1508 to house the remains of its titular saint, beautiful St Roch's Church received a baroque facelift between 1765 and 1771, which included a grand portal flanked by Giovanni Marchiori statues. Bon's rose window was moved to the side of the church, near the architect's original side door. On either side of the main altar are four vast paintings by Tintoretto depict-

THE OTHER RIALTO MARKET
....

No one remembers the original name of **Ponte de le Tette** (Map p278; 🚤San Silvestro), known since the 15th century as 'Tits Bridge'. Back in those days, shadowy porticoes around this bridge sheltered a designated red-light zone where neighbourhood prostitutes were encouraged to display their wares in windows instead of taking their marketing campaigns to the streets in their platform shoes. Between clients, the most ambitious working girls might be found studying: for educated conversation, *cortigiane* (courtesans) might charge 60 times the going rate for basic services from average prostitutes.

Church authorities and French dignitaries repeatedly professed dismay at Venice's lax attitudes towards prostitution, but Venice's idea of a crackdown was to prevent women prostitutes from luring clients by cross-dressing (aka false advertising) and to ban prostitutes from riding in two-oared boats – lucky that gondolas only require one oar. Fees were set by the state and posted in Rialto brothels (soap cost extra), and the rates of high-end *cortigiane* were published in catalogues extolling their various merits. The height of platform shoes was limited to a staggering 30cm by sumptuary laws intended to distinguish socialites from *cortigiane*, with little success.

ing St Roch's life. The saint's casket is positioned above the altar.

⊙ Santa Croce

CA' PESARO   MUSEUM
Map p278 (📞041 72 11 27; www.capesaro.visit muve.it; Fondamenta de Ca' Pesaro 2076; adult/reduced €10/7.50, with Museum Pass free; ⏱10am-5pm Tue-Sun; 🚤San Stae) The stately exterior of this Baldassare Longhena–designed 1710 *palazzo* hides two intriguing art museums that could hardly be more different: the **Galleria Internazionale d'Arte Moderna** and the **Museo d'Arte Orientale**. While the former includes art showcased at La Biennale di Venezia, the latter holds treasures from Prince Enrico di Borbone's epic 1887–89 souvenir-shopping spree across Asia. Competing with the artworks are Ca' Pesaro's fabulous painted ceilings, which hint at the power and prestige of the Pesaro clan.

The 'International Gallery of Modern Art' spans numerous art movements of the 19th and 20th centuries, including the Macchiaioli, expressionists and surrealists. The 1961 De Lisi bequest added Kandinskys and Morandis to the modernist mix of de Chiricos, Mirós and Moores. Later, more treasures accrued from the 1990 Wildt-Scheiwiller bequest, including Wildt's extraordinary sculptures *Man Who Stays Silent* (1899) and *Vir Temporis Acti* (1911). Other collection highlights include Gustav Klimt's *Judith II* (1909), Medrado Rosso's melting waxwork busts, Armando

Pizzinato's timely and troubling *A Spectre Is Haunting Europe* (1949), and Leoncillo Leonardi's forceful, neo-Cubist *Venetian Partisan* (1955), rendered in vividly coloured majolica. With works by Henri Matisse, Max Ernst, Auguste Rodin, Marc Chagall, Ray Lichtenstein and Jeff Koons, Ca' Pesaro outshines even the pricier Peggy Guggenheim Collection.

A phalanx of samurai warriors flanks the creaky attic stairs of the 'Oriental Art Museum', guarding a princely collection of Asian travel mementos. Prince Enrico reached Japan at a time when Edo art was discounted in favour of modern Meiji, and purchased 30,000 objets d'art, including Edo-era *netsukes* (miniature sculptures), weapons, screens and a lacquerware palanquin (litter). Around three-quarters of the collection is Japanese; the remaining quarter includes a small collection of 12th- to 15th-century Islamic ceramics and an intricately carved Chinese chess set from the 18th century.

Temporary exhibitions are regularly held on the middle floor, showcasing modernist and contemporary artists; entry is included in the ticket price.

PALAZZO MOCENIGO   MUSEUM
Map p278 (📞041 72 17 98; www.mocenigo.visit muve.it; Salizada San Stae 1992; adult/reduced €8/5.50, with Museum Pass free; ⏱10am-4pm; 🚤San Stae) Venice received a dazzling addition to its property portfolio in 1945 when Count Alvise Nicolò Mocenigo bequeathed his family's 17th-century *palazzo* to the city. While the ground floor hosts temporary exhibitions, the *piano nobile* (main floor) is

where you'll find a dashing collection of historic fashion, including exquisitely embroidered men's silk waistcoats. Adding to the glamour and intrigue is an exhibition dedicated to the art of fragrance – an ode to Venice's 16th-century status as Europe's capital of perfume.

Palazzo Mocenigo's opulent, chandelier-graced rooms look pretty much as they did at 18th-century A-list parties. Yet even when flirting shamelessly under Jacopo Guarana's *Nuptial Allegory* ceiling (1787) in the Green Living Room, wise guests minded their tongues. The Mocenigos reported philosopher and sometime house guest Giordano Bruno to the Inquisition for heresy; the betrayed philosopher was subsequently tortured and burned at the stake in Rome.

MUSEO DI STORIA NATURALE DI VENEZIA   MUSEUM

Map p278 (Natural History Museum of Venice; ☑041 275 02 06; www.msn.visitmuve.it; Salizada del Fontego dei Turchi 1730; adult/reduced €8/5.50, with Museum Pass free; ☺10am-6pm Tue-Sun; ☻San Stae) Never mind the doge: insatiable curiosity rules Venice, and inside the former Fondaco dei Turchi (Turkish Trading House) it runs wild. The adventure begins upstairs with dinosaurs and prehistoric crocodiles, then dashes through evolution to Venice's great age of exploration, when adventurers such as Marco Polo fetched peculiar specimens from distant lands. There's also a courtyard and charming back garden, which is open during museum hours and ideal for picnics.

Exhibits are extremely well displayed – even the fossil collection looks fascinating – but many of the labels are in Italian only. Upstairs you can out-stare the only complete ouranosaurus skeleton found to date, a macabre menagerie of colonial trophies, a pair of two-headed calves and a mummified Egyptian crocodile priestess flanked by two of her scaly charges. Although the museum's grand finale downstairs is comparatively anti-climactic – a fish tank of Venetian coastal specimens bubbling for attention – it does offer you a close-up glimpse of the large dugout canoe moored at the water door.

Alongside the exit staircase you'll notice marble heraldic symbols of kissing doves and knotted-tail dogs, dating from the building's history as a ducal palace and international trading house. The dukes of Ferrara had the run of this 13th-century mansion until they were elbowed aside in 1621 to make room for Venice's most important trading partner: Turkey. The Ottoman Turks rented the building until 1858, using it as living quarters, a goods warehouse and a place to do business.

CHIESA DI SAN GIACOMO DALL'ORIO   CHURCH

Map p278 (www.chorusvenezia.org; Campo San Giacomo da l'Orio 1457; adult/reduced €3/1.50, with Chorus Pass free; ☺10.30am-4.30pm Mon-Sat; ☻Riva de Biasio) Romanesque St James' Church was founded in the 9th century and completed in Latin-cross form in 1225, with chapels bubbling along the edges. Within the serene gloom of the interior, notable artworks include luminous sacristy paintings by Palma Il Giovane, a rare Lorenzo Lotto *Madonna with Child and Saints* (1546), and an exceptional Paolo Veneziano crucifix (c 1350).

Architectural quirks include decorative pillars, a 14th-century *carena di nave* (ship's keel) ceiling and a 6th-century Byzantine green-marble column looted from Constantinople during the infamous Fourth Crusade.

CHIESA DI SAN SIMEON PICCOLO   CHURCH

Map p281 (www.fsspvenezia.blogspot.com; Fondamente San Simeon Piccolo 698; ☺8am-4pm; ☻Ferrovia) FREE Designed by Giovanni Antonio Scalfarotto and completed in 1738, this domed neoclassical building was one of the last churches to be built in Venice. It's now used for the celebration of the Tridentine (traditional Latin) Mass. For a thoroughly creepy experience, pay €2 for a candle to explore the darkened cross-shaped crypt below, although you might want to stuff your pockets with garlic just in case.

CHIESA DI SAN STAE   CHURCH

Map p278 (www.chorusvenezia.org; Campo San Stae 1981; adult/reduced €3/1.50, with Chorus Pass free; ☺1.45-4.30pm Mon-Sat; ☻San Stae) The influence of Palladio swirls around neoclassical St Eustace's Church (completed in 1709), from the dazzling white, statue-heavy facade facing the Grand Canal to the light-drenched interior. To the left of the main altar, you'll find Giambattista Tiepolo's *Martyrdom of St Bartholomew* (1723) and Sebastiano Ricci's *St Peter Released from Prison* (1724). Be sure to check out the fine carvings on the organ stall above the main entrance.

✕ EATING

San Polo and Santa Croce are crammed with much-loved, high-quality *cicheti* bars, historic *osterie* (taverns) and high-end hotel restaurants. The best *cicheti* bars cluster around the Rialto Market, from where they source their ingredients daily. Popular *osterie* can be found in lanes surrounding key *campi* (squares) such as San Giacomo da l'Orio, San Polo and San Tomà.

✕ San Polo

ALL'ARCO   VENETIAN €

Map p278 (☎041 520 56 66; Calle de l'Ochialer 436; cicheti €2-2.50; ☺9am-2.30pm Mon-Sat; ⛴Rialto Mercato) Search out this authentic neighbourhood bar for some of the best *cicheti* (Venetian tapas) in town. Armed with ingredients from the nearby Rialto Market, father-son team Francesco and Matteo serve miniature masterpieces to the scrum of eager patrons crowding the counter and spilling out onto the street. Even with copious prosecco, hardly any meal here tops €20.

PASTICCERIA RIZZARDINI   PASTRIES €

Map p278 (☎041 522 38 35; Campiello dei Meloni 1415; pastries €1.30-4; ☺7am-8pm Wed-Mon; ⛴San Silvestro) 'From 1742' boasts this tiny corner bakery, whose reputation for cakes, pastries and biscuits has survived many an *acqua alta* – record flood levels are marked by the door. Stop by any time for reliable espresso, indulgent hot chocolate, *spritz* and *pizzette* – but act fast if you want that last slice of tiramisu.

ADAGIO   CAFE €

Map p278 (☎339 5027619; www.facebook.com/dlpcandido; Salizzada San Rocco 3028; cicheti €1-1.50; ☺8am-11pm; ⛴San Tomà) Tucked behind I Frari, this cute and friendly cafe-cum-wine-bar serves delicious, freshly made *cicheti* and pastries throughout the day, along with excellent coffee and wine to wash them down. If you can't nab one of the three small tables inside, either prop up the marble counter or head out into the square.

BASEGÒ   VENETIAN €

Map p278 (☎041 850 02 99; www.basego.it; Campo San Tomà 2863; cicheti €1.50-3; ☺10am-10pm; ⛴⛴; ⛴San Tomà) Focusing on three essen-tial ingredients – good food, good wine and good music – this new-wave *cicheti* bar has rapidly formed a faithful following. Indulge in a feast of lagoon seafood, prosciutto, smoked tuna, salami and cheese heaped on small slices of fresh bread. There's more seating than in most bars of this kind, and a dedicated kids' drawing area.

ANTICO FORNO   PIZZA €

Map p278 (☎041 520 41 10; Rugheta del Ravano 973; pizza slices €3-3.50; ☺11.30am-9pm Mon-Sat; ⛴San Silvestro) The counter at this friendly hole-in-the-wall takeaway is a sea of oven-fresh pizza perfection of both the thin- and thick-crust varieties. Join the queue for staples such as margherita or more imaginative constructions, then devour it standing up at the counter.

LA BOTTIGLIA   SANDWICHES €

Map p278 (☎041 476 24 26; www.facebook.com/labottigliavenezia; Calle de la Chiesa 2537; sandwiches €6; ☺10am-10.30pm; ⛴; ⛴San Tomà) Housed in what was once a butcher's shop, this photogenic deli-style wine bar has an impressive cellar of interesting wines and craft beer. Massive slabs of *panini* are made to order from the excellent selection of cold cuts, cheese and vegetables, and platters are also available. Wash it down with a wine-tasting flight (three for €9.50, five for €15).

GELATERIA IL DOGE   GELATO €

Map p278 (www.gelateriaildoge.com; Campiello San Tomà 2815-2816; 1 scoop €1.80; ☺10am-7.30pm Mar-Oct; ⛴San Tomà) An offshoot of the historic (and some say Venice's best) gelateria in Campo Santa Margherita, Gelateria Il Doge serves delicious flavours such as mango or dark chocolate. It also has vegan options, and does a mean Sicilian *granita* in traditional flavours such as lemon or almond milk.

BAR AI NOMBOLI   SANDWICHES €

Map p278 (☎041 523 09 95; Rio Terà dei Nomboli 2717c; sandwiches €2-6; ☺7am-9pm Sun-Fri, to 3pm Sat; ⛴; ⛴San Tomà) This snappy place is never short of local professors, labourers and clued-in out-of-towners. Crusty rolls are packed with local cheeses, fresh greens, roast vegetables, salami, prosciutto and roast beef. Beyond standard mayo, condiments range from spicy mustard to wild-nettle sauce and fig salsa. Cheap, filling and scrumptious.

SAN POLO & SANTA CROCE EATING

FRARY'S
MIDDLE EASTERN €€

Map p278 (✆041 72 00 50; www.frarys.it; Fondamenta dei Frari 2559; meals €24-32; ⊙11.30am-3pm & 6-10.30pm; 🛜🖉; 🚊San Tomà) Spice things up at this bohemian-spirited bolthole serving Middle Eastern and Mediterranean classics. The antipasto platter might pair Greek *hortopita* (filo pastry stuffed with cheese and vegetables) with Kurdish *kubbe* (fried riceball stuffed with spiced ground meat), while the fragrant mains include classic moussaka and the spicy Jordanian rice dish *maglu'ba*. The menu includes vegan and gluten-free options.

BIRRARIA LA CORTE
INTERNATIONAL €€

Map p278 (✆041 275 05 70; www.birrarialacorte. it; Campo San Polo 2168; pizzas €9.50-15, meals €33-39; ⊙10am-midnight Apr-Oct, 10am-3pm & 6pm-midnight Nov-Mar; 🛜; 🚊San Tomà) This one-time bull stable became a brewery in the 19th century to keep Venice's Austrian occupiers occupied, and beer and beef remain reliable bets. We particularly rate it for its excellent pizza, but there's a big range of international crowd pleasers on offer, including hamburgers, chicken curry, spelt crêpes and lots of Italian dishes too.

AL PONTE STORTO
VENETIAN €€

Map p278 (✆041 528 21 44; www.alpontestorto. com; Calle del Ponte Storto 1278; meals €35-41; ⊙10am-3pm & 6-10pm Tue-Sun; 🛜; 🚊San Silvestro) Once an anarchist clubhouse, intimate, art-slung 'At the Crooked Bridge' serves up scrumptious *cicheti,* whether it's quiche or the famed *polpette* (meatballs). For a more substantial feed, plonk yourself down at a table and tuck into house favourites such as *pappardelle con scampi e radicchio* (pasta with prawns and chicory). In the warmer months, request one of the two canalside tables.

TRATTORIA DA IGNAZIO
VENETIAN €€

Map p278 (✆041 523 48 52; www.trattoriadaignazio.com; Calle dei Saoneri 2749; meals €33-50; ⊙noon-3pm & 7-10pm Sun-Fri; 🚊San Tomà) Dapper white-jacketed waiters serve pristine grilled lagoon fish, fresh pasta and desserts made in-house ('of course') with a proud flourish, on tables bedecked with yellow linen. On cloudy days, homemade crab pasta with a bright Lugana white wine make a fine substitute for sunshine. On sunny days and warm nights, the neighbourhood converges beneath the garden's grape arbour.

SACRO E PROFANO
VENETIAN €€

Map p278 (✆041 523 79 24; Ramo Terzo del Parangon 502; meals €37-44; ⊙noon-3pm & 6pm-midnight Mon-Sat; 🚊Rialto Mercato) Musicians, artists and philosophising regulars make this hideaway, positioned under the arcade leading to the Rialto bridge, exceptionally good for eavesdropping – but once that handmade gnocchi arrives, all talk is reduced to satisfied murmurs. The place is run by a Venetian ska-band leader, which explains the trumpets on the wall and the upbeat, arty scene.

DA FIORE
ITALIAN €€€

Map p278 (✆041 72 13 43; www.dafiore.net; Calle del Scaleter 2202a; meals €61-87, set lunch menus €39-49; ⊙12.30-4.30pm & 7.30pm-12.30am Tue-Sat; 🚊San Stae) Dire Straits was on high rotation last time we visited this Michelin-starred restaurant, which somewhat distracted from the refined ambience created by the expensive Murano glasses and immaculate bowtie-wearing waiters. Regardless, the food is excellent – whether it be something as seemingly simple as a highly memorable caprese salad or one of its signature seafood concoctions.

ANTICHE CARAMPANE
VENETIAN €€€

Map p278 (✆041 524 01 65; www.antichecarampane.com; Rio Terà de le Carampane 1911; meals €55-63; ⊙12.45-2.30pm & 7.30-10.30pm Tue-Sat; 🚊San Stae) Hidden in the once shady lanes behind Ponte de le Tette, this culinary indulgence is hard to find but worth the effort. Once you do, say hello to a market-driven menu of Venetian classics, including *fegato alla veneziana* (veal liver with onions) and lots of seafood. It's never short of a smart, convivial crowd, so it's a good idea to book ahead.

✕ Santa Croce

BACARRETTO
SICILIAN €

Map p278 (✆041 200 76 67; www.facebook.com/bacarrettobistrot.ilsiciliano; Calle de la Chiesa 2098; meals €17-29; ⊙noon-3pm & 7-10pm Mon-Sat; 🚊San Stae) A bijou restaurant whose owner, Marco, is an enthusiastic and knowledgeable connoisseur of Sicilian wine and food. The menu is small, but excellent, with Sicilian classics such as *panelle* (chickpea fritters), *pasta alla norma* (with aubergine and ricotta in tomato sauce) and *involtini di pesce spada* (rolled swordfish). Start with a selection of lightly fried vegetables.

GELATO DI NATURA
GELATO €

Map p278 (📞340 2867178; www.gelatodinatura. com; Calle Larga 1628; 1 scoop €1.50; ⊘10.30am-11pm Feb-Nov; 👪; ⛴Riva di Biasio, San Stae) Along with a dozen other things, Marco Polo is said to have introduced ice cream to Venice after his odyssey to China. At this gelato shop the experimentation continues with vegan versions of your favourite flavours, Japanese rice cakes and the creamiest, small-batch gelato incorporating accredited Italian ingredients such as Bronte pistachios, Piedmontese hazelnuts and Amalfi lemons.

★OSTERIA TREFANTI
VENETIAN €€

Map p278 (📞041 520 17 89; www.osteriatrefanti.it; Fondamenta del Rio Marin o dei Garzoti 888; meals €40-45; ⊘noon-2.30pm & 7-10.30pm Tue-Sun; 📶; ⛴Riva de Biasio) La Serenissima's spice trade lives on at simple, elegant Trefanti, where gnocchi might get an intriguing kick from cinnamon, and turbot is flavoured with almond and coconut. Seafood is the focus; try the 'doge's fettucine', with mussels, scampi and clams. Furnished with recycled copper lamps, the space is small and deservedly popular – so book ahead.

MURO SAN STAE
ITALIAN €€

Map p278 (📞041 524 16 28; www.murovenezia. com; Campiello del Spezier 2048; pizzas €7-15, meals €30-46; ⊘noon-3pm & 6-10.30pm Mon-Fri, noon-10.30pm Sat & Sun; 📶📷; ⛴San Stae) Contemporary and relaxed, versatile Muro plays the role of both pizzeria and restaurant. Tuck into inventive pizzas and seasonal salads, or linger over fresh, flavour-packed mains. Carnivores are especially well catered for, with no shortage of grilled meats and a succulent beef carpaccio, but there are plenty of vegetarian-friendly pizza and pasta options too. There's another branch in **San Polo** (Map p278; 📞041 524 53 10; Rio Terà 2604b; ⛴San Tomà).

OSTERIA LA ZUCCA
ITALIAN €€

Map p278 (📞041 524 15 70; www.lazucca.it; Calle del Tentor 1762; meals €32-38; ⊘noon-2.30pm & 7-10.30pm Mon-Sat; 📷; ⛴San Stae) With its menu of seasonal vegetarian creations and classic meat dishes, this cosy, woody restaurant consistently hits the mark. Herbs and spices are used to great effect in dishes such as the nutmeg-tinged pumpkin and smoked ricotta flan. The small interior can get toasty, so reserve canalside seats in summer. Even in winter you're best to book ahead.

IL REFOLO
ITALIAN €€

Map p278 (📞041 524 00 16; www.facebook.com/ Passito76; Campiello del Piovan 1459; pizzas €15, meals €35; ⊘noon-11pm Mar-Oct; 👪; ⛴Riva di Biasio) With outdoor tables occupying the *campo* in front of San Giacomo dall'Orio, this is a sunny spot from which to watch gondolas drift by. The food, too, is relaxed and unfussy with a menu offering a range of pizzas, pasta and light seafood dishes. Owned by the Martin family of Michelin-starred Da Fiore; expect top-quality ingredients and standout flavours.

OSTERIA MOCENIGO
VENETIAN €€

Map p278 (📞041 523 17 03; Salizada San Stae 1919; meals €25-41; ⊘noon-3pm & 7-10.30pm; 📶👪; ⛴San Stae) Times and dining habits have changed since doges strained waistcoat buttons at neighbouring Palazzo Mocenigo: warm, homely Osteria Mocenigo offers casual lunches and dinners with dishes such fish or vegetable ravioli and grilled meats. Good-value set lunches include pasta, salad, wine and coffee for €12.

AL BACCO FELICE
ITALIAN €€

Map p281 (📞041 528 77 94; Calle dei Amai 197e; pizza €6-13, meals €30-50; ⊘noon-midnight; 👪; ⛴Piazzale Roma) Paper placemats, pop tunes on the radio and glowing customer feedback plastered up the wall: Al Bacco sets a casual, convivial scene for decent, thin-crust pizzas, solid pasta dishes, and unfussy classic mains such as veal scallopini. Pizzas start at a bargain €6, making it an especially popular spot for economising students and families.

★ZANZE XVI
VENETIAN €€€

Map p281 (Trattoria dalla Zanze; 📞041 71 53 94; www.zanze.it; Fondamenta dei Tolentini 231; lunch set menu €25, meals €46-51; ⊘12.30-2.30pm & 7.30-10.30pm Sun & Tue-Fri, 7.30-10.30pm Sat; ❋; ⛴Piazzale Roma) These sophisticated culinary adventurers offer a contemporary spin on Venetian traditions. Opt for a 'surprise' five-course *mare* (seafood; €70) or *terra* (meat and local produce; €50) menu, or leap straight into the eight-course 'soul' menu (€80). If you've got trust issues or a fussy dining partner, there are à la carte options too. The two-course set lunches include coffee.

★GLAM VENETIAN €€€

Map p278 (☎041 523 56 76; www.enricobartolini.
net; Calle Tron 1961; meals €108-168; ☺12.30-
2.30pm & 7.30-10.30pm; ⛴San Stae) Step out of
your water taxi into the canalside garden of
this inventive Michelin-starred restaurant
in the Hotel Palazzo Venart. The contemporary menu focuses on local ingredients,
pepping up Veneto favourites with unusual
spices that would once have graced the tables of this trade-route city. The service and
the wine list are equally impressive.

🍷 DRINKING & NIGHTLIFE

**Sandwiched between the university and
the market, San Polo and Santa Croce
have some cracking bars. Many of them
are hidden in the narrow lanes around
the Rialto Market, while others occupy
strategic corners on sunny *campi* such
as Giacomo da l'Orio, San Cassiano, San
Polo, San Tomà and Campo dei Frari.**

🍴 San Polo

★IL MERCANTE COCKTAIL BAR

Map p278 (☎041 476 73 05; www.ilmercanteven
ezia.com; Campo dei Frari 2564; ☺6pm-1am;
⛴San Tomà) An hour's changeover is all it
takes for historic Caffè dei Frari to transform itself into its night-time guise as
Venice's best cocktail bar. If you can't find
anything that takes your fancy on the adventurous themed cocktail list, the expert
bar team will create something to suit your
mood. In winter, snuggle on a velvet sofa
upstairs.

★CANTINA DO SPADE WINE BAR

Map p278 (☎041 521 05 83; www.cantinadospade.
com; Sotoportego de le Do Spade 860; ☺10am-
3pm & 6-10pm Wed-Mon, 6-10pm Tue; 🛜; ⛴Rialto
Mercato) Famously mentioned in Casanova's
memoirs, cosy 'Two Spades' was founded in
1488 and continues to keep Venice in good
spirits with its bargain Tri-Veneto and Istrian wines and young, laid-back management. Come early for market-fresh *fritture*
(fried battered seafood) and grilled squid,
or linger longer with satisfying, sit-down
dishes such as *bigoli in salsa* (pasta in anchovy and onion sauce).

CANTINA DO MORI WINE BAR

Map p278 (☎041 522 54 01; Calle dei Do Mori
429; ☺8am-7.30pm Mon-Fri, to 5pm Sat; ⛴Rialto
Mercato) You'll feel like you've stepped into
a Rembrandt painting at venerable 'Two
Moors', a dark, rustic bar with roots in the
15th century. Under gleaming, gargantuan
copper pots, nostalgists swill one of around
40 wines by the glass, or slurp prosecco
from old-school champagne coupes. Peckish? Bar bites include pickled onions with
anchovies, succulent *polpette* (meatballs)
and slices of *pecorino*.

CAFFÈ DEL DOGE CAFE

Map p278 (☎041 522 77 87; www.caffedeldoge.
com; Calle dei Cinque 609; ☺7am-7pm; ⛴San
Silvestro) Sniff your way to the affable Doge,
where dedicated drinkers slurp their way
through the menu of speciality imported
coffees, from Ethiopian to Guatemalan,
all roasted on the premises. If you're feel
especially inspired, you can even pick up
a stove-top coffee percolator. Pastries and
viscous hot chocolate are on hand for those
needing a sweet fix.

BARCOLLO BAR

Map p278 (☎041 522 81 58; Campo Cesare Battisti già de la Bella Vienna 219; ☺8.30am-2.30am
Mon-Sat, 10am-2.30am Sun; 🛜; ⛴Rialto Mercato) Its name might mean stagger, but there's
more to this party bar than its heady cocktail sessions and Friday-night DJ sets. Just
steps away from the Rialto Market, it makes
for a handy daytime pit stop for coffee and
a snack. Come evening, however, the cheap
house wine ensures that the boozy crowd
spills out onto the *campo*.

CAFFÈ DEI FRARI CAFE

Map p278 (☎041 476 73 05; Fondamenta dei Frari
2564; ☺9am-5pm; ⛴San Tomà) Take your (ad-
mittedly expensive) espresso with a heap-
ing of history at this atmospheric cafe,
established in 1870, with its Tiffany-style
lamps and elegant mezzanine. At night it
closes and adopts a different mask, reopen-
ing as Il Mercante.

AL MERCÀ WINE BAR

Map p278 (☎346 8340660; Campo Cesare Battisti già de la Bella Vienna 213; ☺10am-2.30pm
& 6-8pm Mon-Thu, to 9.30pm Fri & Sat; ⛴Rialto
Mercato) Discerning drinkers throng to this
cupboard-sized counter on a Rialto Market
square to sip on top-notch prosecco and
other wines by the glass (from €2). Edibles

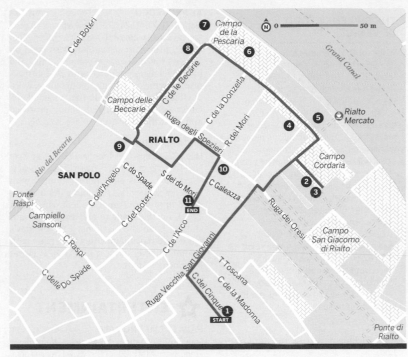

🏃 Neighbourhood Walk
Rialto Culinary Crawl

START CAFFÈ DEL DOGE
END ALL'ARCO
LENGTH 450M; ONE HOUR

The Rialto area has long been the starting point of all things gourmet in Venice, fuelled by its centuries-old market. This walk is designed with grazing and imbibing firmly in mind, so come with an empty stomach. Start as the Venetians do, sipping a coffee standing at the counter of ❶ **Caffè del Doge** (p102), then take busy Ruga Vecchia to Campo Bella Vienna. This little square on the edge of the market is home to the wonderful ❷ **Casa del Parmigiano** (p105). Appetite piqued, order a mini *panini* from the traditional wine bar ❸ **Al Mercà** (p102) next door. As you wander towards the market proper you'll pass ❹ **Macelleria Equina**, a butcher specialising in horse meat, opposite the 16th-century Sansovino-designed ❺ **Fabbriche Nuove** building. Next up is the main outdoor fruit and vegetable section of the ❻ **Rialto Market** (p95), followed by the famous fish market, or ❼ **Pescaria** (p95). Note the marine-themed capitals on the open-sided Gothic building closest to the water, then cross to the larger building on the side canal. Before you enter it, look for the historic ❽ **plaque** outlining the regulations relating to minimum fish sizes. At the other end of the building cut across the square then to the little lane in the far left corner and then take a quick right down the *sotoportego* (covered passage) to 15th-century ❾ **Cantina Do Spade** (p102). Join the ranks of famous former customers such as Casanova and order some seafood *cicheti* (Venetian tapas). Backtrack to the very end of Calle de le Do Spade, take a left and then the third right onto Ruga dei Spezieri – the 'Street of the Spice Merchants'. Continuing the tradition is ❿ **Drogheria Mascari** (p105), the oldest speciality food shop in Venice. Finish up in ⓫ **All'Arco** (p99), San Polo's best and most famous *cicheti* bar.

THE SWEENEY TODD OF VENICE

While most of Venice's streets are named after trades, saints or aristocratic families, the sunny Riva di Biasio has a much darker origin. It takes its name from Biagio Cargnio, a 16th-century butcher known for his sausages and *sguaséto*, a meaty stew that he sold at lunchtime to local workmen. One day a customer found a small bone in his stew, which he soon realised was a human finger, with the fingernail attached. He went straight to the police who raided the shop and found the butchered remains of children out the back.

Biasio's punishment was similarly grisly: he had his hands chopped off before being dragged to Piazza San Marco and beheaded between the Piazzetta's two columns. His body was then quartered and displayed in different parts of the city.

usually include meatballs and mini *panini* (€1.50).

VINERIA ALL'AMARONE   WINE BAR
Map p278 (☑041 523 11 84; www.allamarone.com; Calle dei Sbianchesini 1131; ⏱10am-11pm Thu-Tue; 🛜; 🚤San Silvestro) The warm wood-panelled interior and huge selection of Veneto wines by the glass are just part of the popularity of this friendly bar-cum-restaurant. Other reasons to stop by are generous *cicheti* platters, belly-warming plates of gnocchi and braised beef in red wine, and wine-tasting flights (€31 to €46), which include the heady Amarone from which the bar takes its name.

🍷 Santa Croce

★OSTERIA DA FILO   BAR
Map p278 (Hosteria alla Poppa; ☑041 524 65 54; www.facebook.com/osteriadafilo; Calle del Tentor 1539; ⏱4-11pm Mon-Fri, 11am-11pm Sat & Sun; 🛜; 🚤Riva de Biasio) A living room where drinks are served, this locals' hang-out comes complete with creaky sofas, free wi-fi, abandoned novels and the occasional live-music gig. Drinks are cheap and the Venetian tapas tasty.

AL PROSECCO   WINE BAR
Map p278 (☑041 524 02 22; www.alprosecco.com; Campo San Giacomo da l'Orio 1503; ⏱10am-8pm Mon-Fri, to 5pm Sat; 🚤San Stae) Positioned on Venice's loveliest *campo* (square), this wine bar specialises in *vini naturali* (natural-process wines) – organic, biodynamic, wild-yeast fermented – from Italian winemakers. Order a glass of unfiltered 'cloudy' prosecco and toast the view over a plate of *cicheti*.

BACARETO DA LELE   BAR
Map p281 (Campo dei Tolentini 183; ⏱6am-8pm Mon-Fri, to 2pm Sat; 🚤Piazzale Roma) Pocket-sized Da Lele is perpetually jammed with students and workers, stopping for a cheap, stand-up *ombra* (small glass of wine; from €0.70) on their way to and from the train station. Scan the blackboard for the day's wines and pair them with a little plate with salami, cheese and a roll (€1.60). It closes for much of August.

☆ ENTERTAINMENT

PALAZZETTO BRU ZANE   CLASSICAL MUSIC
Map p278 (Centre du Musique Romantique Française; ☑041 521 10 05; www.bru-zane.com; Campiello del Forner o del Marangon 2368; adult/reduced €15/5; ⏱box office 2.30-5.30pm Mon-Fri; 🚤San Tomà) Pleasure palaces don't get more romantic than this little *palazzo* on concert nights, when exquisite harmonies tickle Sebastiano Ricci angels tumbling across stucco-frosted ceilings. Multi-year restorations returned 17th-century Casino Zane's 100-seat music room to its original function, attracting world-class musicians to enjoy its acoustics. Free guided tours of the building run on Thursdays (in Italian/French/English at 2.30pm/3pm/3.30pm; none in August).

LA CASA DEL CINEMA   CINEMA
Map p278 (Videoteca Pasinetti; ☑041 274 71 40; www.comune.venezia.it; Salizada San Stae 1990; annual membership adult/reduced €35/25; ⏱9am-1pm & 3-10pm Mon-Fri; 🚤San Stae) Venice's public film archive shows original-language art films, including some in English, to members in a modern 50-seat, wood-beamed screening room inside Palazzo Mocenigo (p97). Check online for pre-release previews and revivals with introductions by directors, actors and scholars.

🛍 SHOPPING

The main route linking Campo San Polo and the Rialto Is lined with small boutiques and artisan studios; if you need emergency luggage, this is the place to look. Food stores are focused around the Rialto Market, with high-end shops beneath the arcade leading up to the Rialto bridge. Another artisan hotspot is the area around Campo San Tomà and along Calle Seconda di Saoneri, where you'll find jewellers, glass artists and independent fashion stores.

🛍 San Polo

★ PROCESS COLLETTIVO   GIFTS & SOUVENIRS

Map p278 (📱041 524 31 25; www.rioteradeipen sieri.org; Fondamenta dei Frari 2559a; ⊘10am-8pm; 🚤San Tomà) 🧷 This nonprofit sells goods made by inmates of Venice's prisons as part of a social reintegration program. Toiletries are made from plants grown in the garden of the women's prison on Giudecca, while the satchels and shoulder bags made from recycled advertising hoardings are made at the men's prison in Santa Croce.

IL PAVONE DI PAOLO PELOSIN ARTS & CRAFTS

Map p278 (📱041 522 42 96; Campiello dei Meloni 1478; ⊘9.30am-7pm Tue, Thu, Sat & Sun, 10.45am-7pm Mon & Fri; 🚤San Silvestro) Paolo's hand-bound marbled-paper journals and photo albums make inspired homes for your Venice memories. Recipe books are covered in violet and gold feather patterns, rippled blue sketchbooks conjure seascapes, and paper-wrapped pens seem to catch fire with flickers of orange and red.

DAMOCLE EDIZIONI   BOOKS

Map p278 (📱346 8345720; www.edizionidamocle. com; Calle del Perdon 1311; ⊘10am-1pm & 3-7pm Mon-Fri, 10am-1pm Sat; 🚤San Silvestro) Pocket-sized Damocle is both a bookshop and publisher, translating literary greats and showcasing emerging writing talent. Most of Damocle's creations are bilingual (including books in English) and many feature beautiful artwork.

LA BAUTA   ARTS & CRAFTS

Map p278 (📱041 74 00 95; www.labauta.com; Campo San Tomà 2867; ⊘10.30am-6pm; 🚤San Tomà) Whether it's a unicorn or a steampunk explorer mask you're after, this traditional workshop will see you right. Alternatively you can paint your own plague doctor or sun/moon look in an hour-long session (€40 per person; bookings not required), while learning about Venice's long-standing infatuation with playing dress up.

OH MY BLUE   JEWELLERY

Map p278 (📱041 243 57 41; www.ohmyblue. it; Campo San Tomà 2865; ⊘11am-1pm & 3.30-7.30pm; 🚤San Tomà) In her white-on-white gallery, Elena Rizzi showcases edgy, show-stopping jewellery, accessories and decorative objects from both local and international talent. Expect anything from quartz rings and paper necklaces to sculptural bags.

ALBERTO SARRIA MASKS   ARTS & CRAFTS

Map p278 (📱041 520 72 78; www.masksvenice. com; Ruga Vecchia San Giovanni 777; ⊘10am-7pm; 🚤San Stae) Go Gaga or channel Casanova at this atelier, dedicated to the art of masquerade for over 30 years. Sarria's *commedia dell'arte* masks are worn by theatre companies from Argentina to Osaka – ominous burnished black leather for dramatic leads and harlequin-chequered *cartapesta* (papier mâché) for comic foils, starting from around €25. Beyond the masks is a cast of one-of-a-kind marionettes.

CASA DEL PARMIGIANO   FOOD

Map p278 (📱041 520 65 25; www.aliani-casa delparmigiano.it; Campo Cesare Battisti già de la Bella Vienna 214; ⊘8am-1.30pm Mon-Wed, to 7.30pm Thu-Sat; 🚤Rialto Mercato) Suitably set beside the appetite-piquing Rialto Market, cheery Casa del Parmigiano heaves with coveted cheeses, from potent *parmigiano reggiano* (Parmesan) aged for three years, to rare, local Asiago Stravecchio di Malga. All are kept in good company by fragrant cured meats, *baccalà* (cod) and trays of marinated Sicilian olives.

DROGHERIA MASCARI   FOOD & DRINKS

Map p278 (📱041 522 97 62; www.imascari.com; Ruga dei Spezieri 381; ⊘8am-1pm & 4-7.30pm Mon, Tue & Thu-Sat, 8am-1pm Wed; 🚤Rialto Mercato) Ziggurats of sun-dried tomatoes, leaning towers of star anise and chorus lines of olive oils draw awestruck foodies to Mascari's windows. For small-production Italian wines, don't miss the backroom cantina.

PIED À TERRE   SHOES

Map p278 (📱041 528 55 13; www.piedaterre-venice.com; Sotoportego de Rialto 60; ⊘10am-

LEARN ITALIAN

Founded by Venetian brother and sister Diego and Lucia Cattaneo, the **Venice Italian School** (Map p278; ✆347 9635113; www.veniceitalianschool. com; Campo San Stin 2504, San Polo; 1-/2-week group course €310/550, individual lessons €95; ◉San Tomà) offers excellent, immersive, small-group courses (maximum six students) and one-on-one lessons. The school can also help arrange well-priced accommodation.

12.30pm & 2.30-7.30pm; ◉Rialto Mercato) Pied à Terre's colourful *furlane* (Venetian slippers) are handcrafted with recycled bicycle tyre treads, ideal for finding your footing on a gondola. Choose from velvet, brocade or raw silk in vibrant shades of mustard and ruby, with optional piping. Don't see your size? Shoes can be custom-made and shipped.

OTTICA VASCELLARI   FASHION & ACCESSORIES
Map p278 (✆041 522 93 88; www.otticavascel lari.it; Rugheta del Ravano 1030; ◉9am-12.30pm & 3-7.30pm Mon-Sat, closed Mon Oct-Apr; ◉San Silvestro) Second-generation opticians and first-class stylists, the Vascellari family discern eyewear needs with a glance at your prescription and a long look to assess your face shape and personal style. Angular features demand Vascellari's architectural eyewear with hand-finished, two-tone laminates, while delicate features are set off with sleek specs of ecofriendly cotton-resin – all for less than mass-market brands.

GILBERTO PENZO   ARTS & CRAFTS
Map p278 (✆041 71 93 72; www.veniceboats. com; Calle Seconda dei Saoneri 2681; ◉8.30am-1pm & 3-6pm Mon-Sat; ◉San Tomà) Yes, you actually can take a gondola home in your pocket. Anyone fascinated by the models at the Museo Storico Navale (p131) will go wild here, amid handmade wooden models of Venetian boats, including some that are seaworthy (or at least bathtub worthy). Signor Penzo also creates kits, so crafty types and kids can have a crack at it themselves.

ANATEMA   FASHION & ACCESSORIES
Map p278 (✆041 524 22 21; www.anatema.it; Rio Terà 2603; ◉10am-7pm; ◉San Tomà) Add a Venetian eye for colour to a Japanese flair for sculptural fashion, and here you have it: teal mohair tube scarves that float around the collarbone like clouds, and pleated Thai and Italian silk shawls and bags in shimmering *cangiante* (dual-toned) shades. The Venetian-Japanese design duo behind Anatema brings out new collections each season, from sunhats to wool-felt brooches.

🏛 Santa Croce

PAPEROOWL   ARTS & CRAFTS
Map p278 (✆041 476 19 74; www.paperoowl. com; Calle Longa 2155a; ◉10.30am-6pm Mon-Fri; ◉San Stae) Stefania Giannici's nimble fingers have been practising origami since she was four years old. Now a master of her craft, she folds, prints, rolls and weaves an extraordinary array of paper artworks, ranging from Japanese-style decorative panels to paper wind chimes, *kuzudama* flower balls and chic necklaces that look like Murano glass beads but cost a fraction of the price.

ARTIGIANATO D'ARTE
DI MAURO VIANELLO   GLASS
Map p278 (✆041 520 18 02; www.maurovianello. com; Calle dei Morti 2251; ◉10.30am-6pm Mon-Sat; ◉San Stae) A coral reef's worth of painstakingly detailed glass Nemos, seahorses, starfish, jellyfish and seashells fills the window of this little glass studio. Alternatively you could opt for a biologically accurate reproduction of a delicate butterfly or a glistening snail. Book a demonstration if you want to watch the artist at work (adult/reduced €30/20).

BOTTEGA ORAFA ABC   JEWELLERY
Map p278 (✆041 524 40 01; www.orafaabc.com; Calle del Tentor 1839; ◉9.30am-12.30pm & 3.30-7.30pm Tue-Sat; ◉San Stae) Master of metals, Andrea d'Agostino takes his influence from the Japanese technique of *mokume gane* (meaning 'metal with woodgrain'), masterful examples of which are on display in the Asian gallery of Ca' Pesaro (p97). The result is rings, pendants and bracelets with swirling multicoloured patterns that seem to capture the dappled lagoon waters for all time in silver and gold.

Cannaregio

Neighbourhood Top Five

1 The Ghetto (p109) Exploring the historic island home/prison of Venice's Jewish community, which offered refuge from the Inquisition and sparked a Renaissance in thought.

2 Chiesa di Santa Maria dei Miracoli (p112) Discovering the marble-clad church that marked a turning point in the city's ecclesiastical architecture.

3 Chiesa della Madonna dell'Orto (p111) Paying respects to the genius of Tintoretto at his parish church and burial place, a simple structure filled with the master's works.

4 Ca' d'Oro (p111) Finding Grand Canal photo ops and misappropriated masterpieces in one of Venice's most glorious Gothic *palazzi*.

5 Canalside cicheti bars (p115) Experiencing the very Venetian delight of *aperitivo* seated on broad canal banks that capture the best sunset rays, such as at Vino Vero.

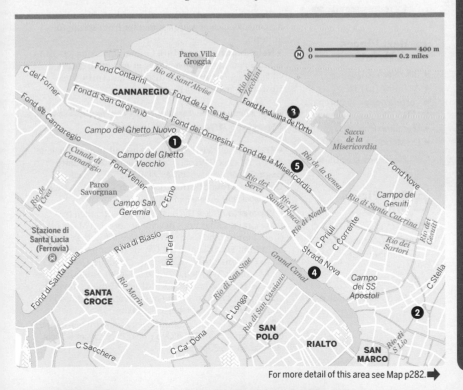

For more detail of this area see Map p282.

Lonely Planet's Top Tip

Napoleon created the pedestrian boulevard that links the train station to the Rialto, and it's a lot like a highway, with rush-hour pedestrian traffic and fast-food and chain stores. At busy times you can avoid a few frustrating blocks by cutting through the Ghetto and following the sunny and scenic *fondamenta* (canal bank) running north of it.

✕ Best Places to Eat

➡ Anice Stellato (p114)

➡ Osteria Boccadoro (p115)

➡ Pasticceria Dal Mas (p113)

➡ Ai Promessi Sposi (p114)

➡ Trattoria Pontini (p113)

For reviews, see p113.➡

◗ Best Places to Drink

➡ Vino Vero (p115)

➡ Al Timon (p115)

➡ Torrefazione Cannaregio (p117)

➡ Marciano Pub (p117)

➡ Un Mondo di Vino (p117)

For reviews, see p115.➡

🔒 Best Places to Shop

➡ Codex Venezia (p119)

➡ Vittorio Costantini (p119)

➡ La Stamperia del Ghetto (p119)

➡ Gianni Basso (p119)

For reviews, see p119.➡

Explore Cannaregio

Cannaregio doesn't have the sex appeal of San Marco, the youth of Dorsoduro or the working-class attitude of Castello. Rather, it's a well-balanced residential neighbourhood of unpretentious, patrician *palazzi* (mansions), picturesque *campi* (squares) and quiet canals. It also has some of the city's best local bars, restaurants and shops.

Settled in the 15th-century when Renaissance town planning was taking effect, Cannaregio is less of a maze than the medieval Rialto, its numerous canals cut in straight lines with broad, pedestrian-friendly *fondamente* (canal banks). The Strada Nova, created in 1871 by filling in canals, slices right through the neighbourhood.

From this pedestrian highway you can reach all of the area's sights: the churches of Madonna dell'Orto (p111), Miracoli (p112) and Gesuiti (p113); the Jewish Ghetto (p109), with its historically important synagogues; and the impressive Gothic gallery of Ca' d'Oro (p111). Come evening you'll appreciate Cannaregio's understated charms even more as locals flock to sun-soaked bars and canalside restaurants along the Cannaregio, Ormesini and Sensa canals.

Local Life

➡ **Shopping secrets** Campo Santa Maria Nova hosts a monthly outdoor antiques market from spring to autumn.

➡ **Neighbourhood nightlife** Cannaregio's timeless calm is broken at night by live music at Al Timon (p115), Al Parlamento (p118), Paradiso Perduto (p118) and Hostaria Bacanera (p117).

Getting There & Away

➡ **Train** All services from the mainland stop at Stazione di Santa Lucia (Ferrovia), where there's a **Deposito Bagagli** (Left Luggage Office; ☎041 78 55 31; ◷6am-11pm) and a **tourist office** (Map p282; ☎041 24 24; www.veneziaunica.it; ◷7am-9pm).

➡ **Vaporetto** Makes the busy Ferrovia stop then two more Grand Canal stops in Cannaregio: San Marcuola (lines 1 and 2) and Ca' d'Oro (1). Lines 4.1, 4.2, 5.1 and 5.2 head from Ferrovia into the Canale di Cannaregio and on to Fondamente Nove, stopping at Guglie, Crea (4.1 and 4.2 only), Tre Archi (5.1 and 5.2 only), Sant'Alvise and Orto on the way. Line 3 heads directly from Ferrovia to all stops on Murano. From Fondamente Nove, lines 12 and 13 head to the northern islands.

➡ **Traghetto** Gondolas shunt back and forth across the Grand Canal from **Ca' d'Oro** (trips €2; ◷7.30am-6.30pm Mon-Sat, 9am-6.30pm Sun).

TOP SIGHT
THE GHETTO

This Cannaregio corner once housed a *getto* (foundry), but its role as Venice's designated Jewish quarter from the 16th to 19th centuries gave the word a whole new meaning. From 1516 onwards, Jewish artisans and lenders tended to Venice's commercial enterprises by day, while at night and on Christian holidays they were restricted to the gated island of Ghetto Nuovo.

Ghetto Life

Jewish people have lived in Venice from at least the 12th century, although it wasn't until 1516 that they were segregated in the Ghetto and subject to a strict sunset curfew. Unlike most European cities of the era, pragmatic Venice granted Jewish communities the right to practise certain professions key to the city's livelihood, including medicine, trade, banking, fashion and publishing.

When the Inquisition forced Jewish communities out of Spain in 1541, many fled to Venice. As new inhabitants crowded in, upper storeys were added to houses, creating mini-high-rises. As numbers grew, the Ghetto was extended into the neighbouring Ghetto Vecchio (Old Foundry) area, creating the confusing situation where the older Jewish area is called the New (Nuovo) Ghetto and the newer is the Old (Vecchio) Ghetto.

While the Ghetto was created as an act of segregation, over time it became a refuge in which Jewish culture and ideas thrived. It was the principal site of Hebrew publishing in Europe; Christians flocked to the sermons of learned rabbi Leon da Modena, as well as rowdy Purim plays; and Ghetto literary salons attracted leading thinkers of all faiths.

When Napoleon conquered the Republic in 1797, the Jewish community experienced six months of freedom before the Austrian administration reimposed discriminatory restrictions. It wasn't until Venice joined with Italy in 1866 that full emancipation was gained. However, Mussolini's 1938 Racial Laws revived the earlier discrimination and in 1943 and 1944, 246 Jewish Venetians were deported to concentration camps; only eight survived. A **memorial** consisting of harrowing bas-reliefs and the names and ages of those killed lines two walls facing Campo del Ghetto Nuovo.

Museo Ebraico

At the Ghetto's heart, the **Museo Ebraico** (Jewish Museum; Map p282; ☑041 71 53 59; www.museoebraico.it; Campo del Ghetto Nuovo 2902b; adult/reduced €8/6, incl tour €12/10; ⊙10am-7pm Sun-Fri Jun-Sep, to 5.30pm Sun-Fri Oct-May; ⛴Guglie) explores the history of Venice's Jewish community and showcases its pivotal contributions to Venetian, Italian and world history. Opened in 1955, it has a small collection of finely worked silverware, precious textiles and other objects used in private prayer and to decorate synagogues, as well as early books published in the Ghetto during the Renaissance.

The museum visit can be combined with a highly recommended guided tour (departing hourly from 10.30am), which visits three of the Ghetto's historic synagogues: the Schola Tedesca, the Schola Canton and either the Schola Italiana (in summer) or the Schola Spagnola (in winter). The museum can also arrange tours to the Antico Cimitero Israelitico (p143) on the Lido.

DON'T MISS

➡ Campo del Ghetto Nuovo
➡ Synagogue tour
➡ Museo Ebraico
➡ Memorial reliefs

TOP TIPS

➡ You can stroll around this peaceful precinct day and night, but the best way to experience the Ghetto is to take one of the guided synagogue tours offered by the Museo Ebraico, departing hourly from 10.30am.

PRACTICALITIES

➡ Map p282, C1
➡ ⛴Guglie

WRITING ON THE WALL

On the wall at No 1131 Calle del Ghetto Vecchio, an official 1704 decree of the Republic forbids Jews who had converted to Christianity from entering into the Ghetto, punishable by 'the rope [hanging], prison, galleys, flogging...and other greater punishments, depending on the judgment of their excellencies (the Executors Against Blasphemy)'. This was to prevent Jews from nominally converting in order to enjoy the freedom of Christians, while secretly continuing their Jewish observances.

GHETTO PUBLISHING

Despite a 10-year censorship order issued by Rome in 1553, Jewish Venetian publishers contributed hundreds of titles popularising new Renaissance ideas on humanist philosophy, medicine and religion – including the first printed Qur'an.

Synagogues

As you enter **Campo del Ghetto Nuovo** from the north, look up: atop private apartments is the wooden cupola of the 1575 **Schola Italiana** (Italian Synagogue). The Italians were the poorest in the Ghetto, having fled from Spanish-controlled southern Italy, and their synagogue is starkly beautiful, with elegantly carved woodwork.

Recognisable from the square by its five long windows, the **Schola Tedesca** (German Synagogue) has been the spiritual home of Venice's Ashkenazi community since 1528. By 16th-century Venetian law, only the German Jewish community could lend money, and the success of this enterprise shows in the handsome decor. The baroque pulpit and carved benches downstairs are topped by a gilded, elliptical women's gallery, modelled after a Venetian opera balcony.

In the corner of the *campo,* behind the entrance to the Museo Ebraica, you'll spot the wonky wooden cupola of the **Schola Canton** (Corner Synagogue), built circa 1531 with gilded rococo interiors added in the 18th century. Though European synagogues typically avoid figurative imagery, this little synagogue makes an exception to the rule with eight charming landscapes inspired by biblical parables.

Over the bridge in **Campo del Ghetto Vecchio**, Sephardic Jewish refugees raised two synagogues that are considered among the most elegant in northern Italy, having been rebuilt in the 17th century. The **Schola Levantina** (Levantine Synagogue), founded in 1541, has a magnificent 17th-century woodworked pulpit (not usually open to the public); the **Schola Spagnola** (Spanish Synagogue), founded around 1580, shows Venetian architectural flourishes such as repeated geometric details, high arched windows, and exuberant marble and carved-wood baroque interiors.

The Ghetto Today

The Ghetto marked its 500th anniversary in 2016, and used the occasion to upgrade the museum and restore significant buildings. Of note is the pretty symbolic garden behind the Schola Spagnola, which is now used as a learning environment.

Today few of Venice's 470-person Jewish community live in the Ghetto, but their children come to the *campo* to play, surrounded by the Ghetto's living legacy of bookshops, art galleries, religious institutions and kosher eateries. For information about local Jewish life, call into the **Jewish Community Info Point** (Map p282; ☑041 523 75 65; www.jvenice.org; Calle del Ghetto Vecchio 1222; ⊗9.30am-5pm Mon-Fri).

⊙ SIGHTS

Sights in this residential quarter are scattered, with the most interesting location – the historic Jewish Ghetto – hidden away in the north. The broad constructed canals north of here get progressively quieter; at night you might even enjoy the rarefied experience of wandering along a deserted canal bank. Ca' d'Oro, the Casino, Chiesa di San Geremia and Chiesa dei Scalzi all take up prime spots on the Grand Canal, south of the busy main thoroughfare, Strada Nova.

THE GHETTO   JEWISH SITE

See p109.

★CHIESA DELLA
MADONNA DELL'ORTO   CHURCH

Map p282 (www.madonnadellorto.org; Campo de la Madonna dell'Orto 3520; adult/reduced €3/2; ⊙10am-5pm Mon-Sat; ⓈOrto) This elegantly spare 1365 brick Gothic church remains one of Venice's best-kept secrets. It was the parish church of Venetian Renaissance painter Tintoretto (1518–94), who is buried in the chapel to the right of the altar. Inside, you'll find two of Tintoretto's finest works: *Presentation of the Virgin in the Temple* and *Last Judgment*, where lost souls attempt to hold back a teal tidal wave while an angel rescues one last person from the ultimate *acqua alta* (high tide).

It also once included a Bellini masterpiece, stolen in 1993 – note the empty space in the side chapel.

★GALLERIA GIORGIO
FRANCHETTI ALLA CA' D'ORO   MUSEUM

Map p282 (⌁041 522 23 49; www.cadoro.org; Calle di Ca' d'Oro 3932; adult/reduced €8.50/2; ⊙8.15am-2pm Mon, to 7.15pm Tue-Sun, 2nd fl 10am-6pm Tue-Sun; ⓈCa' d'Oro) One of the most beautiful buildings on the Grand Canal, with a lacy Gothic facade, 15th-century Ca' d'Oro is resplendent even without the original gold-leaf details that gave the palace its name (Golden House). Baron Franchetti (1865–1922) bequeathed this treasure-box palace to Venice, packed with his collection of masterpieces, many of which were originally plundered from Veneto churches during Napoleon's conquest of Italy. The baron's ashes are interred beneath an ancient purple porphyry column in the magnificent open-sided, mosaic-floored court downstairs.

Napoleon had excellent taste in souvenirs, including bronzes, tapestries, paintings and sculpture ripped (sometimes literally) from church altars. Most were warehoused at Milan's Brera Museum as Napoleonic war trophies until they were reclaimed by Venice for display here. Collection highlights include (when she's not touring the world) Titian's flushed, smouldering *Venus with a Mirror* (c 1550) and Mantegna's arrow-riddled *St Sebastian* (1490). There are also more depictions of the Madonna and Child than seems entirely reasonable.

Step outside onto Ca' d'Oro's double-decker *loggie* (balconies), where Grand Canal views framed by Gothic arcades make the city's most irresistible photo op.

A combined ticket (adult/reduced €13/6.50) that includes the Palazzo Grimani (p127) is available. Admission is free on the first Sunday of each month.

CHIESA DI SAN GEREMIA   CHURCH

Map p282 (⌁041 71 61 81; www.santuariodilucia.it; Campo San Geremia 274; ⊙9am-1pm & 4.30-5pm Wed-Mon, 2.30-5pm Tue; ⓈFerrovia) FREE This hefty-domed 18th-century church contains the body of St Lucy (Santa Lucia), one of the early church's most famous martyrs, who was killed in Syracuse in AD 304. Her body was stolen from Constantinople in 1204 and moved to San Geremia after the Palladian church of Santa Lucia was demolished in the 19th century to make way for the train station. It's now displayed in a glass case in its own chapel (visitable by pre-booked tour only), her face covered by a bronze mask.

CHIESA DEI SCALZI   CHURCH

Map p282 (Chiesa di Santa Maria di Nazareth; ⌁041 71 51 15; www.carmeloveneto.it; Fondamenta dei Scalzi 55-57; suggested donation €1; ⊙7.30-11.50am & 4-6.50pm; ⓈFerrovia) An unexpected outburst of baroque extravagance, this Longhena-designed church (built 1654–80) has a facade by Giuseppe Sardi that ripples with columns and statues in niches. This is an unusual departure for Venice, where baroque ebullience was usually reserved for interiors of Renaissance-leaning buildings – in fact it was a deliberate echo of a style often employed in Rome, intended to help make the Discalced (meaning 'barefoot'; *scalzi* in Italian) Carmelites posted here from Rome feel more at home.

Sadly, the vault frescoes by Tiepolo in two of the side chapels are damaged and his monumental nave ceiling was destroyed by a bomb in 1915. Before the main altar on your left, you might spot the tomb of Venice's last doge, Ludovico Manin, who presided over the dissolution of the Republic in 1797 before the threat of Napoleon and died in ignominy five years later. The altar itself is framed by huge twisted columns of red marble. Also, look out for Longhena's buff statue of St Sebastian in one of the side chapels.

A small shop tucked away beside the sanctuary sells essentials oils, liquors and jams made by the friars. It's possible to arrange a visit to their walled gardens nearby.

CHIESA DI SANT'ALVISE   CHURCH
(Campo Sant'Alvise 3025; adult/reduced €3/1.50, with Chorus Pass free; ⏰10.30am-4.30pm Mon-Sat; 🚤Sant'Alvise) Don't be fooled by the bare brick exterior of this 1388 church, attached to an Augustinian convent. Inside it's a riot of colour, with extraordinary *trompe l'œil* ceiling frescoes and massive canvases all around. Look out for Tiepolo's *La salita al Calvario* (The Road to Calvary), a distressingly human depiction of one of Christ's falls under the weight of the cross.

WILMOTTE FOUNDATION   GALLERY
Map p282 (Fondaco degli Angeli; 🖳041 476 11 60; www.wilmotte.com; Corte Nuova, Fondamenta dell'Abazia 3560; ⏰10am-1.30pm & 2-6pm Tue-Sun; 🚤Madonna dell'Orto) FREE Created by architect and designer Jean-Michel Wilmotte, this foundation aims to nurture the talent of young architects via a series of annual international competitions and exhibitions. Winning work is exhibited in this out-of-the-way gallery – itself a beautifully converted shipyard – and shown alongside fascinating architectural photography from masters such as Gio Ponti and Giorgio Massari.

SCUOLA GRANDE DELLA MISERICORDIA   GALLERY
Map p282 (www.misericordiadivenezia.it; Fondamenta de la Misericordia 3599; ⏰during exhibitions only; 🚤Madonna dell'Orto) One of Venice's seven grand confraternities, the Misericordia was the seat of the wealthy silk weavers guild that commissioned this enormous classical hall. In 1532 Jacopo Sansovino was brought on board, brainstorming the

---

⊙ TOP SIGHT
CHIESA DI SANTA MARIA DEI MIRACOLI

When Nicolò di Pietro's *Madonna* icon started miraculously weeping in its outdoor shrine around 1480, crowd control became impossible. With public fundraising and using marble scavenged from San Marco slag heaps, this magnificent church was built (1481–89) to house the painting. Pietro and Tullio Lombardo's design introduced Renaissance church architecture to Venice.

The father-son team creatively repurposed marbles originally plundered from Egypt to Syria for use on the sides of the Basilica di San Marco. Note the fine scrollwork capitols and Venetian fish-scale patterns framing veined-marble panels. If you look closely at the columns on either side of the sanctuary, you'll spot angels and mermaids carved by Tullio Lombardo.

The lofty vaulted interior and domed apse seem effortless, but they're marvels of Renaissance engineering, achieved without the Gothic device of buttressing. In a prime example of Renaissance humanism, Pier Maria Pennacchi filled each of the 50 wooden coffered ceiling panels with a bright-eyed portrait of a saint or prophet dressed as a Venetian, like a class photo in a school yearbook.

TOP TIPS
➜ The original doors of the organ, depicting the *Annunciation,* were painted by Bellini's studio and are now housed in the **Gallerie dell'Accademia** (p75).

PRACTICALITIES
➜ Map p282, G4

➜ Campo dei Miracoli 6074

➜ adult/reduced €3/1.50, with Chorus Pass free

➜ ⏰10.30am-4.30pm Mon-Sat

➜ 🚤Fondamente Nove

idea of a Roman basilica within a traditional Venetian frame. No expense was spared on the interiors either, which were frescoed by Veronese, Zanchi, Pellegrini and Tintoretto. In 1914 it was taken over by the Reyer Sports Club, providing a beautiful backdrop to their basketball competitions.

I GESUITI
CHURCH

Map p282 (Santa Maria Assunta; ☑041 528 65 79; Salizada dei Specchieri 4882; €1; ☉10.30am-1pm & 3.30-5pm; ⛴Fondamente Nove) Giddily over the top even by rococo standards, this glitzy 18th-century Jesuit church is difficult to take in all at once, with staggering white-and-green intarsia (inlaid marble) walls that look like a version of Venetian flocked wallpaper, marble curtains draped over the pulpit and a marble carpet spilling down the altar stairs. While the ceiling is a riot of gold-and-white stuccowork, gravity is provided by Titian's uncharacteristically gloomy *Martyrdom of St Lawrence*, on the left as you enter the church.

The sacristy is blanketed by 21 impressive works by Jacopo Palma di Giovane.

L'ORATORIO DEI CROCIFERI
CHAPEL

Map p282 (☑041 303 92 11; www.gioiellinascostidivenezia.it; Campo dei Gesuiti 4904; adult/child €3/free; ☉10am-1pm & 2-5pm Thu-Sun; ⛴Fondamente Nove) This plain almshouse is often overlooked in favour of the extravagant Jesuit church opposite. But the 12th-century Order of the Cross that founded it to administer to pilgrims had the patronage of the doge, no less. He gave them a generous endowment, which they used to commission eight monumental canvases by Palma il Giovane, topped by a painted ceiling. Glowing red and gold, they tell the story of the Order and depict aspects of the 16th-century neighbourhood you can still see outside.

LA SPEZIERIA
ALL'ERCOLE D'ORO
HISTORIC BUILDING

Map p282 (☑041 72 06 00; Campo Santa Fosca 2234; ☉9am-12.30pm & 3-7.30pm Mon-Fri, 9am-12.45pm Sat; ⛴Ca' d'Oro) This perfectly preserved 17th-century *spezieria* (pharmacy) illustrates how Venetian medical advice was dispensed three centuries ago, with curatives in antique majolica jars lined up on hand-carved walnut shelves. The ornately panelled room is richly decorated with etchings of wise doctors hanging beneath a gilded wood-beam ceiling in the style of Sansovino. The room is now home to bespoke perfumery the Merchant of Venice, where you can buy signature fragrances in hand-blown Murano glass bottles.

CAMPO DEI MORI
PIAZZA

Map p282 (Square of the Moors; Campo dei Mori; ⛴Orto) Sior Rioba, a gent in an outsized turban, has been hanging out at the corner of Campo dei Mori since the Middle Ages. The square's name is a misnomer, as Rioba and his three buddies are believed to represent the Greek Mastelli family, 12th-century merchants from Morea. The Mastelli brothers became notorious for their eager participation in Doge Dandolo's sacking of Constantinople and, according to legend, Mary Magdalene herself turned them into stone.

✖ EATING

Cannaregio has a great range of restaurants that cater to the area's vibrant residential community. A particular highlight are the excellent *cicheti* (Venetian tapas) bars that line the sunny canal banks at the northern edge of the neighbourhood.

★ PASTICCERIA DAL MAS
BAKERY €

Map p282 (☑041 71 51 01; www.dalmaspasticceria.it; Rio Terà Lista di Spagna 150; pastries €1.30-6.50; ☉7am 9pm; ☑; ⛴Ferrovia) This historic Venetian bakery-cafe sparkles with mirrors, marble and metal trim, fitting for the pastries displayed within. Despite the perpetual morning crush, the efficient team dispenses top-notch coffee and *cornetti* (Italian-style croissants) with admirable equanimity. Come mid-morning for mouthwatering, still-warm quiches. The hot chocolate is also exceptional – hardly surprising given the sibling chocolate shop next door.

★ TRATTORIA PONTINI
TRATTORIA €

Map p282 (☑041 71 41 23; Fondamenta Cannaregio 1268; meals €20-25; ☉11.30am-10.30pm Mon-Sat; ☎; ⛴Guglie) This trattoria is a rare find in Venice: a friendly family-run restaurant serving tasty home-cooked food. As a result, there's often a queue, although you can duck inside and just order *cicheti* at the bar. Otherwise, hold out for excellent seafood antipasto, fluffy heaps of *baccalà* (cod) and polenta, and generous bowls of spaghetti *alla busara* (with crayfish in tomatoes and white wine).

GELATERIA CA' D'ORO
GELATO €

Map p282 (☑041 522 89 82; Strada Nova 4273b; scoops €1.80; ☺10.30am-10pm; ⛴Ca' d'Oro) Foot traffic stops here for spectacularly creamy gelato made in-house daily. For a summer pick-me-up, try the *granita di caffè con panna* (coffee shaved ice with whipped cream).

SULLALUNA
BISTRO €

Map p282 (☑041 72 29 24; Fondamenta de la Misericordia 2535; meals €15-25; ☺8am-11pm Tue-Sat, from 9am Sun; ☏♿; ⛴Madonna dell'Orto) 🍃 Flowers on the windowsill are just one of the thoughtful touches that characterise this bistro and bookshop lined with gorgeous graphic novels, children's books and cookbooks. The inviting space is full of sunshine; tables are adorned with flowers; and the bar serves the owner's organic prosecco alongside herbal teas and coffee. Food has a vegetarian focus and includes salads and mezze plates.

CANTINA AZIENDE AGRICOLE
VENETIAN €

Map p282 (☑333 3458811; www.cantinaaziende agricole.com; Rio Terà Farsetti 1847a; meals €12, cicheti €1.50-1.80; ☺9am-2pm & 5-10pm; ⛴San Marcuola) This friendly hole-in-the-wall *bacaro* (bar) serves an impressive array of local wine to a loyal group of customers who treat the place much like a social club. Join them for a glass of Raboso and heaped platters of *lardo* (cured pork fat), cheese drizzled with honey, *polpette* (meatballs) and deep-fried pumpkin fritters.

PANIFICIO VOLPE GIOVANNI
BAKERY €

Map p282 (☑041 71 51 78; www.facebook.com/PanificioVolpeGiovanni; Calle del Ghetto Vecchio 1143; pastries €1.50-3; ☺7am-7.30pm Mon-Sat, 8.30am-1pm Sun; ⛴Guglie) In addition to unleavened pumpkin and radicchio bread, this kosher bakery sells unusual treats such as crumbly *impade* (biscuity logs flavoured with ground almonds) and *orecchiette di Amman* ('little ears of Amman'; ear-shaped pastries stuffed with chocolate), along with quite possibly the best *cornetti* in Venice.

★ANICE STELLATO
VENETIAN €€

Map p282 (☑041 72 07 44; www.osterianicestel lato.com; Fondamenta de la Sensa 3272; meals €40-50; ☺12.15-2pm & 7.15-10pm Tue-Sat; ⛴Sant'Alvise) Tin lamps, unadorned rustic tables and a small wooden bar set the scene for quality seafood and other Venetian specialities at this excellent canalside *bacaro*.

You can munch on *cicheti* or go for the full menu and swoon over mantis shrimps with pomegranate puree; market-fresh fish; or guinea fowl, radicchio and a decadent port sauce. Reservations recommended.

AI PROMESSI SPOSI
VENETIAN €€

Map p282 (☑041 241 27 47; Calle d'Oca 4367; meals €30-40; ☺noon-2.15pm & 6.30-10.15pm Tue-Sun, 6.30-10.15pm Mon; ⛴Ca' d'Oro) Bantering Venetians thronging the bar are the only permanent fixtures at this neighbourhood *osteria* (casual tavern), where ever-changing menus feature fresh Venetian seafood and Veneto meats at excellent prices. Seasonal standouts include *seppie in umido* (cuttlefish in rich tomato sauce) and house-made pasta, but pace yourself for cloud-like tiramisu and excellent semifreddo.

TRATTORIA DA BEPI GIÀ '54'
VENETIAN €€

Map p282 (☑041 528 50 31; www.dabepi.it; Campo SS Apostoli 4550; meals €25-35; ☺noon-3pm & 7-10pm Fri-Wed; ⛴Ca' d'Oro) Much better than it looks, Da Bepi is a traditional trattoria in the very best sense. The interior is a warm, wood-panelled cocoon, and service is efficient and friendly. Take their advice on the classic Venetian menu and order sweet, steamed spider crab, briny razor clams, grilled turbot with artichokes and, for once, a tiramisu that doesn't disappoint.

ALLE DUE GONDOLETTE
VENETIAN €€

Map p282 (☑041 71 75 23; www.alleduegon dolette.com; Fondamente de le Capuzine 3016; meals €25-35; ☺12.15-2.30pm & 7-10pm Mon-Sat; ⛴Tre Archi) On Fridays it's worth walking the extra mile to this working-class diner for its generous servings of *baccalà* (cod), either creamed with olive oil, lemon and parsley or *alla Vicentina* (braised with onions, anchovies and milk). Other classics on the menu include pasta with octopus, peas and mint, and gnocchi with chicken and *pecorino*.

OSTERIA ALLA VEDOVA
VENETIAN €€

Map p282 (☑041 528 53 24; Calle del Pistor 3912; meals €28-30; ☺11.30am-2.30pm & 6.30-10.30pm Mon-Wed, Fri & Sat, 6.30-10.30pm Sun; ⛴Ca' d'Oro) Culinary convictions run deep here at one of Venice's oldest *osterie* (1891), so you won't find *spritz* or coffee on the menu, or pay more than €2 to snack on one of the signature meatballs. Enjoy superior seasonal *cicheti* with a local crowd at the bar, or call ahead for table service and strictly authentic Venetian dishes.

★ OSTERIA BOCCADORO
VENETIAN €€€

Map p282 (☑041 521 10 21; www.boccadorovenezia.it; Campiello Widmann 5405a; meals €40-55; ☺noon-3pm & 7-11pm Tue-Sun; ☑Fondamente Nove) The sweetly singing birds in this *campo* (square) are probably angling for your leftovers, but they don't stand a chance. Chef-owner Luciano and son Simone's creative *crudi* (raw seafood) are two-bite delights, and cloud-like gnocchi and homemade pasta are gone too soon. Fish is sourced from the lagoon or the Adriatic, and vegetables come from the restaurant's kitchen garden.

OSTERIA DA RIOBA
VENETIAN €€€

Map p282 (☑041 524 43 79; www.darioba.com; Fondamenta de la Misericordia 2553; meals €46-49; ☺12.30-2.30pm & 7.30-10.30pm Tue-Sun; ☑Orto) Taking the lead with fresh seafood and herbs pulled from the family's Sant'Erasmo farm, Da Rioba's inventive kitchen turns out plates as colourful and creative as the artwork on the walls. This is prime date-night territory. In winter cosy up in the wood-beamed interior; in summer sit canalside. Reservations recommended.

MIRAI
JAPANESE €€€

Map p282 (Hotel Principe; ☑041 220 65 17; www.miraivenice.com; Rio Terà Lista di Spagna 146; meals €40-50; ☺7-11pm Tue-Sun; ❂❀; ☑Ferrovia) Despite its historic role as a gateway to the East, Venice has surprisingly few good Asian restaurants. An exception is elegant Mirai, the first Japanese restaurant to open in the city, and still the best. A classic selection of sushi, sashimi, tempura and shisoten is presented on perfectly springy japonica rice. In summer, there's a terrace overlooking the Grand Canal.

TIMON ALL'ANTICA MOLA
VENETIAN €€€

Map p282 (☑041 71 74 92; www.altimon.it; Fondamenta dei Ormesini 2800; meals €50; ☺6pm-12.30am Tue-Sun; ☑San Marcuola) After the success of its first restaurant, specialising in meats, Timon has branched into fish. Stand at the bar for a glass of wine and a selection of *cicheti* or take a seat and tuck into one of the inventive dishes from the menu, such as gnocchi with black cauliflower and squid or grilled eel and creamy beets.

VINI DA GIGIO
VENETIAN €€€

Map p282 (☑041 528 51 40; www.vinidagigio.com; Fondamenta San Felice 3268a; meals €45-50; ☺noon-2.30pm & 7-10.30pm Wed-Sun; ☑Ca' d'Oro) At this characterful canalside *osteria* diners sit deep in conversation at linen-draped tables beneath centuries-old beams. Savour scallops on the half-shell drizzled with a wine reduction, or cuttlefish served with creamy polenta. For wine pairings, ask your host for a recommendation from the hundreds of limited-production labels featured on the wine list.

OSTERIA L'ORTO DEI MORI
ITALIAN €€€

Map p282 (☑041 524 36 77; www.osteriaortodeimori.com; Campo dei Mori 3386; meals €45-50; ☺12.30-3pm & 7-11pm Wed-Mon; ☑Orto) Not since Tintoretto lived next door has this neighbourhood seen so much action, thanks to this bustling *osteria*. Sicilian chef Lorenzo makes fresh pasta daily, including squid atop *tagliolini*. Fish-shaped lamps set a playful mood in an upmarket space.

🍷 DRINKING & 🍸 NIGHTLIFE

The strip lining the canal north of the Ghetto is a wonderful stretch for bar-hopping, taking in swanky wine and *cicheti* places, beer bars and grungy student-populated spots. The scene is lively rather than raucous, and there are a few decent live-music venues scattered about.

★ VINO VERO
WINE BAR

Map p282 (☑041 275 00 44; www.facebook.com/vinoverovenezia; Fondamenta de la Misericordia 2497; ☺noon-midnight Tue-Sun, from 5pm Mon; ☑San Marcuola) Lining the exposed-brick walls of this canalside bar are small-production wines, including a great selection of natural and biodynamic labels. The *cicheti* here lift this place above the ordinary, with arguably the best selection of *crostini* (open-face sandwiches) in the city, including wild-boar sausage with aubergine, gorgonzola drizzled with honey or baba ganoush topped with prosciutto.

★ AL TIMON
WINE BAR

Map p282 (☑041 524 60 66; www.altimon.it; Fondamenta dei Ormesini 2754; ☺5pm-1am; ☑San Marcuola) Find a spot in the wood-lined

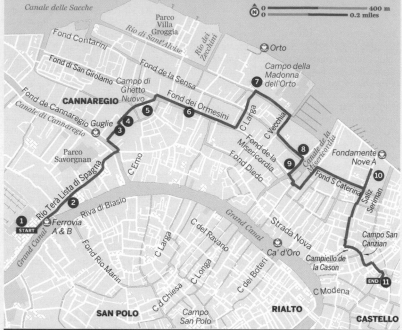

🏃 Neighbourhood Walk
Backstreet Amble

START STAZIONE DI SANTA LUCIA
END CAMPO SANTO MARIA NOVA
LENGTH 3KM; THREE HOURS

Named after the convent that was demolished to make way for it in 1861, **❶ Stazione di Santa Lucia** (p245) is one of the few modernist structures on the Grand Canal. Speed-walk down Rio Terà Lista di Spagna, grabbing a tasty pastry from **❷ Pasticceria Dal Mas** (p113) en route, and cross the 22m-wide Canale di Cannaregio. Turn left and take the third right into the Ghetto Vecchio. Here the crowds vanish and you can relax. Meander up the alley past the grand **❸ Schola Spagnola** (p110) and **❹ Schola Levantina** (p110) synagogues. Notice, too, the *Stolpersteine* commemorating Moisè Calimani in front of door 1146. Continue on to **❺ Campo del Ghetto Nuovo**, where Jewish life thrives. Exit north across the canal and turn right down **❻ Fondamenta dei Ormesini**, where you can browse the windows of art studios

and enjoy a *spritz* in the sun. Turn left up Calle Larga, crossing two canals to reach **❼ Chiesa della Madonna dell'Orto** (p111). Then turn south down Corte Vecchia and left to continue to **❽ Chiesetta della Misericordia**, a 10th-century church with a Renaissance facade from 1659; it's now an exhibition space for the Biennale. It faces the **❾ Scuola Grande della Misericordia** (p112), one of the largest buildings in Venice, once owned by the silk-weavers guild. During temporary exhibitions you can visit its frescoed halls. Move on, east, over the Canale de la Misericordia, left up Calle de la Rachetta and right along Fondamenta Santa Caterina. Emerge in front of the epic **❿ I Gesuiti** (p113), which has a towering angel-clad facade. It's then a straight shot south down Salizada Seriman to Campiello de la Cason, a quick left, over Rio dei Santi through Campo San Canzian, to arrive at Campo Santa Maria Nova with its photogenic view of the **⓫ Chiesa di Santa Maria dei Miracoli** (p112).

interior or, in summer, on the boat moored out the front along the canal, and watch the motley parade of drinkers and dreamers arrive for steak platters and quality wines by the *ombra* (half-glass) or carafe. Musicians play sets canalside when the weather obliges.

★MARCIANO PUB   PUB

Map p282 (☑041 47 62 55; www.facebook.com/marcianopubvenezia; Calle Gheltof o Loredan 1863c; ☺5pm-1am Fri-Wed; ⊠San Marcuola) With its wooden bar and gleaming brass beer taps, this Anglo-Venetian hostelry certainly looks authentic. Marciano takes booze seriously, stocking craft beers from around the globe, including its own brew and samphire-infused gin. The same goes for the food menu of sustainably sourced burgers (€12 to €16) and steaks, including kangaroo and ostrich. There's also an oyster bar and dedicated cocktail area.

★BIRRERIA ZANON   BAR

Map p282 (☑041 476 23 47; Fondamenta dei Ormesini 2735; ☺9am-10pm; ⊠Guglie) There's something of a mini beer craze developing along Fondamenta dei Ormesini, and Birreria Zanon is the latest contender, wooing customers with its sunny setting, laid-back vibe and huge craft-beer selection. Particularly tasty are the *tramezzini* (triangular, stacked sandwiches) on black bread, which go down a treat with a pint of Grimbergen amber ale.

UN MONDO DI VINO   BAR

Map p282 (☑041 521 10 93; www.unmondodivinovenezia.com; Salizada San Canzian 5984a; ☺10am-midnight; ⊠Rialto) Get here early for first crack at marinated artichokes and *sarde in saor* (sardines in sweet and sour sauce), and to claim a few square inches of ledge for your plate and wine glass. There are dozens of wines offered by the glass, so take a chance on a unusual blend or obscure varietal.

TORREFAZIONE CANNAREGIO   CAFE

Map p282 (☑041 71 63 71; www.torrefazionecannaregio.it; Fondamenta dei Ormesini 2804; ☺7am-7.30pm Mon-Sat, 9am-6pm Sun; ⊠Guglie) The only micro-roastery in Venice, this brick-lined cafe perched on a sunny canal bank is filled with house-made roasts including the flagship Remer, an Arabica blend with a smooth, chocolate aftertaste. For those who like more punch there are

Robusta blends, plus some delightful speciality teas. The Marchi family has been roasting since the 1930s; service is knowledgeable and friendly.

HOSTARIA BACANERA   BAR

Map p282 (☑041 260 11 46; Campiello de la Cason 4506; ☺11.30am-3pm & 6-10.30pm Tue-Sun; ☎; ⊠Ca' d'Oro) Hidden behind the SS Apostoli church, this bar-cum-restaurant has a contemporary baroque style with wood beamed ceilings, a signature red banquette, and black bistro chairs set around widely spaced tables. Enjoy *cicheti* (Venetian tapas) and fried snacks from the bar or dine on fragrant plates of fish tortellini, seafood risotto, and tagliatelle with duck *ragù* (meat and tomato sauce). Live bands play on Tuesdays.

OSTERIA AL CICHETO   WINE BAR

Map p282 (☑041 71 60 37; www.osteria-al-cicheto.it; Calle de la Misericordia 367a; ☺11am-3pm & 5.30-10.30pm Mon-Fri, 5.30-10.30pm Sat; ⊠Ferrovia) This wine bar boasts a small but impressive restaurant, but the focus is on wine. It hosts regular wine-tasting evenings, as well as food nights focusing on a single ingredient (pumpkin, for example). No matter when you go, there are always interesting *cicheti* and a fine assortment of wines by the glass.

A LA VECIA PAPUSSA   BAR

Map p282 (☑041 525 60 30; www.alaveciapapussa.it; Fondamenta de la Misericordia 2612; ☺10am-1am; ⊠Orto) This laid-back bar is all bare brick and low lighting; it's one of a handful that remain open until the early hours. Enjoy a selection of drinks, snacks and simple meals at an outdoor table on the lively *fondamente* (canal banks), or rub shoulders with locals in the narrow bar where there are pretty multicoloured wooden chairs and plentiful tables.

OSTERIA AI TRONCHI   BAR

Map p282 (☑041 528 27 27; www.facebook.com/Osteria-Ai-Tronchi; Calle del Spezier 4792; ☺7.30am-11pm Mon-Sat; ⊠Fondamenta Nove) This inviting hole-in-the-wall much frequented by locals has a good selection of wines by the glass (€3 to €4), though a humble *ombra* (small glass of house wine) costs just €1. Bar snacks and sandwiches (€2) are also available. It's just steps from Campo dei Gesuiti.

IRISH PUB
PUB

Map p282 (☎041 099 01 96; www.theirishpub venezia.com; Corte dei Pali Già Testori 3847; ⏰10am-1am; ☎; 🚊Ca' d'Oro) If sedate wine bars aren't really your bag, this reassuringly pub-like place has battered furniture, sports on the TV, tables on the square, Guinness on tap and another 10 European beers to choose from.

EL SBARLEFO
BAR

Map p282 (☎041 523 30 84; www.elsbarlefo.it; Salizada del Pistor 4556c; ⏰10am-11pm; ☎; 🚊Ca' d'Oro) All sorts sidle into this attractive little *cicheti* bar, from local hipsters to candidates for hip replacements, drawn by an excellent wine selection and a tasty array of snacks. The music meanders unpredictably from mellow jazz to early Elvis, but never at volumes that interrupt a decent chat.

BAGATELA
BAR

Map p282 (☎328 7255782; www.bagatelavenezia. com; Fondamente de le Capuzine 2925; ⏰6pm-1am Wed-Sun; 🚊Guglie) Unpretentious and popular, Bagatella is crammed with Cannaregio locals, indie rockers and students. It offers bottled beers, cocktails, board games, sports on the TV and a rather disconcerting skull behind the bar. Pace your alcoholic intake with one of its legendary burgers made with premium Scottona beef.

AL PARLAMENTO
BAR

Map p282 (☎041 244 02 14; www.facebook. com/alParlamento; Fondamenta Savorgnan 511; ⏰7.30am-2am; ☎; 🚊Crea) Entire university careers and international romances are owed to Al Parlamento's powerful espresso, happy-hour cocktails (6pm to 9pm) and excellent overstuffed *tramezzini*. Draped ship ropes accentuate canal views from the large windows at the front. Drop by in the evening and you might catch a live band or DJ set.

LA CANTINA
WINE BAR

Map p282 (☎041 522 82 58; Campo San Felice 3689; ⏰11am-11pm; 🚊Ca' d'Oro) While you can sit down out the back for a serious seafood feast, we prefer to sample the wine and *cicheti* selection while propped up at the bar or on the square at one of the tables fashioned from old wine barrels.

IL SANTO BEVITORE
PUB

Map p282 (☎335 8415771; www.ilsantobevi torepub.com; Calle Zancani 2393a; ⏰4pm-2am;

☎; 🚊Ca' d'Oro) San Marco has its glittering cathedral, but beer lovers prefer pilgrimages to this shrine of the 'Holy Drinker' for 20 brews on tap, including Trappist ales and seasonal stouts. There's also a big range of speciality gin, whisky and vodka. The faithful receive canalside seating, footy matches on TV, free wi-fi and the occasional live band.

☆ ENTERTAINMENT

PARADISO PERDUTO
LIVE MUSIC

Map p282 (☎041 72 05 81; Fondamenta de la Misericordia 2540; ⏰11am-1am Thu-Mon; 🚊Orto) 'Paradise Lost' is a find for anyone craving a cold beer canalside on a hot summer's night. Although the restaurant is also popular, the Paradiso is particularly noted for its Monday-night gigs; Chet Baker, Keith Richards and Vinicio Capossela have all played the small stage.

TEATRO MALIBRAN
THEATRE

Map p282 (☎box office 041 24 24; www.tea trolafenice.it; Calle del Teatro 5873; 🚊Rialto) This pretty 17th-century theatre was built over the ruins of Marco Polo's *palazzo* (mansion). It now shares a classical music, opera and ballet program with La Fenice (p63), as well as hosting an intimate chamber-music season.

CASINÒ DI VENEZIA
CASINO

Map p282 (Ca' Vendramin Calergi; ☎041 529 71 11; www.casinovenezia.it; Calle Vendramin 2040; admission incl gaming token €10; ⏰11am-2.45am Sun-Fri, to 3.15am on Sat; 🚊San Marcuola) Founded in 1638, the world's oldest casino moved into its current palatial home in the 1950s. Slots open at 11am; arrive after 3.30pm wearing your jacket and poker face for gaming tables. Arrive in style with a free water-taxi ride from Piazzale Roma. You must be at least 18 to enter the casino.

The building certainly wasn't lucky for composer Richard Wagner, who died here in 1883; the **Museo Wagner** (☎041 276 04 07; www.casinovenezia.it/en/wagner-museum; Casinò di Venezia 2040; ⏰by appointment) FREE now occupies his suite.

CIRCUITO CINEMA
GIORGIONE MOVIE D'ESSAI
CINEMA

Map p282 (☎041 524 13 20; Rio Terà di Franceschi 4612; ⏰Wed-Mon; 🚊Fondamente Nove)

STUMBLING STONES

Some of the most moving monuments in the Ghetto are so small they are easily missed: *Stolpersteine* (or 'stumbling stones'; www.stolpersteine.eu) are concrete cubes, encased in brass, set in the paving stones outside Jewish homes from which people were taken and deported to Nazi death camps. The 'stones' (*pietra d'inciampo,* in Italian) are inscribed with the names of the inhabitants of each house, and the dates of their birth, deportation and death. Once you become aware of the stones, they will literally stop you in your tracks. Set before homely doorsteps, they are a potent reminder of how normal lives were so cruelly cut short and a community decimated.

The project was started in 1992 by German artist Gunter Demnig, who handmakes each stone. As of October 2018, there were 70,000 *Stolpersteine* in 1200 towns and cities across Europe commemorating victims (Jewish and non-Jewish) of the Holocaust. Venice currently counts 78. Most of them are in and around the Ghetto, but you can spot them all over the city, including on the Lido.

Screenings of international film-festival winners, recently restored classics and family-friendly animations share top billing at this small cinema. There are two screens (one is tiny), showing two or three evening screenings, plus matinees on Sundays.

🛍 SHOPPING

Main thoroughfare Strada Nova is lined with a variety of popular brand and tourist shops, including what might just be the most beautiful supermarket in the world within the former Teatro Italia. Artisanal boutiques and workshops are located in the backstreets and scattered along the outer canal banks.

⭐**CODEX VENEZIA** ART

Map p282 (🔊041 524 61 82; www.codexvenezia.it; Fondamenta degli Ormesini 2799; ☺9.30am-12.30pm & 4-7.30pm Mon-Fri, 9.30am-12.30pm Sat; ⛴San Marcuola) Nelson Kishi's studio contains wonderful prints and original works, mainly in ink on paper, many of them depicting Venetian scenes. Kishi's delicate and intricate cityscapes capture the beauty and bustle of Venice, all packed into this tiny art space.

⭐**VITTORIO COSTANTINI** GLASS

Map p282 (🔊041 522 22 65; www.vittoriocostantini.com; Calle del Fumo 5311; ☺9.30am-1pm & 2.15-5.30pm Mon-Fri; ⛴Fondamente Nove) Kids and adults alike are thrilled at the magical, miniature insects, butterflies, shells and birds that Vittorio Costantini fashions out of glass using a lampwork technique. Some

of the iridescent beetles have bodies made of 21 segments that need to be fused together with dazzling dexterity and speed.

⭐**LA STAMPERIA DEL GHETTO** ARTS & CRAFTS

Map p282 (🔊041 275 02 00; Calle del Ghetto Vecchio 1185a; ☺10am-4pm Sun-Fri; ⛴Guglie) Keep your eyes peeled for Enzo Aboaf's wonderful Ghetto gallery filled with rare original copperplate prints and etchings of the Ghetto and Venice. In among them is a stash of Emanuele 'Lele' Luzzati's highly collectible Chagall-style illustrations. Luzzati was a Genoese Jew who made his name as a theatre designer, but also undertook commissions for posters, books and ceramics.

⭐**FEELIN' VENICE** DESIGN

Map p282 (🔊041 887 86 39; www.feelinvenice.com; Strada Nova 4194; ☺9.30am-8pm; ⛴Ca' d'Oro) Tired of bemoaning the increasing number of tatty souvenir shops, Venetians Mattia and Filippo decided to open a design-led alternative featuring the work of local graphic artists. Their cool, contemporary designs adorn high-quality fabric totes, 100% organic cotton T-shirts, posters, notebooks and graphite pens. If you're looking for a memorable souvenir, this is the place.

GIANNI BASSO STATIONERY

Map p282 (🔊041 523 46 81; Calle del Fumo 5306; ☺9am-1pm & 2-6pm Mon-Fri, 9am-noon Sat; ⛴Fondamente Nove) Gianni Basso doesn't advertise his letterpressing services: the calling cards crowding his workshop window do the trick. From Microsoft COO's to celebrities and royalty, movers and shakers from around the world get their business cards, invitations and stationery printed here. Trained at the Armenian Monastery, Gianni is as much a piece of Venetian history as his miniature print museum next door.

NICOLAO ATELIER
CLOTHING

Map p282 (☑041 520 70 51; www.nicolao.com; Fondamenta de la Misericordia 2590; ⊙9.30am-1pm & 2-6pm Mon-Fri; 🚤San Marcuola) If you're wondering where Cinderella goes to find the perfect ball gown or Prince Charming his tights, look no further than this fairytale wonderland. An exquisite handmade Carnevale outfit will set you back €250 to €300 – and that's just to hire. Out of season the store does brisk business catering to theatres, opera houses and films worldwide.

BALDUCCI BORSE
SHOES

Map p282 (☑041 524 62 33; www.balducciborse.com; Rio Terà San Leonardo 1593; ⊙9.30am-1pm & 2.30-7.30pm; 🚤San Marcuola) Venice isn't known for its leatherwork, but there's always an exception to the rule – and Franco Balducci is it. Step through the door of his Cannaregio workshop and you can smell the quality of the hand-picked Tuscan hides that he fashions on the premises into glossy shoulder bags and women's boots.

ANTICHITÀ AL GHETTO
ANTIQUES

Map p282 (☑041 524 45 92; www.antichitaalghetto.com; Calle del Ghetto Vecchio 1133/4; ⊙10am-7pm; 🚤Guglie) Instead of a souvenir T-shirt, how about taking home a memento of Venetian history: an ancient map of the canal, an etching of Venetian dandies daintily alighting from gondolas or an 18th-century cameo once worn by the most fashionable ladies in the Ghetto.

CA' MACANA ATELIER
ARTS & CRAFTS

Map p282 (☑041 71 86 55; www.camacanaatelier.blogspot.it; Rio Terà San Leonardo 1374; ⊙9am-8pm; 🚤San Marcuola) Resist buying inferior mass-produced Carnevale masks until you've checked out the traditionally made papier-mâché and leather masks at this long-established shop and workshop. The steampunk range is exactly as creepy as you'd hope.

🏃 ACTIVITIES

★PLUM PLUM CREATIONS
ARTS & CRAFTS

Map p282 (☑041 476 54 04; www.plumplumcreations.com; Fondamenta dei Ormesini 2681; ⊙11am-7pm Mon, Wed, Fri & Sat, to 6pm Tue & Thu; 🚤San Marcuola) In the 15th century Venice was such a pioneer of quality printmaking that there were strict penalties for printers who used low-quality paper. Arianna Sautariello preserves this centuries-old tradition in her characterful canalside studio, where you'll find handmade etchings, linocuts, dry points and delicate watercolours. Passionate about the craft, she also offers excellent short courses (€70/120 for four/eight hours).

PAINTING VENICE
ARTS & CRAFTS

(☑340 5445227; www.paintingvenice.com; 2hr private lessons €100, 2-/4-day workshops €280/450) Sign up for a session with professionally trained and practising artists Caroline, Sebastien and Katrin, and strike out into tranquil *campi* (squares) in the tradition of classic *vedutisti* (outdoor artists). Beginners learn the basic concepts, while those with more advanced skills receive tailor-made tuition. A great way to slow down and appreciate the artfulness of each Venetian view.

FALLANI VENEZIA
ARTS & CRAFTS

Map p282 (☑041 523 57 72; www.fallanivenezia.com; Salizada Seriman 4875; courses 1hr €40, 4hr €100-150, 8hr €200-300; 🚤Fondamente Nove) Fiorenzo Fallani's laboratory has been credited with transforming screenprinting from a medium of reproduction to an innovative and creative artistic technique. Courses lead you from printing your own T-shirt to more complex processes using different colours, acetates and frames. Even if you don't fancy taking a course, this is a great place to purchase original art prints of Venice.

BOTTEGA DEL TINTORETTO
ARTS & CRAFTS

Map p282 (☑041 72 20 81; www.tintorettovenezia.it; Fondamenta dei Mori 3400; 5-day courses incl lunch & materials €430; 🚤Orto) During the 1500s Tintoretto operated a printmaking lab on the ground floor of his Cannaregio home. Revived and restored in 1985, the *bottega* once again offers artists a laboratory in which they can practise on historic printing presses, and runs a series of courses in printmaking, bookbinding, watercolours, fresco and sculpture.

Castello

Neighbourhood Top Five

① **Riva degli Schiavoni** (p127) Taking an early-morning or evening stroll along Castello's picturesque waterfront promenade.

② **Zanipolo** (p125) Gawking at the sheer scale of this 14th-century church and admiring the masterworks of painting and sculpture contained within.

③ **Palazzo Grimani** (p127) Viewing classical statuary in this theatrical *palazzo*, which was designed as a stage set around them.

④ **La Biennale di Venezia** (p41) Pondering modern art and ground-breaking architecture in the awesome setting of the Arsenale.

⑤ **Scuola Dalmata di San Giorgio degli Schiavoni** (p130) Basking in the golden glow of Carpaccio's paintings in the club rooms of the city's historic Dalmatian community.

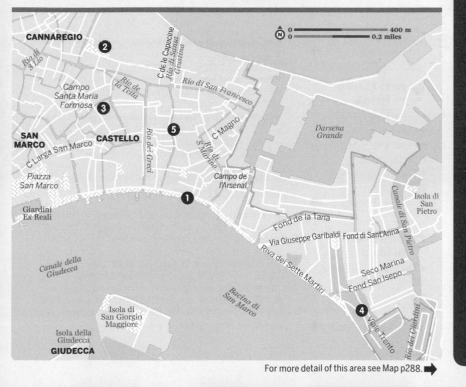

For more detail of this area see Map p288. ➡

Lonely Planet's Top Tip

Venice is always best early in the morning or after the crowds thin in the evening. This is especially true of the **Riva degli Schiavoni** (p127), which is packed from 11am to 7pm with day trippers as cruises disgorge their madding crowds. But if you can get yourself out of bed early enough, the seafront promenade is a magnificent and remarkably solitary spot for a morning constitutional. At the other end of the day, it is a spectacular sundowner spot.

Best Places to Eat

➜ Salvmeria (p131)
➜ CoVino (p132)
➜ Il Ridotto (p133)
➜ Trattoria Corte Sconta (p133)
➜ Osteria da Pampo (p132)

For reviews, see p131.➡

Best Places to Drink

➜ Londra Bar (p134)
➜ El Rèfolo (p134)
➜ Osteria Al Portego (p134)
➜ Strani (p134)
➜ Bar Terrazza Danieli (p134)

For reviews, see p134.➡

Best Places to Shop

➜ Atelier Alessandro Merlin (p136)
➜ Bragorà (p136)
➜ Ballarin (p136)

For reviews, see p136.➡

Explore Castello

Stretching eastwards from San Marco, Castello is the city's most sprawling neighbourhood – exploring its entirety in one blast will test your walking shoes. Start with its most compelling sites – the masterfully grand Zanipolo church (p125), the recently inaugurated Ocean Space (p128) gallery, high-brow Querini Stampalia (p127), frescoed Palazzo Grimani (p127), and blockbuster Bellini artworks in Chiesa di San Francesco della Vigna (p129) and Chiesa di San Zaccaria (p129).

From this impressive start, sights become more modest, reflecting your move into the working-class neighbourhoods around the historic Arsenale (p123) shipyards. While most of this complex is only open for special events, the boats displayed in the Padiglione delle Navi (p124) give a taste of the city's impressive maritime history. Around here, along Via Garibaldi, you're most likely to hear the Venetian dialect, and it's a great place for an *aperitivo* (pre-dinner drink).

Venice's glitzy waterfront promenade, the Riva degli Schiavoni (p127), skirts the entire southern shore of the neighbourhood. It terminates in the pavilion-dotted Giardini Pubblici (p126), which springs to life during the Biennale. Venice's first cathedral (p131) sits just north of the gardens on the island of San Pietro del Castello. Wrap up your exploration by returning at sunset along the Riva dei Partigiani for sweeping views of San Giorgio Maggiore and the Bacino di San Marco.

Local Life

➜**Backstreet bars** Locals drop in all day for *cicheti* (Venetian tapas) at Ossi di Seppia (p132), Salvmeria (p131) and Strani (p134).

➜**Outdoor living** *Nonne* (grandmothers) gather for an afternoon chat while their young charges kick balls across Campo Bandiera e Moro, the Giardini Pubblici (p126) and Parco delle Rimembranze (p126).

Getting There & Away

➜**Vaporetto** Castello is encircled with *vaporetto* stops, with San Zaccaria, Arsenale, Giardini (and its sister stop Giardini Biennale) and Sant'Elena to the south; San Pietro to the east; and Bacini, Celestia and Ospedale to the north. Lines 4.1 and 4.2 stop at all of these; lines 5.1 and 5.2 stop at all but Arsenale. Line 1 links all the southern stops to the Grand Canal and the Lido. The busiest stop is San Zaccaria (also called San Marco San Zaccaria), where multiple jetties spread along the Riva degli Schiavoni.

TOP SIGHT
ARSENALE

SADIK YALCIN/SHUTTERSTOCK ©

For most of the year the public can only gaze and wonder at the grand portal and impassive walls surrounding this historic shipyard and still-functioning naval complex. However, the role the Arsenale has played in Venetian history cannot be underestimated. Founded in 1104, it quickly grew to become Europe's greatest naval installation and the largest productive complex in the world.

An Industrial Revolution

At its 15th- to 17th-century peak, the Arsenale must have made an enormous impression: a ceaseless hive of noise and productivity involving metalworking, timber cutting, rope twisting and lots of boiling black pitch. Indeed, Dante used it as a model for hell in his *Divine Comedy*. Many streets in Castello are still named after its activities: Pece (pitch), Piombo (lead), Ancore (anchors) and Vele (sails).

To sustain it, the city employed a workforce of up to 16,000 highly skilled artisans, and it sat at the very heart of Venice's mercantile and military power, costing the city 10% of its annual income. A unique pre-industrial example of mass production, its centralised organisation, standardised processes and stringent quality control all anticipate the modern factory. Not only was the Arsenale capable of turning out a new galley in a single day, its 45-hectare physical footprint occupied 15% of the city. Even today, it is completely surrounded by 3.2km of crenellated walls.

Perhaps the most revolutionary aspect of the Arsenale was that it used canals as moving assembly lines. The evolving ship would move through the canals from one stage of construction to the next – a system that was not reproduced

BUCINTORO

Seven centuries before *Pimp My Ride,* there was the *bucintoro.* The most lavish creation of the Arsenale, it was the doge's ceremonial galley. The most extravagant version was completed in 1727, and was entirely covered in gold leaf. It had seating for 90 people and required 168 oarsmen to manoeuvre. There's a scale model in the Museo Storico Navale (p131), as well as a few original details salvaged after Napoleonic troops burned it in 1798.

CHANGING SHAPES

At the core of the complex is the Arsenale Vecchio (Old Arsenal), which included storage for the *bucintoro.* Expansion in 1303–04 added La Tana to the Arsenale's southern flank. Used for rope-making, it was refashioned in 1579 by Antonio da Ponte (of Rialto Bridge fame). The Arsenale Nuovo (New Arsenal) was added in 1325, followed in 1473 by the Arsenale Nuovissimo (Very New Arsenal). In the 16th century, production of *galeazze* (large war vessels) required the creation of the deeper Canale delle Galeazze and the Gaggiandre (dry dock).

on such a scale until Henry Ford's car factory in the 20th century. As a result of this innovation, as many as 100 galleys could be in production at once. In addition, consultants such as Galileo helped the Venetians rationalise production and build ships that could be equipped with increasingly powerful munitions.

Porta Magna

Capped by a lion of St Mark that somehow eluded destruction by Napoleon's troops, the Arsenale's ornate landward gate is considered by many to be the earliest example of Renaissance architecture in Venice; it was probably built in 1460. A plaque on the wall celebrates the 1571 victory at Lepanto, and the fenced-in terrace was added in 1692. Below the statues is a row of carved lions; the biggest one, regally seated, was taken as booty by Francesco Morosini from Greece, which must have taken some doing. On the lion's left flank are some very faint Viking runes left behind by Norwegian mercenaries. They boast of their role in helping Byzantium quell a Greek rebellion – the mercenary equivalent of leaving behind a résumé.

Ships Pavilion

An annexe of the Museo Storico Navale, the **Padiglione delle Navi** (Ships Pavilion; ☎041 24 24; www.visit muve.it; Fondamenta de la Madonna 2162c; adult/reduced €10/7.50, incl Museo Storico Navale; ⏰11am-6pm summer, to 5pm winter) is open to the public year-round. This vast 2000-sq-metre warehouse contains a fabulous collection of historic boats, including typical Venetian luggers, gondolas, racing boats, military vessels, a funerary barge and a royal motorboat. The most eye-catching is the *Scalé Reale,* an early-19th-century ceremonial vessel used to ferry King Vittorio Emanuele to Piazza San Marco in 1866 when Venice joined the nascent Kingdom of Italy. It was last used in 1959, when it brought the body of the Venetian pope Pius X to rest at Basilica San Marco.

Exhibition Spaces

Biennale architecture and art exhibitions, as well as special events such as the **Arte Laguna Prize** (www. artelagunaprize.com; Nappe Arsenale Nord; ⏰10am-6pm Mar-Apr), are mounted in the **construction sheds** (Map p290; ⛴Bacini) of the Arsenale. Shows offer a peek inside the former **Corderia** (where ships' cables were made), the **Artiglierie** (gun workshop) and the magnificent arcaded **Gaggiandre** (dry dock), which was fashioned from designs attributed to Jacopo Sansovino. Access to the public areas (as opposed to the military zone, which still operates within the complex) is from the north via the Celestia or Bacini *vaporetto* stops.

TOP SIGHT
ZANIPOLO

Officially the Basilica dei SS Giovanni e Paolo, this huge Dominican church is often called the Venetian Pantheon. It was named after two soldier-martyrs of early Christian Rome, Giovanni and Paolo – elided to Zanipolo in Venetian dialect. After its completion in the 1430s, it became the go-to church for ducal funerals and it contains 25 of their mausoleums. Blockbuster Renaissance artists Gentile and Giovanni Bellini are also buried here.

Architecture

Erected in classic Italian Gothic style in the shape of a Latin cross, Zanipolo is similar in style to the Franciscan Frari in San Polo. Both structures feature red-brick facades with high-contrast detailing in white stone. Designed to make worshippers feel small and reverential, the cavernous interior has three naves and five apses and could accommodate virtually the entire population of 14th-century Castello. The 33m-high nave is supported by 10 massive columns and reinforced by a series of clever cross-beams – necessary because of Venice's waterlogged soil.

Typical of Italian Gothic, the interior has a barn-like simplicity, although there was once an ornate wooden choir that was removed in 1682 to better accommodate official funerals. Then in 1797 Napoleon booted the Dominicans out of their neighbouring friary and its artworks were looted, including Veronese's famous *Supper at the House of Levi* (1573). The rare 15th-century stained-glass windows, created by Bartolomeo Vivarini and Girolamo Mocetto on Murano, remain in the south transept.

TOP TIPS

➡ Zanipolo isn't one of the churches covered by the Chorus Pass; you'll need to buy a separate ticket.

➡ Vespers are sung in the church at 7pm on weekdays.

➡ An excellent antique market is sometimes held in a hall on the church's southern flank.

PRACTICALITIES

➡ Map p288, D2

➡ ☎041 523 59 13

➡ www.basilicasantiovanniepaolo.it

➡ Campo Zanipolo

➡ adult/reduced €3.50/1.50

➡ ⏰9am-6pm Mon-Sat, noon-6pm Sun

➡ 🚤Ospedale

Artistic Masterpieces

In 1867 a fire destroyed paintings by Tintoretto, Palma di Giovanni, Titian and Bellini. Anti-Catholic arson was suspected, but nothing was proven. A second Bellini polyptych, on the second altar in the right aisle, survived intact. Depicting *SS Vincent Ferrer, Christopher and Sebastian,* the work has a vivid sensuousness that was to become a hallmark of Venetian painting. Guido Reni's *San Giuseppe* shows Joseph exchanging adoring looks with baby Jesus. In the **Cappella del Rosario**, Paolo Veronese's *Assunta* ceiling depicts a rosy Madonna ascending a staggering staircase to be crowned by cherubim.

Tombs of the Dogi

Zanipolo was the site of all the doges' funerals from the middle of the 15th century onwards, and the walls are punctuated by 25 of their lavish tombs. From Pietro Lombardo's three-tier monument celebrating the *Ages of Man* for Pietro Mocenigo (1406–76) to the Gothic tomb of Michele Morosini (1308–82) and Andrea Tirali's bombastic *Tomba dei Valier* (1708), they provide an overview of the stylistic development of Venetian art.

The city's history is also on display. The tomb of Leonardo Loredan (1436–1521) shows him shielding Venice with his body against the invading League of Cambria. Sebastiano Venier (1496–1578), the admiral of the victorious fleet in the decisive naval battle of Lepanto in 1571 (and doge in his final year), is buried in the Cappella del Rosario.

TOP SIGHT
GIARDINI PUBBLICI

Venice's first public gardens were laid out between 1808 and 1812 on the orders of Napoleon, who decided the city needed a little breathing space – never mind that an entire residential district had to be demolished to make way for it. The park now stretches from Via Garibaldi, past the Garibaldi monument and through the Napoleonic gardens to Sant'Elena.

Biennale Pavilions

A large portion of the gardens is given over to the Biennale exhibition arena, hosting international art (in odd years) and architecture (even years) events in 29 pavilions, each allocated to a different nation. The pavilions tell a fascinating story of 20th-century architecture – not least because Venetian modernist master Carlo Scarpa contributed to the Biennale from 1948 to 1972, trying to make the best of Duilio Torres' Fascist 1932 Italian Pavilion, now the **Palazzo delle Esposizioni**. Scarpa is also responsible for the daring 1956 raw-concrete-and-glass **Venezuelan Pavilion** and the winsome, bug-shaped **Biglietteria** (Ticket Office). The most recent addition is the 2015 **Australian Pavilion** by starchitects Denton Corker Marshall, the first new pavilion to be built in the garden for 20 years. A black granite box hidden intriguingly amid the foliage, it speaks of the imposition of European settlements on Indigenous Australian land. Note that the entire exhibition area is usually closed to the public outside of the Biennale period.

Serra dei Giardini

This attractive iron-framed **greenhouse** (☑041 296 03 60; www.serradeigiardini.org; Viale Garibaldi 1254; ☺10am-8pm) FREE was built in 1894 to house the palms used in Biennale events. It rapidly expanded into a social hub and a centre for propagation: many plants grown here adorned the municipal flowerbeds of the Lido and the ballrooms of aristocratic *palazzi* (mansions). Restored in 2010, it now has a cafe and hosts well-attended events, exhibitions and workshops.

Monument to the Partisan Woman

Located in the lapping water just along from the Riva dei Sette Martiri – where seven Venetian partisans were publicly executed by the Nazis in 1944 – lies the 1200kg bronze figure of a woman. Sculpted by Augusto Murer, the figure lies on an arrangement of Istrian stone platforms designed by Carlo Scarpa to catch the eye as she appears and disappears beneath the rising and falling tide.

Parco delle Rimembranze

This **memorial park** (Isola di Sant'Elena; 🖪; 🖳Sant'Elena) FREE sits at the eastern limit of the gardens, on the island of Sant'Elena. Planted with umbrella pines, each originally commemorating a fallen WWI soldier, it's a tranquil spot with postcard views of the Bacino di San Marco. Families gather here to sit on the benches, roller skate around the rink and play on the slides and swings. Apart from providing a shady respite in a crowded urban environment, it offers a real slice of Venetian life.

TOP TIPS

➡ Book cheaper early-bird Biennale tickets online before the end of March.

➡ If you want to visit the exhibits over several days you'll need to buy a 'plus ticket' or a one-week multi-entry pass. These can only be bought at the ticket office.

➡ The exhibition area is closed on Mondays, with the exception of the first and last Monday of the Biennale.

➡ Crowds are worst during the Vernissage (first week) and over long holiday weekends.

PRACTICALITIES

➡ Map p290, B4
➡ Riva dei Partigiani
➡ 🖳Giardini

⊙ SIGHTS

Most of Castello's main attractions sit sandwiched between Piazza San Marco and the western edge of the Arsenale. The latter is only accessible during the Biennale or special events. South of the shipyards lies the Giardini Pubblici and the Giardini Biennale, where national pavilions host exhibitions during the annual art and architecture fair. East of here you'll find quiet residential streets and the Basilica di San Pietro di Castello.

ARSENALE   HISTORIC SITE
See p123.

ZANIPOLO   BASILICA
See p125.

GIARDINI PUBBLICI   GARDENS
See p126.

RIVA DEGLI SCHIAVONI   WATERFRONT
Map p288 (🚤San Zaccaria) Stretching east from San Marco, this broad waterfront avenue is one of the world's great promenades. Schiavoni (literally 'Slavs') refers to the people from Dalmatia (the coastal region of present-day Croatia, which once made up a substantial chunk of the Venetian republic) who settled in this part of the city in medieval times.

For centuries, vessels would dock and disembark here, the waterfront a Babel of languages, as traders, dignitaries and sailors arrived from ports around the Mediterranean and beyond. Now it's liberally dotted with market stalls selling souvenir T-shirts, aprons printed with Michelangelo's *David* and mass-produced masks to visitors from even further afield.

PALAZZO GRIMANI   MUSEUM
Map p288 (🗺call centre 041 520 03 45; www. palazzogrimani.org; Ramo Grimani 4858; adult/ reduced €5/2, incl Ca' D'Oro €10/4; ⊙10am-7pm Tue-Sun; 🚤San Zaccaria) The Grimani family built their Renaissance *palazzo* (mansion) in 1568 to showcase the extraordinary Graeco-Roman sculpture collection of Cardinal Giovanni Grimani. Now the basis of the Museo Correr (p62) archaeological section, the antiquities were returned to these theatrical, frescoed halls in May 2019 – after a 430-year absence – on a two-year loan. Gathered from Venetian territories all over the Mediterranean, the sculptures demonstrate the epitome of classical beauty that Renaissance humanists so admired and which the *palazzo* was designed to highlight.

Unusually for Venice, the palace has a Roman-style courtyard, which sheds a flattering light on the interiors and objects displayed within. There is debate about who designed the building. However, it's certain that Giovanni Grimani (1501–93) himself played a large role in the project, which consciously recalls the glories of ancient Rome. Grimani also hired a dream team of fresco painters specialising in grotesques and Pompeii-style mythological scenes. Francesco Salviati applied the glowing Raphael-style colours he'd used in Rome's Palazzo Farnese, while Roman painter Giovanni da Udine, considered among the brightest pupils of Raphael and Giorgione, devoted three rooms to the stories of Ovid.

Nevertheless, the **Sala ai Fogliami** (Foliage Room) is the most memorable room. Painted by Mantovano, ceiling and walls are awash with realistic plant- and birdlife. They even include New World species that had only recently been discovered by Europeans, including two that would come to be staples of Venetian life: tobacco and corn.

A combined ticket is available that includes access to Ca' d'Oro (p111).

FONDAZIONE QUERINI STAMPALIA   MUSEUM
Map p288 (🗺041 271 14 11; www.querinistampa lia.it; Campiello Querini Stampalia 5252; adult/ reduced €14/10; ⊙10am-6pm Tue-Sun; 🚤San Zaccaria) In 1869 Conte Giovanni Querini Stampalia made a gift of his ancestral 16th-century *palazzo* (mansion) to the city on the forward-thinking condition that its 700-year-old library operate late-night openings. Downstairs, savvy drinkers take their *aperitivi* (pre-dinner drinks) in Carlo Scarpa's modernist garden, while the museum's temporary exhibitions, art-filled salons and rare numismatic collection from the Venetian mint offer an interesting insight into how the Venetian aristocracy lived with and collected art.

Located in the upstairs apartments, the museum reflects the 18th-century tastes and interests of the count. Beneath the stuccoed ceilings you'll find rich furnishings and tapestries, Meissen and Sèvres porcelain, marble busts and some 400 paintings. Of these, many are dynastic portraits and conversation pieces, such as Alessandro and Pietro Longhi's genre scenes of masked balls, gambling dens and 18th-century bon vivants. It's a testimony to the richness of the collection that a lovely Tiepolo of St Francis clutching a crucifix is hidden in a small passageway off the bedroom.

Another standout is Giovanni Bellini's arresting *Presentation of Jesus at the Temple*, where the hapless child looks like a toddler mummy, standing up in tightly wrapped swaddling clothes. Other engaging pieces are the 39 winningly naïve *Scenes of Public Life in Venice* by Gabriele Bella (1730–99), which document the city and its customs during the period. Although somewhat crude in their realisation, the subject matter is fascinating.

In November 2018 the museum was further expanded onto the 3rd floor, where Michele de Lucchi refurbished seven new rooms to display artworks on permanent loan from the Intesa Sanpaolo bank. Each room is themed with relevant artworks and period furnishings, stepping you through works by Tintoretto, Pittoni and Creti, Tiepolo, Canaletto, Caffi and Ciardi and sculptures by Arturo Martini. In addition, the bank's glittering numismatic collection is one of the most important collections of coins produced by the Venetian Mint between the late 12th century and when it was shut down in 1866.

CHIESA DI SANTA MARIA FORMOSA   CHURCH

Map p288 (www.chorusvenezia.org; Campo Santa Maria Formosa 5267; adult/reduced €3/1.50, with Chorus Pass free; ☉10.30am-4.30pm; ☻Rialto) Originally built as a thatch-roofed wooden church in the 7th century, Santa Maria Formosa was refashioned by Mauro Codussi in 1492 with new baroque curves that make good on its name (literally 'Buxom St Mary'). The curious moniker is said to derive from a vision of the Madonna appearing in the form of a voluptuous woman to St Magnus, Bishop of Oderzo.

CHIESA DI SAN LIO   CHURCH

Map p288 (Campo San Lio; ☉9am-noon; ☻Rialto) FREE Giandomenico Tiepolo sure knew how to light up a room. Duck into the atmospheric gloom of San Lio's baroque interior and, as your eyes adjust, look up at Tiepolo's magnificent ceiling fresco, *The Glory of the Cross and St Leo IX*. On your left by the main door is Titian's *Apostle James the Great*, but this church is better known for yet another Venetian artist: the great *vedutista* (landscapist) Canaletto, who was baptised and buried in this, his parish church.

SCUOLA GRANDE DI SAN MARCO   NOTABLE BUILDING

Map p288 (www.scuolagrandesanmarco.it; Campo Zanipolo; ☉museum 9.30am-5.30pm Tue-Sat; ☻Ospedale) Instead of simple father-son handyman projects, sculptor Pietro Lombardo and his sons had more ambitious goals: a high-Renaissance marble facade for the most important confraternity in Venice. Mauro Codussi added the finishing touches on this gem. Magnificent lions of St Mark prowl above the portals, while sculpted *trompe l'œil* perspectives beguile the eye. Although the *scuola* now serves as the city's main public hospital, you can visit an intriguing **museum** (€5) of medical instruments and antique books in the palatial gallery upstairs.

While little effort has been made to create a narrative of the objects on display, they are fascinating nonetheless, and the fabulously decorated gallery is reason enough to visit. Also housed here are more than 8000 medical books, including works by early physicians such as Galen and Hippocrates. Best of all is Paduan professor Andreas Vesalius' treatise *De humanicorporisfabrica* (1543), a canonical text on anatomy, which details the fabric of the human body in extraordinarily detailed woodcut engravings.

OCEAN SPACE   GALLERY

Map p288 (Chiesa di San Lorenzo; www.tba21.org; Campo San Lorenzo 5069; ☉11am-7pm Tue-Sun; ☻San Zaccaria) FREE Austrian powerhouse Francesca von Habsburg has restored the epic San Lorenzo church – derelict for nearly a century after suffering damage in WWI – to house the Ocean Space Centre. This cross-disciplinary centre showcases the work of the **TBA21 Academy** and offers a platform to artists, scientists and policymakers tackling the challenge of climate change. Via a programme of lectures, workshops and events, the academy hopes to transform Venice itself into a lab for the future rather than a relic of the past.

The awesome proportions of San Lorenzo, one of the tallest buildings in Venice, are a fitting space for the large-scale contemporary installations. Dating back to the 9th century, the church was rebuilt in the 16th century and formed part of the neighbouring Benedictine monastery, although its bare brick facade was never finished. It is said that Marco Polo and his father, Niccolò, were buried here but that his sarcophagus was misplaced during the rebuilding. At any rate, years of excavation have failed to turn up any hint of the great explorer, although the ghost of his pioneering presence hopefully augurs well for this groundbreaking gallery.

At time of writing, the church was expected to close from November 2019 to March 2020 for further restoration and expansion, including the addition of a new bookshop and workshops.

CHIESA DI SAN FRANCESCO DELLA VIGNA
CHURCH

Map p288 (Campo San Francesco 2786; ⏰8am-12.30pm & 3-7pm; 🚤Celestia) FREE Designed and built by Jacopo Sansovino, with a facade by Palladio, this enchanting Franciscan church is one of Venice's most underappreciated attractions. The Madonna positively glows in Bellini's *Madonna and Saints* (1507) in the **Cappella Santa**, just off the flower-carpeted cloister, while swimming angels and strutting birds steal the scene in the delightful *Virgin and Child Enthroned* (c 1455) by Antonio da Negroponte, near the door to the right of the sanctuary. Bring €0.20 to illuminate them.

Palladio and the Madonna are tough acts to follow, but father-son sculptors Pietro and Tullio Lombardo make their own mark with their 15th-century marble reliefs that recount the lives of Christ and an assortment of saints. Housed in the **Cappella di San Girolamo**, just left of the altar, they are storytelling triumphs. Breezes seem to ripple through carved-marble trees, and lifelike lions seem prepared to pounce right off the wall.

Outside, the free-standing campanile (bell tower) looks like the twin of the more famous one in Piazza San Marco. A portico of classical columns makes the surrounding *campo* (square) look like a proper ancient Roman *agora* (marketplace). This makes a sociable setting for Venice's best annual block party, the **Festa di Francesco della Vigna**, when wine and rustic fare are served up in the church's stately shadow; it's usually held the third week in June.

CHIESA DI SAN ZACCARIA
CHURCH

Map p288 (Campo San Zaccaria 4693; ⏰10am-noon & 4-6pm Mon-Sat, 4-6pm Sun; 🚤San Zacca-

ria) FREE When 15th-century Venetian girls showed more interest in sailors than saints, they were sent to the convent adjoining San Zaccaria. The wealth showered on the church by their grateful parents is evident. Masterpieces by Bellini, Titian, Tintoretto and Van Dyck crowd the walls. The star of the show is undoubtedly Giovanni Bellini's *Madonna Enthroned with Child and Saints* (1505), which graces an altar on the left as you enter, and glows like it's plugged into an outlet.

Bellini was in his 70s when he painted his glowing *Madonna* and had already been confronted by the first achievements of Giorgione (1477–1510), with his softer *sfumato* ('smokey') technique. Bellini's assimilation of the technique is clear in the sunlight that illuminates the saintly arrangement, infusing it with a sense of devout spirituality. The painting is such a treasure that Napoleon whisked it away to Paris for 20 years when he plundered the city in 1797.

To your right, as you enter, the **Cappella di Sant'Atanasio** (admission €1.50) holds Tintoretto's *Birth of St John the Baptist,* while Tiepolo depicts the Holy Family fleeing to Egypt in a typically Venetian boat. Both hang above magnificently crafted choir stalls. Behind this chapel you'll find the Gothic **Cappella di San Tarasio** (also called the Cappella d'Oro, the golden chapel), with impressive Renaissance-style frescoes by Andrea del Castagno and Francesco da Faenza from the 1440s. Some original 12th-century mosaics can be seen by the altar, while a section of the original 9th-century mosaic floor is preserved under glass. Make sure you step down to the eerie flooded crypt, which houses the bodies of eight doges.

CHIESA DI SAN GIORGIO DEI GRECI
CHURCH

Map p288 (☎041 523 95 69; www.ortodossia.it; Campo dei Greci 3412; ⏰9am-1pm & 3-5pm Mon & Wed-Sat; 🚤San Zaccaria) FREE Greek Orthodox refugees who fled to Venice from Turkey with the rise of the Ottoman Empire built this church in the 16th century, using taxes collected on incoming Greek ships. While the exterior is classically Venetian, the interior is Orthodox in style: the aisleless nave is surrounded by wooden stalls and there's a *matroneo* (women's gallery). All eyes, however, are drawn to the golden iconostasis with its 46 icons, most of which were fashioned by 16th-century Cretan artist Michael Danaskinàs.

More fascinating icons can be found in the **Museo delle Icone** (Museum of Icons; Map p288; ☑041 522 65 81; www.istitutoellen ico. org; adult/reduced €4/2; ☉9am-5pm Sat-Mon), housed in the community's neighbouring 17th-century *scuola* (confraternity house), which was designed by Baldassare Longhena. Permission for a Greek confraternity was granted in the late 15th century in acknowledgement of the contribution Greek scholars made to Venice's lucrative printing trade, thus elevating the city to an important seat of Renaissance learning.

The separate, slender bell tower was added in 1582–92 by Simone Sorella. It began to lean right from the start and these days seems poised to dive into the canal at any moment.

LA PIETÀ
CHURCH

Map p288 (☑041 522 21 71; www.pietavenezia. org; Riva degli Schiavoni; €3; ☉10am-6pm Tue-Sun; ☒San Zaccaria) Originally called Chiesa di Santa Maria della Visitazione but fondly nicknamed La Pietà, this harmonious church designed by Giorgio Massari is known for its association with the composer Vivaldi,

who was concertmaster here in the early 18th century. Though the current church was built after Vivaldi's death, its acoustic-friendly oval shape honours his memory, and it is still used as a **concert hall** (☑041 522 11 20; www.chiesavivaldi.it; adult/reduced €28/22.50; ☉concerts 8.30pm). Guided tours (€10) run at noon from Tuesday to Friday.

CHIESA DI SAN GIOVANNI IN BRAGORA
CHURCH

Map p288 (☑041 520 59 06; www.sgbattistain bragora.it; Campo Bandiera e Moro 3790; ☉9-11am & 3.30-5.30pm Mon-Sat, 9.15-11.45am Sun; ☒Arsenale) **FREE** This serene 15th-century brick church harmonises Gothic and Renaissance styles with remarkable ease, setting the tone for a young Antonio Vivaldi, who was baptised here. Look for Bartolomeo Vivarini's 1478 *Enthroned Madonna with St Andrew and John the Baptist,* which shows the Madonna bouncing a delighted baby Jesus on her knee.

CHIESA DI SAN MARTINO
CHURCH

Map p290 (Campo San Martino 2298; ☉9.15am-11.45 & 3.30-6pm Mon-Sat, to 5.30pm Sun; ☒Arsenale) **FREE** Designed by Sansovino, the neighbourhood church of St

---

TOP SIGHT
SCUOLA DALMATA DI SAN GIORGIO DEGLI SCHIAVONI

In the 15th century, Venice annexed Dalmatia – a coastal region of present-day Croatia – and large numbers of Dalmatian Croats, known locally as Schiavoni (Slavs), eventually made their home in the city. They were granted their own *scuola* (religious confraternity) in 1451, hiring Vittore Carpaccio (also of Dalmatian descent) to complete an extraordinary cycle of paintings of Dalmatia's patron saints George, Tryphon and Jerome. Though Carpaccio never left Venice, his scenes with Dalmatian backdrops are minutely detailed. But the real brilliance of his imagined worlds are their engaging narrative power: St George charges a lizard-like dragon across a desert scattered with half-eaten corpses; St Jerome leads his tame-looking lion into a monastery; and St Augustine is distracted from correspondence by a heavenly voice informing him of Jerome's death.

Upstairs is a second chapel, with gilt detailing, a ceiling painted by Bastian de Muran and wall paintings from the school of Palma il Giovane.

Intriguingly, the Scuola Dalmata survived Napoleon's closures and is one of only two confraternities that still operates today.

TOP TIPS

→ Avoid visiting at 1pm during lunch hour.

→ The last entry is generally an hour before closing.

PRACTICALITIES

→ Map p288, F5

→ ☑041 522 88 28

→ Calle dei Furlani 3259a

→ adult/reduced €5/3

→ ☉1.30-5.30pm Mon, 9.30am-5.30pm Tue-Sat, 9.30am-1.30pm Sun

→ ☒San Zaccaria

Martin has a Greek-cross-shaped interior lined with eight chapels and topped by a *trompe l'œil* ceiling by Domenico Bruni. To the right of the church is the former *scuola* (confraternity) of the Ship Caulkers, which sports a bas-relief of Saint Martin dividing his cloak with a poor man.

MUSEO STORICO NAVALE
MUSEUM

Map p290 (Naval History Museum; ☑041 24 24; www.visitmuve.it; Riva San Biagio 2148; adult/reduced incl Padiglione delle Nave €10/7.50; ☺10am-6pm summer, to 5pm winter; ☻Arsenale) Maritime madness spans 42 rooms at this museum of naval history, featuring scale models of Venetian-built vessels as well as Peggy Guggenheim's not-so-minimalist gondola. Downstairs you'll find galleries of fearsome weaponry and 17th-century dioramas of forts and ports. Upstairs you can gawk at a sumptuous model of the *bucintoro*, the doge's gilded ceremonial barge, destroyed by Napoleonic troops in 1798.

BASILICA DI SAN PIETRO DI CASTELLO
CHURCH

Map p290 (www.chorusvenezia.org; Campo San Pietro 2787; adult/reduced €3/1.50, with Chorus Pass free; ☺10.30am-4.30pm Mon-Sat; ☻San Pietro) As interesting as it is, St Peter's would be lucky to scrape into the top 10 of Venice's most impressive churches. Yet it served as the city's cathedral from 1451 until 1807, when Napoleon made the entirely reasonable decision that the Basilica di San Marco was a more worthy choice. St Peter's was founded in the 7th century; a rebuild nearly a thousand years later by one of Palladio's protégés resulted in the classical facade and large dome that stand today.

The most intriguing piece inside the church is **St Peter's Throne**, which according to legend was used by the Apostle in Antioch and once hid the Holy Grail. While the story has all the makings of a Dan Brown novel, there's very little truth to it: the intricately carved stone back is in fact made from a scavenged Muslim tombstone that postdates the saint's death by many centuries. Still, it seems a fitting tale for such a historic location, given that the island of San Pietro (originally known as Olivolo) was one of the first inhabited in Venice, and the original church here was the seat of a Byzantine bishopric as early as 775. The elegant **campanile** of white Istrian stone is older than the current church, having been designed by Codussi in the 15th century.

✖ EATING

The most sprawling *sestiere* (district) in Venice, Castello is largely residential, which means its upmarket restaurants, neighbourhood trattorias and raucous *cicheti* bars offer varied and, usually, better dining choices. Eateries cluster around *campi* (squares), down the narrow *calli* (lanes) around the Arsenale, and along Via Garibaldi.

★SALVMERIA
VENETIAN €

Map p290 (☑041 523 39 71; www.salvmeria.com; Via Garibaldi 1769; meals €15-25; ☺10am-11pm Tue-Sun; ☻Arsenale) Fashioned from an old deli, Marco Ginepri's cool *cichetteria* serves accomplished food and excellent Veneto wines by the glass. Gourmet *cicheti* include fluffy *baccalá* (cod) on polenta, marinated shrimps and Fassone beef with peppers, while main plates include succulent tuna in a sesame crust, warm potato salad with radicchio and belly-warming fish lasagne. Trust them to recommend interesting wine pairings.

DIDOVICH
DELI €

Map p288 (☑041 523 00 17; Campo Santa Marina 5908; pastries €1.10, mains €8-10; ☺7am-7.30pm Mon-Sat; ☻Rialto) With outside seating on pretty Campo Santa Marina, cheerful Didovich offers the rare opportunity to sit down for a cooked breakfast. Otherwise you join the locals propping up the counter, sipping coffee and munching on croissants and *fritelle* (doughnuts). At lunchtime, sweets change to savouries, with an option to take away portions of homemade pasta or *polpette* (meatballs).

PIZZERIA ALLA STREGA
PIZZA €

Map p288 (☑041 528 64 97; www.facebook.com/alla.strega.venezia; Barbaria de le Tole 6418; pizzas €8-9, cicheti platters €14-23; ☺noon-3pm & 6.45-10.30pm Thu-Tue; ☻Ospedale) This hugely popular pizzeria and *cichetteria* has been feeding locals for years. Although best known as a pizza parlour, you can also enjoy a wide range of hearty salads and bar snacks: the famous Venetian *cicheti*. A large platter consists of typical dishes such as *baccalà*, *sarde in saor* (grilled sardines in a sweet and sour sauce) and polenta.

PASTICCERIA DA BONIFACIO
PASTRIES €

Map p288 (☑041 522 75 07; Calle dei Albanesi 4237; pastries €1.10-2; ☺7.30am-6.30pm Fri-Wed; ☻San Zaccaria) Gondoliers and Venetian homemakers flock to this tiny bakery to devour the buttery, just-baked sweetness of almond croissants and take-home boxes of Venetian specialities such as *zaletti* (cornmeal biscuits with sultanas). As afternoon wanes, the bakery turns into a makeshift bar as locals pop in for the signature *spritz* (cocktail made with prosecco) and *mammalucchi* (deep-fried batter balls with candied fruit).

ACIUGHETA
VENETIAN €

Map p288 (☑041 522 42 92; www.aciugheta.com; Campo SS Filippo e Giacomo 4357; meals €20-25; ⊙noon-11pm; 🗟; 🖳San Zaccaria) Just a stone's throw from Piazza San Marco, this is a rarity: a reasonably priced wine bar and restaurant in the most touristy part of town. *Cicheti* (Venetian tapas) at the bar include king prawns *in saor* (marinated with onions) and, for once, good pizza made with organic, stone-ground flour.

CIP CIAP
PIZZA €

Map p288 (☑041 523 66 21; www.cipciappizza.com; Calle del Mondo Novo 5799a; pizza per 100g €1.50; ⊙9am-9pm Wed-Mon; 🖳Rialto) Cip Ciap was one of the first takeaway pizza parlours in Venice and the cooks here take their job seriously enough to dress in traditional chef's whites. Prices are based on weight; expect to pay about €3.50 for a slice.

LE SPIGHE
VEGETARIAN €

Map p290 (☑041 523 81 73; Via Garibaldi 1341; meals €12-15; ⊙10.30am-2.30pm & 5.30-7.30pm Tue-Sat, 10.30am-2.30pm Mon; 🖋; 🖳Giardini) All vegetarian, all organic and largely vegan, this tiny cafe and wholefood shop offers a counter full of salads and grains that are shovelled onto plates and sold by weight – haute cuisine this ain't. Either take yours away to eat in the park or stake a place at the small communal table. The vegan chocolate muffins are surprisingly good.

★COVINO
VENETIAN €€

Map p288 (☑041 241 27 05; www.covinovenezia.com; Calle del Pestrin 3829; fixed-price menu lunch €27-36, dinner €40; ⊙12.45-2.30pm & 7pm-midnight Thu-Mon; 🗟; 🖳Arsenale) Tiny CoVino has only 14 seats but demonstrates bags of ambition with its inventive, seasonal menu inspired by the Venetian terroir. Speciality products are selected from Slow Food Foundation producers, and the charming waiters make enthusiastic recommendations from the wine list. Only a

three-course set menu is available at dinner; however, you can choose from two fixed-price options at lunch.

★GIBRAN
LEBANESE €€

Map p288 (☑375 5997676; Calle del Cafetier 6645; meals €20-35; ⊙11am-3pm & 6.30pm-midnight; 🖳San Zaccaria) Given Venice's globe-trotting history, it's high time the city had a quality Middle Eastern eatery such as this. Cut-brass lanterns hung with Venetian seed pearls cast a warm glow in the cosy wood-beamed interior. Order delicious plates of crunchy fattoush salad, *foul* (boiled beans with garlic and lemon), chicken shish, and fish with pine nuts, almonds and basmati rice.

OSSI DI SEPPIA
OSTERIA €€

Map p288 (☑331 2750934; Calle Seconda de la Fava 6316; meals €25-30; ⊙10am-3pm & 6pm-midnight Thu-Tue; 🖋; 🖳San Zaccaria) It's worth going the extra mile to find this *osteria* (casual tavern) where Venetian neighbours gather to gossip over good glasses of Valpolicella and Malvasia. Settle down to mixed plates of *cicheti* followed by bowls of silky risotto and just-cooked linguine with plump clams. There is a great vegetarian selection here, including oil-drizzled chicory, ratatouille, aubergines, zucchini and frittata.

OSTERIA DA PAMPO
OSTERIA €€

Map p290 (☑041 520 84 19; www.osteriadapampo.com; Calle Chinotto 24; meals €25-35; ⊙noon-2.30pm & 7-10pm Thu-Mon, 7-10pm Wed; 🖳Sant'Elena) This vintage *osteria* (casual tavern) is largely the preserve of Sant'Elena residents who come for the friendly vibe and good seafood. Start with the warm octopus and potato salad followed by baked scabbard fish and vegetables – that's if you can resist the *fritto misto* (mixed fried seafood), for which Da Pampo is famous. Outdoor seating is a plus in summer.

OSTERIA ALLA STAFFA
VENETIAN €€

Map p288 (☑041 523 91 60; www.facebook.com/alla.staffa.it; Calle dell'Ospedale 6397a; meals €30-40; ⊙noon-3pm & 7-11pm Wed-Mon; 🖳Ospedale) With fish fresh from the Rialto every morning and a preference for organic veg and cheese, chef Alberto does a take on Venetian classics that has flavourful foundations. This is traditional cooking taken to the next level, with artful presentation worthy of a modernist masterpiece.

HOSTARIA DA FRANZ
SEAFOOD €€

Map p288 (☏041 522 08 61; www.hostariada franz.com; Salizada San Antonin 3499; meals €35-45; ⊙7-10pm Mon-Fri, 12.30-2pm & 7-10pm Sat & Sun; ⛴San Zaccaria) Known in Venice for its tiramisu, da Franz is also a phenomenal seafood stop. Two dishes spring to mind: the melt-in-mouth *seppie* (cuttlefish) prepared in black ink, and the *anguila* (eel), prepared according to grandma's secret recipes as a grilled fillet.

OSTERIA RUGA DI JAFFA
OSTERIA €€

Map p288 (☏041 241 10 62; www.osteriarugadijaf fa.it; Ruga Giuffa 4864; meals €15-30; ⊙10am-11.30pm; ⛴San Zaccaria) Set on busy Ruga Giuffa, this *osteria* has artsy Murano lamps and seafaring paraphernalia. You should be able to spot it by the gondoliers packing out the tables at lunchtime; they come to feast on lagoon crustaceans, homemade pasta and hearty plates of oven-roasted pork. Plates of *cicheti* can also be taken at the bar with a *spritz*.

ENOITECA MASCARETA
VENETO €€

Map p288 (☏041 523 07 44; www.ostemaurolor enzon.com; Calle Lunga Santa Maria Formosa 5183; meals €35-45; ⊙7pm-2am; ⛴Rialto) Once more of a wine bar than a restaurant, Mascareta is now very much an eatery, serving champagne and oysters or more rustic fare such as guinea fowl. With more than 1000 labels of wine available to try by the glass, however, Enoiteca Mascareta has not betrayed its roots as a top-class vintner.

★TRATTORIA CORTE SCONTA
VENETIAN €€€

Map p288 (☏041 522 70 24; www.cortescon tavenezia.it; Calle del Pestrin 3886; meals €45-55; ⊙12.30-2pm & 7-9.30pm Tue-Sat, closed Jan & Aug; ✳ 🍷; ⛴Arsenale) Well-informed visitors and celebrating locals seek out this vine-covered *corte sconta* (hidden courtyard) for its trademark seafood antipasti and imaginative house-made pasta. Inventive flavour pairings transform the classics: clams zing with ginger; prawn and courgette linguine is recast with an earthy dash of saffron; and the roast eel loops like the Brenta river in a drizzle of balsamic reduction.

IL RIDOTTO
ITALIAN €€€

Map p288 (☏041 520 82 80; www.ilridotto.com; Campo SS Filippo e Giacomo 4509; meals €70-87; ⊙6.45-11pm Thu, noon-2.30pm & 6.45-11pm Fri-Tue; ⛴San Zaccaria) When the octopus start-er looks so beautiful that it elicits gasps, there's no questioning how this small, elegant restaurant gained its Michelin star. Head chef Gianni Bonaccorsi is ably complemented by his Bangladeshi offsider Murshedul Haque, creating a menu that broadens the bounds of Italian cuisine. Tables spill out onto the square but the brick-lined interior is equally appealing.

MET
ITALIAN €€€

Map p288 (☏041 524 00 34; www.metrestau rantvenice.com; Riva degli Schiavoni 4149; experience/veg menu €130/165; ⊙7-10.30pm Tue-Fri, 12.30-2.30pm & 7-10.30pm Sat & Sun; ✳ 🍷🍴; ⛴San Zaccaria) The Hotel Metropole's Michelin-starred restaurant offers an intriguing proposition: at each stage of its multicourse menu you can order a traditional Venetian dish or a theatrical modern interpretation using the same ingredients. The enthusiastic staff will ably assist you in your decision but, either way, you can't go wrong. Jellyfish-like Murano chandeliers add whimsy to an otherwise formal room.

LOCAL
VENETIAN €€€

Map p288 (☏041 241 11 28; www.ristorantelo cal.com; Salizada dei Greci 3303; meals €75; ⊙noon-2pm & 7-10pm Thu-Mon, 7-10pm Wed; ✳; ⛴San Zaccaria) Although he's cooked in fine-dining establishments such as Noma, chef Matteo Tagliapietra grew up on the fishing island of Burano. As such, his simple, seasonal cooking is rooted in the lagoon and his dishes, while creative, remain honest and flavourful. Highlights of the ever-changing menu include gnocchi with mallard, mackerel with red cabbage, and the chocolate *barene* (sandbank) dessert.

AL COVO
VENETIAN €€€

Map p288 (☏041 522 38 12; www.ristoranteal covo.com; Campiello de la Pescaria 3969; meals €42-67; ⊙12.45-3.30pm & 7.30pm-midnight Fri-Tue; ✳; ⛴Arsenale) Chef-owner Cesare Benelli has long been dedicated to the preservation of heritage products and lagoon recipes. Only the freshest seasonal fish gets the Covo treatment, accompanied by artichokes, eggplant, *cipollini* onion and mushrooms from the lagoon larders of Sant'Erasmus, Vignole, Treporti and Cavallino. Meat is also carefully sourced and much of it is Slow Food accredited.

LOVERS' ALLEY

Under the arch of the covered passageway **Sotoportego dei Preti** (Map p288; ⬤Arsenale) is hidden a reddish, heart-shaped stone about the size of a hand. Local lore has it that couples that touch it together will remain in love forever. Not ready to commit just yet? This is also a nice private spot for a smooch.

ALLE CORONE   ITALIAN €€€

Map p288 (📞041 523 22 22; www.hotelaireali.com; Campo della Fava 5527; meals €61-65; ⏱noon-2.30pm & 7-10.30pm; ⬤Rialto) The stupidly romantic view of gondolas floating past the windows helps to distract from the hotel-restaurant vibe of Ai Reali's dining room. The excellent food does its part too, particularly the mixed platter of *cicheti*. Venetian dishes are also showcased in the varied seafood selection on offer.

ALLE TESTIERE   VENETIAN €€€

Map p288 (📞041 522 72 20; www.osteriallestestiere.it; Calle del Mondo Novo 5801; meals €45-60; ⏱12.30-3pm & 7-11pm Tue-Sat; ⬤Rialto) Make a reservation for one of the two evening sittings at this tiny restaurant and come prepared for Bruno Gavagnin's beautifully plated seafood feasts. Subtle spices such as ginger, cinnamon and orange zest recall Venice's trading past with the East.

🍷 DRINKING & NIGHTLIFE

Around sunset, the inhabitants of Castello converge on Via Garibaldi and along the waterfront for the *passeggiata* (evening stroll), then disperse for *aperitivi* (pre-dinner drinks). Cafes in Campo Santa Maria di Formosa, Campo Zanipolo and along Via Garibaldi become prime drinking spots by night – but for cocktails with views, splash out at hotel bars along the Riva degli Schiavoni.

★**LONDRA BAR**   COCKTAIL BAR

Map p288 (📞041 520 05 33; www.londrapalace.com; Hotel Londra Palace, Riva degli Schiavoni 4171; ⏱11am-midnight; 📶; ⬤San Zaccaria) There may be flocks of tourists outside, but the Londra Palace is a haven of serenity and its sleek bar, decked out in wood and white leather, is like a 1st-class cabin of an ocean liner. Furthermore, master mixologist Marino Lucchetti makes inspired cocktails and the bar is popular with locals who come for regular concerts and book launches.

EL RÈFOLO   BAR

Map p290 (www.elrefolo.it; Via Garibaldi 1580; ⏱11.30am-12.30am Tue-Sun; ⬤Giardini) Although the bars along Via Garibaldi may look interchangeable, the queue for El Rèfolo's pavement tables says otherwise. Part of the draw is the ever-friendly Massimiliano dispensing Italian microbrews and glasses of wine, as well as the plump sandwiches and summertime live music.

OSTERIA AL PORTEGO   BAR

Map p288 (📞041 522 90 38; www.osteriaalportego.org; Calle de la Malvasia 6014; ⏱10.30am-2.30pm & 5.30-10.30pm; ⬤Rialto) This walk-in closet somehow manages to distribute wine, craft beer and *cicheti* to the overflowing crowd of young Venetians in approximate order of arrival. Wine is cheap and plentiful, and the bar groans with classic nibbles. If that's not enough, make a dash for one of the five tables around the back where enormous plates of seafood are served.

STRANI   BAR

Map p290 (📞041 099 14 34; Via Garibaldi 1582; ⏱7.30am-1am summer, noon-10pm winter; ⬤Giardini) There's always a party on at Strani thanks to its excellent selection of beers on tap, well-priced glasses of Veneto wines and platters of *sopressa* (soft salami). A plethora of *cicheti* keeps drinkers fuelled for late-night jam sessions with the locals.

BAR TERRAZZA DANIELI   BAR

Map p288 (📞041 522 64 80; www.danielihotelvenice.com; Riva degli Schiavoni 4196; ⏱3-7pm May-Sep; ⬤San Zaccaria) Gondolas glide in to dock along the quay, while across the lagoon the white-marble edifice of Palladio's San Giorgio Maggiore turns from gold to pink in the waters of the canal: this is the late-afternoon scene from the Hotel Danieli's top-floor balcony bar and it definitely calls for a toast. Linger over a *spritz* (cocktail made with prosecco) or cocktail.

BAR DANDOLO   COCKTAIL BAR

Map p288 (📞041 522 64 80; www.danielihotelvenice.com; Riva degli Schiavoni 4196; ⏱9.30am-1am; ⬤San Zaccaria) Dress to the nines and swan

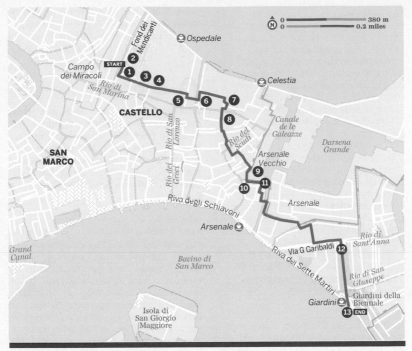

🏃 Neighbourhood Walk
Castello's Byways

START CAMPO ZANIPOLO
END GARDINI PUBBLICI
LENGTH 2.2KM; TWO HOURS

Start in Campo Zanipolo, where you can't miss the **①Bartolomeo Colleoni statue**. Colleoni left Venice a fortune on condition that the city erect a statue in his honour in Piazza San Marco. Venice bent the rules, erecting the statue in front of the **②Scuola Grande di San Marco** (p128) instead. Next door rise the imposing Gothic heights of the treasure-packed Dominican friary, **③Zanipolo** (p125). A block east, you'll pass the **④Ospedaletto**, an orphanage famous for its female musicians. Continue to stroll east down Barbaria de le Tole, past bric-a-brac haven **⑤Ballarin** (p136) and across the canal in front of the **⑥Liceo Scientifico**, which has a fine Longhena facade. Dog-leg left for Palladio's classical **⑦Chiesa di San Francesco della Vigna** (p129). Head under the colonnade lining the square to the

south of the church and cross over Rio di San Francesco. To the left is the graffitied wall of the **⑧Laboratorio Occupato Morion** (p136). Continue past Campo de le Gatte and enter a tight nest of alleys, once housing workers of the **⑨Arsenale** (p123). Turn right at Campo de le Gorne and follow the walls round to **⑩Chiesa di San Martino** (p130). To the right of its doorway is a *bocca di leoni* (mouth of the lion), into which Venetians slipped denunciations of their neighbours. Keep following the Arsenale's walls until you reach the **⑪Porta Magna** (p124). Cross over the wooden bridge, then turn left into Campo de la Tana and drop down Calle Forno into bustling Via Garibaldi. Amble along this sunny promenade to the gates of the Giardini Pubblici, marked by a **⑫monument** to Giuseppe Garibaldi, Italian Independence hero. Continue down the leafy boulevard towards the sweeping views of the Riva Martiri, emerging in front of Carlo Scarpa's moving wave-washed **⑬Monument to the Partisan Woman** (p126).

SANT'ELENA

At the easternmost reaches of central Venice, the island of Sant'Elena is rarely troubled by tourists. Most of it, with the exception of the 12th-century church and monastery of the eponymous saint, was built upon reclaimed swampland dredged up in the process of creating shipping lanes in the early 20th century.

The island took on its current aspect during the 1920s, when it was developed as the city's newest residential area. Deliberately eschewing the modernist trends of its time, the middle-class apartments are echoes of the city's aristocratic palaces, although they lack the quirks and elegant decay that define the rest of Venice.

Today Sant'Elena is a quiet residential quarter and a favourite destination for joggers, thanks to its shady byways and distinct lack of crowds.

straight past the 'hotel guests only' sign to the glamorous bar that fills the grand hall of the 14th-century Palazzo Dandolo. Murano chandeliers reflect off gilt edges and silk furnishings, while snappily dressed staff effortlessly descend with signature Vesper martinis and bottomless bowls of snacks.

ROSA SALVA   CAFE
Map p288 (☑041 522 79 49; www.rosasalva.it; Campo Zanipolo 6779; ☺8am-8pm; ⊛Ospedale) For over a century, Rosa Salva has been serving tea, pastries and ice creams to the passing trade on Campo Zanipolo. Inside the 1930s throwback interior, ladies take *tramezzini* (triangular, stacked sandwiches) and trays of *tè con limone* (tea with lemon) at marble-topped tables while, outside, sunseekers sip *spritz* (cocktail made with prosecco) and children slurp ice creams.

 **ENTERTAINMENT**

LABORATORIO
OCCUPATO MORION   LIVE MUSIC
Map p288 (www.facebook.com/laboratorioccu patomorion; Salizada San Francesco 2951; ⊛Celestia) When not busy staging environmental protests or avant-garde performance art, this counterculture social centre throws one hell of a party, with performances by bands from around the Veneto. Events are announced via posters thrown up around town and on its Facebook page.

🛍 SHOPPING

Castello remains an authentic local neighbourhood. Being relatively far removed from San Marco and the train station, rents here are cheaper, and that means lots of artisan studios and galleries, particularly along Calle del Cafetier, Salizada Sant'Antonin and Via Garibaldi.

★ATELIER
ALESSANDRO MERLIN   HOMEWARES
Map p288 (☑041 522 58 95; Calle del Pestrin 3876; ☺10am-noon & 3-7pm Mon, Tue & Sat, 3-7pm Fri & Sun; ⊛Arsenale) Enjoy your breakfast in the nude, on a horse or atop a jellyfish – Alessandro Merlin paints them all on striking black and white cappuccino cups and saucers. Homoerotic-art lovers will recognise the influence of Tom of Finland in the ultramasculine, well-endowed nude dudes, but the sgraffito technique Alessandro uses on some of his work dates back to Roman times.

BRAGORÀ   FASHION & ACCESSORIES
Map p288 (☑041 319 08 64; www.bragora.it; Salizada Sant'Antonin 3496; ☺9.30am-7.30pm Mon-Sat, 10.30am-6.30pm Sun; ⊛Arsenale) Bragorà is a multipurpose space: part shop, service centre and cultural hub. Its upcycled products include beach bags sewn out of boat sails, toy gondolas fashioned from drink cans, belts made from bike tyres and jewellery crafted from springs. There's an excellent range of witty tees on Venetian themes and you can even print your own.

BALLARIN   ANTIQUES
Map p288 (☑347 7792492; Calle del Cafetier 6482; ☺10am-1pm & 4-6.30pm Mon-Sat; ⊛Ospedale) If you're looking for something distinctively Venetian, check out this Aladdin's cave. An old-fashioned dealer and artisan restorer, Valter Ballarin has a knack for tracking down period furnishings, hand-painted glassware, prints, books, toys and lamps. The best souvenir is a handful of colourful, hand-blown glass flowers from dismembered Murano chandeliers.

VENICE'S SECRET WEAPON: ARSENALOTTI

In an early version of the assembly line, ships built in the Arsenale progressed through sequenced design phases, each staffed by *arsenalotti* (Arsenale workers) specialised in a particular aspect of construction, ranging from hull assembly and pitch application through to sail rigging. Women specialised in sails; children started apprenticeships at age 10, and did their part twisting hemp into rope.

But this wasn't a low-paid, low-status job. The *arsenalotti* were well remunerated, with cradle-to-grave fringe benefits. This helped keep them remarkably faithful to the Republic, and throughout Venetian history, *arsenalotti* repeatedly proved both their loyalty and their brawn during periods of war and rebellion. Using their proven shipbuilding techniques, they also constructed the vast *carena di nave* (ship's keel) ceilings you see in several Venetian churches.

Job requirements for *arsenalotti* included manual dexterity, strength and silence. Even in raucous Castello *bacari* (old-style bars), *arsenalotti* remained carefully vague about the specifics of their workday, in an 'I could tell you, but then I'd have to kill you' kind of way. Shipbuilding processes were top secret, and industrial espionage was considered an act of high treason, punishable by exile or death. For centuries the crenellated walls of the Arsenale hid the feverish activity inside them from view. Even outside the walls, the *arsenalotti* tended to stick to their own kind. They intermarried, and even had their own market gardens to reduce contact with the rest of the city.

I TRE MERCANTI
FOOD

Map p288 (☑041 522 29 01; www.itremercanti.it; Campo de la Guerra 5364; ⊙11am-7.30pm; ⛴San Zaccaria) Stocked with speciality Italian wine, olive oil, jam and pasta, this excellent store has plenty of comestible souvenirs that you could happily lug home with you, but the reality is that most purchases don't make it out of the shop. That's because the legendary homemade macarons and jars of tiramisu demand to be consumed immediately.

PAOLO BRANDOLISIO
ARTS & CRAFTS

Map p288 (☑041 522 41 55; Sotoportego Corte Rota 4725; ⊙9am-1pm & 3-7pm Mon-Fri; ⛴San Zaccaria) Beneath all the marble and gilt, Venice is a city of wood, long supported by its carpenters, caulkers, oar-makers and gilders. Master woodcarver Paolo Brandolisio continues the traditions, crafting the sinuous *forcola* (rowlock) that supports the gondolier's oar. Made of walnut or cherry wood, each is crafted specifically for boat and gondolier. Miniature replicas are on sale in the workroom.

KALIMALA
SHOES

Map p288 (☑041 528 35 96; www.kalimalaven ezia.it; Salizada San Lio 5387; ⊙9.30am-7.30pm Mon-Sat; ⛴Rialto) Sleek belts with brushed-steel buckles, satchels, manbags and knee-high red boots: Kalimala makes beautiful leather goods in practical, modern styles. Shoes, sandals and gloves are crafted from vegetable-cured cowhide and dyed in a mix of earthy tones and vibrant lapis blues. Given the natural tanning and top-flight leather, prices are reasonably reasonable, with handmade shoes starting at €135.

VIZIOVIRTÙ
CHOCOLATE

Map p288 (☑041 275 01 49; www.viziovirtu.com; Calle Forneri 5988; ⊙10am-7pm; ⛴Rialto) Work your way through Venice's most decadent vices at this Willy Wonka–esque shop, where lip-smacking edibles include plague doctor masks. Ganache-filled chocolates come in a five-course meal of flavours, from Barolo wine, pink pepper and balsamic vinegar to wild fennel and Earl Grey.

🏃 ACTIVITIES

★ARTEFACT MOSAIC STUDIO
ARTS & CRAFTS

Map p288 (☑041 877 83 42; www.artefactmo saic.it; Calle del Cafetier 6477a; beginners courses €50-110; ⊙10am-7pm Tue-Sun; ⛴San Zaccaria) After graduating top-of-class at the Scuola Mosaicisti del Friuli, Romuald and Alessandra headed to Venice and established their fascinating mosaic studio. Employing Venetian glass mosaics in a myriad glittering colours, they create unique pieces including some amazingly expressive portraits. Don't miss a visit to this studio or, if you have time, join them for a fascinating workshop.

CASTELLO ACTIVITIES

Giudecca, Lido & the Southern Islands

GIUDECCA | ISOLA DI SAN GIORGIO MAGGIORE | ISOLA DI SAN SERVOLO | ISOLA DI SAN LAZZARO DEGLI ARMENI | LIDO DI VENEZIA | PELLESTRINA

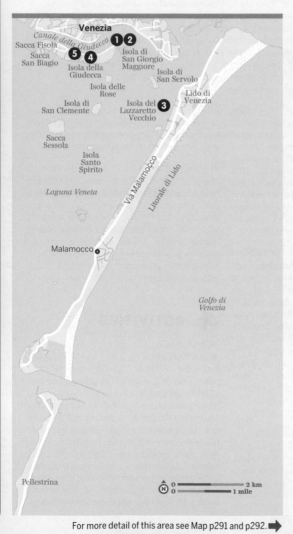

Neighbourhood Top Five

① Chiesa di San Giorgio Maggiore (p140) Immersing yourself in the bright serenity of Palladio's eye-catching church and ascending its *campanile* (bell tower) for spectacular views over San Marco.

② Fondazione Giorgio Cini (p142) Viewing Palladio's cloister, Longhena's elegant library and a precise reproduction of Veronese's vast *Wedding Feast at Cana* in the refectory where it originally hung.

③ Monastero di San Lazzaro degli Armeni (p143) Gaining insights from one of the resident Armenian monks as you tour around their island home.

④ Chiesa del Santissimo Redentore (p141) Giving thanks for Venice's ongoing survival in this impressive, art-filled church.

⑤ La Palanca (p145) Feasting on traditional Venetian seafood in one of Giudecca's excellent eateries, such as this humble bar and local lunching spot.

For more detail of this area see Map p291 and p292.

Explore the Southern Islands

Other cities have suburban sprawl; Venice has medieval monasteries floating in teal-blue waters. To the east and south, the seaward side of the lagoon is sheltered from the Adriatic by Pellestrina and the Lido di Venezia, for centuries the bastions of the city. In the 19th century, the Lido found a new lease of life as a bathing resort and a place of escape from the urban rigours of the Rialto. It's a quick 15-minute boat ride from San Marco, and many people decamp here for weeks in the summer. In winter it's a grim place, with most of its hotels boarded up.

Smaller islands dot the foreground of memorable views back to San Marco. In the past they served as monasteries, quarantine stations, military hospitals and mental asylums. Monks remain on San Giorgio Maggiore and San Lazzaro degli Armeni, while San Servolo is now a university; all three are connected to the *vaporetto* (waterbus) network and can easily be visited. Isola delle Rose and the former women's asylum on San Clemente are now luxury hotels.

Next to San Giorgio Maggiore lies Giudecca, Venice's unofficial seventh *sestiere* (district) – although it's technically part of Dorsoduro. It was once an aristocratic retreat and later the city's industrial centre; it now maintains an interesting balance between luxury and grit.

Local Life

➡ **Island cycling** Rent a bike from **Lido on Bike** (⌨041 526 80 19; www.lidoonbike.it; Gran Viale Santa Maria Elisabetta 21b, Lido; bicycle rental per 90min/day €5/10; ⊙9am-7pm summer; ▣Lido SME) or Venice Rental Services (p249) and hit the excellent cycle paths of the Lido and Pellestrina to get a sense of everyday life in the fishing villages dotted along them.

➡ **Giudecca's back alleys** Away from the main waterfront promenade you'll find parks and tiny squares filled with youngsters kicking balls, oldies holding court on park benches and parents pushing prams.

Getting There & Away

➡ **Vaporetto** Giudecca has four *vaporetto* stops (Sacca Fisola, Palanca, Redentore and Zitelle); lines 2, 4.1 and 4.2 stop at all of them. Line 2 also stops at neighbouring San Giorgio Maggiore. San Lazzaro and San Servolo are both served by line 20 from San Zaccaria. Lines 1, 5.1, 5.2, 6, 10 and 14 all call into Lido SME (Santa Maria Elisabetta), the island's main hub.

➡ **Car Ferry** Line 17 connects Tronchetto to **Lido San Nicolò** and continues on to Punta Sabbioni on the mainland.

Lonely Planet's Top Tip

Instead of braving the lines at San Marco's *campanile*, seek out San Giorgio Maggiore's *campanile*, which offers comparable views for €2 less and a fraction of the wait time.

✗ Best Places to Eat

➡ La Palanca (p145)
➡ Trattoria ai Cacciatori (p145)
➡ Trattoria Altanella (p145)
➡ Favorita (p146)
➡ Magiche Voglie (p145)

For reviews, see p145.➡

♟ Best Places to Drink

➡ Skyline (p146)
➡ Bar 9 (p146)
➡ Osteria da Moro (p146)
➡ Essentiale (p147)
➡ La Palanca (p145)

For reviews, see p146.➡

🔒 Best Places to Shop

➡ Artisti Artigiani del Chiostro (p147)
➡ Fortuny Tessuti Artistici (p147)
➡ Casa dei Tre Oci (p141)
➡ Le Stanze del Vetro (p142)
➡ Mercato della Prigione Femminile (p147)

For reviews, see p147.➡

TOP SIGHT
CHIESA DI SAN GIORGIO MAGGIORE

Designed by Andrea Palladio for maximum dazzle, this Benedictine abbey church was built between 1565 and 1610 and positioned on its own island facing San Marco. Palladio chose white Istrian stone to stand out against the blue lagoon waters, and set it at an angle to create visual drama while also ensuring that it catches the sun all afternoon.

Exterior

Palladio's radical facade gracefully solved the problem bedevilling Renaissance church design: how to graft a triangular, classical pediment onto a Christian church with a high, central nave and lower side aisles. Palladio's solution: use one pediment to crown the nave, and a lower, half-pediment to span each side aisle. The two interlock with rhythmic harmony, while prominent three-quarter columns, deeply incised capitals and sculptural niches create depth with clever shadow-play. Above the facade rises a brick *campanile* with a conical copper spire and a cap of Istrian stone.

Inside

Sunlight enters the church through high thermal windows and is then diffused by acres of white stone. Floors inlaid with white, red and black stone draw the eye toward the altar. With its rigorous application of classical motifs, it's reminiscent of a Roman temple. Two outstanding late works by Tintoretto flank the church's altar. On one side hangs his *Collection of Manna*; on the other side, *Last Supper* depicts Christ and his apostles in a scene that looks suspiciously like a 16th-century Venetian tavern, with a cat and dog angling for scraps.

TOP TIP

→ Take the lift to the top of the bell tower for the views – it's cheaper than San Marco's *campanile* and you won't have to queue.

PRACTICALITIES

→ St George's Church

→ Map p48

→ ☎041 522 78 27

→ www.abbaziasan giorgio.it

→ Isola di San Giorgio Maggiore

→ bell tower adult/ reduced €6/4

→ ⏱9am-6pm

→ 🚤San Giorgio Maggiore

⊙ SIGHTS

The most notable sights on this group of islands are ecclesiastical, including some extraordinary churches and monasteries. Some are still monk-filled, while others have been re-purposed as museums and cultural institutes.

⊙ Giudecca

Giudecca's disputed history begins with its name. The name doesn't connote a historic Jewish enclave (as it does in parts of Southern Italy) but rather it most likely derives from the Venetian *zudega*, meaning 'the judged' – referring to rebel aristocratic families banished here during the 9th century.

Michelangelo fled here from Florence in 1529, though by the time he arrived, the aristocratic Dandolo, Mocenigo and Vendramin families had transformed the island from a prison into a neighbourhood of garden villas. When the nobles headed inland in the 18th century to build villas along the Riviera Brenta, Giudecca's gardens gave way to factories, tenements and military barracks.

In recent years, these large abandoned spaces have attracted a new set of exiles – artists who can no longer afford the rent in central Venice. In 2019, the Giudecca Art District was officially launched, drawing together the island's 11 contemporary art galleries.

CHIESA DEL SANTISSIMO REDENTORE
CHURCH

Map p291 (Church of the Most Holy Redeemer; www.chorusvenezia.org; Campo del SS Redentore 194, Giudecca; adult/reduced €3/1.50, with Chorus Pass free; ☉10.30am-4.30pm Mon-Sat; ⛴Redentore) Built to celebrate the city's deliverance from the Black Death, Palladio's Il Redentore was completed under Antonio da Ponte (of Rialto Bridge fame) in 1592. The theme is taken up in Paolo Piazza's monochrome *Venice's Offering for Liberation from the Plague of 1575–77* (1619), high above the entry door. Look for Tintoretto's *The Flagellation of Christ* (1588) on the third altar to the right.

Survival is never taken for granted in this tidal town, and to give thanks during the Festa del Redentore (p21), Venetians have been making a pilgrimage across the canal on a shaky pontoon bridge from the Zattere on the third weekend in July ever since 1578.

CASA DEI TRE OCI
GALLERY

Map p291 (☏041 241 23 32; www.treoci.org; Fondamenta de le Zitelle 43, Giudecca; adult/reduced €12/10; ☉10am-7pm Wed-Mon; ⛴Zitelle) FREE Acquired by the Fondazione di Venezia in 2000, the fanciful neo-Gothic 'House of Three Eyes' was built in 1913 by artist and photographer Mario de Maria, who conceived its distinctive brick facade with its three unusually shaped arched windows. It now houses his photographic archive and interesting exhibitions of contemporary art, especially photography. The gift shop is worth a browse.

LE ZITELLE
CHURCH

Map p291 (Chiesa di Santa Maria della Presentazione; ☏041 309 66 05; www.gioiellinascostidivenezia.it; Fondamenta de le Zitelle 33, Giudecca; ☉by arrangement; ⛴Zitelle) Designed by Palladio in the late 16th century and built after his death, the Zitelle was a church and almshouse for orphans and poor young women (*zitelle* was local slang for 'old maids'). The church doors are rarely open, but you can get a spa treatment and sleep in the adjoining almshouse. The luxury Bauer Palladio Hotel & Spa (p201) has creatively tweaked the original structure without altering Palladio's blueprint or the original cloister garden.

CHIESA DI SANT'EUFEMIA
CHURCH

Map p291 (St Euphemia's Church; Fondamenta Sant'Eufemia 680, Giudecca; ☉hr vary; ⛴Palanca) Four female saints were venerated in the original AD 890 church here, but Saints Dorothy, Tecla and Erasma weren't as popular as early Christian martyr Euphemia. She was thrown to hungry lions in Chalcedon (present-day Turkey), but after biting off her hand, the lions refused to eat her holy virgin flesh – a hungry bear had fewer scruples. The simple Veneto-Byzantine structure you see today dates from 1371. Frescoes and fine stucco decorate the ceiling of the baroque interior.

Look for the vibrant 1480 painting by Vivirani on the first altar to the right, showing a ringletted St Roch – resplendent in a white pleated mini and blue tights – displaying his muscular plague-scarred thigh to an angel.

GIUDECCA 795
GALLERY

Map p291 (☏340 8798327; www.giudecca795.com; Fondamenta San Biagio 795, Giudecca; ☉6-8pm Tue-Fri & Sun, 4-8pm Sat; ⛴Palanca) FREE Founded to promote local artists of all kinds, this quirky and welcoming gallery displays (and sells) a wide range of works by both established and young artists, most of whom have a strong connection with Venice itself.

GALLERIA MICHELA RIZZO   GALLERY
Map p291 (☑041 839 17 11; www.galleriamichelar izzo.net; Fondamenta San Biagio 800q, Giudecca; ☉11am-6pm Tue-Sat; ☻Palanca) FREE Tucked away in an old industrial complex, this fascinating contemporary-art gallery has long championed local artists, such as Mariateresa Sartori, but it also hosts edgy exhibitions by the likes of Brian Eno and New Yorker Barry X Ball.

☉ Isola di San Giorgio Maggiore

CHIESA DI SAN GIORGIO MAGGIORE
CHURCH
See p140.

LE STANZE DEL VETRO   GALLERY
Map p291 (☑041 522 91 38; www.lestanzedelve tro.org; Isola di San Giorgio Maggiore 8; ☉10am-4.30pm Thu-Tue, extended hours summer; ☻San Giorgio) FREE Once part of a boarding school, 'The Glass Rooms' are now home to a constant flow of temporary exhibitions, all of them based on glass. Often the displays continue outside, with glass installations in the garden. There is a well-stocked gift shop and a fantastic collection of books about glass art.

☉ Isola di San Servolo

Step off *vaporetto* 20 from San Zaccaria and you'll be struck by this little walled island's balmy beauty. Exotic palms and venerable trees sprout within the gardens and there's lots of interesting sculpture scattered about.

Home to Benedictine monks since the 9th century, the island's medicinal flora saw it granted an apothecary's license in 1719 so the monks could better supply the Republic's on-site military hospital. Not long afterwards, in October 1725, San Servolo's first 'insane' patient, Lorenzo Stefani, arrived, starting a trend among aristocratic families to have their afflicted relatives committed. At its peak, the asylum held hundreds of male inmates (the women's asylum was on

---

👁 TOP SIGHT
FONDAZIONE GIORGIO CINI

In 1951, industrialist and art patron Vittorio Cini – a survivor of Dachau – acquired the abbey of San Giorgio and restored it in memory of his son, Giorgio, who died in a plane crash in 1949. Now home to Cini's cultural foundation, the repurposed complex is an architectural treasure incorporating a refectory and cloister by Andrea Palladio, and Baldassare Longhena's monumental staircase and 1671 library. The oldest extant part of the abbey is the Cypress Cloister, completed by Andrea Buora in 1526. The newest is an intricate garden maze, erected in honour of Argentinian writer Jorge Luis Borges.

Veronese's vast *Wedding Feast at Cana* (1563) hung in Palladio's refectory until 1797 when it was looted by Napoleon and sent to the Louvre, where it still resides; an extraordinary full-sized super-high-quality digital copy hangs in its place.

During the Renaissance, Florentine prince Cosimo de' Medici funded the creation of a library here, and the Fondazione continues the Benedictine tradition of scholarship. The Longhena Library has been spectacularly restored, while the impressive Nuova Manica Lunga library now occupies the monks' former dormitory block.

TOP TIP

➜ The complex can only be visited on an hour-long tour with guide and multilingual headset.

PRACTICALITIES

➜ Map p291, F1
➜ ☑041 271 02 37
➜ www.cini.it
➜ Isola di San Giorgio Maggiore
➜ adult/reduced €13/10
➜ ☉tours 10am-6pm daily Apr-Nov, to 4pm Wed-Mon Dec-Mar
➜ ☻San Giorgio Maggiore

the Isola di San Clemente, which is now an exclusive hotel). A large portion of the patients were ex-shiphands and servicemen, many of whom were simply suffering trauma or were afflicted by conditions caused by poverty and poor nutrition.

The psychiatric hospital finally closed its doors in 1978, and in the 1990s the buildings were restored and repurposed. The island is now home to the Venice International University, the Venice Academy of Fine Arts and the international college of the Università Ca' Foscari di Venezia. Visitors can visit the museum, walk around the gardens and make use of the cafe; you might even chance upon an art exhibition.

MUSEO DEL MANICOMIO   MUSEUM
Map p292 (Insane Asylum Museum; ☑041 862 71 67; www.museomanicomio.servizimetropolitani. ve.it; Isola di San Servolo; adult/reduced €6/4.50; ☺10.45am & 2pm Mon-Fri yr-round, plus 3.30-6.30pm Fri, 11.30am-6.30pm Sat & Sun Jun-Sep; ⛴San Servolo) As well as a poignant collection of patients' before-and-after photos, this small museum contains the full paraphernalia of psychiatric treatment of the day, including chains, handcuffs, cages for ice showers, early electro-therapy machines and a rare plethysmograph (the precursor of the lie detector). The visit also takes in an 18th-century pharmacy and church, and a dissection room full of skulls and preserved brains. Tours only take around 30 minutes, but afterwards you're free to potter around the museum.

⊙ Isola di San Lazzaro degli Armeni

Once the site of a Benedictine hospice for pilgrims and then a leper colony, this tiny island was given to Armenian monks fleeing Ottoman persecution in 1717. The entire island is still a working monastery, so access is by tour only.

MONASTERO DI SAN
LAZZARO DEGLI ARMENI   MONASTERY
Map p292 (☑041 526 01 04; Isola di San Lazzaro degli Armeni; adult/reduced €6/4.50; ☺tours 3.25pm; ⛴San Lazzaro) Tours of this historic island monastery are usually conducted by its multilingual Armenian monks, who amply demonstrate the institution's reputation for scholarship. The St Lazarus Monastery is a fascinating repository of Armenian

history, art and culture – and much more besides. Significant manuscripts from its 170,000-item library are on display, alongside curios from Ancient Egypt, Rome, Sumeria and India.

In the 18th century, the monks set up a polyglot printing press here and translated many scientific and literary works into and out of Armenian, publishing 3000 books in a variety of languages. Tours traverse the cloister, refectory, library, museum and glittering church, taking in a ceiling fresco by Tiepolo and a headless Roman statue along the way. An Egyptian mummy and a pair of 15th-century Indian thrones are the quirky main features of the room dedicated to the memory of Lord Byron, who spent six months here in 1816 helping the monks to prepare an English-Armenian dictionary. True to his eccentric nature, he could often be seen swimming from the island to the Grand Canal.

Take the 3.10pm *vaporetto* number 20 from San Zaccaria to arrive in time for the tour; bookings aren't required.

⊙ Lido di Venezia

The Lido is no longer the glamorous bolthole of Hollywood starlets and European aristocracy that it once was, but its groomed beaches, scattering of art nouveau buildings and summering Venetians sipping prosecco beneath candy-striped awnings make it an interesting diversion on a hot day. However, the presence of cars and suburban sprawl can be jarring after the lost-in-time nature of central Venice, and in winter even fading glamour is in short supply.

ANTICO CIMITERO ISRAELITICO   CEMETERY
Map p292 (Ancient Jewish Cemetery; Riviera San Nicolò, Lido; tours €90; ⛴A) This overgrown graveyard was Venice's main Jewish cemetery from 1386 until the 18th century. Tombstones range in design from Venetian Gothic to distinctly Ottoman. Some bear the image of a lion, not of St Mark, but of Castile and León, brought to Venice on the armorials of Sephardic Jews expelled from Spain in 1492. The cemetery can only be visited on a guided tour, arranged through the Museo Ebraico (p109), but you can get a reasonable view through the gate.

PALAZZO DEL CINEMA   NOTABLE BUILDING
Map p292 (www.labiennale.org; Lungomare Marconi 30, Lido; ⛴V) Eugenio Miozzi's angular,

LIDO BEACHES

A near continuous stretch of sand is spread out alongside the seaward side of the Lido. The shallow gradient makes it ideal for toddlers but not great for adults, and despite its somewhat murky appearance, it has been granted Blue Flag status, certifying that the water quality is of a high standard for swimming.

There are only a handful of stretches where the general public can throw a towel down on the sand free of charge. The easiest to reach is the **spiaggia comunale** (Map p292; ⓔLido SME) accessed through the **Blue Moon complex** (Map p292; www.veneziaspiagge. it; Piazzale Bucintoro 1, Lido; ⊗10am-6.30pm summer; ⏵; ⓔLido SME) FREE. The best free stretches are the **Spiaggia di San Nicolò** (⌂041 526 02 36; www.veneziaspiagge.it; Viale Umberto Klinger, Lido; umbrella/lounger per day €15/7.50; ⊗8am-7.30pm; ⏵A) at the north end of the island and the WWF Oasi Dunes degli Alberoni (p144) at the south end.

The rest of the shoreline is occupied by *stabilimenti,* privately managed areas lined with wooden *capannas* (cabins), a relic of the Lido's 1850s bathing scene. Some of them are rented by the same families year in, year out or reserved for guests of seafront hotels. The *stabilimenti* also offer showers, sun lounges and umbrellas (€12 to €18) and small lockers. Rates drop a few euros after 2.30pm.

Rationalist 'Palace of Cinema' was in keeping with the ambitious modernism of the early 1930s, when business tycoon and Fascist minister Count Giuseppe di Volpi cleverly conceived of the Venice Film Festival as a means of fostering the Lido's upmarket tourism industry.

It was an inspired idea in keeping with Volpi's other modernising projects – the Schneider Trophy air race, the casino and an international motorboat race – all of which lured a new breed of moneyed American, English and French holidaymakers.

Inaugurated in August 1932 on the terrace of the Excelsior, the festival was the first of its kind (Cannes was a relative latecomer in 1946) and capitalised on the boom in the film-making industry. So great was its success, in fact, Miozzi's *palazzo* was commissioned within three years and the festival transferred to its new venue in 1938 where it still takes place today.

MALAMOCCO   VILLAGE

(Lido; ⏵A or B) Pass over Ponte di Borgo to explore the canals and *calli* (lanes) of a less overwhelming lagoon town. A miniature version of Venice right down to the lions of St Mark on medieval facades, Malamocco was the lagoon capital from 742 to 811.

WWF OASI DUNES
DEGLI ALBERONI   NATURE RESERVE

Map p292 (www.dunealberoni.it; Piazzale Bagni Alberoni, Lido; ⏵A) FREE Right at the southern tip of the island, the Alberoni pine forest slopes down to the Lido's wildest stretch of beach, home to wildflowers, the *fratino* (Kentish plover) and sea turtles. A 160-hectare expanse of forest and dunes is protected by this 'oasis', although the public can enjoy the shady walking tracks leading to the incongruously plastic-strewn beach. Dogs must be kept on a leash at all times.

◉ Pellestrina

Stretching south of Lido and repeating its long, sinuous shape, Pellestrina is a reminder of what the lagoon might have been like if Venice had never been dreamed of. The 11km-island is home to three tight-knit fishing communities – San Pietro in Volta, Porto Secco and Pellestrina – strung out along the water's edge. There are no hotels, fancy shops or sun loungers here, and only a handful of restaurants and gelato shops. It's mainly just elderly women sitting on their porches and fishermen mending their nets.

Much of Pellestrina's seafront is lined by a remarkable feat of 18th-century engineering known as the *murazzi*. Although not immediately impressive to modern eyes, these massive sea walls represent Herculean handiwork from a pre-industrial age. Designed to keep high seas from crashing into the lagoon, they remain an effective breakwater even today.

The island is blissfully flat, making it ideal biking country. A bike path stretches along the lagoon side of the island, passing candy-striped houses, village churches, boat yards, abandoned industrial buildings and fishermen's shacks built over beds of mussels. There are sandy beaches on the other side of the *murazzi*, but sadly they're often strewn with plastic washed in from the Adriatic.

Bus 11 travels from the Lido SME *vaporetto* stop to Pellestrina via a short hop on a ferry.

EATING

Unsurprisingly, traditional seafood dishes are the main focus in these parts, and both Giudecca and the Lido have some excellent eateries celebrating the local cuisine. You won't find anything on the smaller islets, unless they're attached to one of the private-island hotels.

Giudecca

★LA PALANCA   VENETIAN €€

Map p291 (☑041 528 77 19; www.facebook.com/LaPalancaGiudecca; Fondamenta Sant'Eufemia 448, Giudecca; meals €24-40; ☺7am-8.30pm Mon-Sat; ☜☑; ☒Palanca) Locals of all ages pour into this humble bar for *cicheti* (Venetian tapas*)*, coffee and a *spritz* (prosecco cocktail). However, it's at lunchtime that it really comes into its own, serving surprisingly sophisticated fare like swordfish carpaccio with orange zest alongside more rustic dishes, such as a delicious *pasta e fagioli* (pasta and bean soup). In summer, competition for waterside tables is stiff.

★TRATTORIA AI CACCIATORI   VENETIAN €€

Map p291 (☑328 7363346; www.aicacciatori.it; Fondamenta del Ponte Piccolo 320, Giudecca; meals €34-47; ☺noon-3pm & 6.30-10pm Tue-Sun; ☜; ☒Palanca) If you hadn't guessed from the oversized gun hanging from the ceiling beams, the restaurant is named for the hunters who once bagged lagoon waterfowl. Dishes are hearty but sophisticated, including both game and local seafood.

★TRATTORIA ALTANELLA   VENETIAN €€

Map p291 (☑041 522 77 80; Calle de le Erbe 268, Giudecca; meals €41-46; ☺12.30-2pm & 7.30-9pm Wed-Sun; ☒; ☒Redentore) Founded by fisherfolk in 1920 and still run by the same family, this cosy restaurant serves classic Venetian fare such as potato gnocchi with cuttlefish, stuffed squid and perfectly grilled fish. The vintage interior is hung with paintings, reflecting the restaurant's popularity with local artists, and there are also tables on a flower-fringed balcony jutting out over the canal.

Lido di Venezia

MAGICHE VOGLIE   GELATO €

Map p292 (☑347 7943992; Gran Viale Santa Maria Elisabetta 47g, Lido; cones €2.50-4.50; ☺2.30-9pm Fri-Sun Mar & Oct, 10am-11pm Apr-Sep; ☒Lido SMF) The best ice cream on the Lido is made on the premises of this family-owned gelateria every morning. Decide

---

LIDO STYLE

Between 1857 and WWI, the Lido became the world's most exclusive seaside resort and is still defined by the *stile liberty* (art nouveau) of the period. Walking itineraries around the most extravagant villas are available online at www2.comune.venezia.it/lidoliberty (Italian only). The style reaches an over-the-top apotheosis in the garish 1907 **Grande Albergo Ausonia & Hungaria** (Map p292; ☑041 242 00 60; www.hungaria.it; Gran Viale Santa Maria Elisabetta 28, Lido; ☒Lido SME), decorated with wreath-bearing cherubs and tiles in a particularly nauseating shade of green.

Canny business tycoon Nicolò Spada (founder of the Italian hotel group CIGA) built two vast, extravagant hotels on the Lido. Sitting directly on the beach, the Giovanni Sardi–designed **Hotel Excelsior** (Map p292; ☑041 526 02 01; www.hotelexcelsiorvenezia.com; Lungomare Marconi 41, Lido; r from €328; ☺May-Oct; ☒☜; ☒V), completed in 1908, is a Veneto-Moorish fantasy palace with interiors decorated by Mariano Fortuny. The more conservative **Grand Hotel des Bains** (Map p292; Lungomare Marconi 17, Lido; ☒Lido SME), designed by Francesco Marsich, was finished the following year and recalls the great luxury spas of Baden Baden. It was immortalised in Thomas Mann's best-selling novella *Death in Venice,* which was adapted for the screen by Luchino Visconti in 1971 and filmed in the hotel. Sadly it's now boarded up – an oversized symbol of the beach resort's fall from fashion.

between the soft peaks of New World flavours such as açai berry and caja fruit, or plump for the classic purplish-black cherry or Sicilian pistachio.

GELIDO LATO
GELATO €

Map p292 (☑041 839 06 45; www.gelidolato.it; Via Isola di Cerigo 5, Lido; ice creams from €1.70; ⊘noon-11.30pm; ▣Lido SME) This tiny artisanal ice-cream parlour prides itself on fresh ingredients and interesting flavours, such as cheesecake or walnut and fig. Vegan options available.

EL PECADOR
FOOD TRUCK €

Map p292 (☑324 8373715; Lungomare Gabriele d'Annunzio, Lido; sandwiches €3-6; ⊘10am-2am Apr-Sep; ▣Lido SME) No, you're not suffering from heat stroke – that really is a red double-decker bus parked up against the kerb. What's more, it's dishing out the Lido's finest stuffed sandwiches and *spritz*, so why not take a seat on the canopied top deck?

AL MERCÀ
VENETIAN €€

Map p292 (☑041 243 16 63; www.osteriaalmerca. it; Via Enrico Dandolo 17a, Lido; meals €30-43, 3-course meat/fish menu €15/20; ⊘noon-2.30pm & 6.45-9.30pm daily summer, noon-2.30pm & 6.45-9.30pm Thu-Sat & noon-2.30pm Sun winter; ▣Lido SME) Located in the old Lido fish market, al Mercà is popular with students who come for the abundant *cicheti*, outdoor seating and well-priced wine by the glass. Snack at one of the counters or grab a seat in the *osteria* (casual tavern) for a traditional seafood meal. A good-value set menu is also offered.

TRATTORIA ANDRI
VENETIAN €€

Map p292 (☑041 526 54 82; Via Lepanto 21, Lido; meals €30-38; ⊘6-10pm Tue-Sat, noon-3pm & 6-10pm Sun; ▣Lido SME) Beloved by locals, this charming fish restaurant serves classic Venetian dishes prepared with attention to quality. In summer, book a table on the verdant front verandah.

FAVORITA
VENETIAN €€€

Map p292 (☑041 526 16 26; Via Francesco Duodo 33, Lido; meals €41-55; ⊘7-10.30pm Tue-Thu, 12.30-2.30pm & 7-10.30pm Fri-Sun; ▣A) Favorita has been delivering long, lazy lunches, bottles of fine wine and impeccable service since 1955. The menu is full of traditional Venetian seafood dishes such as *rombo* (turbot) simmered with cherry tomatoes and olives, crab *gnochetti* (mini-gnocchi) and classic fish risotto.

✕ Pellestrina

RISTORANTE DA CELESTE
VENETIAN €€€

(☑041 96 73 55; www.daceleste.it; Via Vianelli 625b, Pellestrina; meals €60-80; ⊘noon-2.30pm & 7-9.15pm Thu-Tue Mar-Oct; ▣11) This simple restaurant halfway along Pellestrina serves lagoon-fresh fish on its pontoon terrace. Go at sunset, when the rose-tinted sky kisses the glassy lagoon, and let Rossano guide you through the best daily offerings, from polenta with tiny shrimp to a whole host of cockles, clams, scallops, spider crab and – the house speciality – fish pie. Reservations essential.

🍷 DRINKING & NIGHTLIFE

Summertime on the Lido brings with it beach bars and barefoot clubs, but at other times there's little to get excited by. True to its divergent nature, Giudecca has a scattering of both cosy local haunts and ritzy hangouts.

SKYLINE
ROOFTOP BAR

Map p291 (☑041 272 33 11; www.skylinebarven ice.it; Fondamenta San Biagio 810, Giudecca; ⊘noon-1am Apr-Oct, 4pm-midnight Nov-Mar; ▣Palanca) From white-sneaker cruise passengers to the €300-sunglasses set, the rooftop bar at the Hilton Molino Stucky wows everyone with its vast panorama over Venice and the lagoon. DJs spin tunes on Friday nights year-round, and on additional nights in summer, when the action moves to the deck and pool. There's occasional live music too.

BAR 9
WINE BAR

Map p292 (☑347 0301575; Via Lepanto 9; ⊘9.30am-12.30am; ▣Lido SME) There's a lot to love about this cosy little place on the Lido's cutest car-free strip: the exposed brick walls, bare-wood bar, interesting art and excellent wine list, for starters. But it's the exceptional *cicheti* that keep us heading back for more.

OSTERIA DA MORO
WINE BAR

Map p291 (☑041 099 58 84; Fondamenta Sant'Eufemia 658, Giudecca; ⊘7am-11pm Wed-Mon; 🛜; ▣Palanca) This bijou bar serves sandwiches and substantial snacks throughout the day, alongside an excellent selection of wine. Large windows make the most of the views across the Giudecca Canal.

ESSENTIALE
BAR

Map p292 (☑041 526 13 16; www.essentialeres taurant.com; Via Sandro Gallo 6, Lido; ☉12.30pm-midnight Tue-Sun; ⬛Lido SME) Sunset photo ops don't come any better than on the terrace of the Habsburg-era Villa Laguna, with views over San Marco framed by a blushing pink sky. While Essentiale is essentially a restaurant, it also caters to the *aperitivo* crowd. And it's very handy to the Lido SME ferry terminal.

DA CRI CRI E TENDINA
BAR

Map p292 (☑041 526 54 28; Via Sandro Gallo 159, Lido; ☉7.30am-9pm Mon-Sat, 8.30am-1pm Sun; 🚉A, B, C) Head to this neighbourhood bar for Veneto wines, beers on tap and a counter full of the island's best *cicheti*. It's best in summer when all the tables are set outside and local card sharks sip their *spritz* and goad each other loudly in Venetian. At lunchtime there's a huge selection of stuffed *panini*.

🛍 SHOPPING

While Lido's main strip, Gran Viale Santa Maria Elisabetta, has plenty of shops, they mainly seem to target rich retirees. Giudecca has a few interesting workshops selling locally produced craft.

ARTISTI ARTIGIANI
DEL CHIOSTRO
ARTS & CRAFTS

Map p291 (Campo San Cosma 620a, Giudecca; ☉hr vary; ⬛Palanca) Dating from the 15th-century, the cloister of the former Convent of Sts Cosmas and Damian has been repurposed as a base for independent artisans to ply their craft. The artisans keep their own hours and not all are open to the public, but loop around and you'll find traditional mask makers, book restorers, painters, metal workers, glass-blowers and many, many cats.

FORTUNY TESSUTI ARTISTICI
HOMEWARES

Map p291 (☑393 8257651; www.fortuny.com; Fondamenta San Biagio 805, Giudecca; ☉10am-6pm Mon-Fri; ⬛Palanca) Marcel Proust waxed rhapsodic over Fortuny's silken cottons printed with art nouveau patterns. At the showroom attached to his still-functioning

factory, visitors can browse 300 textile designs and purchase upholstery fabrics or finished goods such as cushions. For more inspiration, head to the Museo Fortuny (p59).

MERCATO DELLA
PRIGIONE FEMMINILE
MARKET

Map p291 (www.rioteradeipensieri.org; Fondamenta de le Convertite 713, Giudecca; ☉9am-noon Thu; ⬛Palanca) 🌿 Giudecca locals head here early to stock up on organic vegetables grown in the 'Garden of Wonders' in the women's prison and sold on a stand out the front. There are also handmade soaps, shampoos and moisturisers, all made by prisoners on site as part of a social reintegration programme run by a nonprofit cooperative.

MERCATO SETTIMANALE DEL LIDO
MARKET

Map p292 (Area Mercatino delle Quatro Fontane, Lido; ☉7.30am-1pm Tue & Fri; ⬛Lido SME) The Lido's open-air market offers a bit of everything during the Tuesday general market and speciality food products in the Friday Farmers' Markets.

🏃 SPORTS & ACTIVITIES

ACQUOLINA COOKING SCHOOL
COOKING

Map p292 (☑041 526 72 26; www.acquolina.com; Via Lazzaro Mocenigo 10, Lido; half-/full-day courses €170/290; ♿; ⬛Lido) These intimate cookery classes are held by Marika Contaldo in her flower-festooned Lido villa. Serious gourmets will want to consider the multiday culinary vacations, which include cookery lessons interspersed with market visits, lagoon cruises and trips to the Segusa glass factory. Otherwise, there are half- and full day taster courses, the latter including a morning trip to the Rialto Market.

CIRCOLO GOLF VENEZIA
GOLF

Map p292 (☑041 73 13 33; www.circologolfven ezia.it; Strada Vecchia 1, Lido; green fees weekdays/weekends €80/95; ☉9am-4pm; 🚉A) The golf club sits on a 100-hectare site at Alberoni, at the southern end of the island. The original nine-hole course (there are now 18, par 72) was designed by Cruikshank of Glasgow in 1928 and incorporates the walls of the old Alberoni fort as key elements in various holes.

Murano, Burano & the Northern Islands

ISOLA DI SAN MICHELE | MURANO | BURANO & MAZZORBO | TORCELLO | ISOLA DI SAN FRANCESCO DEL DESERTO | SANT'ERASMO | LE VIGNOLE | ISOLA DELLA CERTOSA

Neighbourhood Top Five

1 **Basilica di Santa Maria Assunta** (p150) Engaging with visions of angels, saints and dastardly demons within the golden glow of ancient mosaics in the lagoon's oldest church.

2 **Murano** (p151) Witnessing artistry in action at the island's glass-blowing showrooms, exploring glass-

making history at the Museo del Vetro, and shopping for a unique memento.

3 **Burano** (p152) Watching colourful houses shimmer with delight at their own reflections in the canals, and learning about the island's lacy legacy.

4 **Seafood feasts** (p158) Enjoying the bounty of the

lagoon at restaurants such as Venissa Osteria, where there's the added bonus of vineyard views and rare wine.

5 **Basilica dei SS Maria e Donato** (p151) Checking out more golden mosaics, dragon bones and a spectacular ancient marbled floor.

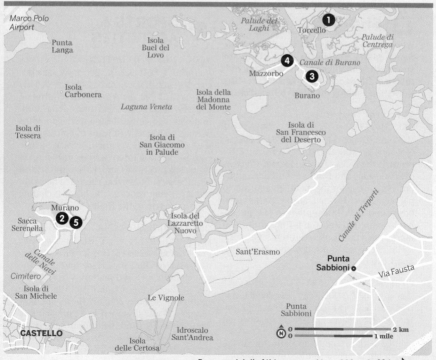

For more detail of this area see Map p293 and p294. ➡

Explore Murano, Burano & the Northern Islands

A multitude of islands dot the northern lagoon like shards of green glass splintering off the mainland. Refugees from the Roman city of Altinum escaped to safety on Torcello in the 5th century when the Mongol hordes descended. There they raised the first church of the lagoon, Santa Maria Assunta (p150), decorating it with glittering mosaics telling cautionary tales in over a million hand-cut glass *tesserae*. From Torcello they gradually spread to the neighbouring islands before largely abandoning them in favour of the new settlement of Venice.

The northernmost islands remain sleepy places today, with only the pretty candy-striped town of Burano attracting significant tourists – and then only during the day. Few bother to cross the bridge to Mazzorbo, although those that do are amply rewarded with some of the region's best food and wine. Only the seriously intrepid visit the lost-in-time friary (p153) on San Francesco del Deserto, or the lagoon gardens on Sant'Erasmo and Le Vignole.

Much closer to Venice, Murano is another story altogether. Here famous glass workshops continue to conjure writhing chandeliers, swirling goblets and gem-bright jewellery from their red-hot furnaces – the modern heirs of Torcello's ancient mosaic makers. But even on this most visited of the northern islands, peace descends after dark.

Local Life

➡ **Peaceful picnics** Pack a picnic to enjoy on Certosa; between the grapevines on Mazzorbo; in the meadow behind the basilica on Torcello; or among the picturesque ruins of Forte Sant'Andrea on Le Vignole.

➡ **Island sleepovers** Stay the night in one of the few inns on Torcello, Burano or Mazzorbo and experience the after-hours peace that usually only the locals enjoy.

Getting There & Away

➡ **Vaporetto** Services run every 10 minutes before 10pm and every 20 to 30 minutes thereafter. Murano has seven stops, and lines 3, 4.1 and 4.2 loop around most of them. Lines 12 (to Mazzorbo, Burano and, sometimes, Torcello) and 13 (to Le Vignole and Sant'Erasmo) stop only at Murano Faro before continuing on to the outlying islands. Aside from line 3 (train station direct), all other lines stop at Fondamente Nove.

Lonely Planet's Top Tip

Hit the outer islands first (boats to Torcello take 50 minutes) before *vaporetti* (small passenger ferries) get crowded, then work your way back to Murano, aiming to hit the shops as crowds start to thin out in the early evening. Murano is only 10 minutes from Venice, so it's fast and easy to reach if you need to return for more glass.

◉ Best Lagoon Photo Ops

➡ Burano canals (p152) Brightly painted houses reflected in the water.

➡ Basilica di Santa Maria Assunta (p150) Lagoon views from the bell tower.

➡ Mazzorbo (p152) Cormorants holding their wings out to dry.

For reviews, see p151.➡

✖ Best Places to Eat

➡ Trattoria al Gatto Nero (p158)

➡ Osteria al Duomo (p158)

➡ Venissa Osteria (p158)

➡ Trattoria Maddalena (p158)

➡ Acquastanca (p158)

For reviews, see p158.➡

🔒 Best Places to Shop

➡ Cesare Toffolo (p159)

➡ ElleElle (p159)

➡ Emilia (p159)

➡ Venini (p159)

➡ Fornace Mian (p159)

For reviews, see p159.➡

TOP SIGHT
BASILICA DI SANTA MARIA ASSUNTA

Life choices are presented in no uncertain terms in the dazzling mosaics of the Assumption Basilica: look ahead to a golden afterlife amid the saints and a beatific Madonna and Child, or turn your back on them to face the wrath of the devil gloating over lost souls.

In existence since the 7th century, this former cathedral is the lagoon's oldest Byzantine-Romanesque structure. The restrained brick exterior betrays no hint of the colourful scene that unfolds as you enter.

In the 12th-century **apse mosaic**, the Madonna and Child hover above the Apostles, standing on a field of Torcello poppies. The **right-hand chapel** is capped with a similarly aged mosaic showing Christ flanked by two angels and Sts Augustine, Ambrose, Martin and Gregory amid richly rendered symbolic plants: lilies (representing purity), wheat and grapes (representing the bread and wine of the Eucharist) and poppies (evoking Torcello's island setting).

On the rear wall, the extraordinary **Last Judgment mosaic** shows the Adriatic as a sea nymph ushering souls lost at sea towards St Peter, while a sneaky devil tips the scales of justice and the Antichrist's minions drag the damned into hell.

Saints line up atop the gilded **iconostasis**, their gravity foiled by a Byzantine screen teeming with peacocks, rabbits and other more fanciful beasts. The polychrome marble floor is another medieval masterpiece, with swirling designs and interlocking wheels symbolising eternal life.

TOP TIPS

➡ Climb the *campanile* (bell tower; €5) for the view over the islands, a fascinating insight into what Venice must have once looked like.

➡ An audio guide (€2) gives further details.

➡ Various combo tickets are offered including the church, *campanile,* audio guide and the neighbouring museum (which is closed on Mondays).

PRACTICALITIES

➡ Map p294, C4

➡ ☏041 73 01 19

➡ Piazza Torcello, Torcello

➡ adult/reduced €5/4, incl museum & campanile €12/10

➡ ⊙10.30am-5.30pm

➡ ⛴Torcello

◉ SIGHTS

Of all the islands, Murano is the easiest to get to and has the most to do, though far-flung Torcello has a cluster of historic sights that rate among the most fascinating in the northern lagoon. Visitors to Torcello would be remiss not to call in to pretty Burano, which is only a short hop away.

◉ Isola di San Michele

This picturesque walled islet, positioned between Murano and the city, is Venice's main cemetery. *Vaporetti* 4.1 and 4.2 stop here, en route between Fondamente Nove and Murano.

CIMITERO DI SAN MICHELE CEMETERY

(Isola di San Michele; ⊗7.30am-6pm Apr-Sep, to 4.30pm Oct-Mar; ⏩Cimitero) **FREE** Until Napoleon established a city cemetery on this little island, Venetians had been buried in parish plots across town – not an ideal solution in a watery city. Today, goths, incorrigible romantics and music lovers pause here to pay respects to Ezra Pound, Joseph Brodsky, Sergei Diaghilev and Igor Stravinsky. Pick up a map from the office to the left of the entrance and join them, but be aware, the map pinpointing of the famous graves isn't accurate.

This is still a functioning graveyard and Venetians are constantly dropping by to pay their respects to their loved ones buried here; hence, photography and picnics aren't permitted. David Chipperfield Architects are in charge of the ongoing extension, which includes striking concrete and basalt 'courtyards'.

Before it was suppressed by Napoleon, the island was home to a Camaldolese monastery. The cloisters remain, as does the 1469 **Chiesa di San Michele in Isola** (€1, open on weekday mornings), one of the first Renaissance churches in Venice. Inside there are impressive carved wooden ceiling bosses, but the architecture is best admired from the ferry to Murano.

◉ Murano

Venetians have been working in glass since the 10th century, but due to the fire hazards of glass-blowing, the industry was moved to the island of Murano in the 13th century. Woe betide the glass-blower with wanderlust: trade secrets were so jealously guarded that any glass worker who left the city was guilty of treason and subject to assassination. Today, glass artisans continue to ply their trade at workshops all over the island, with shops selling their extraordinarily expensive wares lining the Fondamenta dei Vetrai.

Murano is less than 10 minutes from Fondamente Nove by *vaporetto* and services are frequent.

★BASILICA DEI SS MARIA E DONATO CHURCH

Map p293 (www.sandonatomurano.it; Campo San Donato, Murano; ⊗9am-6pm Mon-Sat, 12.30-6pm Sun; ⏩Museo) **FREE** Fire-breathing is the unifying theme of Murano's medieval church, with its astounding 12th-century gilded-glass apse mosaic of the Madonna made in Murano's *fornaci* (furnaces) and the bones of a dragon hanging behind the altar. According to tradition, this beast was slayed by St Donatus of Arezzo, whose mortal remains also rest here. The other masterpiece here is underfoot: a Byzantine-style 12th-century mosaic pavement of waving geometric patterns, griffons, eagles and peacocks rendered in porphyry, serpentine and other precious stones.

MUSEO DEL VETRO MUSEUM

Map p293 (Glass Museum; ☑041 243 49 14; www. museovetro.visitmuve.it; Fondamenta Giustinian 8, Murano; adult/reduced €14/11.50 free with Museum Pass; ⊗10am-5pm; ⏩Museo) Since 1861, Murano's glass-making prowess has been celebrated in Palazzo Giustinian, the home of bishops of Torcello from 1689 until the diocese's dissolution in 1805. Upstairs, eight rooms have beautifully curated displays of objects dating back to the 5th century BC. Back downstairs, rotating contemporary glass exhibits are on show in the Spazio Conterie just beyond the museum shop, which stocks a small selection of top-quality glass gifts, jewellery and art books.

CHIESA DI SAN PIETRO MARTIRE CHURCH

Map p293 (www.sandonatomurano.it; Fondamenta dei Vetrai, Murano; museum €2; ⊗church 9am-5.30pm Mon-Fri, noon-5.30pm Sat & Sun, museum 10am-4pm Mon-Fri; ⏩Museo) **FREE** Take a pause from glass shopping to check out *The Baptism of Christ,* attributed to Tintoretto, in 16th-century St Peter the

A GLIMPSE INTO THE FURNACES

Touts around San Marco and Murano hand out flyers for demonstrations at various furnaces on the island, some of which seem to exist only to cater to tour groups. The experience is extremely touristy but can still be fascinating; the **Glass Cathedral** (Map p293; ☑041 73 69 98; www.santachiaramurano.com; Fondamenta Manin 1; summer/winter €7/5; ⬛Colonna) puts on a good show. **Guarnieri Vetreria Artistica** (Map p293; ☑041 527 43 70; www.vetreriaguarnieri.com; Fondamenta Serenella 4, Murano; ◷9am-4pm; ⬛Colonna) is half the price, but the presentations are half as long. Note that some places offer 'free' demonstrations, but you may be asked for 'donations' for the workers or aggressively upsold in the attached shop.

Few of the top artisans offer tours, but if you're looking at shelling out thousands for a chandelier or two, chances are they'll be amenable to showing you around.

Martyr's Church. The parish museum has the usual collection of religious art, vestments, processional artefacts and reliquaries. Of more interest is the extraordinary 17th-century panelling in the sacristy, featuring 33 carved wooden characters including Nero with his fiddle and a suitably macabre Prometheus.

◉ Burano & Mazzorbo

Once Venice's lofty architecture leaves you feeling overwhelmed, Burano brings you back to your senses with a reviving shock of colour. The 50-minute ferry ride on line 12 from the Fondamente Nove is packed with amateur photographers preparing to bound into Burano's backstreets, snapping away at pea-green stockings hung to dry between hot-pink and royal-blue houses.

Burano is famed for its handmade lace, which once graced the décolletage and ruffs of European aristocracy. Unfortunately, the ornate styles and expensive tablewear fell out of vogue in lean post-WWII times and the industry has since suffered a decline. Some women still maintain the traditions, but few production houses remain; with a couple of notable exceptions, most of the lace for sale in local shops is of the imported, machine-made variety.

If you fancy a stroll, hop across the 60m bridge to Burano's even quieter sister island, Mazzorbo. Little more than a broad grassy knoll, Mazzorbo is a great place for a picnic or a long, lazy lunch. Line 12 also stops at Mazzorbo, and line 9 runs a shuttle between Burano and Torcello.

MUSEO DEL MERLETTO   MUSEUM
Map p294 (Lace Museum; ☑041 73 00 34; www.museomerletto.visitmuve.it; Piazza Galuppi 185, Burano; adult/reduced €5/3.50, with Museum Pass free; ◷10am-5pm; ⬛Burano) Burano's Lace Museum tells the story of a craft that cut across social boundaries, endured for centuries and evoked the epitome of sophistication reached during the Republic's heyday. Lace-making was both a creative expression and a highly lucrative craft, although the skill was nearly lost several times as handmade lace went in and out of fashion.

CHIESA DI SAN MARTINO   CHURCH
Map p294 (☑041 73 00 96; www.parrocchiadiburano.weebly.com; Piazza Galuppi, Burano; ◷8am-noon & 3-7pm; ⬛Burano) FREE Sixteenth-century St Martin's Church, with its worryingly wonky 53m-high *campanile*, is worth a peek for Giambattista Tiepolo's 1725 *La Crocifissione* (near the rear on the left), showing the Madonna collapsed at the foot of the Cross, grey with grief. The 19th-century Russian icon near the main altar is the *Madonna di Kazan,* a masterpiece of enamelwork with astonishingly bright, lifelike eyes.

CHIESA DI SANTA CATERINA   CHURCH
Map p294 (☑041 73 01 69; www.parrocchiadimazzorbo.weebly.com; Isola di Mazzorbo 32; ◷9am-7pm summer, to 5pm winter; ⬛Mazzorbo) Mazzorbo's late 13th-century Romanesque St Catherine's Church is the only one of the island's 10 medieval churches to survive. Call in to see its wooden *carena di nave* (ship's hull) ceiling; chances are you'll have the church all to yourself.

◉ Torcello

On the pastoral island of Torcello, sheep vastly outnumber the 14 or so human residents. This bucolic backwater was once a

Byzantine metropolis of 20,000, but rivalry with its offshoot Venice and a succession of malaria epidemics systematically reduced its population. Of its original nine churches and two abbeys, all that remain are the Basilica di Santa Maria Assunta (p150) and the 11th-century Chiesa di Santa Fosca.

Not all line 12 *vaporetto* services stop at Torcello, but those that do provide a direct link to Burano, Mazzorbo, Murano and Fondamente Nove. The more frequent line 9 shuttles to and from Burano.

BASILICA DI SANTA MARIA ASSUNTA
CHURCH

See p150.

MUSEO DI TORCELLO
MUSEUM

Map p294 (☑041 73 07 61; www.museoditorcello.provincia.venezia.it; Piazza Torcello, Torcello; adult/reduced €3/1.50, incl basilica €8/6; ⊙10.30am-5.30pm Tue-Sun; ⚓Torcello) Occupying two buildings across the square from the Basilica di Santa Maria Assunta, this museum is dedicated to Torcello's venerable history. The main building, the 13th-century Palazzo del Consiglio, displays mainly religious art recovered from the island's many long-lost churches. The annexe focuses on ancient archaeological treasures, many of which were discovered in the abandoned Roman city of Altinum (Altino) on the mainland. The collection includes tiny Egyptian figurines, Etruscan bronzes, Greek pottery and some lovely Roman cameos.

CHIESA DI SANTA FOSCA
CHURCH

Map p294 (Piazza Torcello, Torcello; ⊙10am-4.30pm; ⚓Torcello) **FREE** Literally overshadowed by Torcello's famous basilica, to which it's connected by a colonnaded walkway, this interesting round Byzantine-style church dates from the 11th century. It's relatively unadorned inside, with plain brick walls, a domed wooden roof and Corinthian columns in grey marble.

TRONO D'ATTILA
HISTORIC SITE

Map p294 (Attila's Throne; Piazza Torcello, Torcello; ⚓Torcello) This 5th-century marble throne is said to have been used by Attila the Hun when his horde swept south, terrorising the Roman city of Altino. In fact, the Huns never reached Torcello and the throne was the seat of the *magister mili-*

REGATTA REVELRY

The biggest event in the northern lagoon calendar is the 32km Vogalonga long row from Venice to Murano and Burano and back each May or June. It's a fabulously festive occasion when hundreds of enthusiasts take to the waters in their wooden *batèla* (flat-bottomed boat) and motorised boats are banned from the lagoon for the day.

Plan in advance and find a grassy picnic spot on Mazzorbo. If you'd like to have a go yourself, get in touch with **Row Venice** (Map p282; ☑347 7250637; www.rowvenice.org; Fondamenta Contarini; 90min lessons per 1-2 people €85, 3/4 people 120/140; ⚓Orto), who'll soon show you how to wield an oar like a gondolier.

tum, the military governor of the island, used when administering justice.

⊙ Isola di San Francesco del Deserto

Given that the Venetian lagoon is situated on one of the most important bird migration routes in Europe, it seems only fitting that Francis of Assisi, the saint so famous for talking to birds, should have sought respite here after his journey to Palestine in 1220. After the saint's death Jacopo Michiel, the owner of the island, donated it to the Franciscan order. In 1420 the friars were forced to desert the island (hence the name) due to rampant malaria, but in 1856 Monsignor Portogruaro brought them back and here they have remained ever since.

To get to the island you'll need to hire a private boat or water taxi (approximately €80 to €100 return for up to four people, including the 40- to 60-minute wait time) or book a seat aboard the 2.30pm shuttle from Burano operated by **Laguna Fla** (☑347 9922959; www.lagunaflaline.it; return €10, min 4 people).

CONVENTO DI SAN FRANCESCO DEL DESERTO
MONASTERY

(☑041 528 68 63; www.sanfrancescodeldeserto.it; Isola di San Francesco del Deserto; donations appreciated; ⊘9-11am & 3-5pm Tue-Sun) FREE Franciscan friars offer free tours of their secluded island home, which still retains some of its 13th-century elements, including the first cloister. As this is a place of contemplation, visitors are asked to speak in hushed tones as they are led around the two cloisters and into the serene chapel where St Francis himself is said to have prayed. Best of all are the peaceful, cypress-scented gardens with their dreamlike views of Burano.

It pays to phone ahead to ensure there's a friar available.

⊙ Sant'Erasmo

Sant'Erasmo is known as the *orto di Venezia* (Venice's garden), and if you're visiting in early May, don't miss the **Festa del Carciofo Violetto** (⊘May), when the island celebrates the first crop of its purple-hued artichokes. At 4.5km from tip to toe, Sant'Erasmo is as long as Venice, although it's just 1km at its widest point. Seven-hundred-and-fifty farmers still plough its fields, supplying not only artichokes but also asparagus, squash and tomatoes to the Rialto Market and Venice's restaurants.

Once a rural retreat for aristocrats, the island now provides a largely tourist-free refuge for Venetian families who moor their boats along its mudbanks and picnic on its narrow 'beaches'. Essential shots of coffee and pizza lunches are provided by the seasonal bar behind the **beach** (Via dei Forti, Sant'Erasmo; ⚲Capannone), while bikes (€5 for two hours, €1 every hour thereafter) can be rented at the island's only accommodation, Il Lato Azzurro (p202).

Vaporetto 13 from Fondamente Nove and Murano docks at Capannone, Chiesa and Punto Vela. In summer, line 18 departs from Murano and the Lido and stops near the partly ruined **Torre Massimiliana** (Maximilian's Tower; Via dei Forti, Sant'Erasmo; ⊘hr vary; ⚲Capannone), a 19th-century Austrian fort sometimes used for art exhibitions. There's a small beach nearby.

⊙ Le Vignole

Welcome to the Venetian countryside! Together the two islands of Vignole Vecchie and Vignole Nuove produced the doge's wine, and their 50 inhabitants still make a living mainly from agriculture. Like that of nearby Sant'Erasmo, the landscape is covered in fields, groves and vineyards, and people are few and far between. *Vaporetto* 13 runs to Le Vignole from Fondamente Nove via Murano (Faro stop).

At the island's southeastern tip a promontory ends in the Isola di Sant'Andrea, the location of the best-preserved fort on the lagoon: 16th-century **Forte Sant'Andrea**.

ISOLA DEL LAZZARETTO NUOVO

Every summer since 1988, amateur archaeologists, university graduates and school-children have made the journey out to the island of **Lazzaretto Nuovo** (⌀041 244 40 11; www.lazzarettonuovo.com; tour €5; ⊘tours 9.45am & 4.30pm Sat & Sun Apr-Oct; ⚲Lazzaretto Nuovo) to work on one of the most fascinating historic sites in the lagoon, the **Tezon Grande**.

The island was used as a quarantine depot for the Republic between 1468 and the 1700s, and the 16th-century Tezon is the largest public building in the lagoon after the Corderie at the Arsenale. Around its perimeter, excavations have revealed one-room cells where travelling merchants waited out their 40-day exile, trying to avoid the plague while city officials fumigated their cargoes. Archaeological groups have catalogued hundreds of artefacts and uncovered extensive graffiti describing harrowing voyages from Cyprus and Constantinople.

Budding Indiana Jones wannabes can enjoy an active role in the Lazzaretto's rehabilitation during the archaeological **summer camps** (€490 per week including food and lodging).

On weekends in the warmer months the island may be visited on a **guided tour**, focusing on its history, archaeology and nature. Take the *vaporetto* 13 service leaving from Fondamente Nove D at 9.25am or 4.05pm and request the stop.

EXPLORING THE LAGOON

Seeing and understanding something of the lagoon's patchwork of shifting mudflats is integral to understanding Venice. Unesco recognised this by specifically including the 550-sq-km expanse – the largest coastal wetland in Europe – in its designation of Venice as a World Heritage Site in 1987.

Rich in unique flora and fauna, the tidal *barene* (shoals) and salt marshes are part of the city's psyche. Between September and January over 130,000 migrating birds nest, dive and dabble in the shallows, while year-round fishermen tend their nets and traps, and city-council workers dredge canals and reinforce the shifting islands of cord-grass and saltwort so essential to the lagoon's survival.

The easiest and cheapest way to explore the lagoon is to island hop with a *vaporetto* day pass. A boat tour, such as those offered by **Terra e Acqua** (☑347 4205004; www.veneziainbarca.it; ⊙day trips from €400), will take you to harder-to-reach places, such as the island friary of San Francesco del Deserto (p153). Otherwise you can rent your own vessel with **CBV** (Classic Boats Venice; ☑041 523 67 20; www.classicboats-venice.com; Isola della Certosa; 1/2/3/4/8hr rental €80/130/180/225/295; ⊙9am-7pm Apr-Feb; ☑Certosa) ⌀ or **Brussa Is Boat** (Map p282; ☑041 71 57 87; www.brussaisboat.it; Fondamenta Labia 331; 7m boat per hr/day incl fuel €43/196; ⊙7.30am-5.30pm Mon-Fri, to 12.30pm Sat & Sun; ☑Ferrovia) and go it alone. If you don't mind working up a sweat, both **Venice Kayak** (☑346 4771327; www.venicekayak.com; Vento di Venezia, Isola della Certosa; half-/full-day tours €95/125) and **SUP in Venice** (Map p282; ☑389 9851866; www.supinvenice.com; Fondamenta Contarini 3535; tours from €70; ⊙Apr-Oct; ☑Orto) also offer lagoon excursions.

⊙ Isola della Certosa

Once home to Carthusian monks (hence the island's name), La Certosa was the site of a grand monastery, its church graced with ducal tombs and rich artworks. All of that was lost, however, when the island was taken over by the military in the 19th century. Even the cloister was purchased by Prince Charles of Prussia and rebuilt in his summer castle in Berlin in 1850.

Today, thanks to EU funding and a public-private partnership, the island has been revived as a marina and lush public park under the **Vento di Venezia** (☑041 520 85 88; www.ventodivenezia.it; Isola della Certosa; ☑Certosa) umbrella. The marina complex includes a hotel, an alfresco restaurant-bar and a sailing club, which runs regattas and a summertime Sail Camp for children. However the biggest appeal is that's it's a pretty place for a stroll or a picnic, away from the crowds. Chances are, aside from a few dog walkers and joggers, you'll have the paths to yourself.

Vaporetto line 4.1/4.2 stops on request in Certosa between 6am and 8.30pm, while 5.1/5.2 takes up the service after 8.30pm. To signal that you want to be picked up from the island, push the signal button at the wharf for the direction in which you want to go.

✕ EATING

Seafood features highly in traditional Venetian cuisine and no more so than in this part of the lagoon. The northern islands offer some culinary highlights, so make time for a long, lazy lunch away from the tourist hustle of the city.

AI BISATEI
VENETIAN €

Map p293 (☑041 73 95 28; Campo San Bernardo 6, Murano; meals €18-27; ⊙11.30am-3pm Thu-Tue; ☑Venier) Seek out this vintage *osteria* (casual tavern) where glass-blowers head for plates of *frittura mista* (mixed fried fish), seafood risotto and spaghetti *vongole* (with clams). If you're dining alone, you're likely to be seated with a local – a good opportunity to practise your Italian, if you have any. Service is friendly and efficient, and the food, while simple, is very tasty.

★ OSTERIA AL DUOMO
ITALIAN €€

Map p293 (☑041 527 43 03; www.osteriaalduomo.com; Fondamenta Maschio 20-21, Murano; meals €23-46; ⊙11am-10.30pm; ⊛⌀⌘; ☑Museo) Opened in 1903 by the parish priest as a co-op grocery shop, this *osteria* is still collectively owned by 50 Muranese families. Don't be surprised, then, by the friendly

(Continued on page 158)

Venetian Artistry

Glass

Venetians have been working in crystal and glass since the 10th century, though fire hazards prompted the move of the city's furnaces to Murano in the 13th century. Trade secrets were closely guarded: no glass-worker would leave the city on pain of assassination for treason. By the 15th century Murano glass-makers were setting standards that couldn't be equalled anywhere in the world. They monopolised the manufacture of mirrors for centuries, and in the 17th century their skill at producing jewel-bright crystal led to a ban on the production of false gems out of glass. Murano's history of innovation and high standard of artistry are well displayed at the island's **Museo del Vetro** (p151).

Today on Murano centuries of tradition are upheld in **Cesare Toffolo's** winged goblets (p159) and **Davide Penso's lampworked glass beads** (p160), while striking modern glass designs by Nason Moretti at **ElleElle** (p159), **Marina e Susanna Sent** (p159) and **Venini** (p159) keep the tradition moving forward.

Paper

Embossing and marbling began in the 14th century as part of Venice's burgeoning publishing industry, but these bookbinding techniques and *ebru* (Turkish marbled paper) endpapers have taken on lives of their own. Artisan **Paolo Olbi** (p86) continues Venice's long tradition of creating unique marbled and embossed notebooks and journals, while **Gianni Basso** (p119) uses 18th-century book symbols to make letter-pressed business cards with old-world flair.

1. Hand-blown Murano glass **2.** Textile samples from Fortuny **3.** Weaving velvet

Textiles

Anything that stands still long enough in this city is liable to end up swagged, tasselled and upholstered. Venetian lace was a fashion must for centuries as Burano's **Lace Museum** (p152) attests, and **Bevilacqua** (p71) still weaves luxe tapestries.

But the modern master of Venetian bohemian textiles is **Fortuny** (p147), whose showroom on Giudecca features hand-stamped wall coverings created in strict accordance with top-secret techniques. But though the methods are secret, Fortuny's inspiration isn't: it covers the walls of his home studio, from Persian armour to portraits of socialites who tossed aside their corsets for Fortuny's Delphi gowns – now available for modern boho goddesses at **Venetia Studium** (p72).

TOP FIVE NON-TOURISTY SOUVENIRS

➡ Contemporary handwoven tablewear and bed linen from **Chiarastella Cattana** (p70)

➡ Handprinted linocuts and etchings at **Plum Plum Creations** (p120)

➡ Blown-glass soap-bubble necklaces from **Marina e Susanna Sent** (p159)

➡ Lux, hand-stamped velvet evening bags in gold and mulberry from **Venetia Studium** (p72)

➡ Bronze figurines of the Lion of St Mark from the **Fonderie Valese foundry** (p71)

(Continued from page 155)

vibe, honest bowls of pasta (the swordfish, olive and tomato spaghetti is excellent) and some of the best pizza in Venice. In summer, sit out in the walled garden.

★TRATTORIA MADDALENA VENETIAN €€
Map p294 (✆041 73 01 51; www.trattoriamaddalena.com; Fondamenta di Santa Caterina 7b, Mazzorbo; meals €26-46; ⊙noon-3pm & 7-9pm Fri-Wed; ⓖMazzorbo) Just a footbridge away from Burano's crowds, this pretty restaurant is a great place for a lazy seafood lunch. Relax by the canal or in the garden out the back. It pays to call ahead, as the hours are sporadic in the low-season.

BUSA ALLA TORRE VENETIAN €€
Map p293 (✆041 73 96 62; Campo Santo Stefano 3, Murano; meals €28-40, set menu €16; ⊙11.30am-3.30pm; ⓖFaro) Glassy-eyed shoppers are drawn to this classic eatery for its sunny disposition and great-value two-course set menu (not available Sunday). Arrive early for piazza seating with tempting views of glass showrooms, and settle in for seasonal lagoon treats like seafood soup and *sepie alla venexiana* (squid in black sauce).

★TRATTORIA AL GATTO NERO VENETIAN €€€
Map p294 (✆041 73 01 20; www.gattonero.com; Fondamenta della Giudecca 88, Burano; meals €42-70; ⊙12.30-3pm & 7.30-9pm Tue-Sun; ⓖBurano) Don't expect fancy tricks from this 'Black Cat' – just excellent, traditional fare. Once you've tried the homemade *tagliolini* (ribbon pasta) with spider crab, whole grilled fish and perfect house-baked biscuits, the ferry ride to Burano seems a minor inconvenience. Call ahead and plead for canalside seating.

★VENISSA OSTERIA VENETIAN €€€
Map p294 (✆041 527 22 81; www.venissa.it; Fondamenta Santa Caterina 3, Mazzorbo; meals €37-56; ⊙noon-4pm & 7-9pm daily Apr-Nov, Thu-Mon Dec-Mar; ⓖMazzorbo) A more affordable companion piece to its Michelin-starred sister, this upmarket *osteria* offers updates on Venetian classics such as marinated fish, duck tagliatelle and *bigoli* (thick wholemeal pasta with anchovies). Splash out on a glass of dorona,

the prestigious golden-hued wine varietal only grown here.

ACQUASTANCA VENETIAN €€€
Map p293 (✆041 319 51 25; www.acquastanca.it; Fondamenta Manin 48, Murano; meals €48-54; ⊙10am-4pm & 7-10pm Mon & Fri, 10am-4pm Tue-Thu & Sat, extended in summer; ⓖFaro) A modern sensibility imbues both the decor and the menu at this wonderful little restaurant. Seafood features prominently on a menu that includes octopus with chickpeas and a panoply of pasta.

LOCANDA CIPRIANI VENETIAN €€€
Map p294 (✆041 73 01 50; www.locandacipriani.com; Piazza Torcello 29, Torcello; meals €54-69; ⊙noon-3pm Wed-Mon Mar-Dec, plus 6-11pm Fri & Sat Apr-Sep; ⓖTorcello) Run by the Cipriani family since 1935, the Locanda is Harry's Bar gone rustic, with a wood-beamed dining room opening onto a pretty garden. The kitchen delivers pillowy gnocchi, perfectly cooked fish and decadent chocolate mousse.

🛍 SHOPPING

Murano glass ranges from the sublime to the completely ridiculous (clown-crammed cars and parrots in trees are popular), and you'll see both as you walk down the main strip of showrooms on Fondamenta dei Vetrai. Sales staff will let you handle pieces if you ask first, but move with care – what you break, you buy. On Burano, Via Galuppi is lined with lace shops. Look for *'fatto a Burano'* (made in Burano) and 'Vero Artistico Murano' guarantees, since almost all of the less-expensive stock is imported. Authentic goods are expensive.

★CESARE TOFFOLO GLASS
Map p293 (✆041 73 64 60; www.toffolo.com; Fondamenta dei Vetrai 37, Murano; ⊙10am-6pm; ⓖColonna) Miniatures are the trademarks of this Murano glass-blower, but you'll also find chiselled cobalt-blue vases, glossy black candlesticks and drinking glasses so fine that they seem to be made out of air.

★ELLEELLE GLASS
Map p293 (✆041 527 48 66; www.elleellemurano.com; Fondamenta Manin 52, Murano; ⊙10.30am-6pm; ⓖFaro) Nason Moretti has been making modernist magic happen in glass since the

VENISSA: A MAZZORBO RENAISSANCE

• •

During the Renaissance, most of the wine served at Venice's high tables came from vineyards on the lagoon islands. The king of all was dorona, a local varietal that was golden hued and imbued with the delicate flavours of peach and apricot.

Devastating floods all but wiped out the dorona vines, and the wine of the doges was nearly lost for ever. That is, until Gianluca Bisol, a prosecco producer from Valdobbiadene, heard of an ancient vineyard enclosed by medieval walls on Mazzorbo (p152). He rented the land from the city and set about rehabilitating the orchard and vegetable patches, restoring the brick-lined *peschiera* (cultivated fish pond), and reintroducing the rare dorona grape from just 88 vines that had survived on Torcello.

Once he'd reclaimed Venissa's garden and left it in the care of a team of Burano pensioners, he turned his attention to the farm buildings, which he converted into a contemporary six-room guesthouse (p202) and an osteria. Since then a Michelin-starred **restaurant** (Map p294; ☏041 527 22 81; www.venissa.it; Fondamenta Santa Caterina 3, Mazzorbo; set menu €110-175; ⏱12.30-2pm & 7.30-9pm Wed-Mon Apr-Oct; ☷Mazzorbo) has been added in the garden and they've converted five historic cottages on neighbouring Burano into an *albergo diffuso* (multivenue hotel), Casa Burano (p202).

As for the dorona? It's exceptional – as demonstrated by the prestigious wine awards that it has won since its first vintage in 2010. Given the low volumes produced and the fact that it's sold in individually etched and numbered Murano glass bottles embossed with gold leaf, it's virtually impossible to buy. However, you can sample a glass over dinner at Venissa for a mere €25 – a worthwhile investment.

1950s, and the third-generation glass designers are in fine form in this showroom. Everything is signed, including an exquisite range of hand-blown drinking glasses, jugs, bowls, vases, tealight holders, decanters and lamps.

EMILIA ARTS & CRAFTS

Map p294 (☏041 73 52 99; www.emiliaburano.it; Via Galuppi 205, Burano; ⏱9.30am-7pm; ☷Burano) Doyenne Emilia di Ammendola, a third-generation lace-maker, has passed on her skills to her children who are continuing the family tradition in this flagship store; there's another on Calle San Mauro and a branch in Los Angeles. There's a family museum upstairs.

VENINI GLASS

Map p293 (☏041 273 72 04; www.venini.it; Fondamenta dei Vetrai 47, Murano; ⏱9.30am-6pm Mon-Sat; ☷Colonna) Even if you don't have the cash to buy a Venini, pop into this gallery to see Murano glass at its finest. Of the big houses, Venini remains the most chic, having embraced modernist trends since the 1930s, and its enviable range is bolstered by collaborations with design greats such as Carlo Scarpa, Tadao Ando and Gae Aulenti.

FORNACE MIAN GLASS

Map p293 (☏041 73 94 23; www.fornace mian.com; Fondamenta da Mula 143, Murano;

⏱9.30am-5.30pm; ☷Venier) Shuffle past the typical Murano kitsch (glass pandas, parrots in trees etc) and you'll find one of the best ranges of classic stemware on the island. If there isn't enough of your favourite design in stock, it can be made to order and shipped internationally.

MARINA E SUSANNA SENT STUDIO GLASS

Map p293 (☏041 527 46 65; www.marinaesusan nasent.com; Fondamenta Serenella 20, Murano; ⏱10am-5pm Mon-Fri; ☷Colonna) This striking space dedicated to the work of the pioneering Sent sisters is as sleek as their jewellery. The collection is displayed in colour groups and neatly stashed in drawers. Other shops can be found in **Dorsoduro** (Map p284; ☏041 520 81 36; www.marinaesusannasent.com; Campo San Vio 669; ⏱10am-6.30pm; ☷Accademia), San Polo and San Marco (p71).

DAVIDE PENSO GLASS

Map p293 (☏041 73 98 19; www.davidepenso. com; Fondamenta Riva Longa 48, Murano; ⏱10am-6pm Mon-Sat; ☷Museo) Davide Penso has taken the art of bead making to dizzying heights with exhibits at the Museo Correr, Boston's Fine Arts Museum and the San Marco Museum of Japan. Made using the lampworking process, each bead is worked into striking geometric forms and individually painted in matt colours.

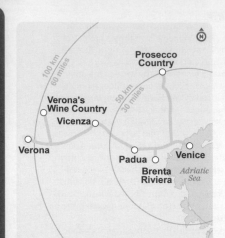

Day Trips from Venice

Brenta Riviera p161
The 18th-century Venetian elites gambled away their summers in Palladian-style villas.

Padua p162
A vibrant university town with a treasure trove of fresco cycles from its medieval golden age.

Vicenza p168
Palladio's adopted home is defined by the architect's classical restraint, while its countryside is dotted with his elegant villas.

Prosecco Country p172
Just the spot for a glass of *prosecco* with hard-working locals in one of the Veneto's most underrated areas.

Verona p176
Romeo and Juliet were fictional, but Verona's real history lives on in its Roman arena, Romanesque churches and Renaissance churches.

Verona's Wine Country p182
Valpolicella yields some of Italy's biggest, boldest reds, while Soave delivers crisp, refreshing whites.

Brenta Riviera

Explore

Every 13 June for 300 years, summer officially kicked off with a traffic jam along the Grand Canal, as a flotilla of fashionable Venetians headed to their villas along the banks of the Brenta. Ball gowns and poker chairs were loaded onto barges for dalliances that stretched until November. The annual party ended when Napoleon arrived in 1797, but 80 villas still strike elegant poses along the Brenta, and six of them are now open to the public at various times of the year.

The Best...

➡ **Sight** Villa Foscari

➡ **Place to Eat** Osteria da Conte (p162)

➡ **Place to Drink** I Molini del Dolo (p162)

Top Tip

All the villas along the Brenta show their best architectural face to the river. Even today the best way to experience the riviera is on a flat-bottomed riverboat.

Getting There & Away

➡ **Boat** Organised boat tours leave from both Venice and Padua.

➡ **Bus** ACTV's Venezia–Padova Extraurbane bus 53 leaves from Venice's Piazzale Roma about every half-hour, stopping at key Brenta villages en route to Padua.

➡ **Train** Venice–Padua train services stop at Dolo (€3.55, 25 minutes, one to three per hour).

➡ **Car & Motorcycle** Take SS11 from Mestre-Venezia towards Padua and take the A4 autostrada towards Dolo/Padua.

Need to Know

➡ **Area Code** 041

➡ **Location** 15km to 30km west of Venice

⊙ SIGHTS

Many visitors opt to self-drive around the Riviera Brenta, but its network of cycling routes also makes it a great place to explore on two wheels.

VILLA FOSCARI   HISTORIC BUILDING

(☑041 5203 9662; www.lamalcontenta.com; Via dei Turisti 9, Malcontenta; adult/reduced €10/8; ⊙9am-noon Tue, Wed & Fri-Sun Apr-Oct) The most romantic Brenta villa, the Palladio-designed, Unesco-listed Villa Foscari (built 1555–60) got its nickname La Malcontenta from a grande dame of the Foscari clan who was reputedly exiled here for cheating on her husband – though these bright, highly sociable salons hardly constitute a punishment. The villa was abandoned for years, but Giovanni Zelotti's frescoes have now been restored to daydream-inducing splendour.

VILLA WIDMANN
REZZONICO FOSCARI   HISTORIC BUILDING

(☑041 42 49 73; https://villawidmann.servizime tropolitani.ve.it; Via Nazionale 420, Mira; adult/ reduced €5.50/4.50; ⊙10am-1pm & 1.30-4.30pm Tue-Sun May-Oct) To appreciate both gardening and Venetian-style social engineering, stop just west of Oriago at Villa Widmann Rezzonico Foscari. Originally owned by Persian-Venetian nobility, the 18th-century villa captures the Brenta's last days of rococo decadence, with Murano sea-monster chandeliers and a frescoed grand ballroom with upper viewing gallery. Head to the gallery to reach the upstairs ladies' gambling parlour where, according to local lore, villas were once gambled away in high-stakes games.

VILLA BARCHESSA
VALMARANA   HISTORIC BUILDING

(☑041 426 63 87; www.villavalmarana.net; Via Valmarana 11, Mira; adult/reduced €6/5; ⊙10am-6pm Tue-Sun Mar-Oct, to 4.30pm Sat & Sun Nov-Feb, or by appointment during the week) Debuting on

---

❶ BRENTA BY BIKE

The scenic Brenta Riviera plains make an easy, enjoyable bicycle ride, and you can speed past those tour boats along 150km of cycling routes. **Veloce** (☑0586 40 42 04; www.rentalbikeitaly. com; touring/mountain/racing bicycle per day €20/25/35; ⊙8am-8pm) is a friendly bike-rental outlet with branches in many Veneto towns offering mountain and city bikes, plus pre-loaded GPS units (€10), guided tours (€80 per person), roadside assistance and advice in English on itineraries and local restaurants. Bikes need to be pre-booked.

RIVER CRUISES

Watch 50 villas drift by on the **Il Burchiello** (☑049 876 02 33; www.ilburchiello.it; half-day cruise adult/child €70/55; ☉Tue-Sun Apr-Nov) barge, a modern version of the pleasure boats that cruised up and down the Brenta ferrying aristocrats to and from their country villas. Full-day cruises run between Venice and Padua, stopping at Malcontenta, Widmann (or Barchessa Valmarana) and Pisani villas.

From Venice, cruises depart from Pontile della Pietà pier on Riva degli Schiavoni (Tuesday, Thursday and Saturday). From Padua, cruises depart from Pontile del Portello pier (Wednesday, Friday and Sunday). There are also half-day tours stopping at one or two villas, running to Oriago from Venice (Tuesday, Thursday and Saturday) and Padua (Wednesday, Friday and Sunday), and from Oriago to Venice (Wednesday, Friday and Sunday) and Padua (Tuesday, Thursday and Saturday). Book online.

the riviera in the 17th century, Villa Barchessa Valmarana was commissioned by Vicenza's aristocratic Valmarana family. You'll find them enjoying *la dolce vita* (the sweet life) in the villa's fanciful frescoes, painstakingly restored in 1964. These days, the building is mainly used as a function centre, but is still fully accessible to the public.

VILLA PISANI NAZIONALE   HISTORIC BUILDING
(☑049 50 20 74; www.villapisani.beniculturali.it; Via Doge Pisani 7, Stra; adult/reduced €10/5, park only €7.50/4.50; ☉9am-8pm Tue-Sun Apr-Sep, to 6pm Oct, to 5pm Nov-Mar) To keep hard-partying Venetian nobles in line, Doge Alvise Pisani provided a Versailles-like reminder of who was in charge. The 1774, 114-room Villa Pisani Nazionale is surrounded by huge gardens, a labyrinthine hedge maze, and pools to reflect the doge's glory. Here you'll find the bathroom with a tiny wooden throne used by Napoleon; the sagging bed where new king Vittorio Emanuele II slept; and, ironically, the reception hall where Mussolini and Hitler met in 1934 under Tiepolo's ceiling depicting the *Geniuses of Peace*.

VILLA FOSCARINI ROSSI   HISTORIC BUILDING
(☑049 980 10 91; www.museodellacalzatura.it; Via Doge Pisani 1/2, Stra; adult/reduced €7/5; ☉9am-1pm & 2-6pm Mon-Fri, 2.30-6pm Sat & Sun Apr-Oct, 9am-1pm & 2-6pm Mon-Fri Nov-Mar) Well-heeled Venetians wouldn't have dreamed of decamping to the Brenta without their favourite cobblers, sparking a local tradition of shoemaking. Today, 538 companies produce around 19 million pairs of shoes annually. Their lasting contribution is celebrated with a **Shoemakers' Museum** at this 18th-century villa, its collection including 18th-century slippers and kicks created for trendsetter Marlene Dietrich. Admission includes access to the villa's 17th-century *foresteria* (guesthouse), which wows with allegorical frescoes by Pietro Liberi and *trompe l'œil* effects by Domenico de Bruni.

✖ EATING & DRINKING

OSTERIA DA CONTE   VENETIAN €€
(☑049 47 95 71; Via Caltana 133, Mira; meals €25-35; ☉noon-2pm & 8-10pm Tue-Sat) An unlikely bastion of culinary sophistication lodged practically underneath an overpass, Da Conte has one of the most interesting wine lists in the region, plus creative takes on regional cuisine, from shrimps with black sesame and pumpkin puree to gnocchi in veal-cheek *ragù*. If it's on the menu, end your meal with the faultless *zabaglione* (egg and Marsala custard).

I MOLINI DEL DOLO   WINE BAR
(www.molinidolo.com; Via Garibaldi 3, Dolo; meals €20-25; ☉10am-2am Tue-Sun) Adorned with hulking wooden machinery, this atmospheric, canalside wine bar occupies a restored 16th-century mill. Swill a coffee, or settle in with a regional *vino* and a selection of cheeses and cured meats, from local *porchetta* to rustic *ventricina* salami from Italy's south. If the weather's warm, keep the waterwheel company on the alfresco patio.

Padua

Explore
Though less than an hour from Venice, Padua (Padova in Italian) seems a world away with its medieval marketplaces,

Fascist-era facades and hip student population. As a medieval city-state and home to Italy's second-oldest university, Padua challenged both Venice and Verona for regional hegemony. A series of extraordinary fresco cycles recalls this golden age – including in Giotto's blockbuster Cappella degli Scrovegni, Menabuoi's heavenly gathering in the baptistry and Titian's *St Anthony* in the Scoletta del Santo. For centuries, Padua and Verona fought for dominance over the Veneto plains. But Venice finally occupied Padua permanently in 1405.

As a strategic military-industrial centre, Padua became a parade ground for Mussolini speeches, an Allied bombing target and a secret Italian Resistance hub (at its university). Even today, Padua remains an important industrial city – its industrial zone employs some 50,000 people – a dynamic university town and an important pilgrimage centre.

The Best...

→ **Sight** Cappella degli Scrovegni
→ **Place to Eat** Belle Parti (p168)
→ **Place to Drink** Caffè Pedrocchi (p167)

Top Tip

Reservations are required to see Giotto's extraordinary Cappella degli Scrovegni. Book a few weeks ahead for summer weekends and during school holidays.

Getting There & Away

→ **Car & Motorcycle** Padua can be reached via the congested Turin–Trieste A4 or the Padua–Bologna A13. There is a restricted-access ZTL zone covering the centre of the city, but cars are allowed entry to drop luggage at hotels. Check www.parcheggipadova.it for information on secure parking lots.

→ **Train** By far the easiest way to reach Padua from Venice (€4.35 to €19, 25 to 50 minutes, one to nine per hour). The station is about 500m north of Cappella degli Scrovegni and linked to the centre by a monorail.

Getting Around

→ Bikes are the preferred mode of transport in Padua and the **GoodBike Padova** (☑800 20 43 03; www.goodbikepadova.it) bike-sharing scheme has a network of 25 stations dotted around the city. To use it, subscribe online, where you can pay a flat fee of €8/13 for 24/48 hours.

→ It is easy to get to all the sights by foot from the train and bus stations, but the city's unusual single-branch monorail running from the train station passes within 100m of all the main sights. Tickets (€1.30) are available at tobacconists and newsstands.

Need to Know

→ **Area Code** 049
→ **Location** 37km west of Venice
→ **Tourist Office** (☑049 520 74 15; www.turismopadova.it; Vicolo Pedrocchi; ⊙9am-7pm Mon-Sat, 10am-4pm Sun)

⊙ SIGHTS

★**CAPPELLA DEGLI SCROVEGNI**   CHAPEL
(Scrovegni Chapel; ☑049 201 00 20; www.cappelladegliscrovegni.it; Piazza Eremitani 8; adult/reduced €13/8, night ticket €8/6; ⊙9am-7pm, night ticket 7-10pm) Padua's version of the Sistine Chapel, the Cappella degli Scrovegni houses one of Italy's great Renaissance masterpieces – a striking cycle of Giotto frescoes. Dante, da Vinci and Vasari all honour Giotto as the artist who ended the Dark Ages with these 1303–05 paintings, whose humanistic depiction of biblical figures was especially well suited to the chapel Enrico Scrovegni commissioned in memory of his father (who as a moneylender was denied a Christian burial).

It's a simple brick building, with little indication from the outside of what lies within. It took Giotto two years to finish the frescoes, which tell the story of Christ from Annunciation to Ascension. Scrovegni's chapel once adjoined the family mansion (demolished in 1824) – the city of Padua acquired the chapel in 1881.

Giotto's moving, modern approach helped change how people saw themselves: no longer as lowly vassals, but as vessels for the divine, however flawed. And where medieval churchgoers had been accustomed to blank stares from saints perched on high thrones, Giotto introduced biblical figures as characters in recognisable settings. Onlookers gossip as middle-aged Anne tenderly kisses Joachim, and Jesus stares down Judas as the traitor puckers up for

Padua

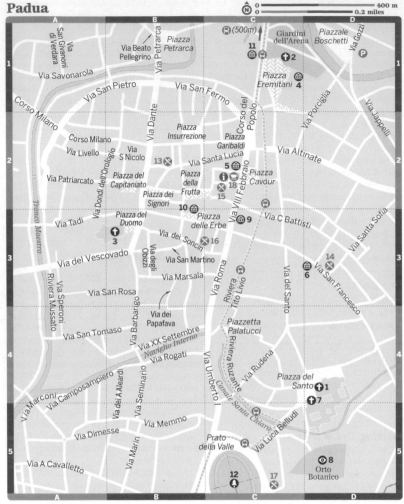

the fateful kiss. Giotto also used unusual techniques such as impasto, building paint up into 3D forms. A 10-minute introductory video provides some helpful insights before you enter the church itself.

Visits must be booked. Tickets are available at the Musei Civici agli Eremitani (p167), where you access the chapel, or at the tourist office. Chapel visits last 15 to 20 minutes (depending on the time of year), plus another 10 minutes for the video. Arrive at least 15 to 30 minutes before your tour starts, or an hour before if you want to tour the Musei Civici agli Eremitani beforehand.

★ **PALAZZO BO** HISTORIC BUILDING
(☎049 827 39 39; www.unipd.it/en/guided tours; Via VIII Febbraio 2; adult/reduced €7/4; ⊙see website for tour times) This Renaissance *palazzo* (mansion) is the seat of Padua's history-making university. Founded by renegade scholars from Bologna seeking greater intellectual freedom, the university has employed some of Italy's greatest and most controversial thinkers, including Copernicus, Galileo, Casanova and the world's first female doctor of philosophy, Eleonora Lucrezia Cornaro Piscopia (her statue graces the stairs). Admission is on a 45-minute

Padua

guided tour only, which includes a visit to the world's first **anatomy theatre** and the Aula Magna (Great Hall) where Galileo lectured.

Today, Palazzo Bo is home to the Rector's offices, libraries, and the halls used for ceremonies and the discussion of dissertations. They blend the historic buildings with Rationalist renovations and modifications made by Italy's great rationalist architect, Gio Ponti, in the 1930s and '40s. During the renovation, Ponti called on artists, such as Campigli, Pendini and Severini, to fresco the Rector's offices, while at the entrance to the New Courtyard stands Arturo Martini's statue of Palinurus, which is dedicated to the partisan Masaccio and commemorates the Italian Resistance movement.

Note also the six Stumbling Stones (*stolpersteine*) embedded in the cobblestones in front of the entrance; they commemorate Jewish students who were arrested here and deported to Auschwitz.

★MUSME   MUSEUM
(www.musme.it; Via San Francesco 94; adult/reduced/child €10/8/6; ⊙2.30-7pm Tue-Fri,

9.30am-7pm Sat & Sun) Padua's Museum of Medical History is a fascinating mash-up of historical artefacts and high-tech exhibits that detail the city's outsized contribution to world medicine between the 16th and 18th centuries. Virtual guides representing Padua's most famous physicians narrate the university's greatest discoveries in thematic displays covering how the human body functions, fails and is treated. The journey ends in an Anatomical Theatre, mimicking the original theatre in Palazzo Bo, where a giant mannequin lies on a dissection table ready for an augmented-reality investigation.

The building resonates with history, too. It was the city's first public hospital, San Francesco il Grande, financed by wealthy heiress Sibilia de'Cetto and Baldo Bonafari da Piombino and built in 1414. It replaced the medieval hospices and can reasonably be called the first hospital as it was here that medical students started to learn clinical practice at a patient's bedside, thus laying the foundations for the modern, academic approach towards medicine.

Among the great names who studied, researched and taught here are Andrea Vesalius, father of modern anatomy; Giovanni Morgagni, father of modern pathology; Prospero Alpini, pioneering botanist, Prefect of the Botanical Garden and the father of modern pharmacology; and Santorio Santorio, the physician and inventor, who introduced the quantitative approach into medicine and invented several medical instruments in order to measure physiological symptoms, including the thermometer. Part science centre, part museum, it is an understandable hit with kids.

PRATO DELLA VALLE   PARK
(Prato della Valle) At the southern edge of the historical centre, this odd, elliptical garden was long used as a communal sports ground. Today it's a popular spot for locals wanting to soak up some summer rays and students swotting for exams. Framing the space is a slim canal lined by 78 statues of the great and good of Paduan history, plus 10 empty pedestals. Ten Venetian doges once occupied them, but Napoleon had them removed after he took Venice in 1797.

ORTO BOTANICO   GARDENS
(☑049 827 39 39; www.ortobotanicopd.it; Via dell'Orto Botanico 15; adult/reduced €10/8, with PadovaCard €5; ⊙9am-7pm Tue-Sun Apr-Sep, to

ℹ DISCOUNT PASS

A **PadovaCard** (€16/21 per 48/72 hours) gives one adult and one child under 14 free use of city public transport and access to almost all of Padua's major attractions, including the Cappella degli Scrovegni (plus €1 booking fee; reservations essential). PadovaCards are available at Padua tourist offices, Musei Civici agli Eremitani and the hotels listed on the PadovaCard section of the tourist-office website (www.turismopadova.it).

6pm Oct, to 5pm Nov-Mar) Planted in 1545 by Padua University's medical faculty to study the medicinal properties of rare plants, Padua's World Heritage–listed Orto Botanico is the world's original botanical garden. The oldest tree is nicknamed 'Goethe's palm'; planted in 1585, it was mentioned by the German writer in *Italienische Reise* (Italian Journey). The garden is still used as a learning and research environment; studies now focus on the preservation of rare indigenous plants and the maintenance of biodiversity, which is celebrated in the high-tech **Garden of Biodiversity**.

BASILICA DI SANT'ANTONIO CHURCH
(Il Santo; ☎049 822 56 52; www.basilicadelsanto.org; Piazza del Santo; ⊘6.20am-6.45pm Mon-Sat, to 7.45pm Sun) **FREE** A pilgrimage site and the burial place of St Anthony of Padua (1193–1231), this huge church was begun in 1232, its polyglot style incorporating rising eastern domes atop a Gothic brick structure crammed with Renaissance treasures. Behind the high altar, nine radiating chapels punctuate a broad ambulatory homing in on the **Cappella delle Reliquie** (Relics Chapel), where the relics of St Anthony reside.

You'll also notice dozens of people clustering along the left transept waiting their turn to enter the **Cappella del Santo**, where Anthony's tomb is covered with requests and thanks for the saint's intercession in curing illness and recovering lost objects. The chapel itself is a light-filled Renaissance confection lined with nine panels vividly depicting the story of Anthony's life in extraordinary relief sculptures. The panels are attributed to the Padua-born Lombardo brothers and were completed around 1510.

Other notable works include the lifelike 1360s crucifix by Veronese master Altichiero da Zevio in the frescoed **Cappella di San Giacomo**; the wonderful 1528 sacristy fresco of St Anthony preaching to spellbound fish by a follower of Girolamo Tessari; and 15th-century high altar reliefs by Florentine Renaissance master Donatello (ask guards for access).

Through the south door of the basilica you reach the attached monastery with its five wonderfully peaceful cloisters. The oldest (13th century) is the **Chiostro della Magnolia**, so called because of the magnificent tree in its centre. The complex also holds a large gift shop selling icons and St Anthony souvenirs to pilgrims.

ORATORIO DI SAN GIORGIO & SCUOLA DEL SANTO CHURCH
(☎049 822 56 52; www.santantonio.org; Piazza del Santo; adult/reduced €5/4; ⊘9am-1pm & 2-6pm Tue-Sun, to 5pm Oct-Mar) Anywhere else, the fresco cycle of the Oratorio di San Giorgio and the paintings in the Scuola del Santo would be considered highlights, but in Padua they must contend with Giotto's Scrovegni brilliance. This means you'll have Altichiero da Zevio and Jacopo Avanzi's jewel-like, 14th-century frescoes of St George, St Lucy and St Catherine all to yourself, while upstairs in the *scuola* (confraternity house), Titian paintings are seldom viewed in such tranquillity.

DUOMO CATHEDRAL
(Basilica Cattedrale di Santa Maria Assunta; ☎049 65 69 14; Piazza Duomo; baptistry €3; ⊘7am-noon & 4-7.30pm Mon-Fri, 7am-7pm Sat, 8.30am-8pm Sun, baptistry 10am-6pm) Built from a much-altered design of Michelangelo's, the rather industrial facade and whitewashed symmetry of Padua's duomo is a far cry from its rival in Piazza San Marco. Pop in quickly for Giuliano Vangi's contemporary chancel crucifix and sculptures before visiting the adjoining 13th-century **baptistry**, a Romanesque gem frescoed with luminous biblical scenes by Giusto de' Menabuoi. Hundreds of saints congregate in the cupola, posed as though for a school graduation photo, exchanging glances and stealing looks at the Madonna.

PALAZZO DELLA RAGIONE HISTORIC BUILDING
(☎049 820 50 06; Piazza delle Erbe; adult/reduced €6/4; ⊘9am-7pm Tue-Sun Feb-Oct, to 6pm Nov-Jan) Ancient Padua can be glimpsed in

elegant twin squares (one the fruit market, the other the vegetable market) separated by the triple-decker Gothic Palazzo della Ragione, the city's tribunal dating from 1218. Inside Il Salone (the Great Hall), frescoes by Giotto acolytes Giusto de' Menabuoi and Nicolò Miretto depict the astrological theories of Padovan professor Pietro d'Abano, with images representing the months, seasons, saints, animals and noteworthy Paduans (not necessarily in that order).

MUSEO DEL RISORGIMENTO E DELL'ETÀ CONTEMPORANEA   MUSEUM

(☑049 878 12 31; Galleria Pedrocchi 11; adult/reduced €4/2; ⊙9.30am-12.30pm & 3.30-6pm Tue-Sun) Since 1831, this neoclassical landmark has been a favourite of Stendhal and other pillars of Padua's cafe society for the heart-poundingly powerful coffee and *caffè correto* (coffee-based cocktails) served at the ground-floor **Caffè Pedrocchi** (☑049 878 12 31; www.caffepedrocchi.it; Via VIII Febbraio 15; ⊙8am-midnight Sun-Thu, to 1am Fri & Sat). The grand 1st floor – decorated in styles ranging from ancient Egyptian to imperial – houses the museum, recounting local and national history from the fall of Venice in 1797 until the republican constitution of 1848 in original documents, images and mementos.

MUSEI CIVICI AGLI EREMITANI   MUSEUM

(☑049 820 45 51; Piazza Eremitani 8; adult/reduced €10/8; ⊙9am-7pm Tue-Sun) The ground floor of this monastery houses artefacts dating from Padua's Roman and pre-Roman past, including some delicate glass, serviceable Roman surgical instruments and Etruscan bronze figures. Upstairs, a rambling but interesting collection boasts a few notable 14th- to 18th-century works by Bellini, Giorgione, Tintoretto and Veronese. Among the showstoppers are a monster Brussels tapestry and an 18th-century painting by Georgio Fossati that shows the Prato della Valle (p165) when it was still a sports ground.

PALAZZO ZUCKERMANN   GALLERY

(☑049 820 56 64; Corso Garibaldi 33; adult/reduced €10/8; ⊙10am-7pm Tue-Sun) The ground and 1st floors of the early-20th-century Palazzo Zuckermann are home to the **Museo d'Arti Applicate e Decorative**, with an eclectic assortment of decorative and applied arts spanning several centuries of flatware, furniture, fashion and jewellery. On the 2nd floor is the **Museo Bot-**

tacin, a treasury of finely worked historic coins and medals, kept company by a modest collection of 19th-century paintings and sculpture.

✗ EATING

With its spectacular produce markets and demanding locals, Padua is well served with some excellent and well-priced *osterie* (casual taverns or eateries) and traditional restaurants. Street food is also popular here, with many of the stands in the covered market also selling snacks and quick bites.

DALLA ZITA   STREET FOOD €

(☑049 65 49 92; Via Gorizia 12; snacks €4.50-6.50, coffee €1; ⊙9am-8pm Mon-Fri) So small that around five people fill the place while standing, this unmarked street-food bar is Padua's best spot when you need to eat on the hop. Choose from the large menu of sandwiches stuck to the wall on multicoloured sticky notes, or if your Italian and patience is up to it, customise your very own *panini*. Gets very busy at lunchtime.

ZAIRO   ITALIAN €

(☑049 66 38 03; www.zairo.net; Prato della Valle 51; pizzas €4-9.40, meals €25; ⊙noon-2.30pm & 7pm-1am Tue-Sun) The fresco above the kitchen door at this sweeping, chintzily over-the-top restaurant-pizzeria dates back to 1673, but most people come for Zairo's long menu of cheap pizzas while on a break from the Prato della Valle park on its doorstep.

★DA NANE DELLA GIULIA   OSTERIA €€

(☑049 66 07 42; Via Santa Sofia 1; meals €25-30; ⊙12.30-2pm & 7pm-midnight Wed-Sun; ☑) Enter the blood-red, candlelit dining room of Padua's oldest tavern and you'll immediately be transported back to another era. Diners settle in at dark wooden tables beneath vaulted ceilings and peruse the seasonal, local menu. It includes traditional dishes such as chicken in red grappa with pancetta and polenta and vegetarian-friendly plates of white asparagus, courgettes and local cheese.

OSTERIA DEI FABBRI   OSTERIA €€

(☑049 65 03 36; Via dei Fabbri 13; meals €30; ⊙noon-3pm & 7-11pm, closed Sun dinner) Rustic wooden tables, wine-filled tumblers and a single-sheet menu packed with hearty dishes keep things real at dei Fabbri. Slurp on

LOCAL KNOWLEDGE

TO MARKET

One of the most enjoyable activities in Padua (Padova) is browsing the markets in **Piazza delle Erbe** and **Piazza della Frutta**, which operate very much as they've done since the Middle Ages. Dividing them is Europe's oldest covered market, housed in the Gothic Palazzo della Ragione (p166). The *palazzo* (mansion) arcades – known locally as **Sotto il Salone** – rumble with specialist butchers, cheesemakers, fishmongers, *salumerie* (delicatessens or sausage shops) and fresh-pasta producers. The markets are open all day, every day, except Sunday, although the best time to visit is before midday.

superlative *zuppe* (soups) such as sweet red-onion soup, or tuck into comforting meat dishes such as oven-roasted pork shank with Marsala, sultanas and polenta.

★**BELLE PARTI**   ITALIAN **€€€**
(☑049 875 18 22; www.ristorantebelleparti.it; Via Belle Parti 11; meals €50; ⊙12.30-2.30pm & 7.30-10.30pm Mon-Sat) Prime seasonal produce, impeccable wines and near-faultless service meld into one unforgettable whole at this stellar fine-dining restaurant, resplendent with 18th-century antiques and 19th-century oil paintings. Seafood is the forte, with standout dishes including an arresting *gran piatto di crudità di mare* (raw seafood platter). Dress to impress and book ahead.

Vicenza

Explore

When Palladio escaped an oppressive employer in his native Padua, few would have guessed the humble stonecutter would, within a few decades, transform not only his adoptive city but also the history of European architecture. By luck, a local count recognised his talents in the 1520s and sent him to study the ruins in Rome. When he returned to Vicenza, the autodidact began producing his extraordinary buildings,

structures that marry sophistication and rustic simplicity, reverent classicism and bold innovation. His genius would turn Vicenza and its surrounding villas into one grand Unesco World Heritage Site. And yet, the Veneto's fourth-largest city is more than just elegant porticoes and balustrades – its dynamic exhibitions, bars and restaurants provide a satisfying dose of modern vibrancy.

The Best...
➜ **Sight** La Rotonda
➜ **Place to Eat** Al Pestello (p171)
➜ **Place to Drink** Bar Borsa (p171)

Top Tip
Palladio's Teatro Olimpico was built for live performances, and that is still the best way to absorb the complex harmonies of the space.

Getting There & Away
➜ **Train** Trains are the easiest way to reach Vicenza from Venice (€6.50 to €18, 45 to 80 minutes, up to five hourly). Trains also connect with Padua and Verona.
➜ **Car & Motorcycle** Vicenza lies just off the A4 connecting Milan with Venice, while the SR11 connects Vicenza with Verona and Padua. There are several larger car parks skirting the historic centre, including the underground Park Verdi just north of the train station (enter from Viale dell'Ippodromo). For real-time updates on available parking spaces, see www.aimmobilita.it/it/mobilita/auto/parcheggi_a_sbarra.

Need to Know
➜ **Area Code** 0444
➜ **Location** 62km west of Venice
➜ **Tourist Office** (☑0444 32 08 54; www.vicenzae.org; Piazza Matteotti 12; ⊙9am-5.30pm)

◉ SIGHTS

★**LA ROTONDA**   HISTORIC BUILDING
(☑049 879 13 80; www.villalarotonda.it; Via della Rotonda 45; adult/child villa & gardens €10/5, gardens €5/free; ⊙villa 10am-noon & 3-6pm Wed & Sat mid-Mar–mid-Nov, gardens 10am-noon &

3-6pm Tue-Sun year-round) No matter how you look at it, this villa is a showstopper: the namesake dome caps a square base, with identical colonnaded facades on all four sides. This is one of Palladio's most admired creations, inspiring variations across Europe and the USA, including Thomas Jefferson's Monticello. Inside, the circular central hall is covered from the walls to the soaring cupola with *trompe l'œil* frescoes. Catch bus 8 (€1.30, €2 on board) from in front of Vicenza's train station, or simply walk (about 25 minutes).

★PALAZZO LEONI MONTANARI   MUSEUM
(⏲800 578875; www.gallerieditalia.com; Contrà di Santa Corona 25; adult/reduced €5/3, or free with MuseumCard; ⊙10am-6pm Tue-Sun) An extraordinary collection of treasures awaits inside Palazzo Leoni Montanari,including ancient pottery from Magna Graecia and grand salons filled with Canaletto's misty lagoon landscapes and Pietro Longhi's 18th-century satires. A recent addition is Agostino Fasolato's astounding *The Fall of the Rebel Angels,* carved from a single block of Carrara marble and featuring no less than 60 angels and demons in nail-biting battle. Topping it all off is a superb collection of 400 Russian icons.

★TEATRO OLIMPICO   THEATRE
(⏲0444 96 43 80; www.teatrolimpicovicenza.it; Piazza Matteotti 11; adult/reduced €11/8, or free with MuseumCard; ⊙9am-5pm Tue-Sun Sep-Jun, 10am-6pm Jul & Aug) Behind a walled garden lies a Renaissance marvel: the Teatro Olimpico, which Palladio began in 1580 with inspiration from Roman amphitheatres. Vincenzo Scamozzi finished the elliptical theatre after Palladio's death, adding a stage set modelled on the ancient Greek city of Thebes, with streets built in steep perspective to give the illusion of a city sprawling towards a distant horizon.

PALAZZO CHIERICATI   MUSEUM
(⏲0444 22 28 11; www.museicivicivicenza.it; Piazza Matteotti 37/39; adult/reduced €7/5; ⊙9am-5pm Tue-Sun Sep-Jun, 10am-6pm Tue-Sun Jul & Aug) Vicenza's civic art museum occupies one of Palladio's finest buildings, designed in 1550. The ground floor, used for temporary exhibitions, is where you'll find the **Sala dal Firmamento** (Salon of the Skies) and its blush-inducing ceiling fresco of Diana and an up-skirted Helios by Domenico Brusasorci. Highlights in the up-

VICENZA JAZZ

Vicenza's biggest annual event is the **jazz festival** (⏲0444 22 15 41; www.vicenzajazz.org; ⊙mid-May) that takes place at the Teatro Olimpico and at several other venues for a week in mid-May, attracting top names from the Italian scene.

stairs galleries include Anthony Van Dyck's allegorical *The Four Ages of Man* and Alessandro Maganza's remarkably contemporary *Portrait of Maddalena Campiglia.*

PALLADIO MUSEUM   MUSEUM
(Palazzo Barbarano; ⏲0444 32 30 14; www.palladiomuseum.org; Contrà Porti 11; adult/reduced €8/6, or free with MuseumCard; ⊙10am-6pm Tue-Sun) To better understand architect Andrea Palladio and his legacy, explore the frescoed halls of this modern museum. Artefacts include historical copies of Palladio's celebrated *Quattro libri dell'architettura* (Four Books of Architecture; 1570) and intriguing architectural models of his lauded *palazzi* and villas, as well as video footage of experts discussing various aspects of the maverick's craft and genius.

PIAZZA DEI SIGNORI   SQUARE
The heart of historic Vicenza is Piazza dei Signori, where Palladio lightens the mood of government buildings with his trademark play of light and shadow. Dazzling white Piovene stone (a local limestone) arches frame shady double arcades at the Basilica Palladiana while, across the piazza, white stone and stucco grace the exposed red-brick colonnade of the 1571-designed **Loggia del Capitaniato**.

BASILICA PALLADIANA   GALLERY
(⏲0444 22 21 22; ww.museicivicivicenza.it; Piazza dei Signori; basilica adult/reduced €4/2, exhibitions €10-13; ⊙10am-4pm Tue-Sun) Now a venue for world-class exhibitions, the Palladian Basilica is capped with an enormous copper dome reminiscent of the hull of a ship. The building, modelled on a Roman basilica, once housed the law courts and Council of Four Hundred. Palladio was lucky to secure the commission in 1549 (it took his patron 50 years of lobbying the council), which involved restructuring the original, 15th-century *palazzo* and adding a double order

Vicenza

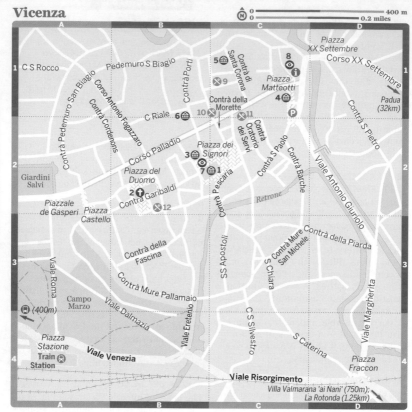

of loggias, supported by Tuscan and Ionic columns topped by soaring statuary.

MUSEO DEL GIOIELLO
MUSEUM

(☑0444 32 07 99; www.museodelgioiello.it; Piazza dei Signori; adult/reduced €8/6; ⊗3-7pm Mon-Fri, 11am-7pm Sat & Sun) Vicenza's expertise in jewellery dates back to 600 BC when the Vicentini were crafting clothing fasteners, called fibula. This museum celebrates that centuries-long tradition with an elegant museum set within the Basilica Palladiana. Rotating exhibitions of historic and contemporary bijouterie showcase 7th-century bejewelled funerary crosses, 15th-century silk and gold harness belts, 1920s costume jewellery, and avant-garde creations from visionaries such as Evart Nijland and Lucy Sarneel.

VILLA VALMARANA
'AI NANI'
HISTORIC BUILDING

(☑0444 32 18 03; www.villavalmarana.com; Via dei Nani 8; adult/reduced €10/6; ⊗10am-6pm Mar-Oct) From La Rotonda, a charming footpath leads about 500m to the neoclassical elegance of Villa Valmarana 'ai Nani', nicknamed after the 17 statues of dwarves ('ai Nani') around the perimeter walls. Step inside for 18th-century frescoes by Giambattista Tiepolo and his son Giandomenico. Giambattista painted the Palazzina wing with his signature mythological epics, while his offspring executed the rural, carnival and Chinese themes adorning the *foresteria* (guesthouse).

DUOMO
CATHEDRAL

(Cattedrale di Santa Maria Annunciata; Piazza del Duomo; ⊗7.30am-8pm) **FREE** Designed by Lorenzo di Bologna, construction of Vicenza's cathedral began in the late 15th century. In the mid-16th century, Andrea Palladio added his own touches to the incomplete building, most notably the cupola, inspired by the dome of the Pantheon in Rome. Aside from the pink-hued

Vicenza

facade, the clean-cut cathedral you see today is a 20th-century reconstruction, the building having been heavily bombed during WWII.

✘ EATING & DRINKING

Vicenza's historic centre is full of atmospheric taverns, lively cafes and bars, and some very good contemporary restaurants catering to an affluent dining audience. The city's signature dish is, somewhat surprisingly, *bacalà alla vicentina:* codfish, poached in milk with anchovies.

★SÒTOBOTEGA
VENETIAN €

(☑0444 54 44 14; www.gastronomiailceppo.com; Corso Palladio 196; meals €25, set tasting menus €26; ◎11.30am-3.30pm) Drop into cult-status deli **Gastronomia Il Ceppo** (prepared dishes per 100g from around €2.50; ◎8am-7.45pm Tue-Sat, 9am-4pm Sun) for picnic provisions, or head down into its cellar for sensational sit-down dishes like expertly crafted *bigoli* (a type of pasta) with the sauce of the day, or the star of the show, *bacalà alla vicentina,* Vicenza's signature codfish dish. Some 500 mostly Italian wines line the walls, and transparent floor panels reveal an ancient Roman footpath and the foundations of an 11th-century dwelling.

RESTAURANT RIGHETTI
VENETIAN €

(☑0444 54 31 35; www.selfrighetti.it; Piazza del Duomo 3; meals €10-15; ◎noon-3pm & 7pm-midnight Mon-Fri) This rare self-service restaurant offers an honest, daily-changing menu of local pasta and meat for knock-down prices (*primi* €4, *secondi* €5), plus salads, desserts and cheap wine. Despite the abundance of seats, you'll be forced to join an Italian queue at feeding time when it's packed out. No English spoken.

★AL PESTELLO
VENETIAN €€

(☑0444 32 37 21; Contrà San Stefano 3; meals €35; ◎7.30-11.45pm Mon & Wed-Fri, 12.30-2pm & 7.30-11.45pm Sat & Sun; ☏) Homely Al Pestello dishes out intriguing, lesser-known *cucina vicentina* such as *la panà* (bread soup), red-wine-braised donkey and *bresaola* 'lollies' filled with grappa-flavoured Grana Padano and mascarpone. The kitchen is obsessed with local ingredients, right down to the Colli Berici truffles, while the collection of harder-to-find *digestivi* makes for an enlightening epilogue. Book ahead.

★FUORIMODENA
EMILIAN €€

(☑0444 33 09 94; www.fuorimodena.it; Contrà San Gaetano da Thiene 8; meals €40-45; ◎7.30-11.30pm Tue-Sun; ✿) Two hundred kilometres separate Vicenza and Modena, but enter this restaurant and you'll enjoy the finest Emilian cooking courtesy of Lorenzo Roncaccioli, whose grandparents emigrated here in 1949. Exquisite plates of the Culatello di Zibello DOP (aged for 32 months) are followed by *passatelli* pasta with Zocca chestnuts and saffron, and then delicate guinea fowl with creamy polenta and chargrilled fennel.

BAR BORSA
BAR

(☑0444 54 45 83; www.barborsa.com; Basilica Palladiana, Piazza dei Signori 26; ◎6pm-2am Mon, 10am-2am Tue-Sun; ☏) Decked out in all manner of knickknacks and illuminated by flickering candlelight, hip Bar Borsa covers all bases, from coffee and juices to *aperitivo* and cocktails. Likewise, flavoursome food options span breakfast, brunch, lunch, snacks and dinner, with DJs spinning tunes on Fridays and Saturdays and jazz sessions almost any night of the week.

Prosecco Country

Explore

In the foothills of the Alps, the area between Conegliano and Valdobbiadene is the toast of the Veneto. The vine-draped hillsides hereabouts produce prosecco, a dry, crisp white wine made in *spumante* (bubbly), *frizzante* (sparkling) and still varieties. In 2009, Conegliano's prosecco was promoted to DOCG (guaranteed-quality) status, Italy's highest oenological distinction.

Plot a tasting tour along La Strada del Prosecco from Conegliano to Valdobbiadene to see what all the fuss is about. It is Italy's oldest wine route and covers 120 wine producers in 60km.

The Best...

→ **Sight** Villa di Masèr (p175)

→ **Place to Eat** Due Mori (p176)

→ **Place to Drink** Cantina Bisol (p173)

Top Tip

Running through a landscape of rolling vineyards, **La Strada di Prosecco** is a driving route that takes you from Conegliano to Valdobbiadene via some of the region's best wineries. A dedicated website (www.coneglianovaldobbiadene.it) provides an itinerary, background information on prosecco, and details about stops along the way.

Getting There & Away

→ **Car** Your own wheels are your best option for getting around the region at a reasonable pace and visiting wineries and farmstays. The A27 heads directly north from Mestre to Conegliano.

→ **Train** Head from Venice to the Mestre station, where there are two to three trains per hour to Conegliano (€5.10, 50 minutes).

Need to Know

→ **Area Code** 0423

→ **Location** Conegliano is 53km north of Venice; Bassano del Grappa is 58km northwest of Venice

→ **Tourist Office** (☑0438 2 12 30; Via XX Settembre 132; ☺9am-1pm Tue & Wed, to 1pm & 2-6pm Thu-Sun)

◉ SIGHTS

◉ Conegliano

If you've ever admired the paintings of sweet Madonnas and saints by local boy Giovanni Battista Cima (aka Cima da Conegliano), you'll most likely feel a sense of déjà vu when you arrive in the town of Conegliano. Draped attractively over a prominent hill in the foothills of the Alps, the town and the surrounding countryside were Giovanni's go-to backdrops, and it's no wonder given their sense of timeless pastoral beauty. These days Conegliano remains a sleepy rural town and is the starting point for Italy's oldest wine route, **La Strada del Prosecco** (The Prosecco Road; www.coneglianovaldobbiadene.it).

CASTELLO DI CONEGLIANO   CASTLE
(Piazzale San Leonardo; ☺24hr) **FREE** Head up steep Calle Madonna della Neve, following

---

THE PROSECCO LOWDOWN

Prosecco can be traced back to the Romans. It was then known as 'Pucino' and was shipped directly to the court of Empress Livia from Aquileia, where it was produced with grapes from the Carso. In the 16th century, during the time of the Venetian Republic, the vines were transferred to the sunny hillsides just north of the Piave river between the towns of Valdobbiadene, Conegliano and Vittorio Veneto.

You can spot a good prosecco by its straw-like yellow colouring, which is touched with a tinge of green. Its bubbles should be tiny, numerous and long-lasting in your glass. On the nose it is fragrant with the scent of white fruits and freshly mown grass, while in the mouth it is crisp and aromatic. These characteristics are not long lasting, so don't hang on to bottles of prosecco too long. Instead, drink it young when it is full of fizz.

WINERIES

Tucked in a broad curve of the Piave river between the towns of Conegliano, Vittorio Veneto and Valdobbiadene, prosecco country is deeply rural. Narrow country roads meander through a patchwork of vineyards, the majority of which are small, family-run affairs. Tastings, which can be arranged between Monday and Saturday, should be booked in advance and you'll need your own set of wheels to get between vineyards. Alternatively, tour operators in Venice, Padua and Asolo can help organise visits.

Cantina Bisol (☑0423 90 47 37; www.bisol.it; Via Follo 33, Santo Stefano di Valdobbiadene; ☺10am-1pm & 3-6pm Mon-Sat, 10am-1pm Sun) Twenty-one generations of the Bisol family have been striving to produce the best prosecco in the world since 1542. Their vineyard, the most important in the area, occupies steep hillsides angled towards the sun, making them perfect for Glera-grape growing. Tastings take place in the atmospheric underground cellars. Their signature labels are the award-winning Cartizze Dry and Jeio Brut.

Azienda Agricola Barichel (☑0423 97 57 43; www.barichel.it; Via Roccat e Ferrari 12, Valdobbiadene) Like the prodigal son, ultra-marathon runner and vintner Ivan Geronazzo returned to his grandfather's vineyard in Valdobbiadene after years of working at larger, high-capacity wineries. Here he tends his 7 hectares by hand, producing up to 60,000 bottles of natural, *frizzante*, extra dry and brut prosecco with a pale, straw-yellow colour and apple-and-pear fragrances. Prices range from €5 to €8 per bottle.

Azienda Agricola Frozza (☑0423 98 70 69; www.frozza.it; Via Martiri 31, Colbertaldo di Vidor; ☺8.30am-12.30pm Mon-Sat) Galera vines have grown on this sunny Colbertaldo hillside for hundreds of years, and six generations of the Frozza family have tended them since 1870. The result: prosecco with a remarkable fragrance and complexity. The 2011 brut is a particularly good vintage. Expect fruity fragrances supported by a well-structured, mineral-rich body. Prices range from €5 to €8 per bottle. Book tastings.

Vignaioli Contra Soarda (☑0424 50 55 62; www.contrasoarda.it; Strada Soarda 26, San Michele di Bassano del Grappa; tastings per person €25; ☺6.30-11pm Mon-Thu, 5.30pm-midnight Fri & Sat; ☏) Grappa isn't the only reason to visit Bassano: there are also some exceptional vineyards such as Contra Soarda. Located in a volcanic zone at the start of the Valsugana Valley, the vineyard's autochthonous Garganega, Marzemino and Grupello wines are award-winning, as is the ecofriendly cellar, which is tucked into the hillside.

---

an intact section of 13th-century defensive walls all the way to a summit, where the last remaining tower of Conegliano's 10th-century castle dominates an attractive set of gardens. The tower is home to a small museum (adult/reduced €2.50/1.50), but the real joy here is the views across the surrounding hills. It's also a superb place to unfurl the picnic blanket, or to spend a sleepy afternoon in the company of a good book.

DUOMO CHURCH
(Duomo di Santa Maria Annunziata e San Leonardo; Via XX Settembre 42; ☺10am-noon & 3-7pm) **FREE** Conegliano's Duomo would be wholly unremarkable were it not for some early works by Veneto artists. The most notable is a 1492–93 altarpiece by local master Cima da Conegliano.

⊙ Asolo

Known as the 'town of 100 vistas' for its panoramic hillside location, the medieval walled town of Asolo has long been a favourite of literary types. Robert Browning bought a house here, but the ultimate local celebrity is Caterina Corner, the 15th-century queen of Cyprus, who was given the town, its castle (now used as a theatre) and the surrounding county in exchange for her abdication. She promptly became queen of the literary set, holding salons that featured writer and later cardinal Pietro Bembo.

DAY TRIPS FROM VENICE PROSECCO COUNTRY

GYPSOTHECA E MUSEO ANTONIO CANOVA

Antonio Canova was Italy's master of neoclassical sculpture. He made marble come alive, and you can see his fascinating modelling technique at the beautiful **Gypsotheca** (☑ 0423 54 43 23; www.museocanova.it; Via Canova 74, Possagno; adult/reduced €10/6; ◷ 9.30am-6pm Tue-Sat, to 7pm Sun), fashioned by modernist master Carlo Scarpa in 1957. Inside, plaster casts reveal the laborious process through which Canova arrived at his glossy, seemingly effortless marbles. Rough clay models give way to plaster figures cast in gesso, which were then used to map out the final marble in minute detail with small nails.

After visiting the Gypsotheca you can head over to Canova's house or just enjoy the beautiful garden and its *belvedere* (viewpoint).

ROCCA
RUINS

(☑ 329 8508512; €2; ◷ 10am-7pm Sat & Sun Apr-Jun, Sep & Oct, 10am-noon & 3-7pm Sat & Sun Jul & Aug, 10am-5pm Sat & Sun Nov-Mar) Perched on the summit of Monte Ricco and looking down on central Asolo are the hulking ruins of a fortress dating back to the 12th to early 13th centuries. The still-visible cistern well was constructed between the 13th and 14th centuries, while the heavily restored buttresses offer a breathtaking panorama that takes in soft green hills, snow-capped mountains and the industrious Po Valley. At the time of writing, the fortress was closed for maintenance work.

MUSEO CIVICO DI ASOLO
MUSEUM

(☑ 0423 95 23 13; www.asolo.it; Via Regina Cornaro 74; adult/reduced €5/4; ◷ 9.30am-12.30pm & 3-6pm Sat & Sun) Explore Asolo's Roman past and wander through a small collection of paintings, including a pair of Tintoretto portraits. The museum also includes rooms devoted to actress Eleonora Duse (1858–1924) and British traveller and writer Freya Stark (1893–1993), who retreated to Asolo between Middle Eastern forays.

VILLA FREYA
GARDENS

(☑ 0423 56 54 78; www.bellasolo.it; Via Forestuzzo; adult/reduced €3/2; ◷ 1st 3 Sat each month, closed Aug & Dec) When she wasn't exploring the furthest reaches of the Empty Quarter or negotiating with future Arab heads of state, legendary explorer and travel writer Freya Stark retired to Asolo to tend her flower-filled gardens. Inevitably she brought back exotic botanical specimens, which still thrive on the sunny slopes that originally formed part of a Roman theatre complex. The ticket price includes a guided tour by **BellAsolo** (☑ 0423 56 54 78; www.bellasolo.it; Via Schiavonesca Marosticana 15;

English-speaking guide half-/full-day €130/230) at 10am and 11am.

◉ Bassano del Grappa

Bassano del Grappa sits charmingly on the banks of the river Brenta as it winds its way free from Alpine foothills through the Veneto plains to the Venetian lagoon. The town is famous for its namesake spirit, grappa – a distillation made from the discarded skins, pulp, seeds and stems of winemaking – although there is plenty to enjoy in this lovely Veneto town with its Palladian architecture and ancient historic core.

Subject to Venetian rule between 1404 and 1815, Bassano has long been a flourishing manufacturing town, while in the 18th century the local Remondini printing house grew to become the largest in Europe. But the strategic location that gave Bassano its commercial edge also put it on the front line in both world wars. In 1928, the town's name was changed to Bassano del Grappa in honour of the thousands of soldiers who died in the battle of Monte Grappa.

★ SACRARIO MILITARE DEL MONTE GRAPPA
MEMORIAL

No battle defines Italy's struggle in the Great War better than the 1917–18 battle of Monte Grappa. Despite being severely weakened after the battles of Caporetto and Isonzo, Italian Alpine brigades mounted a heroic stand atop this barren mountain and finally brought a halt to the Austro-Hungarian advance. The savage conflict claimed the lives of 22,910 troops, who are now entombed in this memorial, which caps the summit and is studded with bronze plaques commemorating the deceased.

The epic ossuary, designed by Giovanni Greppi and Giannino Castiglioni in 1935, mimics the natural slope of the mountain in five concentric stone rings that are positioned on top of one another to form a pyramid, which is capped by a small sanctuary, the **Madoninna del Grappa**. Both Italian and Austro-Hungarian troops are buried in niches dug into the stone, although the two sides are separated by a longitudinal avenue called the **Strada Eroica** (Heroic Way).

Look out for the grave bearing the name, Peter Pan, which is often adorned with flowers and toys. Although little is known about this 21-year old Austrian soldier, the poignant connection between him and the ever-youthful fictional character is self-evident: both will remain forever young on Monte Grappa, known locally as Alpe Madre (Mother Alp).

Near the memorial, there is a cave with a sculpture by Augusto Murer called *Al Partigiano*. It was erected in 1974 in memory of WWII partisans who also sought shelter on Monte Grappa and were burned alive by the retreating Nazis after the Armistice was signed.

The memorial is 32km northeast of Bassano del Grappa. You'll need a car to reach it.

★ **PALAZZO STURM**   MUSEUM

(✆0424 51 99 40; www.museibassano.it; Via Schiavonetti 40; adult/reduced €5/3.50; ◷9am-1pm & 3-6pm Mon-Sat, 10am-7pm Sun) Pretty Palazzo Sturm sits overlooking the Brenta river. It was built in the mid-18th century by wealthy industrialist and silk merchant Vincenzo Ferrari, who decorated it with bourgeoisie baroque frescoes by Veronese painter Giorgio Anselmi. Set against this florid pastel backdrop is a permanent collection of extravagant (and outlandish) historic ceramics and a fascinating exhibit celebrating Bassano's world-famous printers, the Remondinis. Aside from the detailed description of the printing process, there are stunning etchings and woodcuts by Dürer, Mantegna and Tiepolo.

PONTE DEGLI ALPINI   BRIDGE

Spanning the river is Palladio's photogenic 1569 wooden bridge. Fragile as it seems, it is cleverly engineered to withstand the rush of spring meltwaters from Monte Grappa. It's always been critical in times of war: Napoleon bivouacked here and during WWII the bridge was destroyed by the Germans, only to be reconstructed by the Italian Alpine brigade, who adopted it as their emblem.

POLI MUSEO DELLA GRAPPA   MUSEUM

(✆0424 52 44 26; www.poligrappa.com; Via Gamba 6; ◷museum 9am-7.30pm, distillery guided tours 9am-1pm & 2-6pm Mon-Fri) **FREE** Explore four centuries of Bassano's high-octane libation at this interactive museum, which includes tastings and the chance to tour the distillery of esteemed producer Poli (book tours online; €3 per person). Although grappa is made all over Italy, and indeed inferior versions are distilled well beyond the peninsula, the people of the Veneto have been doing it since at least the 16th century. In fact, an institute of grappa distillers was created in Venice in 1601.

WORTH A DETOUR

VILLA DI MASÈR

A World Heritage Site, the 16th-century **Villa di Masèr** (Villa Barbaro; ✆0423 92 30 04; www.villadimaser.it; Via Cornuda 7, Maser; adult/reduced €9/7; ◷10am-6pm Tue-Sat, from 11am Sun Apr-Oct, 11am-5pm Sat & Sun Nov-Mar; ℙ) is a spectacular monument to the Venetian *bea vita* (good life). Designed by the inimitable Andrea Palladio, its sublimely elegant exterior is matched by Paolo Veronese's wildly imaginative *trompe l'œil* architecture inside. Vines crawl up the Stanza di Baccho; a watchdog keeps an eye on the painted door of the Stanza di Canuccio (Little Dog Room); and in a corner of the frescoed grand salon, the painter has apparently forgotten his spattered shoes and broom.

Until the 1850s the villa's wines were stored beneath the porticos. But, on expanding the vineyards' wine production, the Giacomelli's built a separate cantina, where you can book tastings (€4.50 per person) and a light lunch (€6.50 to €9.50 per person). Situated in the heart of the Montello and Colli Asolani DOC area, the wines on offer include the award-winning Manzoni Bianco and the villa's signature Maserino Rosso, both of which are cultivated according to strict ecofriendly regulations.

You'll find it bedded down in a vineyard 7km northeast of Asolo.

MUSEO CIVICO
MUSEUM

(☎0424 51 99 01; www.museibassano.it; Piazza Garibaldi 34; adult/reduced €7/5; ⊙10am-7pm Wed-Mon) Bassano del Grappa's Museo Civico is beautifully housed around the cloisters of the Convento di San Francesco. Endowed in 1828 by the naturalist Giambattista Brocchi, the museum features an extensive archaeological collection alongside 500 paintings, including masterpieces such as the 1545 *Flight into Egypt* by local son Jacopo Bassano.

✖ EATING

Agriturismi offer some of the best dining in these parts, though there are plenty of other restaurants and *osterie* in the towns between Valdobbiadene and Conegliano.

AGRITURISMO DA OTTAVIO
VENETIAN €

(☎0423 98 11 13; Via Campion 2, San Giovanni di Valdobbiadene; meals €15-20; ⊙noon-3pm Sat, Sun & holidays, closed Sep; ℗) Prosecco is typically drunk with *sopressa,* a fresh local salami, as the sparkling *spumante* cleans the palate and refreshes the mouth. There's no better way to test this than at Da Ottavio, where everything on the table, *sopressa* and prosecco included, is homemade by the Spada family.

OSTERIA ALLA CANEVA
VENETIAN €

(☎335 5423560; Via G Matteotti 34, Bassano del Grappa; dishes €20-30; ⊙9.30am-3pm & 5.30pm-midnight Wed-Sun, 9.30am-3pm Mon) This is an old-school favourite, featuring hanging pots, worn wooden tables and inter-generational regulars washing down rustic regional grub with a glass or three of *vino* from local wineries such as Vigneto Due Santi di Zonta. Food options lean towards cured meats and pasta dishes like fettuccine with artichokes. For a light bite, don't miss the *baccala cicchetti* (salted-cod tapas).

AL CASTELLO
CAFE €€

(☎0438 2 23 79; www.ristorantealcastello.it; Piazzale San Leonardo 7, Conegliano; meals €30-40; ⊙12.15-2.15pm & 7.30-10pm Wed-Sun, 12.15-2.15pm Mon) In the grounds of the *castello,* the combination of good Italian food and the incredible views across the surrounding hills make this place well worth the hike uphill from the centre. Go for the full experience, involving duck *tagliata* (sliced grilled meat) with orange sauce or codfish Vicentina.

LOCANDA BAGGIO DA NINO
VENETO €€

(☎0423 52 96 48; www.locandabaggio.it; Via Bassane 1, Asolo; meals €30-40; ⊙12.30-2.30pm Wed-Sun & 7.30-10pm Tue-Sun) Run by the Baggio family, who welcome each guest personally and make sure only the finest ingredients go into the food they serve. The menu is a delightful read featuring suckling pig, guinea fowl, pizzas, octopus and lamb, and the family even make their own souvenirs and examples of local produce to take away.

★DUE MORI
ITALIAN €€€

(☎0423 95 09 53; www.2mori.it; Piazza Gabriele D'Annunzio 5; meals €40-50; ⊙12.30-2.30pm & 7.30-9.30pm Tue-Sun) If ever there was a table with a view, the dining room of Due Mori provides it, with floor-to-ceiling windows overlooking Asolo and the layered Veneto hillsides. Nor does the food disappoint. Refined rustic dishes are cooked on a wood-burning stove that yields a delicious depth of flavour. Try the ravioli with poison-oak leaves and ricotta, or the rich guinea fowl *ragù.*

Verona

Explore

Best known for its Shakespeare associations, Verona attracts a multinational gaggle of tourists to its pretty piazzas and knot of lanes, most in search of Romeo, Juliet and all that. But beyond the heart-shaped kitsch and Renaissance romance, Verona is a bustling centre, its heart dominated by a mammoth, remarkably well-preserved 1st-century amphitheatre, the venue for the city's annual summer opera festival. Add to that countless churches, a couple of architecturally fascinating bridges over the Adige, regional wine and food from the Veneto hinterland and some impressive art, and Verona shapes up as one of northern Italy's most attractive cities. And all this just a short hop from the shores of stunning Lake Garda.

The Best...

➡ **Sight** Roman Arena (p177)

➡ **Place to Eat** Locanda 4 Cuochi (p181)

➡ **Place to Drink** Antica Bottega del Vino (p181)

Top Tip

VeronaCard (per 24/48 hours €20/25; www.veronatouristoffice.it) is available at tourist sights, tobacconists and numerous hotels, and offers access to most major monuments and churches, unlimited use of town buses, and discounted tickets to selected concerts and opera and theatre productions.

If you're planning on seeing Verona's four main churches – the Duomo, San Zeno, Sant'Anastasia and San Fermo – invest in a **cumulative ticket** (adult/reduced €6/5, valid until end December). Included in the ticket is an audio guide in six languages.

Getting There & Away

➡ **Train** Verona Porta Nuova station is a major stop on the Italian rail network with direct services to numerous northern Italian towns and cities, including Venice (€9.50 to €25, 70 minutes to 2¼ hours, one to four hourly), Padua and Vicenza.

➡ **Car & Motorcycle** Verona is at the intersection of the A4 (Turin–Trieste) and A22 motorways. Traffic is restricted in the historic centre, although guests of hotels are allowed entry to drop off bags.

➡ **Bus** The intercity bus station is in front of the train station. Buses run to Padua, Vicenza and Venice.

Need to Know

➡ **Area Code** 045

➡ **Location** 120km west of Venice

➡ **Tourist Office** (☑045 806 86 80; www.veronatouristoffice.it; Via degli Alpini 9; ☺8am-7pm Mon-Sat, 10am-6pm Sun)

◉ SIGHTS

★ROMAN ARENA RUINS

(☑045 800 32 04; Piazza Brà; adult/reduced €10/7.50; ☺8.30am-7.30pm Tue-Sun, 1.30-7.30pm Mon) Built of pink-tinged marble in the 1st century AD, Verona's Roman amphitheatre survived a 12th-century earthquake to become the city's legendary open-air opera house, with seating for 30,000 people. You can visit the arena year-round, though it's at its best during the summer opera festival (p40). In winter months, concerts are held at the **Teatro Filarmonico** (☑045

800 28 80; www.arena.it; Via dei Mutilati 4; tickets from €25). From October to May, admission is €1 on the first Sunday of the month.

The eighth-biggest amphitheatre in the Roman Empire and predating the Colosseum in Rome, nothing of the incredible inside is visible from outside. Pass through the dingy ancient corridors, wide enough to drive a gladiator's chariot, to re-emerge into the massive, sunlit stone arena, at least 50 levels of seating rising from the mammoth, oval showground. Note the amphitheatre is completely open so this is not a great place to visit in the rain.

★GIARDINO GIUSTI GARDENS

(☑045 803 40 29; http://giardinogiusti.com; Via Giardino Giusti 2; adult/reduced €8.50/5; ☺9am-7pm) Across the river from the historic centre, these sculpted gardens are considered a masterpiece of Renaissance landscaping, and are named after the noble family that has tended them since opening the gardens to the public in 1591. The vegetation is an Italianate mix of the manicured and natural, graced by soaring cypresses, one of which the German poet Goethe immortalised in his travel writings.

According to local legend, lovers who manage to find each other in the gardens' petite labyrinth are destined to stay together. If you do, whisper sweet nothings while gazing out at the city from the *belvedere* (lookout), accessed from the back of the gardens. Forget the Casa di Giulietta, this is where the real romance is in Verona.

★GALLERIA D'ARTE MODERNA ACHILLE FORTI GALLERY

(Palazzo della Ragione; ☑045 800 19 03; https://gam.comune.verona.it; Cortile Mercato Vecchio; adult/reduced €4/2.50, incl Torre dei Lamberti €8/5; ☺10am-6pm Tue-Fri, 11am-7pm Sat & Sun) In the shadow of the Torre dei Lamberti, the Romanesque Palazzo della Ragione is home to Verona's jewel-box Gallery of Modern Art. Reached via the Gothic **Scala della Ragione** (Stairs of Reason), the collection of paintings and sculpture spans the period from 1840 to 1940 and includes influential Italian artists such as Giorgio Morandi and Umberto Boccioni. Among the numerous highlights are Francesco Hayez' arresting portrait *Meditazione* (Meditation), Angelo Dall'Oca's haunting *Foglie cadenti* (Falling Leaves) and Ettore Berladini's darkly humorous *I vecchi* (Old Men).

Verona

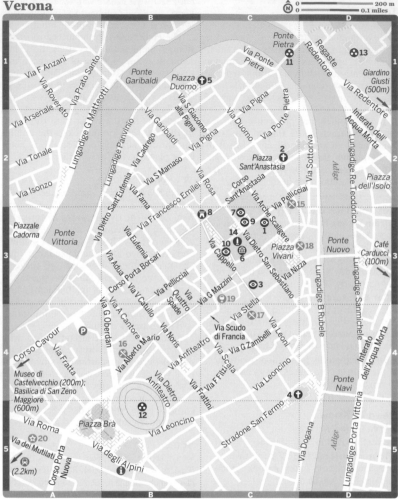

The gallery's architectural pièce de résistance is the vaulted **Cappella dei Notai** (Chapel of Notaries), bursting with late-17th and early-18th-century biblical scenes executed by Alessandro Marchesini, Giambattista Bellotti, Santo Prunati and Louis Dorigny.

★ MUSEO DI CASTELVECCHIO   MUSEUM
(☎045 806 26 11; https://museodicastelvec chio.comune.verona.it; Corso Castelvecchio 2; adult/reduced €6/4.50, free with VeronaCard; ⏱1.30-7.30pm Mon, 8.30am-7.30pm Tue-Sun) Bristling with fishtail battlements along the river Adige, Castelvecchio was built in the 1350s by Cangrande II. Severely damaged by Napoleon and WWII bombings, the fortress was reinvented by architect Carlo Scarpa, who constructed bridges over exposed foundations, filled gaping holes with glass panels, and balanced a statue of Cangrande I above the courtyard on a concrete gangplank. The complex is now home to a diverse collection of statuary, frescoes, jewellery, medieval artefacts and paintings.

Scarpa's modern reworking of the interior comes as a surprise after the austere medieval exterior and provides a contrasting backdrop for the exhibits. Highlights include some wonderful 14th-century glass,

Verona

the Pisanello room with its well-preserved frescoes, the collection of Flemish art and works by Renaissance Veronese and Venetian painters. Look out for the Cangrande coat of arms throughout – Cangrande means 'Top Dog' and the family's comedy shield features two dogs climbing a ladder! After viewing the exhibition, clamber out onto the ramparts for views of the river and old city defences.

TORRE DEI LAMBERTI   TOWER
(☑045 927 30 27; Via della Costa 1; adult/reduced incl Galleria d'Arte Moderna Achille Forti €8/5, with VeronaCard €1; ⊙10am-6pm Mon-Fri, 11am-7pm Sat & Sun) One of Verona's most popular attractions, this 84m-high watchtower provides panoramic views of Verona and nearby mountains. Begun in the 12th century and finished in 1463 – too late to notice invading Venetians – it sports an octagonal bell tower whose two bells retain their ancient names: Rengo once called meetings of the city council, while Marangona warned citizens of fire. A lift whisks you up two-thirds of the way, but you have to walk the last few storeys.

BASILICA DI SAN ZENO
MAGGIORE   BASILICA
(www.basilicasanzeno.it; Piazza San Zeno; €3; ⊙8.30am-6pm Mon-Sat, 12.30-6pm Sun Mar-Oct, 10am-1pm & 1.30-5pm Mon-Sat, 12.30-5pm Sun Nov-Feb) A masterpiece of Romanesque architecture, the striped brick-and-stone basilica was built in honour of the city's patron saint. Enter through the flower-filled cloister into the nave – a vast space lined with

12th- to 15th-century frescoes. Painstaking restoration has revived Mantegna's 1457–59 *Majesty of the Virgin* altarpiece, painted with such astonishing perspective that you actually believe there are garlands of fresh fruit hanging behind the Madonna's throne.

Under the rose window depicting the Wheel of Fortune you'll find meticulously detailed 12th-century bronze doors, which include a scene of an exorcism with a demon being yanked from a woman's mouth. Beneath the main altar lies a brooding crypt, with faces carved into medieval capitals and St Zeno's corpse glowing in a transparent sarcophagus.

CHIESA DI SAN FERMO   CHURCH
(Stradone San Fermo; €3, free with VeronaCard; ⊙10am-6pm Mon-Sat, 1-6pm Sun Mar-Oct, to 5pm Nov-Feb) At the river end of Via Leoni, Chiesa di San Fermo is actually two churches in one: Franciscan monks raised the 13th-century Gothic church right over an original 11th-century Romanesque structure. Inside the main Gothic church, you'll notice a magnificent timber *carena di nave,* a ceiling reminiscent of an upturned boat's hull. In the right transept are 14th-century frescoes, including some fragments depicting episodes in the life of St Francis. Stairs from the cloister lead underground to the spare but atmospheric Romanesque church below.

CASA DI GIULIETTA   NOTABLE BUILDING
(Juliet's House; ☑045 803 43 03; Via Cappello 23; adult/reduced €6/4.50, free with VeronaCard; ⊙1.30-7.30pm Mon, 8.30am-7.30pm Tue-Sun) Juliet's house is a spectacle, but not for the

ℹ️ BIKE TOURS

Simonetta Bike Tours (📞 045 222 65 29; www.simonettabiketours.it) operates a variety of pedal-powered jaunts around Verona, one involving cycling and rafting on the Adige. It also arranges longer bike tours of the Veneto, Lake Garda and the Dolomites. A three-hour bike tour around Verona costs €35 per person.

reasons you might imagine – entering the courtyard off Via Cappello, you are greeted by a young multinational crowd, everyone milling around in the tiny space trying to take selfies with the well-rubbed bronze of Juliet. The walls are lined up to 2m high with love notes, many attached with chewing gum. Above you is the famous balcony, tourists taking their turn to have pics taken against the 'romantic background'.

The actual house is not worth the entrance fee – it's virtually empty and swamped with visitors who can hardly pass on the narrow stairs. There are only a couple of interesting exhibits inside, including the bed that featured in Zeffirelli's 1968 film, and a few Renaissance costumes. The gift shop opposite reaches the height of heart-shaped kitsch.

PIAZZA DELLE ERBE   SQUARE
Originally a Roman forum, Piazza delle Erbe is ringed with buzzing cafes and some of Verona's most sumptuous buildings, including the elegantly baroque **Palazzo Maffei**, which now houses several shops at its northern end. Just off the piazza, the monumental arch known as the **Arco della Costa** is hung with a whale's rib. Legend holds that the rib will fall on the first just person to walk beneath it. So far, it remains intact, despite visits by popes and kings.

PIAZZA DEI SIGNORI   SQUARE
Verona's beautiful open-air salon is ringed by a series of elegant Renaissance *palazzi*. Chief among these are the **Palazzo degli Scaligeri** (aka Palazzo Podestà), the 14th-century residence of Cangrande I Della Scala; the arched **Loggia del Consiglio**, built in the 15th century as the city council chambers; and the brick and tufa stone **Palazzo della Ragione**. In the middle of the piazza is a famous statue of **Dante**, who was given

refuge in Verona after he was exiled from Florence in 1302.

Most of the piazza's buildings are off limits to the public, but you can visit the 12th-century **Palazzo della Ragione**, on your left as you enter from the Arco della Costa, which has housed a modern art gallery since April 2014. Next door, the **Palazzo del Capitano** is fronted by a cobbled square with two huge round windows in the ground, which reveal the excavated Roman and medieval basements beneath. To the northeast loom the **Arche Scaligere** (Via Arche Scaligere), the ornate, Gothic funerary monuments of the Della Scala family.

BASILICA DI SANT'ANASTASIA   BASILICA
(www.chieseverona.it; Piazza di Sant'Anastasia; €3, free with VeronaCard; ⏰ 9am-6pm Mon-Sat, 1-6pm Sun Mar-Oct, to 5pm Nov-Feb) Dating from the 13th to 15th centuries and featuring an elegantly decorated vaulted ceiling, the Gothic Basilica di Sant'Anastasia is Verona's largest church and a showcase for local art. The multitude of frescoes is overwhelming, but don't overlook Pisanello's storybook-quality fresco *St George and the Princess* above the entrance to the **Pellegrini Chapel**, or the 1495 **holy water font** featuring a hunchback carved by Paolo Veronese's father, Gabriele Caliari.

DUOMO   CATHEDRAL
(Cattedrale Santa Maria Matricolare; 📞 045 59 28 13; Piazza Duomo; €3, free with VeronaCard; ⏰ 10am-5.30pm Mon-Sat, 1.30-5.30pm Sun Mar-Oct, to 5pm Nov-Feb) Verona's 12th-century *duomo* is a striking Romanesque creation, with bug-eyed statues of Charlemagne's paladins Roland and Oliver, crafted by medieval master Nicolò, on the west porch. Nothing about this sober facade hints at the extravagant 16th- to 17th-century frescoed interior with angels aloft amid *trompe l'œil* architecture. At the left end of the nave is the **Cartolari-Nichesola Chapel**, designed by Renaissance master Jacopo Sansovino and featuring a vibrant Titian *Assumption*.

PONTE PIETRA   ARCHAEOLOGICAL SITE
(Via Ponte Pietra) At the northern edge of the city centre, this bridge is a quiet but remarkable testament to the Italians' love of their artistic heritage. Two of the bridge's arches date from the Roman Republican era in the 1st century BC, while the other three were replaced in the 13th century. The ancient bridge remained largely intact

until 1945, when retreating German troops blew it up. Locals fished the fragments out of the river, and painstakingly rebuilt the bridge stone by stone in the 1950s.

TEATRO ROMANO E MUSEO ARCHEOLOGICO
ARCHAEOLOGICAL SITE

(☎045 800 03 60; Regaste Redentore 2; adult/reduced €4.50/3, with VeronaCard free; ◷8.30am-7.30pm Tue-Sun, 1.30-7.30pm Mon) Just north of the historic centre you'll find a **Roman theatre**. Built in the 1st century BC, it is cunningly carved into the hillside at a strategic spot overlooking a bend in the river. Take the lift at the back of the theatre to the former convent above, which houses an interesting collection of Greek and Roman pieces.

EATING

★PASTICCERIA FLEGO
CAFE €

(☎045 803 24 71; www.pasticceriaflego.com; Via Stella 13; pastries €1.30-1.60; ◷7.30am-7.30pm Tue-Sun) The gold standard for pastry in Verona is Flego, where you'll find at least 10 different croissant options every morning, including the divine myrtle-berry croissant, alongside the classic Risino, a typical Veronese cake made with rice. It also specialises in coffee and macarons and, come lunchtime, offers a range of savoury puff-pastry snacks, salads and sandwiches.

HOSTARIA LA VECCHIA FONTANINA
TRATTORIA €

(☎045 59 11 59; www.ristorantevecchiafontanina.com; Piazzetta Chiavica 5; meals €20-25; ◷10.30am-3.30pm & 6.30-11pm) With tables on a pint-sized piazza, cosy indoor rooms and excellent food, this historic, knick-knack-filled eatery stands out from the crowd. The menu features typical Veronese dishes alongside a number of more unusual creations such as *bigoli con ortica e ricotta affumicata* (thick spaghetti with nettles and smoked ricotta) and several heavenly desserts. Queuing to get in is normal.

★CAFÉ CARDUCCI
BISTRO €€

(☎045 803 06 04; www.cafecarducci.it; Via Carducci 12; meals €25-45; ◷7am-3pm & 5-11pm Mon-Sat; ⚅) A charming 1920s-style bistro where stylish diners relax in the mirror-lined interior at linen-topped tables set with candles and plates of exquisitely sweet salami and local cheeses. The menu is as classic as the surroundings, offering risotto in an Amarone reduction and black rice with scallops. In cherry season, don't miss the cream ice cream with Bigarreau cherries doused in grappa.

★LOCANDA 4 CUOCHI
ITALIAN €€

(☎045 803 03 11; www.locanda4cuochi.it; Via Alberto Mario 12; meals €40, 3-course set menu €43; ◷12.30-2.30pm & 7.30-10.30pm, closed lunch Mon & Tue; ☎) With its open kitchen, urbane vibe and hotshot chefs, you're right to expect great things from Locanda. Culinary acrobatics play second fiddle to prime produce cooked with skill and subtle twists. Whether it's perfectly crisp suckling pig lacquered with liquorice, or an epilogue of *gianduja* ganache with sesame crumble and banana, you will be gastronomically impressed.

★PESCHERIA I MASENINI
SEAFOOD €€€

(☎045 929 80 15; www.imasenini.com; Piazzetta Pescheria 9; meals €40-50; ◷12.40-2pm & 7.40-10pm, closed Sun evening & Mon) Located on the piazza where Verona's Roman fish market once held sway, softly lit Masenini quietly serves up Verona's most imaginative, modern fish dishes. Inspired flavour combinations might see fresh sea-bass carpaccio paired with zesty green apple and pink pepper, black-ink gnocchi schmoozing with lobster *ragù*, or sliced amberjack de lightfully matched with crumbed almonds, honey, spinach and raspberries.

🍷 DRINKING & NIGHTLIFE

Piazza delle Erbe is ringed with cafes and bars and fills with a fashionable drinking crowd come early evening. Or head to the river, for a *spritz* with a view. For a less touristy experience, head across the Ponte Nuova to Veronetta, where students and locals prefer to hang out.

★ANTICA BOTTEGA DEL VINO
WINE BAR

(☎045 800 45 35; www.bottegavini.it; Vicolo Scudo di Francia 3; ◷11am-1am) While *vino* is the primary consideration at this historic, baronial-style wine bar (the cellar holds around 18,000 bottles), the linen-lined tables promise a satisfying feed. Ask the sommelier to recommend a worthy vintage to go with your braised donkey, Vicenza-style codfish or Venetian liver – some of the best wines here are bottled specifically for the *bottega*.

Verona's Wine Country

Explore

A drive through Verona's hinterland is a lesson in fine wine. To the north and northwest are Valpolicella vineyards, which predate the arrival of the Romans, and east on the road to Vicenza lie the white-wine producers of Soave.

The Best...

➡ **Sight** Villa della Torre

➡ **Place to Eat** Enoteca della Valpolicella (p185)

➡ **Place to Drink** 1898 Cantina di Soave

Top Tip

If you don't want to rent a car, **Pagus** (📞327 7965380; www.pagusvalpolicella.net; Via San Giuseppe 18; group tour half day €75-95, full day €120-140; ⊙10am-1pm & 2-6pm Mon-Fri, to 1pm Sat) offers tours of Valpolicella and Soave, leaving regularly from Verona. Tours include visits to unusual rural sites, impromptu rambles, lunches in local restaurants and, of course, wine tastings. They can also be customised.

Getting There & Away

➡ **Car & Motorcycle** A car is essential for getting to Valpolicella and even though Soave is accessible by public transport, a car is needed for exploring the surrounding vineyards. Valpolicella, situated 20km northwest of Verona, can be reached via the SP1 and SP4; while Soave is a 40-minute drive east along the A4/E70 motorway.

Need to Know

➡ **Area Code** 045

➡ **Location** Soave and Valpolicella are 85km and 140km west of Venice, respectively

➡ **Tourist Offices Soave** (📞045 619

07 73; www.soaveturismo.it; Piazza Foro Boario I; ⊙10am-4pm Tue-Fri, to 2pm Sat & Sun); **Valpolicella** (📞045 770 19 20; www.valpolicellaweb.it; Via Ingelheim 7, San Pietro in Cariano; ⊙9am-1pm Mon-Fri)

◉ SIGHTS & ACTIVITIES

◉ Soave

East of Verona and an easy day trip, Soave serves its namesake DOC (Denominazione di Origine Controllate) white wine in a storybook setting. The town is entirely encircled by medieval fortifications, including 24 bristling watchtowers guarding a medieval castle. Wine is the main reason to come here, with tastings available throughout the year.

CASTELLO DI SOAVE   CASTLE

(📞045 768 00 36; www.castellodisoave.it; adult/reduced €7/4; ⊙9am-noon & 3-6.30pm Apr-Oct, to noon & 2-4pm Nov-Mar) Built on a medieval base by Verona's fratricidal Scaligeri family, the Castello complex encompasses an early-Renaissance villa, grassy courtyards, the remnants of a Romanesque church and the Mastio (the defensive tower, apparently used as a dungeon – during restoration, a mound of human bones was unearthed here). The highlight for most, however, will be the panoramas of the surrounding countryside from the many rampart viewing points.

⭐ **1898 CANTINA DI SOAVE**   WINE

(📞045 613 98 45; www.cantinasoave.it; Via Covergnino 7; ⊙9am-7pm Mon-Sat May-Sep, 8.30am-12.30pm & 2.30-7pm Mon-Sat Oct-Apr) Going strong for over a century and once an official supplier to Italian royalty, this cooperative of 2000 Soave producers is a must-visit. It is housed in a small hamlet, Borgo Rocca Sveva, set against the castle wall, where you can visit the cellars, wine shop and botanical garden. Book tours.

⭐ **SUAVIA**   WINE

(📞045 767 50 89; www.suavia.it; Via Centro 14, Fittà; ⊙9am-1pm & 2.30-6.30pm Mon-Fri, to 1pm Sat & by appointment) Soave is not known as a complex white, but this trailblazing winery, located 8km outside Soave via the SP58, has been changing the viticultural landscape in recent years. Don't miss the award-winning DOC Monte Carbonare Soave Classico, with its mineral, ocean-breeze finish. Book tours.

AZIENDA AGRICOLA COFFELE   WINE
(☑045 768 00 07; www.coffele.it; Via Roma 5; wine tasting €12-25; ◷9.30am-7.30pm Mon-Sat, 10am-1pm & 2-7pm Sun) Across from the old-town church, this family-run winery offers tastings of lemon-zesty DOC Soave Classico and an elegant, creamy DOC Coffele Ca' Visco Classico. The family also rents out rooms among vineyards a few kilometres from town. Book wine tastings in advance; at least a day ahead in winter and about a week ahead in summer.

⊙ Valpolicella

The 'valley of many cellars', from which Valpolicella gets its name, has been in the business of wine production since the ancient Greeks introduced their *passito* technique (the use of partially dried grapes) to create the blockbuster flavours we still enjoy in the region's Amarone and Recioto wines.

Situated in the foothills of Monte Lessini, the valleys benefit from a happy microclimate created by the enormous body of Lake Garda to the west and cooling breezes from the Alps to the north. No wonder Veronese nobility got busy building weekend retreats here. Many of them, like the extraordinary Villa della Torre, still house noble wineries, while others have been transformed into idyllic places to stay and eat.

★VILLA DELLA TORRE   HISTORIC BUILDING
(☑045 683 20 70; www.villadellatorre.it; Via della Torre 25, Fumane; villa guided tours €10, with wine tasting & snack €30-40; ◷villa tours 11am & 4pm Mon-Sat by appointment; ℗) The jewel in the Allegrini crown, this historic villa dates to the mid-16th century and was built by intellectual and humanist Giulio della Torre. Numerous starchitects contributed to its construction: the classically inspired peristyle and fish pond are attributed to Giulio Romana (of Palazzo Te fame), the chapel to Michele Sanmicheli, and the monstrous, gaping-mouthed fireplaces to Bartolomeo Ridolfi and Giovanni Battista Scultori.

VILLA SEREGO ALIGHIERI   WINERY
(☑045 770 36 22; www.seregoalighieri.it; Via Giare 277, Località Gargagnago; tours & tastings €18; ◷by appointment) Fleeing false charges of corruption in Florence, Italy's great medieval poet Dante Alighieri escaped to Verona and the protection of the Scala family. With the family settled in the Veneto, his son Pietro acquired a grand villa in 1353, the Casal dei Ronchi, which remains in the family today and forms the Villa Serego winery. Tours of the property and winery can be booked and are well worth it just to hear the fascinating story.

PIEVE DI SAN GIORGIO   CHURCH
(www.infovalpolicella.it; Piazza della Pieve 22, San Giorgio di Valpolicella; ◷7am-8pm summer, 8am-5pm winter) FREE In the tiny hilltop village of San Giorgio, around 6km northwest of San Pietro in Cariano, you'll find this fresco-filled, cloistered 8th-century Romanesque church. Not old enough for you? In the little garden to its left you can also see a few fragments of an ancient Roman temple.

PIEVE DI SAN FLORIANO   CHURCH
(Via della Pieve 49, Località San Floriano; ◷7.30am-7.30pm) FREE Considered one of the most attractive Romanesque churches in the region, this austere place of worship dates back to between the 10th and 13th centuries. Particularly impressive are the cloisters, a peaceful stone oasis with a truly ancient feel.

★DAMOLI   WINE
(☑340 8762680; www.damolivini.com; Via Jago di Mezzo 5, Negrar; tastings per person €30; ◷by appointment) The Damoli family have been cultivating wines in Negrar since 1623, first as tenant farmers and then as owners of their own small vineyard. Their passion and dedication show in their classic Amarones and the three-hour-long tastings where Lara Damoli explains the attention to detail in their production process. The award-winning Checo wine is also extremely well priced at €30.

★GIUSEPPE QUINTARELLI   WINE
(☑045 750 00 16; giuseppe.quintarelli@tin.it; Via Cerè 1, Negrar; wine tastings per person €30; ◷by appointment) The late Giuseppe Quintarelli put the Valpolicella region on the world wine map, and his benchmark estate is now run by daughter Fiorenza and her family. Quintarelli's extraordinary, limited-production Amarone – made using Corvina, Corvinone, Rondinella, cabernet, Nebbiolo, Croatina and Sangiovese grapes –

ℹ VALPOLICELLA WINERIES

Details of wineries, restaurants and themed itineraries can be found at www.stradadelvinovalpolicella.it.

is a Holy Grail for serious oenophiles. Given how expensive and hard to find the estate's wines are, the €30 tasting is fantastic value for money.

ALLEGRINI
WINE

(☑045 683 20 11; www.allegrini.it; Via Giare 9/11, Fumane; vineyard tour per person €60; ☺by appointment) The Allegrini family has been tending vines in Fumane, Sant'Ambrogio and San Pietro since the 16th century. Pride of place goes to the *cru* wines produced from Corvinia and Rondinella grapes grown on the La Grola hillside (La Poja, La Grola and Palazzo della Torre). Tours of Allegrini's six different vineyards are possible for wine enthusiasts and explore the details of terroir and cultivation; otherwise, wine tastings are held in the historic 16th-century Villa della Torre (p183).

VILLA MOSCONI BERTANI
WINE

(☑045 602 07 44; www.mosconibertani.it; Via Novare, Arbizzano; tours €9, tastings €22-35; ☺wine tastings & tours 2pm & 4pm Sun-Fri, & 10am Tue-Sun) This lovely winery housed in a small manor offers both wine tastings and tours of the neoclassical building, a historic landmark, which boasts a richly frescoed chamber designed for operatic performances. There is a choice of four tasting sessions, most of them involving superior Valpolicello wines such as Lepia Soave DOC, Amarone Classico DOCG and Torre Pieve chardonnay. Pre-booking is advised.

ZÝMĒ
WINE

(☑045 770 11 08; www.zyme.it; Via Cà del Pipa 1, San Pietro in Cariano; wine tastings €20; ☺shop 9am-6pm Mon-Sat, tastings by appointment) An award-winning winery with striking contemporary architecture and an ancient quarry-turned-cellar. Celestino Gaspari, who founded the winery in 2003, is a dreamer, known for big blend wines. The most famous of these is Zýmē's signature Harlequin, an opulent IGP wine made using 15 local grape varieties (11 red, four white). Other notable wines to taste include Kairos and Oseleta. Book wine tastings in advance.

FRATELLI VOGADORI
WINE

(☑328 9417228; www.amaronevalpolicella.org; Via Vigolo 16, Negrar; tastings per person €25; ☺8am-noon & 1-6pm Mon-Sat, 8am-noon Sun; ⓢ) 🥬 The eponymous brothers (*fratelli*) of Vogadori produce organic wines using unusual native varieties such as Oseleta and Negrara. The result: the wonderfully full-bodied Amarone Riserva Forlago (2004) and the deservedly famous 2007 Recioto della Valpolicella, which pairs wickedly with dark chocolate cake. Cellar-door wine-tasting sessions take place throughout the day; book ahead. Rooms are also available (doubles €70).

MASSIMAGO
WINE

(☑045 888 01 43; http://massimago.com; Via Giare 21, Mezzane di Sotto; wine tastings €10-30, ☺9am-8pm Mon-Fri, tastings by appointment) Presiding over the cutting-edge of Valpolicella viticulture is the dynamic Camilla Chauvenet, who took over this winery when she was just 20 years old, and has since been turning out lighter, more modern versions of the classics, including an unusual rosé and a sparkling variety. The on-site four-room boutique **hotel** (d €100-140, 4-person apt €180-200) is as elegant and refined as the wines. Call or email ahead for wine tastings, which are preferred in the afternoon.

MONTECARIANO CELLARS
WINE

(☑045 683 83 35; www.montecariano.it; Via Valena 3, San Pietro in Cariano; tastings per person €25; ☺9am-12.30pm & 3-5pm Mon-Fri by appointment) Sample award-winning Amarone at this winery in the town of San Pietro in Cariano, just off central Piazza San Giuseppe.

TEZZA
WINE

(☑045 55 02 67; www.tezzawines.it; Stradella Maioli, Valpantena; tastings per person €15-25; ☺wine tastings by appointment) Bordering the historic heart of Valpolicella is the beautiful Valpantena valley, where the Tezza brothers cultivate 25 hectares using a mixture of traditional and modern methods. Some of the vines are planted in the high pergola style, hanging high to protect them from the sun and humidity, and producing wines that are intense, tannic and unusually dry.

VALENTINA CUBI
WINE

(☑045 770 18 06; www.valentinacubi.it; Località Casterna 60, Fumane; wine tastings €20; ☺9.30am-12.30pm & 3-6pm Mon-Fri, to 1pm Sat

Church in Valpolicella (p183)

by appointment; [image]) [image] The eponymous Valentina Cubi is blazing a trail with her state-of-the-art, 10-hectare, certified organic winery. Cubi uses biodynamic methods and, subject to the quality of the year's harvest, produces one of the few 'natural', sulphate-free Valpolicellas. To discover more, bed down in one of the farm's smart rooms (double €120).

✗ EATING

TRATTORIA ALLA ROCCA   TRATTORIA €
([image]045 768 02 35; Corso Vittorio Emanuele II 155, Soave; meals €15-20; ⊘noon-2pm & 7-10.15pm Tue-Sat, 7-10.15pm Sun) Cheap and cheerful Alla Rocca is known as La Bigoleria because it focuses on the region's signature pasta *(bigoli)* served with dozens of different sauces. The slow-cooked wild-boar sauce is particularly good and plentiful.

★ENOTECA DELLA VALPOLICELLA   VENETIAN €€
([image]045 683 91 46; www.enotecadellavalpolicella.it; Via Osan 47, Fumane; meals €25-35; ⊘noon-2.30pm & 7pm-midnight Tue-Sat, to 3pm Sun) Gastronomes flock to the town of Fumane, just a few kilometres north of San Pietro in Cariano, where an ancient farmhouse has found renewed vigour as a rustically elegant restaurant. Put your trust in gracious owners Ada and Carlotta, who will eagerly guide you through the day's menu, a showcase for fresh, local produce.

★OSTERIA NUMERO UNO   OSTERIA €€
([image]045 770 13 75; www.osterianumero1.com, Via Flaminio Pellegrini 2, Fumane; meals €20-30; ⊘noon-2.30pm & 7-10.30pm Thu-Mon) The archetypal *osteria* with a wooden bar packed with overall-clad vintners and delicious aromas wafting out of the kitchen. Glasses of Valpolicella (around 120 types) range from just €2 to €5 for a good Amarone. Pair them with salty speck and belly-filling duck with wild garlic and gnocchi.

TRATTORIA CAPRINI   TRATTORIA €€
([image]045 750 05 11; www.trattoriacaprini.it; Via Zanotti 9, Torbe; meals €30; ⊘noon-2.30pm & 7-10pm Thu-Tue) A little north of Negrar in the hamlet of Torbe, family-run Caprini serves heart-warming fare you wish your mamma could make. Many menu items are homemade, including the delicious *lasagnetta* with hand-rolled pasta, and a *ragù* of beef, tomato, porcini and finferlo mushrooms. Downstairs, beside the fire of the old *pistoria* (bakery), you can sample some 200 Valpolicella labels.

LOCANDA LO SCUDO   ITALIAN €€
([image]045 768 07 66; www.loscudo.vr.it; Via Covergnino 9; meals €35; ⊘noon-2.30pm & 7.30-10.30pm Tue-Sat, to 2.30pm Sun; [image]) Just outside the medieval walls of Soave, Lo Scudo is half country inn and half high-powered gastronomy. Cult classics include a risotto of scallops and porcini mushrooms, though – if it's on the menu – only a fool would resist the extraordinary dish of tortelloni stuffed with local pumpkin, Grana Padano, cinnamon, mustard and Amaretto, and topped with crispy fried sage.

Magnificent Palladio

When it comes to coffee-table archi-tecture, no one beats Andrea Palladio. As you flip through photos of his villas, concerns about your own problematic living space begins to dissolve, and you find yourself strolling through more harmonious country. Nature is governed by pleasing symmetries. Roman rigour is soothed by rustic charms. He managed to synthesise the classical past without doggedly copying it, creating buildings that were at once inviting, useful and incomparably elegant. From London to St Petersburg, his work – cleverly disseminated by his *I Quattro Libri*, a how-to guide for other architects – shaped the way Europe thought about architecture.

And yet when Palladio turned 30 in 1538, he was little more than a glorified stonecutter in Vicenza. His big break came when nobleman and amateur architect Giangiorgio Trissino recognised his potential and noticed his inclination towards mathematics. He introduced Palladio to the work of Roman architectural theorist Vitruvius, and sent him to Rome (1545–47) to sketch both crumbling antiquities and new works such as Michelangelo's dome for St Peter's.

Something mysterious happened on those trips, because when Palladio returned to Vicenza he was forging a new way of thinking about architecture – one that focused on the relationship between ratios to create spatial harmony. So a room in which the shorter wall was one-half (1:2), two-thirds (2:3) or three-quarters (3:4) the length of the longer would feel more satisfying because it was rationally

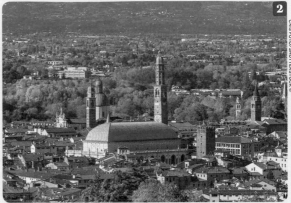

1. Teatro Olimpico
(p169)
2. Basilica Palladiana
(p169)
3. La Rotonda (p168)

harmonious. Like Pallas Athena, the goddess of wisdom, from whom he took his name, Palladio's ideas seemed to spring fully formed from his head.

This search for perfection was never at odds with practicality. In his villas, he squeezed stables beneath elegant drawing rooms. Lacking funds to line San Giorgio Maggiore with marble, he came up with a superior solution: humble stucco walls that fill the church with an ethereal softness. Constraint provided the path to innovation.

A Palladian villa never masters its landscape like, say, Versailles. Palladio makes his mark tactfully, as if he has merely gathered the natural forces of the land and translated them into an ideal, and distinctly human, response. His Rotonda, for example, crowns a rise in the terrain, and looks out on it from four identical facades. Nothing like it had been built before. Yet when you see it in situ, it seems to be the inevitable outcome of the site itself.

PALLADIAN HIGHLIGHTS

Basilica Palladiana (p169) Top-notch art gallery modelled on a Roman basilica.
La Rotonda (p168) Palladio's most inspired design, copied the world over.
Villa di Masèr (p175) Butter-yellow villa set against a green hillside; Palladio's prettiest composition.
Villa Foscari (p161) River-facing facade with soaring Ionic columns that draw the eye and spirits upwards.
Teatro Olimpico (p169) Palladio's visionary elliptical theatre.

Sleeping

Venice was once known for charmingly decrepit hotels where English poets quietly expired, but new design-literate B&Bs and boutique hotels are spiffing up historic palaces. In peak seasons quality hotels fill up fast. In summer, many people decamp to the Lido where prices are more reasonable and swimming is an option after hot days in the Rialto.

More Options than Ever

Venice offers plenty of luxe hotels along the Grand Canal and Riva degli Schiavone, and there's also a growing inventory of boutique sleeps. At the same time, the internet has made it much easier for locals to rent out their homes (or extra rooms) and short-term rentals are increasingly popular.

For budget travellers, Venice offers a range of *foresterie* (hostels). Some bunks even have canal or garden views. During summer, university housing also opens to tourists.

Location, Location, Location

Although Venice is a small city, getting around it amid tourist crowds and on slow *vaporetti* (small passenger ferries) can take time, so plan where you stay carefully. Easy access to the Grand Canal or a convenient *vaporetto* stop is key, although San Marco has all the best sights, and *sestieri* (districts) such as Dorsoduro, Cannaregio and Castello have all the best restaurants and bars. For those on a budget, Giudecca, Murano and the Lido are all within 15 to 30 minutes of the Rialto and are cheaper, quieter and more authentically Venetian.

Season Matters

In low season – November, early December, and January to March (except around New Year's, Carnevale and Easter) – you can expect discounts of 20% or more off peak rates. Even in high season, midweek rates tend to be lower than weekend ones. By contrast, expect to pay a hefty premium during Carnevale, New Year's and Easter.

The rates provided should be considered a guide, since hotels make constant adjustments according to season, day of week and holidays of varying importance. Booking directly with hotels nearly always guarantees the best price, as you won't be covering the 15% to 20% commissions levied by online sites.

Amenities

In general, rooms in Venice tend to be small – and sometimes dark or awkwardly shaped as per the quirks of ancient *palazzi* (mansions). Unless otherwise stated, guestrooms come with private bathroom, often with a shower rather than a bathtub. Business centres are rarely well equipped, even in swanky hotels. Only a few large hotels have a pool – mostly on the Lido or private islands. While increasingly available, wi-fi doesn't always penetrate thick stone walls and may only be available in common areas.

Buyer Beware

Not all hotels in Venice are grand: some are cramped, frayed and draughty, with lackadaisical service. Budget and midrange places around the train station tend to be especially dreary – sometimes despite glowing internet 'reviews'. Note also that many hotels boast of 'Venetian-style' rooms. Sometimes this implies real antiques and Murano chandeliers, but it can mean a kitsch version of baroque in rooms whose former charms have been remodelled out of existence. Lonely Planet's Top Choices

Lonely Planet's Top Choices

Hotel Nani Mocenigo Palace (p194) Lavish suites in a doge's palace.

Cima Rosa (p197) A stylish bolthole with luxurious suites and Grand Canal views.

Al Ponte Antico (p199) A silk-swathed *palazzo* (mansion) with dreamy views of the Rialto bridge.

Corte di Gabriela (p191) Cool, contemporary interiors framed by 19th-century elegance.

Novecento (p192) Plush, bohemian-chic getaway ideal for modern Marco Polos.

Rosa Salva Hotel (p192) Venetian style with a modern twist in San Marco.

Best by Budget

€

B&B San Marco (p199) Rooms in a Venetian home with canal views.

Ca' Barba (p195) Smart, wood-beamed rooms and a smiling host.

Casa Burano (p202) Make yourself at home in a fisher's cottage.

€€

Giardino dei Melograni (p198) Bight, modern digs with canal views in the heart of the Ghetto.

Locanda Fiorita (p191) A boutique hotel with elegant rooms and wisteria-draped terraces.

Residenza de L'Osmarin (p199) A true B&B with quilted bedspreads and a slap-up breakfast.

Hotel Bucintoro (p199) Ship-shape wood-panelled rooms with lagoon views.

€€€

Gritti Palace (p191) Artful suites in Venice's finest Grand Canal palace.

Hotel Nani Mocenigo Palace (p194) Frescoed halls and silk-draped rooms in a 15th-century palace.

Palazzo Abadessa (p199) Frescoed rooms, canal views and a lily-scented garden.

Hotel Moresco (p194) Off-the-beaten-track luxury on the quiet Rio Novo.

Best for Design

Palazzo Cristo (p200) Sets the benchmark for modern Venetian luxury.

Corte di Gabriela (p191) Design greats bring palace living into the 21st century.

DD724 (p194) Designer digs filled with modern art in Dorsoduro.

Best for Romance

Al Ponte Antico (p199) A Grand Canal hideaway worthy of Casanova.

Oltre Il Giardino (p196) Effortless elegance with a whimsical, artistic soul.

Ai Cavalieri di Venezia (p200) Venetian opulence, love-bird terraces and a rooftop spa.

Best for Heritage

Gritti Palace (p191) A prestigious, landmark hotel full of opulent details.

Hotel Nani Mocenigo Palace (p194) A 15th-century Gothic palace with a secret garden.

Palazzo Abadessa (p199) A frescoed palace ready for romance since 1540.

NEED TO KNOW

Price Ranges

The following price ranges refer to a double room with bathroom. Unless otherwise stated, breakfast is included in the price.

€	less than €110
€€	€110–200
€€€	more than €200

Reservations

➡ Book ahead at weekends and any time during high season and major events.

➡ The best, and best-value, hotels are always in high demand; book well ahead.

➡ Check individual hotel websites for online deals.

➡ Confirm arrival at least 72 hours in advance, especially during high season.

Getting to Your Accommodation

➡ Try to arrive during daylight to avoid getting lost.

➡ Get directions from your accommodation, plus a detailed map.

➡ Though expensive, water-taxis can be worth the price for night arrivals or if you're heavily laden.

Breakfast

Except in higher-end places, breakfast tends to be utilitarian. *Affittacamere* (rooms for rent) generally don't offer breakfast because of strict dining codes. However, you're never far from a great local cafe.

Where to Stay

NEIGHBOURHOOD	FOR	AGAINST
San Marco	Historic and design hotels in central location, optimal for sightseeing and shopping.	Rooms often small with little natural light; streets crowded and noisy in the morning; fewer good restaurant options.
Dorsoduro	Lively art and student scenes, with design hotels near museums and seaside getaways along Zattere.	Lively student scene can mean noise echoing from Campo Santa Margherita until 2am, especially on weekends.
San Polo & Santa Croce	Top value on spacious B&Bs and opulent boutique hotels with prime local dining, the Rialto Market, drinking and shopping; convenient to train and bus.	Easy to get lost in maze of streets, and it may be a long walk to major sights and a *vaporetto* stop.
Cannaregio	Venice's best deals on B&Bs with character and hotels convenient to the train and bus stop, with canal-bank happy hours and restaurants frequented by locals.	Long walk or *vaporetto* ride to San Marco sightseeing; pedestrian traffic between train station and Rialto.
Castello	Calmer and fewer tourists as you move away from San Marco; good budget options close to San Marco and the park.	The eastern fringes near Sant'Elena are far away from key sights and devoid of services.
Giudecca, Lido & the Southern Islands	Good value for money; beaches within walking distance in summer; fewer tourists.	Far from the action, especially at night; must rely on expensive *vaporetti* and less frequent services at night.
Murano, Burano & the Northern Islands	Murano is a crowd-free, good-value alternative base within 10 minutes of Cannaregio. Outer islands are remote, but great for gourmet weekend retreats.	Limited eating and drinking options; outer islands are far from Venice; very quiet in low season.

PHILIP LEE HARVEY/LONELY PLANET ©

Lido di Venezia (p143)

SLEEPING SAN MARCO

🛏 San Marco

★LOCANDA FIORITA   BOUTIQUE HOTEL €€
Map p274 (☑041 523 47 54; www.locandafiorita.
com; Campiello Novo 3457a; d €80-180; ✴🏠;
🚤San Samuele) Few budget digs can match
this smart 10-room hotel with flower-
draped terraces and dreamy views of Chiesa di Santo Stefano from its rooms. Petite
bedrooms offer a chic, updated take on
Venetian style, with Rubelli-style fabrics
and period furnishings. Room 10 has a private terrace. Head out for *aperitivo* on the
roof terrace of adjoining B&B Bloom (same
management) and breakfast in Campiello
Novo.

ALBERGO SAN SAMUELE   HOTEL €€
Map p274 (☑041 520 51 65; www.hotelsansamu
ele.com; Salizada San Samuele 3358; d €140-175,
s/d without bathroom €96/105; @🏠; 🚤San
Samuele) These neat and friendly digs offer
10 modernised rooms (three of which share
bathrooms) with cool terrazzo floors and
comfortable beds at very reasonable prices
for Venice. There's no air-con and breakfast
isn't served, but there's free tea and coffee
and you're steps away from cafe-fringed
Campo San Stefano.

B&B AL TEATRO   B&B €€
Map p274 (☑333 9182494; www.bedandbreak
fastalteatro.com; Fondamenta de la Fenice 2554;
d from €170; 🏠; 🚤Giglio) With La Fenice opera house for your neighbour and a chorus
of singing *gondolieri* passing beneath your
windows, you'll need to book early to nab
one of the three rooms in Eleonora's 15th-
century family home. Inside, old-world elegance meets a minimalist style with white
linen and Murano chandeliers. Eleonora
hosts breakfast every morning, sharing recommendations over freshly brewed coffee.

HOTEL FLORA   HOTEL €€
Map p274 (☑041 520 58 44; www.hotelflora.it;
Calle dei Bergamaschi 2283a; s/d from €150/170;
✴🏠; 🚤Giglio) Down a lane from glitzy
Calle Larga XXII Marzo, this ivy-covered
retreat quietly outclasses brash designer
neighbours with its delightful tearoom
and breakfasts served around the garden
fountain. Guest rooms feature antique mirrors, fluffy duvets atop hand-carved beds
and tiled bathrooms with apothecary-style
amenities. Damask-clad superior rooms
overlook the garden. Strollers and teatime

for kids are complimentary; babysitting
available.

AI BARETERI   GUESTHOUSE €€
Map p274 (☑041 523 22 33; www.bareteri.it;
Calle di Mezzo 4966; d €150-185; ✴🏠; 🚤Rialto)
There are no views to speak of and its decor is dated, but this great old place is well
positioned in a quiet back lane midway between Rialto and Piazza San Marco. The 12
well-kept rooms have terrazzo floors and
en-suite bathrooms, although the shower
stalls are of the kind that tend to shoot water all over the floor.

GIÒ & GIÒ   B&B €€
Map p274 (☑347 3665016; www.giogiovenice.
com; Calle de le Ostreghe 2439; d from €150-
160, s from €200; ✴🏠; 🚤Giglio) Restrained
baroque may sound like an oxymoron,
but here you have it: burl-wood bedsteads,
pearl-grey silk draperies, polished parquet
floors and spotlit art. Packaged breakfasts
are available in the shared kitchen. It's ide
ally located near Piazza San Marco, along a
side canal; angle for rooms overlooking the
gondola stop, and wake to choruses of '*Vol-
are, oh-oh-oooooh!*'.

REZIDENZA CORTE ANTICA   B&B €€
Map p274 (☑335 1863555; www.residenzacor
teantica.com; Calle Frutarol 2876; d €160-200;
✴🏠; 🚤Accademia) A tasteful renovation
showcases the ancient wooden beams and
stone staircases of this historic Venetian
house, hidden down a small lane at the
western edge of San Marco. Each of its
three classic rooms is simply decorated
with wooden floorboards, Murano chandeliers and vintage wrought-iron beds –
including one four-poster – dressed with
white linens.

★GRITTI PALACE   HOTEL €€€
Map p274 (☑041 79 46 11; www.thegrittipalace.
com; Campo di Santa Maria del Giglio 2467; r from
€874; ✴🏠; 🚤Giglio) Guests at the Gritti Palace on the Grand Canal don't need to leave
their balconies to sightsee. This landmark
1525 doge's palace features Grand Canal
rooms with Rubelli silk damask lining,
antique fainting couches, stucco ceilings,
hand-painted vanities and bathrooms
sheathed in rare marble.

★CORTE DI GABRIELA   HOTEL €€€
Map p274 (☑041 523 50 77; www.cortedigabriela.
com; Calle dei Avvocati 3836; r from €300; ✴🏠;

Sant'Angelo) Corte di Gabriela is a 19th-century *palazzo,* but there's nothing traditional about its 11 rooms, which inventively play with the palace's historic features. Frescoed ceilings and terrazzo floors meet with contemporary design pieces, high-spec gadgets and a modern colour palette. The central wisteria-draped courtyard is super romantic and the lavish breakfast is one of the best in Venice.

★ NOVECENTO — BOUTIQUE HOTEL €€€

Map p274 (041 241 37 65; www.novecento. biz; Calle del Dose 2683/84; d from €215; ⊛⬚; Giglio) Run by the Romanelli family for more than 50 years, this hotel is a home away from home. Nine individually designed rooms are inspired by designer Mario Fortuny and come finished with Turkish kilim pillows, velvet draperies and carved bedsteads. You can mingle with creative fellow travellers around the honesty bar, while the garden is a lovely spot in which to linger over breakfast.

★ ROSA SALVA HOTEL — BOUTIQUE HOTEL €€€

Map p274 (041 241 33 23; www.rosasalvahotel. it; Calle Fiubera 951; d from €205; ⊛⬚; San Marco) Run by the same family as the well-regarded Rosa Salva pastry shop next door, this high-standard hotel features contemporary rooms the colour of a good cappuccino, finished with beautiful parquet floors, large beds with coil-spring mattresses, luxe drapes and large wardrobes. Service is highly personal, and breakfast includes a selection of divine pastries from its cafe next door.

B&B BLOOM & SETTIMO CIELO — B&B €€€

Map p274 (340 1498872; www.bloom-venice. com; Campiello Santo Stefano 3470; d €110-260; ⊛⬚; Sant'Angelo) Occupying the top floor of a historic home overlooking Santo Stefano, Bloom has glam-rock rooms in shocking scarlet, fuchsia and gold damask, with leather bedsteads, and breakfast served on a sunny terrace. Downstairs, sister B&B Settimo Cielo (Seventh Heaven) is artfully romantic. Both properties share the top-floor library and living room, and the fabulous roof terrace overlooking Campo Santo Stefano.

CA' DEL NOBILE — HOTEL €€€

Map p274 (041 528 34 73; www.cadelnobile. com; Rio Terà de le Colonne 987; d €209-369; ⊛⬚; Rialto) Move over, Casanova – Ca' del Nobile makes romantic getaways easy. The exposed-brick Casanova room has a canopied bed; cosy standards have wood-beamed ceilings and sleigh beds; and deluxe rooms have room for daybeds and cribs.

🛏 Dorsoduro

CA' DEL BROCCHI — HERITAGE HOTEL €

Map p284 (041 522 69 89; www.cadelbrocchi. it; Rio Terà San Vio 470; r/ste from €89/149; ⊛⬚; Spirito Santo) A colourful character inhabiting a quiet side street in Dorsoduro's museum district, Ca' del Brocchi has small yet over-the-top baroque-styled rooms – tasselled, gilt to the hilt and upholstery padded, with matching scrollwork wallpaper. Lower-level rooms have porthole-sized windows; better options have garden views,

---

APARTMENT RENTALS

Holiday rentals are booming in Venice thanks to online outfits such as Airbnb and Vrbo. In fact, so prolific are these sites that the issue of short-term rentals has become a political hot potato, with residents saying they're being driven out of the historic centre as landlords turn properties over to tourists to reap higher incomes.

That said, short term rentals are a cost-effective option for groups and families – just be sure that your landlord is legally registered and does not rent out multiple properties, which indicates agency activity. A good place to start is the community-powered home-sharing website Fairbnb (p196), which operates on ethical criteria.

Neighbourhoods to consider include Cannaregio, Castello, Dorsoduro, Giudecca and Murano, away from the crowded centre. Always check reviews for issues such as noise and accessibility, as many apartments don't have lifts. In most cases, the city's tourist tax has to be paid separately, in cash.

Foyer of the Grilli Palace (p191)

balconies and/or Jacuzzi tubs. Babysitting and cradles are available for families.

LE TERESE
B&B €

Map p284 (☑041 523 17 28; www.leterese.com; Campiello Tron 1902; r €100; ✴☎; ⬛Santa Marta) Join architectural duo Antonella and Mauro in their 18th-century granary on the Rio Terese for a dose of local living. There are just two rooms overlooking the canal and both are stylishly decorated with bright feature walls and Persian rugs. The large, tiled bathroom is shared, which just adds to the home-away-from-home feeling.

SILK ROAD
HOSTEL €

Map p284 (☑388 1196816; www.silkroadhostel.com; Calle Corteloto 1420e; dm/s/d from €49/66/110; ☎; ⬛San Basilio) Breathe easy along the Giudecca Canal in this clean, hassle-free hostel, complete with communal kitchen and, best of all, no curfew. Both of the airy, four-bed dorms (one mixed gender, one female only) come with water views, and there are private rooms to boot; bathrooms are shared. The hostel is down the block from a supermarket, canalside cafes and *vaporetto* stops.

LA CHICCA
B&B €€

Map p284 (☑041 522 55 35; www.lachicca-venezia.com; Calle Franchi 644; d €170; ✴☎; ⬛Accademia) It's neatly wedged between Dorsoduro's trifecta of museums – Accademia, Peggy Guggenheim and Punta della Dogana – yet all you'll hear at night in this elegant B&B is the lapping of the canal at the end of the lane. Hosts Sabrina and Massimo are helpful, and their damask-clad, terrazzo-floored guestrooms are glitzy and spacious.

HOTEL GALLERIA
HERITAGE HOTEL €€

Map p284 (☑041 523 24 89; www.hotelgalleria.it, Campo de la Carità 878a; s/d from €123/152; ☎; ⬛Accademia) Occupying a floor of an 18th-century *palazzo* alongside the Accademia bridge, this classic hotel is decked out with floral silk wallpaper and imposing period furnishings. Book ahead, especially for rooms 7 and 9, two well-priced but small doubles with sublime Grand Canal views. Room 10 sleeps four and comes with an original ceiling fresco. Breakfast is served in the rooms.

CA' DELLA CORTE
B&B €€

Map p284 (☑041 71 58 77; www.cadellacorte.com; Corte Surian 3560; r from €135; ✴☎; ⬛Piazzale Roma) Live like a Venetian in this 16th-century family home with a Liberty frescoed salon, piano room, self-service bar, top-floor terrace, and breakfast delivered to your room. Stay in wood-beamed garrets, chandelier-lit superior rooms or feng shui eco-rooms. Sporty types should ask helpful staff to organise sailing, tennis and horse-riding on the Lido; babysitting and shiatsu massage are also available.

CORTE VECCHIA
B&B €€

Map p284 (☑335 7449238; www.cortevecchia. net; Rio Terà San Vio 462; s/d from €80/123; ✳☎; ⚓Spirito Santo) Corte Vecchia is a stylish steal a stone's throw from Peggy Guggenheim, the Accademia and Punta della Dogana. Choose from a snug single with an en suite, and two good-sized doubles – one with an en suite, the other with an external private bathroom. All are simple and nicely decorated with contemporary and vintage objects. There's also a tranquil, shared lounge.

DORSODURO461
B&B €€

Map p284 (☑041 528 61 72; www.dorsoduro461. com; Rio Terà San Vio 461; s/d €100/130; ✳☎; ⚓Spirito Santo) Get to know Venice from the inside out at Silvia and Francesco's homestyle B&B, around the corner from Peggy Guggenheim's place. Your hosts' shared love of books, antique restoration and design is obvious in the bookshelf-lined breakfast room and three well-curated guestrooms, with Kartell lamps perched atop 19th-century poker tables.

LA CALCINA
HERITAGE HOTEL €€

Map p284 (☑041 520 64 66; www.lacalcina. com; Fondamenta Zattere ai Gesuati 780; s/d from €104/135; ✳@☎; ⚓Zattere) This little hotel offers breezy roof-garden breakfasts, a canalside restaurant, and panoramas of Palladio's Redentore church across Giudecca Canal. Antique armoires and brocade bedspreads come as standard in parquet-floored guestrooms. Bathrooms are clean though tired and uninspiring. Book ahead for waterfront rooms – especially room 2, where John Ruskin wrote his classic *The Stones of Venice* (1876).

LOCANDA SAN BARNABA
HERITAGE HOTEL €€

Map p284 (☑041 241 12 33; www.locanda-san-barnaba.com; Calle del Traghetto 2786; s/d from €115/175; ✳☎; ⚓Ca' Rezzonico) The stage is set for intrigue at this 16th-century *palazzo*, with its frescoed grand salon, hidden courtyard garden and cupboards concealing a secret staircase. Ask for the romantic wood-beamed Il Poeta Fanatico room; Campiello, with skylight views of a neighbouring bell tower; or the superior Il Cavaliere e la Dama, for 18th-century frescoed ceilings and balconies dangling over the canal.

PENSIONE ACCADEMIA VILLA MARAVEGE
HERITAGE HOTEL €€

Map p284 (☑041 521 01 88; www.pensioneac cademia.it; Fondamenta Bollani 1058; s/d from €111/164; ✳@☎; ⚓Accademia) Step through the ivy-covered gate of this 17th-century garden villa just off the Grand Canal, and you'll forget you're a block from the Accademia. Although some of the 27 guestrooms are small, all are effortlessly elegant, with parquet floors, antique desks and shiny bathrooms – some have canal views. Buffet breakfasts are served outside in summer.

★HOTEL MORESCO
BOUTIQUE HOTEL €€€

Map p284 (☑041 244 02 02; www.hotelmoresco venice.com; Fondamente del Passamonte 3499; r/ste from €223/372; ✳☎; ⚓Piazzale Roma) A complimentary glass of prosecco at check-in and a daily happy hour in the walled garden will give you an idea of the welcoming and friendly service you'll encounter at this lovely hotel. Rooms are similarly well cared for, with fine fabrics, elaborate wallpapers, plush sofas and sleek modern bathrooms. Staff can help with all manner of things, and do.

★DD724
DESIGN HOTEL €€€

Map p284 (☑041 277 02 62; www.thecharm inghouse.com; Ramo da Mura 724; s/d from €160/308; ✳☎; ⚓Accademia) A flock of lacy black butterflies greets guests at this artsy retreat, tucked behind the Guggenheim. Art is liberally strewn about the six luxurious rooms in the main building and three in a nearby annexe. Some have views over Peggy Guggenheim's garden, with the San Marco campanile visible in the distance.

★HOTEL NANI MOCENIGO PALACE
HERITAGE HOTEL €€€

Map p284 (☑041 520 01 45; www.hotelnani mocenigo.com; Fondamenta Nani 960; s/d from €163/200; ✳☎; ⚓Accademia) Live like a doge in a 15th-century Venetian-Gothic palace that once belonged to one of the most famous of them: Agostino Barbarigo, who was responsible for commissioning some of the most significant buildings on Piazza San Marco. This gorgeous hotel, just steps from the Accademia, offers a variety of tastefully furnished rooms and charming communal spaces, including a hidden garden.

CA' MARIA ADELE
BOUTIQUE HOTEL €€€

Map p284 (☑0415203078; www.camariaadele.it;
Rio Terà dei Catecumeni 111; r/ste from €462/770;
⬛Salute) If your vision of Venice includes a palace full of crushed velvet, gold wallpaper, mad Murano chandeliers and marbled bathrooms, then this decadent boutique hotel is for you. It's quietly situated overlooking a canal and offers an impressive level of personal service. Unsurprisingly, it's full of lovebirds who can be found canoodling on the 2nd-floor terrace.

PALAZZO VENEZIANO
HOTEL €€€

Map p284 (☑041 277 87 19; www.palazzoveneziano.com; Fondamenta Zattere al Ponte Longo 1413; r/ste from €210/323; ✳🌐; ⬛San Basilio) Overlooking the Giudecca Canal at the front and the impossibly picturesque Ognissanti canal at the rear, this large hotel offers a large variety of swish rooms, some of which have terraces with outdoor spa pools. The bar is cosy and there is outdoor seating under copper palm trees in the warmer months.

CA' PISANI
DESIGN HOTEL €€€

Map p284 (☑041 240 14 11; www.capisanihotel.it; Rio Terà Antonio Foscarini 979a; r/ste from €206/316; ✳🌐; ⬛Accademia) Sprawl out in style right behind the Accademia, and luxuriate in sleigh beds, Jacuzzi tubs and walk-in closets. Mood lighting and soundproofed walls make downstairs deco-accented rooms right for romance; families will appreciate top-floor rooms with sleeping lofts. Venetian winters require in-house Turkish steam baths, while summers mean roof-terrace sunning and patio breakfasts. It's a hushed, elegant, antiques-laced retreat.

NH RIO NOVO
HOTEL €€€

Map p284 (☑041 275 35 11; www.nh-hotels.com; Calle Larga Ragusei 3489e; r from €230; ✳; ⬛Piazzale Roma) Though jarring in a Venetian context, this clean-lined 1950s brick building has crisp, white rooms, some with canal views. Communal areas are modern and spacious, with comfortable sofas to lounge in, and the breakfast bar has a cheerful vibe. It's tucked away in a quiet street but close to transport hub Piazzale Roma. Skip breakfast and you'll save around €35.

🛏 San Polo & Santa Croce

⭐CA' BARBA
B&B €

Map p278 (☑328 2144979; www.cabarba.com; Calle Ca' Michiel 1825; r/ste/apt from €106/123/166; ✳🌐; ⬛Rialto Mercato) Hidden down a quiet lane just around the corner from Rialto Market, this B&B offers exceptionally good value with four spacious rooms with wooden ceiling beams, black-and-white Venice photographs, modern bathrooms, coffee machines and huge smart TVs. A breakfast basket is delivered to the room every day. Host Alessandro is a good source of advice, even loaning out Venice-themed books.

AL GALLION
B&B €

Map p278 (☑041 524 47 43; www.algallion.com; Calle Gallion 1126; r €75-110; 🌐; ⬛Riva de Biasio) A couple of bridges away at train-station hotels, weary tourists wait at front desks – but at this 16th-century family home, you'll be chatting and sipping espresso in the living room. The whitewashed guest room is handsomely furnished with walnut desks, cheerful yellow bedspreads and terrazzo floors; the bathroom is down the corridor.

HAVEN HOSTEL
HOSTEL €

Map p278 (☑347 0268037; www.havenhostel.com; Campo San Tomà 2846; s €50; ☺Jul & Aug; 🌐; ⬛San Tomà) During the academic year, the Haven is home to Ca' Foscari University students, but in summer it throws open its doors to travellers. The rooms are somewhat spartan and can get stiflingly hot, but most of the twins have en-suite bathrooms. There's also a communal kitchen, dining area and common room with a TV and limited wi-fi.

L'IMBARCADERO
HOSTEL €

Map p278 (☑329 1350271; http://imbarcadero.hostelvenice.net; Calle Zen 1268; dm €51; 🌐; ⬛Riva de Biasio) A five-minute walk from the train station, this friendly hostel in Santa Croce offers worn but comfortable mixed and female-only dorms with single beds and the occasional Grand Canal view. Prices include use of a communal kitchen and wi-fi.

⭐AL PONTE MOCENIGO
HERITAGE HOTEL €€

Map p278 (☑041 524 47 97; www.alpontemocenigo.com; Fondamenta Rimpetto Mocenigo 2063; r

BOOKING SERVICES

➜ **Luxrest Venice** (Map p288; ☏041 296 05 61; www.luxrest-venice.com; Ponte del Pistor 5990, Castello) Carefully curated, hand-picked selection of apartments.

➜ **Lonely Planet** (lonelyplanet.com/ italy/venice/hotels) Expert author reviews, user feedback, booking engine.

➜ **Venice Prestige** (www.veniceprestige.com) Venetian apartments to rent in aristocratic palaces in the best locations in town.

➜ **Views on Venice** (☏041 241 11 49; www.viewsonvenice.com) Apartments picked for their personality, character and view, of course.

➜ **Fairbnb Venice** (https://fairbnb.coop/venice) A community-powered home-sharing platform where 50% of booking fees support local projects.

€144-191; ❄🛜; 🚤San Stae) A doge of a deal near the Grand Canal, this historic *palazzo* is just steps from the San Stae *vaporetto* stop. Reached via a petite bridge, this little oasis offers elegant guest rooms, some with Murano chandeliers illuminating high wood-beamed ceilings, four-poster beds, gilt-edged armoires and salon seating. Ask for a room overlooking either Rio San Stae or the courtyard.

⭐**IL GIARDINO DI GIULIA**   B&B €€
Map p278 (☏041 200 77 86; www.ilgiardinodigiulia.com; Salizada de la Chiesa 965; s/d €70/120; ❄🛜; 🚤Riva de Biasio) The three atmospheric guest rooms at the bottom of this tower-like house have wooden beams and antique furniture, and each has its own theme: maritime, rock music or Italian actor Marcello Mastroianni. It's a reflection of the personality of charming, chatty owner Marco Busetto, who also happens to serve some of the best B&B breakfasts in Venice.

OLTRE IL GIARDINO   BOUTIQUE HOTEL €€
Map p278 (☏041 275 00 15; www.oltreilgiardino-venezia.com; Fondamenta Contarini 2542; d/ste from €180/280; ❄🛜; 🚤San Tomà) Live the dream in this garden villa, the 1920s home of Alma Mahler, the composer's widow. Hidden behind a lush walled garden, its six high-ceilinged guest rooms and suites mar-

ry historic charm with modern comfort: marquetry composer's desks, candelabras and 19th-century poker chairs sit alongside flat-screen TVs and designer bathrooms, while outside, pomegranate trees flower.

CA' DELLA SCIMMIA   APARTMENT €€
Map p278 (☏342 8508498; www.myveniceapartment.com; Calle de la Scimia o de la Spade 230; apt from €182; 🚤Rialto Mercato) The My Venice Apartment crew rents units in six locations around Venice, but we particularly like this block for its back-lane location right at the centre of it all – just steps from the Rialto Market and Rialto Bridge. The four apartments are modern and well furnished, with cooking and laundry facilities; only one has any views to speak of.

CAMPIELLO ZEN   B&B €€
Map p278 (☏041 71 03 65; www.campiellozen.com; Rio Terà 1285; r from €180; ❄🛜; 🚤Riva de Biasio) Hotels would have you believe Venetians live a twee existence in fussy brocade-upholstered pink salons, but this B&B in a traditional family home treats guests to comfortable beds, handsome antique wardrobes, quirky wall niches and every modern convenience, especially in the bathrooms. It's handy to the train and *vaporetto,* but blissfully off the tourist track.

SANTA CROCE
BOUTIQUE HOTEL   BOUTIQUE HOTEL €€
Map p278 (☏041 740 112; www.santacroceboutiquehotel.com; Campo Nazario Sauro 980; r/ste from €181/334; ❄🛜; 🚤Riva di Biasio) Close to the train and bus stations, this hotel is nevertheless a quiet haven. It offers just 15 rooms and suites, tastefully furnished with velvets, silks and Murano glass, and sleek bathrooms with designer fittings. A pretty courtyard offers a bucolic retreat while the plush bar offers refreshments. Attentive staff go out of their way to make your stay easy and pleasurable.

CA' ANGELI   BOUTIQUE HOTEL €€
Map p278 (☏041 523 24 80; www.caangeli.it; Calle del Traghetto de la Madoneta 1434; s/d/ste from €166/175/227; ❄🛜; 🚤San Silvestro) Murano glass chandeliers, a Louis XIV love-seat and namesake 16th-century angels set a refined tone at this restored, canalside *palazzo.* Guestrooms are spacious, and some have terrazzo or brightly tiled floors. The breakfast room looks out onto the Grand Canal.

CA' ZUSTO
BOUTIQUE HOTEL €€

Map p278 (☏041 524 29 91; www.hotelcazusto
venezia.it; Campo Rielo 1359; s/d/ste from
€90/118/211; ✳🛜; ⚓Riva di Biasio) Gothic
goes pop at this palace, whose stately Veneto-Byzantine exterior disguises a colourful
wild streak. Designer Gianmarco Cavag-
nino serves up 22 brightly striped, harem-
styled suites named after Turkish prin-
cesses. Pedestal tables flank baroque beds
fit for pashas, and Jacuzzis soothe frazzled
darlings in the deluxe rooms.

LA VILLEGGIATURA
B&B €€

Map p278 (☏041 524 46 73; www.lavilleggiatura.
it; Calle dei Bolteri 1569; r/ste from €159/199;
✳🛜; ⚓Rialto Mercato) This charming B&B
has six large, light-filled rooms and suites
decorated with verve around different
musical or historical themes. The choicest
rooms are on the *piano nobile* (main floor)
and enjoy pretty views, king-sized beds
and generous bathrooms with bathtubs.
Breakfast is taken at a communal table
where guests are pampered by their genial
hostess.

HOTEL AL DUCA DI VENEZIA
HERITAGE HOTEL €€

Map p278 (☏041 812 30 69; www.alducadlveri
ezia.com; Salizada del Fontego dei Turchi 1739;
r/apt from €150/200; ✳🛜; ⚓San Stae) Bedrooms swagged with damask and Murano
chandeliers are Venetian bordello-chic,
honouring the courtesans that once ruled
nearby Rialto backstreets. Get an insider's
view of Venice at the family-friendly kitch
enette apartments, conveniently close to
Campo San Giacomo da l'Orio happy hours.
Reception is open 24 hours; babysitting,
laundry and wheelchair-accessible rooms
are available.

PENSIONE GUERRATO
HERITAGE HOTEL €€

Map p278 (☏041 522 71 31; www.hotelguerrato.
com; Calle Drio la Scimia 240a; r €150, without
bathroom €100, apt €160-280; ✳🛜; ⚓Rialto
Mercato) In a 1227 building that was once a
hostel for knights and merchants, the smart
guestrooms here haven't lost their sense of
history – some have frescoes or glimpses of
the Grand Canal. Sparkling modern bathrooms, a prime Rialto Market location and
helpful owners add to the package. There
are also three good-value apartments with
kitchens, sleeping four to eight people.

HOTEL AL SOLE
HERITAGE HOTEL €€

Map p281 (☏041 244 03 28; www.alsolehotels.
com; Fondamenta Minotto 134-136; s/d/ste from
€117/135/216; ✳@🛜; ⚓Piazzale Roma) This
gorgeous 15-century Venetian Gothic palace is now a traditional family-run hotel.
The decor is a little old fashioned, but the
rooms are comfortable and spacious. There
is a pretty courtyard as well as canal views
from some of the rooms.

★CIMA ROSA
B&B €€€

Map p278 (☏041 099 52 71; www.cimarosaven-
ezia.com; Calle e Corte Dandolo 1958; r/ste from
€225/365; ✳🛜; ⚓San Stae) Although many
B&Bs promise a 'living in Venice' experience, Cima Rosa, in the northern reaches of
Santa Croce, delivers it in spades. There are
just two doubles and one suite in this 15th-
century *palazzo*, all with beamed ceilings
and most with Grand Canal views. Breakfast is in the stylish downstairs lounge. Let
owner Brittany plan an insider's itinerary
for you.

★HOTEL CANAL GRANDE
HERITAGE HOTEL €€€

Map p281 (☏041 244 01 48; www.hotelcanal-
grande.it; Campo San Simeon Grande 932; s/d/
ste from €208/215/288; ✳🛜; ⚓Riva de Biasio)
The 24 sumptuous rooms are split between
a Grand Canal *palazzo* and a humbler
building a few doors down, but both swirl
with old Venetian glamour. There are can-
opy beds, damask wall claddings, Murano
sconces, and even the TVs are cunningly
hidden within gilded Venetian mirrors.
Breakfasts are served on a deck jutting ro-
mantically over the canal.

HOTEL PALAZZO VENART
HERITAGE HOTEL €€€

Map p278 (☏041 523 37 84; www.palazzovenart.
com; Calle Tron 1961; r/ste from €319/697; ✳🛜;
⚓San Stae) Glamorous yet discreet, this
16th-century Grand Canal *palazzo* has hidden gardens front and rear, and its own
Michelin-starred restaurant. The 18 rooms
and suites are opulent but still tasteful,
with plenty of velvet, gold and marble on
display. It's an ideal destination for a budg-
et-be-damned romantic getaway.

PALAZZO BARBARIGO
DESIGN HOTEL €€€

Map p278 (☏041 74 01 72; www.palazzobar-
barigo.com; Calle Corner 2765; r/ste from
€252/351; ✳🛜; ⚓San Tomà) Brooding, chic
and seductive, Barbarigo delivers 18 plush
guestrooms combining modern elegance

and intrigue – think dark, contemporary furniture, sumptuous velvets, feathered lamps and the odd fainting couch. Whether you opt for a suite overlooking the Grand Canal or a standard room overlooking Rio di San Polo, you can indulge in the sleek bathrooms, positively royal breakfasts and smart, attentive service.

🛏 Cannaregio

WE CROCIFERI   HOSTEL €

Map p282 (📞041 528 61 03; www.we-gastameco. com; Campo dei Gesuiti 4878; s/tw/apt from €30/80/109; ❄@📶; ⛴Fondamente Nove) In contrast to the bombastic Gesuiti church next door, this convent-turned-barracks-turned-hostel provides minimalist white rooms overlooking a cloister. Used as university digs throughout the year, there's a friendly vibe to the place, with a buzzy on-site cafe (breakfast costs an additional €7), bar, laundry and communal kitchen. Look out for interesting events and gigs on the noticeboard in the entrance.

CA' DOGARESSA   BOUTIQUE HOTEL €

Map p282 (📞041 275 94 41; www.cadogaressa. com; Fondamenta di Cannaregio 1018; d €85-130; ❄@📶; ⛴Guglie) Venetian charm abounds at this family-run canalside inn. Rooms have princess beds, gilt mirrors, chandeliers and modern bathrooms. The views from the roof terrace and breakfasts by the canal in summer are memorable perks. An annexe around the corner can be rented as a three-bedroom apartment or as individual rooms; breakfast isn't offered and the bathrooms are shared.

★LOCANDA CA' LE VELE   B&B €€

Map p282 (📞041 241 39 60; www.locandalevele. com; Calle de le Vele 3969; d €122-148, ste €165-183; ❄📶; ⛴Ca' d'Oro) The lane may be quiet and the house may look demure but inside it's Venetian glam all the way. The six guest rooms are a surprisingly stylish riot of terrazzo floors, damask furnishings, Murano glass sconces and ornate gilded beds with busy covers. Pay a little extra for a canal view.

★GIARDINO DEI MELOGRANI   HOTEL €€

Map p282 (📞041 822 61 31; www.pardesrimonim. net; Campo del Ghetto Nuovo 2874; d €160-200, tr €230-260; ⏱Feb-Dec; ❄📶; ⛴Guglie) Run by Venice's Jewish community, to which all proceeds go, the 'Garden of Pomegranates' is a sparkling kosher residence. You don't have to be Jewish to enjoy the 20 modern rooms, with artwork themed around local plants. Some have canal views while others face the *campo* (square). Families may prefer the brand-new one- and three-bedroom apartments, also located in the Ghetto.

3749 PONTE CHIODO   B&B €€

Map p282 (📞041 241 39 35; www.pontechiodo. it; Calle de la Rachetta 3749; d €130-180; ❄📶; ⛴Ca' d'Oro) This charming little B&B offers six sweet rooms with period furnishings, views over the canal and a private front garden. It takes its name from the bridge at the back door – the only remaining one without parapets. All bridges in Venice were once like this before too many drunks took the plunge and the government decreed new safety measures.

ALLO SQUERO   B&B €€

Map p282 (📞041 523 69 73; www.allosquero.it; Corte dello Squero 4692; d €120; 📶; ⛴Fondamente Nove) Dock for the night at this historic gondola *squero* (shipyard), converted into a garden retreat. Gondolas float right by the windows of two of the rooms. All have their own bathrooms, although one is accessed from the corridor. Hosts Andrea and Hiroko offer Venice-insider tips over cappuccino and pastry breakfasts in the fragrant wisteria-filled garden. Cots and cribs are available.

CA' POZZO   HOTEL €€

Map p282 (📞041 524 05 04; www.capozzoinn. com; Calle de Ca' Pozzo 1279; d €125-140; ❄@; ⛴Guglie) Recover from Venice's sensory onslaught at this low-slung minimalist-chic hotel hidden down a dead-end lane near the Ghetto. Sleek, contemporary guest rooms feature platform beds, abstract artwork and cube-shaped bathroom fixtures.

CASA BASEGGIO   B&B €€

Map p282 (📞348 3432069; www.casabaseggio. it; Fondamenta dell'Abazia 3556; d €110-125; 📶; ⛴Orto) *Venexianárse* (become Venetian) at this converted family home in a quiet Cannaregio corner, handy to happy-hour hotspots. The house is situated in a wing of the Misericordia abbey, and from the 1st floor there are views through the cypresses into the abbey garden. As well as two bedrooms upstairs, there's a self-contained flat on the ground floor.

HOTEL LA FORCOLA
HOTEL €€

Map p282 (☑041 524 14 84; www.laforcolahotel.
com; Calle del Magazzen 2353; s €100-130, d
€150-200; ❉❈; ⌖San Marcuola) Set in a quiet
location overlooking the San Marcuola
canal, this family-run hotel has 23 rooms
furnished in a smart neoclassical style with
striped wallpaper, gathered cream curtains
and satin-effect bed covers. Suites offer
more space and better views. There's also a
small dining room downstairs where a generous breakfast buffet is laid out. Staff are
kind and helpful.

★AL PONTE ANTICO
BOUTIQUE HOTEL €€€

Map p282 (☑041 241 19 44; www.alponteantico.
com; Calle de l'Aseo 5768; d €330; ❉❈; ⌖Ri-
alto) Like a courtesan's boudoir, this 16th-
century *palazzo* (mansion) is swathed in
damask wall coverings, heavy silk curtains
and thick, plush carpets. A smiling host
greets you at the padded, golden reception
desk and whisks you up to large, unabash-
edly lavish rooms with enough gilt to sat-
isfy Louis XIV. In the evening, romance
blossoms on the terrace, framed by views
of Rialto Bridge.

★PALAZZO ABADESSA
BOUTIQUE HOTEL €€€

Map p282 (☑041 241 37 84; www.abadessa.com;
Calle Priuli 4011; r €225-335; ❉❈; ⌖Ca' d'Oro)
Evenings seem enchanted in this opulent
1540 *palazzo,* where staff fluff pillows, ply
guests with prosecco, arrange water taxis
to the opera and plot irresistible marriage
proposals. Classic guest rooms feature
beds fit for royalty, silk-damask-clad walls,
Murano glass lamps and wood-beamed
ceilings. Frescoed superior rooms have
18th-century vanities and canal vistas.
Breakfast is served in the tree-shaded, lily-
perfumed garden.

EUROSTARS RESIDENZA
CANNAREGIO
HOTEL €€€

(☑041 524 43 32; www.eurostarshotels.co.uk;
Calle dei Riformati 3210a; d €195-280; ❉❈;
⌖Sant'Alvise) The Eurostars chain has got a
lot right at this converted convent with a
charming cloister garden on the Sant'Alvise
canal. Decor has been stripped back to reveal brick walls and wooden beams against
which is set modern furniture and beds
dressed in white linens. There is a 24-hour
concierge, interconnected family rooms,
babysitting services, and rooms accessible
to travellers with disabilities.

⌕ Castello

★AI TAGLIAPIETRA
B&B €

Map p288 (www.aitagliapietra.com; Salita Zorzi
4943; s €70, d €75-110; ❈; ⌖San Zaccaria) Ai
Tagliapietra is exactly what a B&B should
be: well located, welcoming, unpretentious,
comfortable and very reasonably priced.
This is all down to excellent host Lorenzo,
who knows what travellers need and is on
hand to supply good coffee, fresh breakfasts
and excellent recommendations. There are
only three simple, but smart, rooms so book
early to avoid disappointment.

B&B SAN MARCO
B&B €

Map p288 (☑041 522 75 89; www.realvenice.it;
Fondamente San Giorgio dei Schiavoni 3385l; r
€135, without bathroom €105-135; ❉; ⌖San Zaccaria) Alice and Marco welcome you warmly
to their home overlooking Carpaccio's frescoed Scuola Dalmata. The 3rd-floor apartment (no lift), with its parquet floors and
large windows, is furnished with family antiques and offers photogenic views over the
terracotta rooftops and canals. The hosts
live upstairs, so they're always on hand
with great recommendations.

ALLOGGI BARBARIA
B&B €

Map p288 (☑041 522 27 50; www.alloggibarbaria.
it; Calle de le Capucine 6573; d €75-125; ❉❈;
⌖Ospedale) Located near the Fondamente
Nove, this *pensione* isn't easy to find – but
that's part of its charm, and so are the intrepid fellow travellers you'll meet over
breakfast on a shared balcony. All six rooms
are simple but tidy, bright and airy.

★RESIDENZA DE L'OSMARIN
B&B €€

Map p288 (☑347 450 1440; www.residenzadelos
marin.com; Calle Rota 4960; d €170-250; ❉❈;
⌖San Zaccaria) This B&B is good value, especially considering it is barely 300m from
Piazza San Marco. Rooms – one with a
roof terrace and another with a courtyard-
facing terrace – are quaintly decorated with
quilted bedspreads, painted wardrobes and
period furnishings. The hosts make guests
feel welcome with slap-up breakfasts of
homemade cakes, brioche and platters of
ham and cheese.

HOTEL BUCINTORO
BOUTIQUE HOTEL €€

Map p290 (☑041 528 99 09; www.hotelbucin
toro.com; Riva San Biasio 2135a; d €130-260; ❈;
⌖Arsenale) Set at the southern end of the

STUDENT STAYS

From July to mid-September the city's university accommodation is available to rent through Hostels Club (041 524 67 42; www.hostelsclub.com). Singles, doubles and triples are available. Prices run from around €35 to €45 per person per night. Residence halls are located in Cannaregio, Castello, San Polo, Dorsoduro and Giudecca.

Riva, all 20 rooms in this modest hotel offer spectacular views with a modest price tag. Styled like a ship's cabin, they're finished in glossy, dark-wood panelling and decorated with nautical pictures, and bathrooms are covered in coloured marbles reminiscent of the lagoon.

CA' DEI DOGI   BOUTIQUE HOTEL €€

Map p288 (✏041 241 37 51; www.cadeidogi.it; Corte Santa Scolastica 4242; s €95-125, d €165-250; ❇❂; ⬇San Zaccaria) Even the nearby Bridge of Sighs can't dampen the high spirits of the sunny Ca' dei Dogi, with guestroom windows sneaking peeks into the convent cloisters next door. Streamlined, modern rooms look like ship cabins, with tilted wood-beamed ceilings, dressers that look like steamer trunks, and compact mosaic-covered bathrooms – ask for the one with the terrace and Jacuzzi.

HOTEL SANT'ANTONIN   HOTEL €€

Map p288 (✏041 523 16 21; www.hotelsant antonin.com; Fondamenta dei Furlani 3299; d €165-250; ❇❂; ⬇San Zaccaria) Enjoy patrician pleasures at this 16th-century *palazzo* perched on a canal near the Greek church. Grand proportions make for light, spacious rooms, with cool terrazzo floors, geranium-draped balconies, frescoed ceilings and impressive furnishings. Trip down the stone staircase and out into one of the largest private gardens in Venice, complete with a pretty stone pergola and gurgling fountain.

PALAZZO SCHIAVONI   APARTMENT €€

Map p288 (✏041 241 12 75; www.palazzoschi avoni.com; Fondamenta dei Furlani 3288; 1-bed apt from €160; ❇❂; ⬇San Zaccaria) The refurbishment of this 15th-century *palazzo* (mansion) into an apartment hotel retained many of its period features while paying close attention to guest comforts. Apart-

ments are fitted with kitchens and generous living spaces.

AI CAVALIERI DI VENEZIA   HOTEL €€€

Map p288 (✏041 241 10 64; www.hotelaicavalieri. com; Calle Borgolocco 6108; d €260-440; ❇❂; ⬇Rialto) Venetian glam is dialled up to the max in this luxurious *palazzo* (mansion) hotel, yet it somehow avoids slipping into tackiness. Rooms are dripping in gilt, silk damask wall coverings and sparkling Murano chandeliers – and with canals on two sides, you've got an excellent chance of a watery view.

HOTEL DANIELI   HOTEL €€€

Map p288 (✏041 522 64 80; www.danielihotel venice.com; Riva degli Schiavoni 4196; d €485-1200; ❇❂; ⬇San Zaccaria) As eccentric and luxurious as Venice itself, the Danieli has attracted bohemians, minor royalty and their millionaire lovers for more than a century. The hotel sprawls through three landmark buildings: the frescoed, antique-filled 14th-century *casa vecchia* (old house), built for Doge Enrico Dandolo; the 18th-century gilt-to-the-hilt *casa nuova* (new house); and the Danielino, a Fascist edifice with a modern-luxe interior redesign.

PALAZZO CRISTO   APARTMENT €€€

Map p288 (✏331 4299308; https://palazzo cristo.com; Campo SS Giovanni e Paolo 6805a; ste from €450; ❂; ⬇Fondamenta Nove) This stunning *palazzo* offers three extravagant suites with eye-popping views of the Scuola Grande di San Marco. Despite dating to the 13th-century, the suites are exemplars of luxurious contemporary design, kitted out in exquisite materials and furnished with custom-made modern pieces. There's a concierge service, but you'll need to pop down to the square for breakfast.

AQUA PALACE   LUXURY HOTEL €€€

Map p288 (Palazzo Scalfarotto; ✏041 296 04 42; www.aquapalace.it; Calle de la Malvasia 5492; d €180-340; ❇❂; ⬇Rialto) With its exotic, spice-route vibe and burnished colour palate of gold, bronze and grey, the Aqua Palace is a heady mix of modern amenities and Eastern romance. Expect aristocratic proportions in the suites: acres of weighty fabric and bathrooms marbled within an inch of their lives. Complete with its own private gondola pier, this is the hotel for lovebirds.

🛏 Giudecca, Lido & the Southern Islands

VILLA VENICE MOVIE   HOTEL €

Map p292 (✆041 73 15 98; www.villavenicemovie.
com; Via Lorenzo Marcello 26b; r from €79; ❄🖃;
🖃A, B, C, V) You might find yourself waking
up in a room with a red perspex chandelier,
Holly Golightly–inspired wallpaper and
framed Grace Kelly portraits at this glee-
fully camp six-room hotel. It's situated on
a quiet canal not far from the Palazzo del
Cinema, which explains the screen-goddess
obsession. Ample free bikes make exploring
the Lido and Pellestrina a breeze.

CAMPLUS LIVING REDENTORE   HOSTEL €

Map p291 (✆041 522 53 96; www.campusliving.
it; Calle de le Cape 194, Giudecca; s/d €56/76;
🖃; 🛳Redentore) The Redentore's remaining
Capuchin friars still tend their extensive
gardens, but they no longer have use for this
large accommodation block next to them.
University students fill the 1st floor during
term time, but during summer the entire
building is turned over to travellers. The en-
suite cells are spartan but clean, and there
are kitchen and laundry facilities.

GENERATOR   HOSTEL €

Map p291 (✆041 877 82 88; www.generatorhos
tels.com; Fondamenta de la Croce 86, Giudecca;
dm/r from €36/153; ❄@🖃; 🛳Zitelle) Generator rocks a sharp, contemporary interior including a fabulous kooky-kitsch bar-
restaurant with crazy wallpaper, Murano
chandeliers and a pool table. Try to score a
bunk by the window – you might even wake
up to a San Marco view. Sheets, blanket and
a pillow are provided; breakfast is an additional €6.50 (there's no kitchen).

CAMPING SAN NICOLÒ   CAMPGROUND €

(✆041 526 74 15; www.campingsannicolo.com;
Via dei Sanmicheli 14, Lido; campsite per tent/
caravan €15/55; ⊙May-Sep; 🖃A) Tucked into
a pretty corner of the island, this small,
clean campsite has room for tents and
campervans. Bikes, tents, sleeping bags and
mobile homes are available for rent.

★AL REDENTORE
DI VENEZIA   APARTMENT €€

Map p291 (✆041 522 94 02; www.alredentoredi-
venezia.com; Fondamenta del Ponte Longo 234a,
Giudecca; apt from €163; ❄🖃; 🛳Redentore)
These eight self-contained apartments
blend modern facilities with antique-style
furnishings, and then throw in marble-
tiled bathrooms, top-quality pillows and
high-end bath products. All are generously
proportioned and some have views across
the water to Dorsoduro and San Marco.

VILLA INES   B&B €€

Map p292 (✆041 526 72 26; www.villa-ines.
com; Via Lazzaro Mocenigo 10, Lido; r/ste from
€120/170; ⊙Mar-Oct; P❄🖃; 🛳Lido SME)
Gorgeous gardens surround this quintes-
sential Liberty-style villa. It belongs to
the Seguso family, one of Murano's most
famous glass-blowing dynasties, so the
fittings are predictably top-notch: Seguso
chandeliers, enormous beds, flat-screen
TVs and Jacuzzi bathtubs. Hostess Marika
is a chef and runs the Acquolina Cooking
School (p147) on-site; a delicious breakfast
is included with direct bookings.

JW MARRIOTT VENICE   HOTEL €€€

(✆041 852 13 00; www.jwvenice.com; Isola delle
Rose; r/ste from €352/572; ❄🖃🏊) This bucolic haven inhabits a 16-hectare private
island, 20 minutes from San Marco Giardinetti via a free private shuttle. While the
minimalist interiors are elegant in the extreme, it's the rooftop spa and pools, with
their four-poster loungers and unimpeded
views across the lagoon, that really steal the
show. The spa centre and acclaimed restaurant are open to nonguests.

BAUER PALLADIO
HOTEL & SPA   HERITAGE HOTEL €€€

Map p291 (✆041 520 70 22; www.palladiohotel-
spa.com; Fondamenta de le Zitelle 33, Giudecca;
r/ste from €250/350; ⊙Mar-Oct; ❄🖃; 🛳Zitelle)
Slink into this serene Palladio-designed former almshouse and pamper yourself with
a spa session or indulge in a James Bond
fantasy on the private boat to San Marco.
Many of the serene and comfortable rooms
have garden terraces or canal views.

BELMOND HOTEL CIPRIANI   HOTEL €€€

Map p291 (✆041 24 08 01; www.belmond.com;
Fondamenta de le Zitelle 10, Giudecca; r from
€810; ⊙Apr-Oct; ❄🖃🏊; 🛳Zitelle) The heart-
stoppingly expensive Cipriani offers 95 luxurious rooms and suites – all with private
balconies overlooking flower-filled gardens
– along with Venice's best swimming pool
and a Michelin-starred restaurant.

Colourful buildings in Burano (p152)

🛏 Murano, Burano & the Northern Islands

CASA BURANO   COTTAGE €

(📞041 527 22 81; www.casaburano.it; Burano; r/ste from €108/144; ❄🛜) Wake up in one of Burano's famous candy-coloured houses, courtesy of the stylish folks at Venissa (p202) who have converted five classic homes into an *albergo diffuso* – basically a spread-out hotel (not self-catering apartments). There's no reception; you'll be met at the ferry and led to your canalside cottage. Rooms are spacious and chic, and breakfast baskets are delivered daily.

IL LATO AZZURRO   B&B €

(📞041 523 06 42; www.latoazzurro.it; Via dei Forti 13, Sant'Erasmo; dm/s/d €35/60/88; 🛜; 🚤Capannone) Sleep among the artichokes on Venice's garden isle of Sant'Erasmo in a red-roofed country villa, 25 minutes by boat from central Venice. Spacious guestrooms with wrought-iron beds open onto a wraparound verandah. Meals are largely homegrown, bicycles are available and the lagoon laps at the end of the lane – bite-prone guests should bring mosquito repellent.

★VILLA LINA   B&B €€

Map p293 (📞041 73 90 36; www.villalinavenezia.com; Calle Dietro gli Orti 12, Murano; r from €160; ❄🛜; 🚤Colonna) Finding 16th-century Villa Lina in the grounds of the Nason Moretti glassworks is like chancing upon a wonderful secret. The home of Carlo Nason and his wife Evi has a mod 1950s vibe and is scattered with Carlo's glass designs. Bedrooms

are large, comfortable and contemporary, and the flower-filled garden backs directly on to the Serenella Canal.

★MURANO PALACE   HOTEL €€

Map p293 (📞041 73 96 55; www.muranopalace.com; Ramo dei Vetrai 77, Murano; r €110-195; ❄🛜; 🚤Faro) Come here for designer fabulousness at an outlet price. Jewel-toned colour schemes and (naturally) Murano glass chandeliers illuminate high-ceilinged, wooden-floored rooms, and there are free drinks and snacks in the minibar. Expect canal views and unparalleled art-glass shopping in the vicinity, but an eerie calm descends once the shops close around 6pm.

VENISSA WINE RESORT   INN €€

Map p294 (📞041 527 22 81; www.venissa.it; Fondamenta di Santa Caterina 3, Mazzorbo; r/ste from €153/216; ❄🛜; 🚤Mazzorbo) Gourmet getaways are made in the shade of the vineyards at Venissa, which offers some of the lagoon's best dining as well as six Scandinavian-chic rooms under the farmhouse rafters.

LOCANDA CIPRIANI   INN €€€

Map p294 (📞041 73 01 50; www.locandacipriani.com; Piazza Torcello 29, Torcello; s/d/ste €140/240/300; 🕑Wed-Mon Mar-Dec; ❄; 🚤Torcello) Not much has changed since this rustic wine shop was transformed into an inn in 1934 by Harry's Bar founder Giuseppe Cipriani. The six spacious rooms are more like suites, with books and easy chairs in lieu of TVs. You're bound to find inspiration in Hemingway's favourite room, Santa Fosca, with its creaky oak floors and balcony overlooking the garden.

Understand Venice & the Veneto

Venice Today

It seems that everyone wants a piece of Venice, from selfie-stick-wielding tourists and foreign entrepreneurs, to self-interested politicians and the rising Adriatic Sea. As La Serenissima sails further into the 21st century, new challenges are stirring up rather choppy seas. How does a city reconcile its magnetism with its fragility, its individuality with an increasingly homogenised, globalised world?

Best on Film

Casino Royale (2006) James Bond hits the Grand Canal (don't worry, that palace survived).
Bread & Tulips (2000) A housewife starts life anew in Venice.
Fellini's Casanova (1976) Fellini's take on Venice's seducer with Donald Sutherland tops Lasse Halström's with Heath Ledger.
Don't Look Now (1973) A couple's demons follow them to Venice in Nicolas Roeg's taut thriller.
Death in Venice (1971) Luchino Visconti's version of Thomas Mann's story: a Mahler-esque composer, an infatuation and a deadly disease.

Best in Print

Stabat Mater (Tiziano Scarpa; 2009) Winner of Italy's top literary prize; based on Antonio Vivaldi's orphan-girl orchestra.
Venice Revealed (Paolo Barbaro; 2001) An intimate profile of the city and a passionate plea for its salvation.
Watermark (Joseph Brodsky; 1992) The Nobel Laureate's 17-year fascination with Venice spills onto every page.
Venice, An Interior (Javier Marías; 1988) How history and geography have shaped real and imagined spaces.

#Venexodus

Tempers are fraying in La Serenissima as the rising tide of tourism – 25 million per annum – threatens to overwhelm the city. Of the 53,835 residents who remain (down from 102,000 in 1976), life in the world's most beautiful city is woeful, featuring low-wage employment, limited housing, neglected civic infrastructure, political disenfranchisement and a declining quality of life.

Top of the list of grievances is the lack of affordable housing, which is forcing young Venetians out of their island home and over to mainland Mestre, from where 40,000 of them currently commute. The liberalisation of the rental sector in 2013 and the unregulated growth of home-rental websites mean fewer apartments are available to rent, and at ever-increasing prices. After all, when tourists will pay €1000 a week to rent an apartment, renting to locals for a quarter of the price is hardly an enticing prospect.

Soaring real-estate prices have also precipitated the closure of essential businesses. In 2019, the Association of Craftsmen reported a 50% collapse in small businesses and a 38% rise in fast-food outlets, while only 29 stalls remain at the Rialto Market (down from 104 in 1994), whose survival is now in question for the first time in its centuries-long history. Furthermore, schools, libraries and the hospital are underfunded, while valuable public properties (such as islands, parks and palaces) are sold off cheaply to cover city debts.

A Showdown at Unesco

These challenges are propelling an increasing number of grassroots organisations – including Venessia (www.venessia.com), Generazione90 (www.facebook.com/generazione90), Venezia Cambia (www.veneziacambia.org), Gruppo 25 Aprile (www.gruppo25aprile.org) and We Are Here Venice (https://wearaherevenice.org) – to raise public awareness and lobby politicians to take action. Their chief demands: immediate measures to tackle the housing crisis; a complete ban of cruise ships from the lagoon; regulation on the speed and number of boats; and the creation of a sustainable tourism strategy.

Their efforts have succeeded in bringing the city's problems to global attention. In 2015, Icomos (International Council on Monuments and Sites) published a damning report on the degradation of the city, which has led to the possibility of Unesco placing the city on its list of Endangered Heritage Sites in 2017 unless the administration delivers a plan for the protection of the city and the lagoon.

In response, Mayor Brugnaro announced the €457 million 'Pact of Venice' aimed at revitalising the city. Although there has been limited concrete action to date, there are signs of change with the renovation of some bridges and canal banks and the resurrection of long-abandoned canal-maintenance. In addition, temporary-access gates around Piazza San Marco can now be introduced when overcrowding threatens and in 2019 a €6 to €10 tax on day trippers was announced along with a ban on cruise ships bigger then 55,000 tons in the Giudecca canal (due to come into effect in 2021).

People Power

Although most Venetians don't think these measures go nearly far enough in addressing the crisis, they demonstrate that the work of citizen groups is bearing fruit, particularly in a changing world where environmental concerns and issues of sustainability are becoming ever-more-pressing political priorities.

Furthermore, historically, Venice was a pioneering sustainable city so a blueprint for the future already exists, and young Venetians passionately believe it can be so again. This belief underpins progressive new initiatives, such as Fairbnb Venice, Venezia Autentica, Design.Ve, CBV's restored electric boats, the launch of Giudecca Art District and the new Ocean Space centre. Furthermore, hotels such as Novecento and Hotel Flora are addressing the pressing issue of plastic waste by providing guests with a map of Venice's historic water wells and encouraging the use of water flasks. They estimate that between them they can save 36,000 bottles annually, a staggering figure when extrapolated to Venice's 750-plus hotels.

Travellers, too, have a positive role to play. Venice needs and welcomes visitors willing to play their part in being engaged and considerate guests. Staying in officially registered accommodation, eating in local restaurants, buying products made by local artisans and exploring the city's hidden corners, quiet islands and magical lagoon, all contribute to a healthier and happier city.

if Venice were 100 people

14 would be under 18 years old
60 would be 18 to 64 years old
26 would be 65 years old or older

ethnicity
(% of population)

91 Italian
3 Eastern European
South Asian
1 East Asian
4 Other

population per sq km

VENICE   ITALY

≈ 200 people

History

For centuries Venice dominated trade on the Mediterranean through wily diplomacy, assisted by its mighty navy. When its maritime empire passed its high-water mark, Venice refused to concede defeat on the world stage. Instead the city itself became a stage, attracting global audiences with its vivid visual art, baroque music, opera, independent thinkers and parties without parallel. In its audacious 1000-year history, Venice has not only remained above sea level, but repeatedly risen to the occasion.

From Swamp to Empire

A malarial swamp seems like a strange place to found an empire, unless you consider the circumstances. The Veneti, who had dominated this northern part of the Adriatic coast since at least 800 BC, had been Roman citizens since 49 BC and were not in the habit of war. But between the 5th and 6th centuries AD, when Visigoths, Huns and Lombards started to sack Veneto towns such as Altinum and Aquileia, many Veneti fled to the murky wetlands of the lagoon. They settled first on the island of Torcello before spreading out to the surrounding islands and finally the Rivoalto (meaning 'high bank', shortened to Rialto).

By AD 466, these nascent island communities had elected tribunes and formed a loose federation. When Emperor Justinian claimed Italy's northeast coast for the Byzantine (Eastern Roman) Empire in 540, Venetia (roughly today's Veneto region) sent elected representatives to the regional Byzantine headquarters in Ravenna. This council reported to the capital, Constantinople (today's İstanbul), but as Byzantine power waned in the early 8th century, Venice seized the opportunity for independence.

In 726 the people of Venice elected Orso Ipato as their *dux* (Latin for leader; in English, 'duke'; in Venetian, 'doge'), the first of 118 elected Venetian doges that would lead the city for more than 1000 years. Like some of his successors, Orso tried to turn his appointment into a hereditary monarchy. He was assassinated for overstepping his bounds. At first, no one held the doge's hot seat for long: Orso's successor, Teodato, managed to transfer the ducal capital to Malamocco on the Lido in 742

TIMELINE	AD 452	7th–9th centuries	726
	The Huns, led by Attila, sack the Roman cities of Aquileia and Altinum on the mainland, and their inhabitants take refuge in the islands of the lagoon.	Glassmaking furnaces on Torcello get fired up, creating the basilica's Byzantine glass-mosaic masterpieces.	Orso Ipato becomes the first Venetian doge to be elected without Constantinople's blessing. The Byzantines consider Ipato's election an act of rebellion. Ipato is assassinated in 737.

before being deposed. Gradually the office of the doge was understood as an elected office, kept in check by two councillors and the Arengo (a popular assembly).

When the Franks invaded the lagoon in 809, they were surprised by resistance led by Agnello Partecipazio from Rivoalto, a shallow area of the lagoon inaccessible to most seafaring vessels. Partecipazio's success led to his election as doge and the establishment of a fortress on the eventual site of the Palazzo Ducale. Thus the cluster of islets around Rivoalto became the focus of community development. Land was drained, earth was lifted above the tides with wooden pylons driven into the soft silt, and soon Venetians rose above their swampy circumstances.

War & Spoils

Once terra firma was established, Venice set about shoring up its business interests. When consummate diplomat Pietro II Orseolo was elected doge in 991, he positioned Venice as a neutral party between the western Holy Roman Empire and the Byzantine Empire controlled by Constantinople, and won the medieval equivalent of most-favoured-nation status from both competing empires.

Even at the outset of the Crusades, La Serenissima ('The Most Serene' Venetian Republic) maintained its strategic neutrality, continuing to trade with Muslim leaders from Syria to Spain while its port served as the launching pad for crusaders bent on wresting the Holy Land from Muslim control. With rivals Genoa and Pisa vying for lucrative contracts to equip crusaders, Venice established the world's first assembly lines in the Arsenale (p123), capable of turning out a warship a day. Officially, the city state remained above the fray, joining crusading naval operations only sporadically – and almost always in return for trade concessions.

With Venice starting to have a hold on the Byzantine economy, emperor Manuel I Comnenus played on Venetian-Genoese rivalries, staging an 1171 assault on Constantinople's Genoese colony and blaming it on the city's Venetian residents, who were promptly clapped into irons. Venice sent a fleet to the rescue, but the crew contracted plague from stowaway rats, and the ships limped home without having fired a shot.

Meanwhile, Venice was under threat by land from Holy Roman Emperor Frederick I (Frederick Barbarossa), who had plans to force Italy and the pope to recognise his authority. After several strikes, Barbarossa found northern Italy tough territory to control. When his army was struck by plague in 1167, Barbarossa was forced to withdraw to Pavia – only to discover that 15 Italian city-states, including Venice, had formed the Lombard League against him. Barbarossa met with spectacular

828	957	1094	1096
According to legend, the corpse of St Mark the Evangelist is smuggled from Alexandria (Egypt) to Venice in a pork shipment. St Mark is adopted as the patron saint of Venice.	Holy Roman Emperor Otto the Great recognises key trading rights for Venice, cutting the Byzantine empire out of Venice's increasingly lucrative deals.	Basilica di San Marco is completed in its current form. The doge's spectacular Chiesa d'Oro (Church of Gold) extols the glory of Venice, St Mark and the city's finest artisans.	Byzantine emperor Alexios I Comnenus hands the administration of Dalmatia (present-day Croatia) over to the Venetian Republic.

THE STOLEN SAINT

By the 9th century, Venice had all the makings of an independent trading centre – ports, a defensible position against Charlemagne and the Franks, leadership to settle inevitable trade disputes – but no glorious shrine to mark the city's place on the world map. So Venice did what any ambitious, God-fearing medieval city would do: it procured a patron saint. Under Byzantine rule, St Theodore (San Teodoro) had fulfilled the role. But according to local legend, the evangelist St Mark (San Marco) had visited the lagoon islands and been told by an angel that his body would rest there – and some Venetian merchants decided to realise this prophecy.

In AD 828, Venetian smugglers stole St Mark's body from its resting place in Alexandria (Egypt), apparently hiding the holy corpse in a load of pork to deter inspection by Muslim customs officials. Venice summoned the best artisans from Byzantium and beyond to enshrine these relics in an official ducal church that would impress visitors with the power and glory of Venice. The usual medieval construction setbacks of riots and fires thrice destroyed exterior mosaics and weakened the underlying structure, and St Mark's bones were misplaced twice in the mayhem; they now rest safely in their sarcophagus within the main altar of the Basilica di San Marco (p52).

The winged lion of St Mark was officially adopted as the emblem of the Venetian Republic, symbolically setting Venice apart from Constantinople and Rome.

Those found guilty of crimes against the doge were bludgeoned or decapitated. Severed heads were placed atop columns outside the Palazzo Ducale and sundry body parts displayed in *sestieri* (districts) for exactly three nights and four days, until they started to smell.

defeat and, even worse, excommunication. Venice quickly recognised that it could only handle one holy war at a time and, through diplomatic manoeuvres, convinced Pope Alexander III and the repentant emperor to make peace in Venice in 1177.

The Dodgy Doge

For fast talking, even the shrewdest Venetian merchant couldn't top doge Enrico Dandolo. The doddering nonagenarian might have seemed like an easy mark to Franks seeking Venice's support in the Fourth Crusade, but the doge drove a hard bargain: Venice would provide a fleet to carry 30,000 crusaders, but not for less than 84,000 silver marks – approximately double the yearly income of the king of England at the time.

Only one-third of the proposed Frankish forces turned up in Venice the following year, and their leaders couldn't pay. But Venice had the ships ready, and figured it had kept its side of the bargain. To cover the balance due, Dandolo suggested that the crusaders might help Venice out with a few tasks on the way to Palestine. This included invading Dalmatia and a detour to Constantinople in 1203 that would last a year, while Venetian and Frankish forces thoroughly pillaged the place.

1105	1172	1203–4	1205
Venice loses the Dalmatian towns of Zadar, Trogir and Split to the Hungarians. The Venetians and Hungarians tussle over the cities for the next 40 years.	Venice establishes a Maggior Consiglio, instituting a form of communal civic leadership that limits the powers of the doge.	Doge Dandolo promises to transport Frankish crusaders to the Holy Land but heads to Constantinople; his forces massacre and pillage, then return to Venice with booty.	Without the protection of the Byzantine Empire, Ragusa (Dubrovnik) falls to Venice – which controls the city for the next 153 years.

Finally Dandolo claimed that Constantinople had been suitably claimed for Christendom – never mind that it already was under Christian rule. At age 96, the doge declared himself 'Lord of a Quarter and a Half-Quarter of the Roman Empire' of Byzantium. This title conveniently granted Venice three-eighths of the spoils, including the monumental gilt-bronze horses now in Basilica di San Marco (p52). Venetian ships opted to head home loaded with booty instead of onward to Christian duty, leaving the Franks to straggle onwards to the Crusades.

Venice Versus Genoa

The puppet emperor whom Dandolo put on the throne in Constantinople didn't last long: the Genoese conspired with the Byzantines to overthrow the pro-Venetian regime. Having taken Constantinople for all it was worth, Venice set its sights on distant shores. Through the overland trip of native son Marco Polo in 1271–91, Venetian trade routes extended all the way to China. Rival Genoa's routes to the New World were proving slower to yield returns, and that impatient empire cast an envious eye on Venice's spice- and silk-trade routes.

In 1372 Genoa and Venice finally came to blows over an incident in Cyprus, initiating eight years of maritime warfare that took a toll on Venice. To make matters worse, plague decimated Venice in the 1370s Genoa's allies Padua and Hungary took the opportunity to seize Venetian territories on the mainland, and in 1379 a Genoese fleet appeared off the Lido. Venetian commander Carlo Zeno's war fleet had been sent out to patrol the Mediterranean, leaving the city outflanked and outnumbered.

But the Genoese made a strategic mistake: instead of invading, Genoa attempted to starve the city. With stores of grain saved for just such an occasion, Venice worked day and night to build new ships and defences around the islands. Mustering all of Venice's might, Venetian commander Vettor Pisani mounted a counterattack on the Genoese fleet – but his forces were inadequate. All hope seemed lost, until ships flying the banner of the lion of St Mark appeared on the horizon. Carlo Zeno had returned. Venice ousted the Genoese, exerting control over the Adriatic and a backyard that stretched from Dalmatia (Croatia) to Bergamo (northern Italy).

Rats & Redemption

As a maritime empire, ships came and went through Venice's ports daily, carrying salt, silks, spices and an unintentional import: rats infested with fleas carrying bubonic plague. In 1348 the city was still recovering from an earthquake that had destroyed houses and drained the Grand

---

Byzantine Splendour

Basilica di San Marco (San Marco)

Basilica di Santa Maria Assunta (Torcello)

Basilica dei SS Maria e Donato (Murano)

HISTORY FROM SWAMP TO EMPIRE

In 1271, traders Niccolò and Maffeo Polo departed for Shangdu (Xanadu), the court of Kublai Khan, with Niccolò's 17-year-old son, Marco. They returned in 1295 and Marco's detailed account of their experiences (*Il milione* or *Travels of Marco Polo*) became a sensation throughout Europe.

1212	1297	1310	1348–49
Venice takes control of the Greek island of Crete from their rival, Genoa. Venetian rule of the island would continue for over 450 years.	Membership of the Maggior Consiglio is restricted to only those whose families are already members, creating a hereditary ruling elite.	With rebellion afoot, a temporary security force called the Consiglio dei Dieci is convened; it lasts almost five centuries, effectively running Venice for 200 years.	A horrific bout of the Black Death hits Venice, killing some 60% of the population. Venetian doctors observe that the worst-hit areas are by Dorsoduro's docks, where rats arrive.

Canal, when the plague struck. Soon as many as 600 people were dying every day, and undertakers' barges raised the rueful cry: *'Corpi morti! Corpi morti!'* (Bring out your dead!). Within a year, more than 50,000 Venetians died.

No one was sure how the disease had spread, but Venice took the unprecedented step of appointing three public health officials to manage the crisis. Observing that outbreaks seemed to coincide with incoming shipments, Venice decided in 1403 to intercept all incoming ships arriving from infected areas on Isola di Lazzaretto Vecchio. Before any ship was allowed to enter the city, it was required to undergo inspection, and its passengers had to wait for a *quarantena* (40-day period) while Venetian doctors monitored them for signs of plague. This was the world's first organised quarantine station, setting a precedent that has saved untold lives from plague and other infectious diseases since.

While the plague struck Italy's mainland as many as 50 more times before 1500, the outbreaks often seemed to miraculously bypass Venice. The city's faithful chalked up their salvation to divine intervention, and built the spectacular churches of Il Redentore (p141) and Basilica di Santa Maria della Salute (p78) as monumental acts of gratitude.

Traders & Traitors

Like the architecture of its signature Basilica di San Marco (p52), the Venetian empire was dazzlingly multicultural. Venice turned arrivals from every nation and creed into trading partners with a common credo: as long as everyone was making money, cultural boundaries need not apply. Dalmatians, Armenians, Turks, Greeks and Germans became neighbours along the Grand Canal, and Jewish and Muslim refugees and other groups widely persecuted in Europe settled into established communities in Venice.

Commerce provided a common bond. At the height of Venice's maritime prowess, 300 shipbuilding companies in the Arsenale had 16,000 employees. By the mid-15th century, Venice's maritime ventures had left the city swathed in golden mosaics, rustling silks and incense. In case of trade disputes or feuds among neighbours, La Serenissima instigated a complex political system of checks, balances and elections, with the doge as the executive presiding over council matters.

Yet inside the red-velvet cloak of its ruling elite, Venice was hiding an iron hand. Venice's shadowy secret service, the Consiglio dei Dieci (Council of Ten), thwarted conspiracies by deploying Venetian James Bonds throughout the city and major European capitals. Venice had no qualms about spying on its own citizens, and trials, torture and execu-

---

Multicultural Landmarks

The Ghetto (Cannaregio)

Museo delle Icone (Castello)

Scuola Dalmata di San Giorgio degli Schiavoni (Castello)

Monastero di San Lazzaro degli Armeni (Southern Islands)

Fondaco dei Tedeschi (San Marco)

In 1444 the second incarnation of the Rialto Bridge collapsed under the weight of spectators watching a wedding flotilla. It took 148 years before the current stone replacement by Antonio da Ponte was completed.

1403	1420	1470	1492
The world's first quarantine stations are established with proceeds from Venice's salt monopoly, saving lives by limiting contact with the bubonic plague.	Venice retakes control of Dalmatia (not including Dubrovnik), having 'purchased' it from King Ladislaus of Naples in 1409 for 100,000 ducats.	Cyprus is the latest of Venice's conquests, which now stretch across the mainland to Bergamo, along the Adriatic and through the Aegean to Crete.	Genoese Cristoforo Colombo's voyage kicks off the age of discovery and Venice's long slide into obsolescence, as the Portuguese and Spanish bypass its customs controls.

tions were carried out in secret. Still, compared with its neighbours at the time, Venice remained a haven of tolerance.

Friendly Foes

Never mind that Venice sacked Constantinople, or that Constantinople sided with Genoa against Venice: warfare wasn't enough to deter the two maritime powers from doing brisk business. When Constantinople fell to Ottoman rule in 1453, business carried on as usual. The rival powers understood one another very well; the Venetian language was widely spoken across the eastern Mediterranean.

After Suleiman the Magnificent captured Cyprus in 1571, Venice sensed its maritime power slipping, and allied with the papal states, Spain and even arch-rival Genoa to keep the Ottoman sultan at bay. The same year a huge allied fleet (much of it provided by Venice) routed the Turks off Lepanto (Greece) and Sebastiano Venier and his Venetian fleet sailed home with 100 Turkish women as war trophies.

Legend has it that when Turkish troops took over the island of Paros, the prisoners of war included Cecilia Venier-Baffo, who was apparently the illegitimate daughter of Venice's noble Venier family, a niece of the doge, and possibly the cousin of Sebastiano (of Lepanto fame). Cecilia became the favourite wife of sultan Salim II in Constantinople, and when he died in 1574 she took control as Nurbanu Sultan (Princess of Light). Regent of sultan Murad III, she was a faithful pen pal of Elizabeth I of Britain and Catherine de' Medici of France. According to historian Alberto Toso Fei, Nurbanu Sultan's policies were so favourable to Venetian interests that the Venetian senate set aside special funds to fulfil her wishes for Venetian specialities, from lapdogs to golden cushions. Genoa wasn't pleased by her favouritism, and in 1582 she was poisoned by what appeared to have been Genoese assassins.

The Age of Decadence

While Italy's city-states continued to plot against one another, they were increasingly eclipsed by marriages cementing alliances among France, England and the Habsburg Empire. As it lost ground to these European nation states and the seas to pirates and Ottomans, Venice took a different tack, and began conquering Europe by charm.

Sensations & Scandals

Venice's star attractions were its parties, music, women and art. Nunneries in Venice held soirées to rival those in its *ridotti* (casinos), and Carnevale lasted up to three months. Claudio Monteverdi was hired as choir director of San Marco in 1613, introducing multipart harmonies

Venetian party planners outdid themselves with the 1574 reception for Henry III of France. The king's barge was greeted with glass-blowers performing on rafts, bevvies of Venetian beauties dressed in white, a 1200-dish meal and decorations provided by an all-star committee of Palladio, Veronese and Tintoretto.

John Julius Norwich's *History of Venice* (1977, 1981) is an engrossing account of the city's maritime empire. Peter Ackroyd's *Venice: Pure City* (2009) is a highly evocative read. Joanne M Ferraro's *Venice: History of the Floating City* (2012) takes a more intellectual approach.

HISTORY THE AGE OF DECADENCE

1494	1498	1501	1508
Aldo Manuzio founds Aldine Press, introducing mass-market paperbacks, including Dante's *Divine Comedy*. By 1500, one in six books published in Europe is printed in Venice.	Portuguese explorer Vasco da Gama sails around the Cape of Good Hope, and the boom in trans-Atlantic trade shuts out many Venetian merchants.	The Magistrato alle Acque is created in order to maintain and regulate the delicate hydrological balance of the lagoon, on which Venice's security and fortune is built.	The Holy Roman Empire, papal states, Spain and France form the League of Cambrai against Venice – but with Venice cutting side deals, the ensuing war doesn't change the map much.

and historical operas with crowd-pleasing tragicomic scenes. Monteverdi's style of opera caught on: by the end of the 17th century, Venice's season included as many as 30 operas.

New orchestras required musicians, but Venice came up with a ready workforce: orphan girls. Circumstances had conspired to produce an unprecedented number of Venetian orphans: on the one hand was the plague, and on the other were scandalous masquerade parties and flourishing prostitution. Funds poured in from anonymous donors to support *ospedaletti* (orphanages), and the great baroque composers Antonio Vivaldi and Domenico Cimarosa were hired to lead orphan orchestras. The Venetian state took on the care and musical training of the city's orphan girls, who earned their keep by performing at public functions and *ospedaletti* fundraising galas. Visiting diplomats treated to orphan concerts were well advised to tip the orphan performers: you never knew whose illegitimate daughter you might be insulting otherwise.

Pulling Rank: The Pope & the Doge

Rome repeatedly censured Venice for depicting holy subjects in an earthy, Venetian light, and for playing toe-tapping tunes in churches – but such admonishments were largely ignored. According to late-16th-century gossip, Cardinal Camillo Borghese had had a beef with the Venetian ambassador to Rome, Leonardo Donà, ever since the two exchanged heated words in the Roman halls of power. The cardinal

> Individual Venetians involved in the sacking of the Christian cities of Zadar and Constantinople during the Fourth Crusade were excommunicated from the Church in 1202. However, on five subsequent occasions between 1284 and 1606, the Pope placed the entire city under an interdict (restricting sacraments) for openly defying orders.

VENICE'S 'HONEST COURTESANS'

High praise, high pay and even high honours: Venice's *cortigiane oneste* (honest courtesans) earned the title not by offering a fair price, but by providing added value with style, education and wit that reflected well on their patrons. They were not always beautiful or young, but *cortigiane oneste* were well educated, dazzling their admirers with poetry, music, philosophical insights and apt social critiques. In the 16th century, some Venetian families of limited means spared no expense on their daughters' educations: beyond an advantageous marriage or career, educated women who become *cortigiane oneste* could command prices 60 times those of the average *cortigiana di lume* ('courtesan of the lamp' – street prostitute).

Far from hiding their trade, a catalogue of 210 of Venice's *piu honorate cortigiane* (most honoured courtesans) was published in 1565, listing contact information and going rates, payable directly to the courtesan's servant, her mother or, occasionally, her husband. A *cortigiana onesta* might circulate in Venetian society as the known mistress of one or more admirers, who compensated her for her company rather than services rendered, and with an allowance rather than pay per hour. Syphilis was an occupational hazard, and special hospices were founded for infirm courtesans.

1516	1571	1575–6	1630
A proclamation declares that Jewish residents of Venice are to live in a designated zone called the Ghetto, with closed gates and guards after dark.	Venice and the Holy League of Catholic states defeat Ottoman forces at the naval Battle of Lepanto, thanks in part to a technical advantage: cannons and guns versus archers.	Plague claims many lives, including Titian's. Quarantine aids Venice's recovery; a new painting cycle by Tintoretto is dedicated to San Rocco, patron saint of the plague-stricken.	The plague kills a third of Venice's population within 16 months. With few leaders surviving, the republic allows wealthy Venetians to buy their way into the Golden Book of nobility.

PRINCE OF PLEASURE

Never was a hedonist born at a better time and in a more appropriate place. Eighteenth-century Venice was well into its new career as the pleasure capital of Europe when Giacomo Casanova (1725–98) arrived on the scene. He was abandoned as a young boy, and became a gambler and rake while studying law in Padua. He graduated by age 17 to take up a position with the Church in Venice, but adventuring soon became Casanova's primary career. His charm won him warm welcomes into the homes of wealthy patrons – and the beds of their wives, lovers and daughters.

Venice was a licentious place, but political limits still applied. Casanova's dalliances with Freemasonry and banned books were considered nothing less than a threat to the state. After an evening foursome with the French ambassador and a couple of nuns, Casanova was arrested on the convenient charge of 'outrages against religion' and dragged to the Palazzo Ducale's dreaded attic prison. Sentenced to five years in a flea-infested cell, Casanova complained bitterly, and promptly escaped through the roof of his cell, entered the palace, and breezed past the guards in the morning.

Casanova fled Venice to make his fortune in Paris and served briefly as a French spy. But his extracurricular habits caused him no end of trouble: he went broke in Germany, survived a duel in Poland, fathered and abandoned several children, and contracted venereal diseases in England. Late in life, he returned to Venice as a celebrity, and served the government as a spy – but he was exiled for publishing a satire of the nobility. He wound up as a librarian in an isolated castle in Bohemia, where boredom drove him to finally write his memoirs. In the end, he concluded, 'I can say I have lived.'

hissed that, were he pope, he'd excommunicate the entire Venetian populace. 'And I would thumb my nose at the excommunication,' retorted Donà.

As fate would have it, by 1606 cardinal and ambassador were promoted to Pope Paul V and doge of Venice, respectively. Rome had never appreciated Venice's insistence on reserving a degree of control over Church matters, and when Venice claimed that zoning laws required its approval of Church expansion plans within the city, Pope Paul V issued a papal bull excommunicating the city-state. As promised, the doge defied the bull, ordering all churches to remain open on Venetian territory. Any church that obeyed the bull would have its doors permanently closed, property seized and clergy exiled from Venice.

Venetian-born monk and philosopher Paolo Sarpi convincingly argued Venice's case, claiming Venice's right to self-determination came directly from God, not through Rome. Before the excommunication could cause further loss of Church property in Venice, or other Catholic territories became convinced by Sarpi's argument, Pope Paul V rescinded his bull.

1669	1718	1797	1807
The Venetian colony of Crete is lost to the Ottoman Turks, yet the two powers continue to trade with one another – despite repeated objections from Rome.	Venice and Austria sign the Treaty of Passarowitz with the Ottoman Empire, splitting prime coastal territory and leaving Venice with nominal control and some Ionian islands.	Napoleon enters the city and the Venetian Republic is extinguished. The segregation of Jewish Venetians briefly comes to an end.	Napoleon suppresses religious orders to quell dissent. Some churches are eventually reconsecrated – but many aren't, serving instead as archives or tourist attractions.

But the power struggle didn't stop there. Venice conducted an official 1767 audit of 11 million golden ducats in revenues rendered to Rome in the previous decade, and decided to cut its losses: 127 Veneto monasteries and convents were closed, cutting the local clerical population in half and redirecting millions of ducats to Venice's coffers.

Venice's former leper colony of San Lazzaro degli Armeni became a monastery, founded by Armenian refugees in 1717, and frescoed Palazzo Zenobio remains an Armenian cultural centre and popular venue for concerts and Carnevale.

Red Lights, White Widows & Grey Areas

While Roman clerics furiously scribbled their disapproval, Venetian trends stealthily took over drawing rooms across the continent. Venetian women's lavish finery, staggering platform shoes up to 50cm high and masculine quiff hairdos scandalised visiting European nobility, until Venice felt obliged to enact sumptuary laws preventing women from wearing manly hairstyles and blinding displays of jewels on dipping décolletages. Venetian noblewomen complained to the doge and the pope, and the restrictions were soon dropped.

With trade revenues and the value of the Venetian ducat slipping in the 16th century, Venice's fleshpots brought in far too much valuable foreign currency to be outlawed. Instead, Venice opted for regulation and taxation. Rather than baring all in the rough-and-ready streets around the Rialto, prostitutes could only display their wares from the waist up in windows, or sit bare-legged on window sills. Venice decreed that to distinguish themselves from noblewomen who increasingly dressed like them, ladies of the night should ride in gondolas with red lights. By the end of the 16th century, the town was flush with some 12,000 registered prostitutes, creating a literal red-light district.

Beyond red lights ringing the Rialto, 16th- to 18th-century visitors encountered broad grey areas in Venetian social mores. As free-spirited, financially independent Venetian women took lovers, there became a certain fluidity surrounding the definition of a *cortigiana* (courtesan). With their husbands at sea for months or years, Venice's 'white widows' took young, handsome *cicisbei* (manservants) to tend their needs. Not coincidentally, Venetian ladies occasionally fell into religious fervours entailing a trimester-long period of seclusion.

Many Venetians dropped the mask of propriety altogether, openly cohabiting with lovers year-round and acknowledging illegitimate heirs in their wills. By the 18th century, less than 40% of Venetian nobles bothered with the formality of marriage.

From Occupation to Revolution

When Napoleon arrived in 1797, Venice had been reduced by plague and circumstances from its 16th-century peak population of around 190,000 to fewer than 140,000 people. Venetian warships managed to deter one French ship by the Lido, but when Napoleon made it clear he intended to destroy the city if it resisted, the Maggior Consiglio (Great Council) decreed the end of the republic. The doge reportedly doffed the signature cap of his office with a sigh, saying, 'I won't be needing

1814	1836	1846	1848
Austria takes Venice as a war trophy and imposes order with thousands of troops, a house-numbering system and heavy taxes that push Venice to the brink of starvation.	Fire guts Venice's legendary opera house, but a new version soon rises from the ashes. When La Fenice (The Phoenix) burns again in 1996, an exact replica of this second house is built.	The first train crosses to Venice from the mainland. The feat is bittersweet: churches are demolished for the station, trains bring occupying Austrian troops and Venetians foot the bill.	Daniele Manin leads an anti-Austrian rebellion and declares Venice a republic. Austrians retake the city in 1849, and Venice remains under Austrian control for 17 years.

this anymore.' Rioting citizens were incensed by such cowardice, but French forces soon ended the insurrection, and began systematically plundering the city.

Though Napoleon only controlled Venice for a total of about 11 years, on and off, the impact of his reign is still visible. Napoleon grabbed any Venetian art masterpiece that wasn't nailed down, lifted restrictions on the Jewish Ghetto and filled in canals in order to create wider streets to facilitate the movement of troops and commerce. Napoleon lost control of Venice to the Austrians in 1814, and two years later one-quarter of Venice's population was destitute.

Austria had grand plans for the city, and expected impoverished Venetians to foot the bill. They were obliged to house Austrian soldiers, who spent off-duty hours indulging in their new happy-hour invention, the *spritz* (a prosecco-and-bitters cocktail). Finding their way back home afterwards was a challenge in Venetian *calli* (lanes), so the Austrians implemented a street-numbering system. To improve shipping access for reinforcements and supplies, they dredged and deepened entrances to the lagoon, and began a train bridge in 1841 – all with Venetian labour and special Venetian taxes. To make way for the new train station in 1846, *scuole* (religious confraternities), a palace and the church containing the body of St Lucy were demolished.

When a young lawyer named Daniele Manin suggested reforms to Venice's puppet administration in 1848, he was tossed into prison – sparking a popular uprising against the Austrians that would last 17 months. Austria responded by bombarding and blockading the city. In July, Austria began a 24-day artillery bombardment, raining some 23,000 shells down on the city and its increasingly famished and cholera-stricken populace, until Manin finally managed to negotiate a surrender to Austria with a guarantee of no reprisals. Yet the indignity of Austria's suppression continued to fester, and when presented with the option in 1866, the people of Venice and the Veneto voted to join the new independent Kingdom of Italy under King Vittorio Emanuele II.

Life During Wartime

Glamorous Venice gradually took on a workaday aspect in the 19th century, with factories springing up on Giudecca, along the fringes of Cannaregio and around Mestre and Padua, and textile industries setting up shop around Vicenza and Treviso. As an increasingly strategic industrial area, Venice began to seem like a port worth reclaiming. But when Austro-Hungarian forces advanced on Venice, they were confronted by Italy's naval marines. Two days after Italy declared war on Austria in 1915, air raids on the city began, and would continue inter-

In 1703 Antonio Vivaldi became the musical director at La Pietà, composing many concertos for the resident orchestra comprised of orphan girls. He was fired in 1709 but swiftly recalled, to Venice's immense benefit.

In *The Wings of the Dove* (1902), a dapper con man and sickly heiress meet in Venice, with predictable consequences – but Henry James' gorgeous storytelling makes for riveting reading.

HISTORY LIFE DURING WARTIME

1866	1895	1907	1918
Venice and the Veneto join the new Kingdom of Italy. The unification of Italy is complete when Rome is made the capital in 1870.	The first Biennale reasserts the city's role as global tastemaker. Other nations are eventually invited, though a provocative Picasso is removed from the Spanish pavilion in 1910.	Under the Italian government, the Magistrato alle Acque becomes part of the Ministry of Public Works and operational functions are devolved to the Consorzio Venezia Nuova.	Austro-Hungarian planes drop almost 300 bombs on Venice in WWI, but their aim is off, resulting in mercifully little loss of life or damage to property.

mittently throughout WWI until 1918. Venice was lucky: the bombardments caused little damage.

When Mussolini rose to power after WWI, he was determined to turn the Veneto into a modern industrial powerhouse and a model Fascist society – despite Venice's famously laissez-faire outlook. Mussolini constructed a road causeway from the mainland to Venice, literally bringing the city into line with the rest of Italy. While Italy's largest Fascist rallies were held in Padua, with up to 300,000 participants, Italian Resistance leaders met in Padua's parks to plot uprisings throughout northern Italy. When Mussolini's grip on the region began to weaken during WWII, partisans joined Allied troops to wrest the Veneto from Fascist control.

Venice emerged relatively unscathed from Allied bombing campaigns that targeted mainland industrial sites, and was liberated by New Zealand troops in 1945 – but the mass deportation of Venice's Jewish population in 1943 had all but annihilated that historic community. When the Veneto began to rebound after the war, many Venetians left for the mainland, Milan and other postwar economic centres. The legendary lagoon city seemed mired in the mud, unable to reconcile its recent history with its past grandeur, and unsure of its future.

Director Luchino Visconti takes on the novella by Nobel Prize winner Thomas Mann with the story of a Mahler-esque composer, an infatuation and a deadly outbreak in *Death in Venice* (1971).

The Magistrato alle Acque (Water Magistrate) was the second-most important role in the Venetian Republic (after the doge), and his word was law on anything to do with the lagoon.

Keeping Venice Afloat

No one comes to Venice and fails to be struck by the uniqueness of the city. However, fewer people consider the utterly unique character of the lagoon in which it stands, despite the fact that it is the only lagoon in the world to have retained its equilibrium for over 1000 years.

Master of the Waters

By its very nature a lagoon is an unstable system, tending either towards erosion or, if the silt-bearing rivers prevail, towards swamps and then fields. In order to prevent either of these two fates, the Republic of Venice brought to bear all its resources and technological know-how and enforced them autocratically under the aegis of the Magistrato alle Acque (Master of the Waters), which was established in 1501. This specially empowered office had absolute responsibility for ensuring the hydraulic health of the lagoon.

Between the 14th and 16th centuries when the Brenta, Sila and Piave rivers threatened to overwhelm the lagoon with silt, the magistrates ordered they be rerouted. Later, in the 18th century, they engineered the construction of Pellestrina's impressive *murazzi* (sea walls). To ensure the ebb and flow of the tides dealt effectively with the city's sewage, the three mouths to the sea were kept open just enough; and ships were

1932	1933	1943	1948
The world's first film festival is initially considered a dubious ploy for attention, but Greta Garbo, Clark Gable and 23,000 moviegoers prove the formula a success.	Mussolini opens the Ponte della Libertà (Freedom Bridge) from Mestre to Venice. The 4km-long, two-lane highway remains the only access to Venice by car.	Under the Nazi occupation, 256 Jewish Venetians are rounded up and deported to concentration camps.	Peggy Guggenheim arrives with major Modernists, renewing interest in Italian art, reclaiming Futurism from the Fascists and championing Venetian abstract expressionism.

required to unload cannons and cargo at Pola and the Lido to reduce weight in order to navigate the *ghebbi* (capillary canals) that ensured the city's security against both enemies and the force of the tidal influx. Anyone who sunk *briccole* (navigation poles) without permission was sent directly to prison, and in 1505 the Senate enacted a fine of 100 ducats (a colossal amount) for any unauthorised person who tampered with the lagoon in any way. Through this careful management the lagoon not only survived but thrived.

When the Republic fell in 1797 the unified management of the lagoon collapsed. Instead, Napoleonic, Austrian and Italian governments introduced new systems that validated the concept of private property. A third of the lagoon was reclaimed for agricultural use and aquaculture, and in 1917 the industrial zone of Marghera was constructed. To allow cargo ships to access Marghera, a deep-water channel, the Vittorio Emanuele, was dug in 1925, with two additional channels – the Canale Malamocco-Marghera and the Canale dei Petroli – dredged in the mid-1960s.

As the area into which high tides could expand and the area of absorbent capillary canals was reduced, the level of the *acque alte* (high waters) increased. Then in 1966, a catastrophic flood hit. For hours the waters reached more than 2m above sea level and the world feared that Venice would drown. Fifty organisations worldwide rallied to preserve the city, raising €50 million to cover 1500 restoration projects. Unesco took fright at the threatened loss and in 1987 awarded Venice and its lagoon World Heritage status.

Modern Lagoon Politics

More importantly for the city, in 1973, Italy passed the first 'special' law for Venice, wherein the Italian state recognised the vital task of maintaining the lagoon in order to safeguard the city from environmental disaster. Debates were held, studies commissioned and it was agreed that any further reduction in the area of the lagoon should be forbidden. A plan to build a third industrial zone was abandoned and ideas were discussed as to how best to regulate the increased force of the tides.

It was decided to commission a system of barriers – MoSE (Modulo Sperimentale Elettromeccanico) – at the three mouths of the lagoon, which could be raised to prevent flooding during high tides. Initial costs were estimated at €1.5 billion with a completion date set for 1995. Since then decades of controversy have ensued, culminating in the exposure of a huge corruption scandal in 2014 that saw the arrest of the city's mayor, undermined the scientific soundness of the idea and resulted in the dissolution of the 500-year-old Magistrato alle Acque,

One of Italy's most beloved graphic novels, *Corto Maltese: Fable of Venice* (originally published in 1967) follows Hugo Pratt's cosmopolitan sea captain as he cracks the mysteries of the *calli* (lanes).

HISTORY KEEPING VENICE AFLOAT

1955	1966	1973	1978
Venice opens Italy's first museum of Jewish history, the Museo Ebraico, in the historic Ghetto. The museum opens the Ghetto's synagogues and Lido cemetery to visitors.	Record floods cause widespread damage and unleash debate on measures to protect Venice. Admirers around the world rally to save the city, and rescue its treasures from lagoon muck.	Italy's first 'special' law for Venice is enacted. It promises to protect urban settlements while maintaining the physical continuity of the lagoon.	The Patriarch of Venice, Cardinal Albino Luciani, surprises most observers when he is elected as Pope John Paul I. He dies of a heart attack after 33 days in the role.

As a cosmopolitan port city, Venice has always been a crowded place. Today, the city accommodates a daily average of around 144,000 residents and visitors combined, which still falls short of the 190,000 residents the city housed at its 16th-century peak.

also implicated in the scandal. Some academics and hydrologists argue that relying on the mechanical fix of MoSE is an inadequate solution for a dynamic system like a lagoon, which needs constant regulation and effective, unitary environmental planning, as the Republic once provided. MoSE is now not expected to be fully completed until 2022 and the price tag has risen to €5.5 billion.

But just as public opinion questions the efficacy of MoSE as a solution, Venice faces another rising tide – the boom in tourism. In 1999, cruise-ship passengers accounted for only 100,000 visitors a year to Venice. By 2012 the Port Authority published figures of 2.26 million arrivals. In protest, Venetians took to the Giudecca Canal in rowboats and gondolas, symbolically blocking the entry of ships they argue endanger the very foundations of their city. Their cause was taken up by Unesco, which threatened to place Venice on their list of endangered heritage sites unless the big ships were banned. Eventually the protestors won a partial victory: in 2017 it was announced that, within four years, outsized ships (greater than 96,000 tonnes) would have to dock at the unlovely nearby port of Marghera, and only ships less than 55,000 tonnes would be allowed to traverse the Giudecca Canal. Polls show that most Venetians would prefer the ships to be banned entirely.

Venice sorely misses the dedicated, centralised governance of the Republic – the lagoon now covers four provinces and is dependent on the policies and finances of nine different city and town councils. Venice also has to negotiate over the direct stake of the national government in its museums, airport, railway station and port. As a result the city and its lagoon continue to degrade, with the city estimated to be sinking at a rate of 2mm a year. The floor of the lagoon on which Venice stands may gradually be washed out to sea, transforming the lagoon into a bay, with the city in danger of subsidence or actual collapse into the water as the foundations are undermined.

1996	2012	2014	2019
La Fenice burns down for the second time; two electricians are found guilty of arson. A €90-million replica of the 19th-century opera house is completed in 2003.	Venetians target the cruise industry in protests held under the banner 'No Grandi Navi' (No Large Ships). The following year, dozens of small protest vessels blockade the Giudecca canal.	MoSE is mired in scandal. Venice mayor Giorgio Orsoni is arrested, the city council suspended and the venerable office of Magistrato alle Acque is dissolved.	The city announces a tax on day trippers, aiming to curb numbers and to recoup some of the costs associated with catering to them.

Architecture

So what exactly is Venetian architecture? Everyone has a pet period in Venice's architectural history, and hardly anyone agrees which is Venice's defining moment. Nineteenth-century critic John Ruskin waxed rhapsodic about Venetian Gothic and detested Palladio; Palladians rebuffed baroque; fans of rococo were scandalised by the Lido's louche Liberty style; and pretty much everyone recoiled at the inclinations of industry to strip Venice of ornamentation. Now that the latest architectural trend is creative repurposing, it's all making a comeback.

Engineering Marvels

Over the centuries, Venetian architecture has evolved into such a dazzling composite of materials, styles and influences that you might overlook its singular defining feature: it's built on water. Thousands of wooden pylons sunk into lagoon mud support stone foundations, built up with elegant brickwork and rustic ceiling beams, low *sotoportegi* (passageways) and lofty loggias, grand water gates and hidden *corti* (courtyards). Instead of disguising or wallpapering over these essential Venetian structural elements, modern architects have begun highlighting them. With this approach, the Fondazione Giorgio Cini (p142) converted a monastery into a cultural centre, Tadao Andō turned Punta della Dogana (p80) customs houses into a contemporary-art showplace, and Renzo Piano transformed historic Magazzini del Sale (Salt Warehouses) into a rotating gallery space for Fondazione Vedova (p81). With original load-bearing supports and brickwork exposed to public admiration, Venice's new-old architecture seems more fresh and vital than ever.

Most Divine Religious Buildings

Basilica di San Marco (San Marco)

Basilica di Santa Maria della Salute (Dorsoduro)

Chiesa di Santa Maria dei Miracoli (Cannaregio)

Schola Spagnola (Cannaregio)

Veneto-Byzantine

If Venice seems to have unfair aesthetic advantages, it did have an early start: cosmopolitan flair has made Venetian architecture a standout since the 7th century. While Venice proper was still a motley, muddy outpost of refugee settlements, the nearby island of Torcello was a booming Byzantine trade hub of 20,000 to 30,000 people.

At its spiritual centre was the Basilica di Santa Maria Assunta (p150), which from afar looks like a Byzantine-style basilica on loan from Ravenna. But look closely: those 7th-to-9th-century apses have Romanesque arches, and the iconostasis separating the central nave from the presbytery is straight out of an Eastern Orthodox church. Back in Torcello's heyday, traders from France, Greece or Turkey could have stepped off their boats and into this church, and all felt at home. To signal to visitors that they had arrived in a powerful trading centre, Santa Maria Assunta glitters with 12th-to-13th-century golden mosaics.

Excavations have revealed Torcello glassworks dating from the 7th century, and those furnaces would have been kept glowing through the night to produce the thousands of tiny glass tesserae (tiles) needed to create the mesmerising *Madonna* hovering over the altar – not to

Next to bridges, Venice's most common architectural features are its *poggi* (well-heads). Before Venice's aqueduct was constructed, more than 6000 wells collected and filtered rainwater for public use. Even today, overflow happy-hour crowds at neighbourhood *bacari* (bars) schmooze and toast around 600 surviving ancient watering holes.

Venetians avoid walking between the San Marco pillars, where criminals were once executed. According to legend, anyone wandering between these pillars will meet an untimely demise – doomed Marin Falier was beheaded eight months after supposedly passing between them to accept the post of doge.

mention the rather alarmingly detailed *Last Judgment* mosaic, with hellfire licking at the dancing feet of the damned.

Breakout Byzantine Style

When Venice made its definitive break with the Byzantine empire in the 9th century, it needed a landmark to set the city apart, and a platform to launch its golden age of maritime commerce. Basilica di San Marco (p52) captures Venice's grand designs in five vast gold-mosaic domes, refracting stray sunbeams like an indoor fireworks display. Even today, the sight elicits audible gasps from crowds of international admirers. The basilica began with a triple nave in the 9th century, but after a fire two wings were added to form a Greek cross in an idea borrowed from the Church of the Holy Apostles in Constantinople. The finest artisans from around the Mediterranean were brought in to raise the basilica's dazzle factor to jaw-dropping, creating the 11th-to-13th-century marble relief masterpieces over the Romanesque entry arches and the intricate Islamic geometry of the inlaid semiprecious stone floors from the 12th to 13th century.

Since the basilica was the official chapel of the doge, every time Venice conquered new territory by commerce or force, the basilica displayed the doge's share of the loot – hence the walls of polychrome marble pilfered from Egypt and 2nd-century Roman bronze horses looted from Constantinople's hippodrome in 1204. The basilica's ornament shifted over the centuries from Gothic to Renaissance, but the message to visiting dignitaries remained the same: the glory above may be God's, but the power below rested with the doge.

Romanesque

Romanesque architecture was all the rage across Western Europe in the 9th century, from the Lombard plains to Tuscany, southern France to northeast Spain, and later, Germany and England. While the materials ranged from basic brick to elaborate marble, Romanesque rounded archways, barrel-vaulted ceilings, triple naves and calming cloisters came to define early-medieval church architecture. This austere, classical style was a deliberate reference to the Roman Empire and early martyrs who sacrificed all for the Church. But in case the architecture failed to send the message, sculptural reliefs were added, heralding heroism on entry portals – and putting the fear of the devil into unbelievers, with angels and demons carved into stone capitals in creepy crypts.

As Venice became a maritime empire in the 13th century, many of the city's smaller Byzantine and early Romanesque buildings were swept away to make room for International Gothic grandeur. The finest examples of Romanesque in the Veneto – and possibly in northern Italy – are Verona's vast 12th- to 14th-century Basilica di San Zeno Maggiore (p179) and Padua's frescoed jewel of a Romanesque baptistry. Within Venice, Romanesque simplicity awaits at Chiesa di San Giacomo dell'Orio.

Venetian Gothic

Soaring spires and flying buttresses rose above Paris in the 12th century, making the rest of Europe suddenly seem small and squat by comparison. Soon every European capital was trying to top Paris with Gothic marvels of their own, featuring deceptively delicate ribbed cross-vaulting that distributed the weight of stone walls and allowed openings for vast stained-glass windows.

Europe's medieval superpowers used this grand international style to showcase their splendour and status. Venice one-upped its neighbours, not with height but by inventing its own version of Gothic. Venice had been trading across the Mediterranean with partners from Lebanon to North Africa for centuries, and the constant exchange of building materials, engineering innovations and aesthetic ideals led to a creative cross-pollination in Western and Middle Eastern architecture. Instead of framing windows with the ordinary ogive (pointed) arch common to France and Germany, Venice added an elegantly tapered, Moorish flourish to its arches, with a trilobate (three-lobed) shape that became a signature of Venetian Gothic, as exemplified on the facade of Ca' d'Oro (p111) and numerous other buildings along the Grand Canal.

Brick Gothic

While Tuscany, like France and Germany, used marble for Gothic cathedrals, Venice showcased a more austere, cerebral style with clever brickwork and a Latin cross plan at I Frari (p94), completed in 1443 after a century's work, and Zanipolo (p125), consecrated in 1430. The more fanciful brick Madonna dell'Orto (p111) was built on 10th-century foundations, but its facade was lightened up with lacy white porphyry ornament in 1460–64. This white stone framing red brick may have Middle Eastern origins: the style is pronounced in Yemen, where Venice's Marco Polo established trade relations in the 13th century.

Secular Gothic

Gothic architecture was so complicated and expensive that it was usually reserved for churches in wealthy parishes – but Venice decided that if it was good enough for God, then it was good enough for the doge. A rare and extravagant secular Gothic construction, the Palazzo Ducale (p55) was built in grand Venetian Gothic style beginning in 1340, with refinements and extensions continuing through the 15th century. The palace was just finished when a fire swept through the building in 1577, leaving Venice with a tricky choice: rebuild in the original *gotico fiorito* (flamboyant Gothic) style, or go with the trendy new Renaissance style proposed by Palladio and his peers. The choice was Gothic, but instead of brick, the facade was a puzzle-work of white Istrian stone and pink Veronese marble, with a delicate, lofty white loggia facing the Grand Canal.

While the doge's palace is a show-stopper, many Venetian nobles weren't living too shabbily themselves by the 14th century. Even stripped of its original gilding, the Ca' d'Oro (p111) is a Grand Canal highlight. The typical Venetian noble family's *palazzo* (palace) had a water gate that gave access from boats to a courtyard or ground floor, with the grand reception hall usually on the *piano nobile* ('noble' or 1st floor). The *piano nobile* was built to impress, with light streaming through double-height loggia windows and balustraded balconies. The 2nd floor might also feature an elegant arcade topped with Venetian Gothic marble arches and trefoils, with crenellation crowning the roofline like a whimsical tiara.

Renaissance

For centuries Gothic cathedrals soared to the skies, pointing the eye and aspirations heavenward – but as the Renaissance ushered in an era of reason and humanism, architecture became more grounded and rational. Venice wasn't immediately sold on this radical new Tuscan world view, but the revival of classical ideals was soon popularised by the University of Padua and Venetian publishing houses.

With the study of classical philosophy came a fresh appreciation for strict classical order, harmonious geometry and human-scale

ARCHITECTURE RENAISSANCE

More than 1000 years of architectural history are covered on the short trip down the Grand Canal, with 200 palaces ranging from Venetian Gothic with Moorish flourishes (Ca' d'Oro) to neoclassical (Palazzo Grassi), baroque (Chiesa di Santa Maria delle Salute), modernist (Stazione di Santa Lucia) and contemporary (Ponte di Calatrava).

proportions. A prime early example in Venice is the 1489 Chiesa di Santa Maria dei Miracoli (p112), a small church and great achievement by sculptor-architect Pietro Lombardo (1435–1515) with his sons Tullio and Antonio. The exterior is clad in veined multicolour marbles apparently 'borrowed' from Basilica di San Marco's slag-heap, kept in check by a steady rhythm of Corinthian pilasters. The stark marble interiors set off a joyous profusion of finely worked sculpture, and the coffered ceiling is filled in with portraits of saints in contemporary Venetian garb. This is ecclesiastical architecture come down to earth, intimate and approachable.

Sansovino's Humanist Architecture

Born in Florence and well versed in classical architecture in Rome, Jacopo Sansovino (1486–1570) was a champion of the Renaissance as Venice's *proto* (official city architect). His best works reveal not just a shift in aesthetics but a sea change in thinking. While the Gothic ideal was a staggeringly tall spire topped by a cross, his Biblioteca Nazionale Marciana (p62) is a role-model Renaissance landmark: a low, flat-roofed monument to learning, embellished with statues of great men. Great men are also the theme of Sansovino's Scala dei Giganti in the Palazzo Ducale (p55), a staircase reserved for Venetian dignitaries and an unmistakable metaphorical reminder that in order to ascend to the heights of power, one must stand on the shoulders of giants.

VENICE'S MOST CONTROVERSIAL BRIDGES

Ponte di Calatrava Officially known as Ponte della Costituzione (Constitution Bridge), Spanish architect Santiago Calatrava's contemporary bridge between Piazzale Roma and Ferrovia was commissioned for €4 million in 1999, and for a decade was variously denounced as unnecessary, inappropriate, wheelchair-inaccessible and torture for anyone with luggage. Though the bridge cost more than triple the original estimate, it also received private backing, hence its local nickname 'Benetton Bridge'.

Ponte di Rialto The original wooden structure (1255) burned during a 1310 revolt, and its replacement collapsed under spectators watching a wedding parade in 1444. The state couldn't gather funds for a 1551 stone bridge project pitched by Palladio, Sansovino and Michelangelo, and the task fell to Antonio da Ponte in 1588. Cost over-runs were enormous: as the stonework settled, the bridge cracked, and legend has it that only a deal with the Devil allowed da Ponte to finish by 1592.

Ponte dei Pugni Turf battles were regularly fought on Dorsoduro's 'Bridge of the Fists' between residents of Venice's north end, the Nicolotti, and its south end, the Castellani. Deadly brawls evolved into full-contact boxing matches, with starting footholds marked in the corners of the bridge. Bouts ended with fighters bloodied, bruised and bobbing in the canal. King Henry III of France apparently enjoyed the spectacle, but escalation into deadly knife fights in 1705 ended the practice.

Ponte delle Tette 'Tits Bridge' got its name in the late 15th century, when neighbourhood prostitutes were encouraged to display their wares in the windows of buildings above the bridge instead of taking their marketing campaigns to the streets. According to contemporary logic, this display was intended to curb a dramatic increase in sodomy.

Ponte dei Sospiri Built by Antonio Contino in 1600 and given its 'Bridge of Sighs' nickname by Lord Byron, the bridge connects the upper storeys of the Palazzo Ducale and Priggione Nove (New Prisons). According to Byron's conceit, doomed prisoners would sigh at their last glimpse of lovely Venice through the bridge's windows – but as you'll notice on Palazzo Ducale visits, the lagoon is scarcely visible through the stonework-screened windows.

Instead of striving for the skies, Renaissance architecture reached for the horizon. Sansovino changed the skyline of Venice with his work on 15 buildings, including the serenely splendid Chiesa di San Francesco della Vigna (p129), completed with a colonnaded facade by Palladio and sculptural flourishes by Pietro and Tullio Lombardo. Thankfully, however, one of Sansovino's most ambitious projects never came to fruition: his plan to turn Piazza San Marco into a Roman forum.

Renaissance Palaces

As the Renaissance swept into Venice, the changes became noticeable along the Grand Canal: pointed Gothic arcades relaxed into rounded archways, repeated geometric forms and serene order replaced Gothic trefoils, and palaces became anchored by bevelled blocks of rough-hewn, rusticated marble. One Renaissance trendsetter was Bergamo-born Mauro Codussi (c 1440–1504), whose pleasing classical vocabulary applied equally to churches, the 15th-century Torre dell'Orologio (Clock Tower) (p59) and several Grand Canal palaces, including Ca' Vendramin Calergi, better known today as Casinò di Venezia (p118).

Michele Sanmicheli (1484–1559) was from Verona but, like Sansovino, he worked in Rome, fleeing its sacking in 1527. The Venetian Republic kept him busy engineering defence works for the city, including Le Vignole's Forte Sant'Andrea, also known as the Castello da Mar (Sea Castle). Even Sanmicheli's private commissions have an imposing imperial Roman grandeur; the Grand Canal's Palazzo Grimani (built 1557–59) incorporates a triumphal arch on the ground floor, and feels more suited to its current use as the city's appeal court than a 16th-century pleasure palace. Sanmicheli is also occasionally credited with the other Renaissance Palazzo Grimani (p127) in Castello, along with Sansovino – but Venetian Renaissance man Giovanni Grimani seems to have mostly designed his own home as a suitably classical showcase for his collection of ancient Roman statuary, now in the Museo Correr (p62).

Palladio

As the baroque began to graft flourishes and curlicues onto basic Renaissance shapes, Padua-born Andrea Palladio (1508–80) carefully stripped them away, and in doing so laid the basis for modern architecture. His facades are an open-book study of classical architecture, with rigorously elemental geometry – a triangular pediment supported by round columns atop a rectangle of stairs – that lends an irresistible logic to the graceful exteriors of San Giorgio Maggiore (p140) and Il Redentore (p141).

Critic John Ruskin detested Renaissance architecture in general and Palladio in particular, and ranted about San Giorgio Maggiore in his three-volume book *The Stones of Venice* (1851–53): 'It is impossible to conceive a design more gross, more barbarous, more childish in conception, more servile in plagiarism, more insipid in result, more contemptible under every point of rational regard.' But don't take his word for it: Palladio's blinding white Istrian-stone facades may seem stoic from afar, but up close they become relatable, with billowing ceilings and an easy grace that anticipated baroque and high modernism.

Palladio's influence eventually spread around the world and Palladian architecture, as it came to be known, became especially popular in the USA, where it can be seen in the Rotunda of the University of Virginia and in the neoclassical proportions of the White House.

Top Palladio Designs

Chiesa di San Giorgio Maggiore (Southern Islands)

Chiesa del Santissimo Redentore (Giudecca)

Facade of Chiesa di San Francesco della Vigna (Castello)

Le Zitelle (Giudecca)

1. Mosaics, Basilica di San Marco **2.** Basilica di Santa Maria della Salute **3.** Palazzo Ducale **4.** Venezuelan Pavilion, Giardini Pubblici

Architectural Marvels

Basilica di San Marco

Only if angels and pirates founded an architecture firm could there ever be another building like **Venice's cathedral** (p52). Saints tip-toe across gold mosaics inside bubble domes, gilded horses pilfered from Constantinople gallop off the loggia, and priceless marbles lining the walls and floors are on exceedingly long-term loan from Syria and Egypt.

Basilica di Santa Maria della Salute

The **sublime white dome** (p78) defies gravity, but thousands of wooden poles underfoot are doing the heavy lifting, creating an ingenious foundation for Baldassare Longhena's white Istrian stone masterpiece, influenced by mystical cabbala designs and rumoured to have curative powers.

Palazzo Ducale

Town halls don't get grander than this **pink palace** (p55). Other medieval cities reserved Gothic graces for cathedrals, but Venice went all out to impress visiting dignitaries and potential business partners with pink Veronese marble and gilt staircases – you'd never guess there were spies and prisoners hidden upstairs.

Biennale Pavilions

International relations never looked better than in Venice's **Giardini Pubblici** (p126), where Biennale pavilions are purpose-built to reflect national architectural identities from Hungary (futuristic folklore hut) to Korea (creative industrial complex). Venetian modernist Carlo Scarpa steals the show with his Venezuelan Pavilion.

Chiesa di Santa Maria dei Miracoli

Pietro Lombardo and sons worked wonders from San Marco's marble slag-heap, creating this small **corner church** (p112), a masterpiece of Renaissance repurposing.

Baroque & Neoclassical

In other parts of Europe, baroque architecture seemed lightweight: an assemblage of frills and thrills, with no underlying Renaissance reason or gravitas. But baroque's buoyant spirits made perfect sense along the Grand Canal, where white-stone party palaces with tiers of ornament looked like floating wedding cakes. Baldassare Longhena (1598–1682) stepped into the role of the city's official architect at a moment when the city was breathing a sigh of relief at surviving the Black Death, providing the architectural antidote to Venice's dark days with the white bubble-dome of Basilica di Santa Maria della Salute (p78). Another Longhena-designed marvel is Ca' Rezzonico (p79), a wonder of sunny salons graced with spectacular Tiepolo ceilings. Soaring grandeur and mystical geometry in the interior of the Ghetto's Schola Spagnola synagogue (p110) have led many to attribute it to Longhena, too.

Neoclassicism & Napoleon

Venice's bridge to the mainland was built by the Austrians at Venetian taxpayers' expense in 1841–46, enabling troop and supply transport by railway. Propped up by 222 arches, the bridge spans 2.7km. Explosives were originally planted under the piers, to be detonated in case of threat.

Venice didn't lose track of Renaissance harmonies completely under all that ornament, and in the 18th century muscular neoclassicism came into vogue. Inspired by Palladio, Giorgio Massari (c 1686–1766) created the Chiesa dei Gesuati as high theatre, setting the stage for Tiepolo's *trompe l'œil* ceilings. He built the gracious Palazzo Grassi (p63) with salons arranged around a balustraded central light well, and brought to completion Longhena's Ca' Rezzonico on the Grand Canal.

Napoleon roared into Venice like a bully in 1797, itching to rearrange its face. The emperor's first order of architectural business was demolishing Sansovino's Chiesa di San Geminiano to construct a monument in his own glory: the Ala Napoleonica (now Museo Correr) by Giovanni Antonio Selva (1753–1819). Napoleon had an entire district with four churches bulldozed to make way for the Giardini Pubblici (p126) and Via Garibaldi in Castello. Though Napoleon ruled Venice for only 11 years, French boulevards appeared where there were once churches across the city. Among others, Sant'Angelo, San Basilio, Santa Croce, Santa Maria Nova, Santa Marina, San Mattio, San Paterniano, San Severo, San Stin, Santa Ternita and San Vito disappeared under the ambitions of the Gallic ruler.

The 20th Century

Wagering which of Venice's brick *campanili* (bell towers) will next fall victim to shifting *barene* (mud banks) is a morbid Venetian pastime – but don't bet on the leaning tower of San Giorgio dei Greci, which has slouched since 1592. San Marco's *campanile* stood ramrod-straight until its 1902 collapse.

After Giudecca's baroque buildings were torn down for factories and the Ferrovia (train station) erected, the city took decades to recover from the shock. Venice reverted to 19th-century *venezianitá,* the tendency to tack on exaggerated Venetian elements from a range of periods – a Gothic trefoil arch here, a baroque cupola there. Rather than harmonising these disparate architectural elements, interiors were swagged in silk damask and moodlit with Murano chandeliers. The resulting hodgepodge seemed to signal the end of Venice's architectural glory days.

From Liberty Flounce to Fascist Sobriety

After nearly a century dominated by French and Austrian influence, Venice let loose on the Lido with the bohemian decadence of *stile Liberty* (Liberty style, or Italian art nouveau). Ironwork vegetation wound around balconies of seaside villas and wild fantasy took root at grand hotels, including Giovanni Sardi's 1898–1908 Byzantine-Moorish Excelsior (p145) and Guido Sullam's garish Ausonia & Hungaria (p145). Eclectic references to Japanese art, organic patterns from nature and past Venetian styles give Lido buildings cosmopolitan flair with *stile Liberty* tiles, stained glass, ironwork and murals.

By the 1930s, the Liberty party was well and truly over. The Fascists arrived to lay down the law on the Lido, applying a strict, functional neoclassicism even to entertainment venues such as the 1937–38 Palazzo del Cinema (p143) and the **former Casinò**. Fascist architecture makes occasional awkward appearances in central Venice too, notably the Bauer hotel (p201) and the extension to the Hotel Danieli (p200), which represent an architectural oxymoron: the strict Fascist luxury-deco hotel.

Scarpa's High Modernism

The Biennale introduced new international architecture to Venice, but high modernism remained mostly an imported style until it was championed by Venice's own Carlo Scarpa (1906–78). Instead of creating seamless modern surfaces, Scarpa frequently exposed underlying structural elements and added unexpectedly poetic twists. At Negozio Olivetti (p62), mosaic and water channels mimic *acqua alta* (high tide) across the floor, a floating staircase makes ascent seem effortless, and internal balconies jut out mid-air like diving boards into the infinite. Scarpa's concrete-slab Venezuelan Pavilion was ahead of its time by a half-century, and inevitably steals the show at Biennales.

Modernist architecture aficionados make pilgrimages outside Venice to see Scarpa's Brioni Tomb near Asolo, and Museo di Castelvecchio (p178) in Verona. Scarpa's smaller works can be spotted all over Venice: the cricket-shaped former ticket booth at the Biennale, the entry and gardens of Palazzo Querini Stampalia, spare restorations within the Gallerie dell'Accademia (p75), the elegant *boiserie* (panelling) inside the Aula Mario Baratto at Ca' Foscari University, as well as the playful main gate at the Tolentini complex of the Università Iuav di Venezia.

Best Modern Design

Biennale pavilions (Castello)

Punta della Dogana (Dorsoduro)

Negozio Olivetti (San Marco)

Fondazione Giorgio Cini (Southern Islands)

Palazzo Grassi (San Marco)

Contemporary Venice

Modernism was not without its critics, especially among Venice's preservationists. But when a disastrous flood hit Venice in 1966, architecture aficionados around the globe put aside their differences, and aided Venetians in bailing out *palazzi* and reinforcing foundations across the city. With the support of Unesco and funding from 24 affiliated organisations worldwide, Venice has completed more than 1500 restoration projects in 40 years.

Today the city is open to a broader range of styles, though controversy is never far behind. Divisive projects that never left the drawing board include a 1953 design for student housing on the Grand Canal by Frank Lloyd Wright, Le Corbusier's 1964 plans for a hospital in Cannaregio, Louis Kahn's 1968 Palazzo dei Congressi project for the Giardini Pubblici, and the 2011 Palais Lumière, a three-finned skyscraper proposed by fashion designer Pierre Cardin and his architect nephew Rodrigo Basilicati. Planned for the industrial, mainland area of Porto Marghera, the 60-storey project ignited widespread opposition in Venice, with many Venetians arguing that its enormous scale and sci-fi design was highly inappropriate in the historic lagoon. Old also triumphed over new in the 2003 reconstruction of La Fenice, which opted for a €90 million replica of the 19th-century opera house instead of an edgier, modernised version proposed by the late architect Gae Aulenti.

Old is the New New

Despite the constraints of history, strict building codes, and the practical challenges of construction with materials transported by boat, lifted by crane and hauled by handcart, a surprising number of projects have turned Venice into a portfolio of contemporary architecture.

MIT-trained Italian architect Cino Zucchi kicked off the creative revival of Giudecca in 1995 with his conversion of 19th-century brick factories and waterfront warehouses into art spaces and studio lofts. A decade later, a triangular WWII bunker and bombs warehouse found new purpose as Teatro Junghans (p239), a hotspot for experimental theatre.

London-based firm David Chipperfield Architects has breathed new life into the cemetery island of San Michele with its sleek contemporary extensions. Among them is the House of the Dead, a bold, basalt-clad burial complex consisting of four open courtyards. The most striking of these is the Courtyard of the Four Evangelists. Featuring a black concrete colonnade, the courtyard's walls and pavement are inlaid with text from the gospels. The next stage of the project will see a new island flanking the existing one. Separated by a canal, this supporting island is set to include gardens at water level and a series of elegant, sculpted mausoleums.

Meanwhile, rebirth of the artistic kind underscores Fondazione Giorgio Cini's redevelopment of the monastery (p142) on Isola di San Giorgio Maggiore, one that has transformed the island into a global cultural centre. Among its numerous features is a garden maze dedicated to Argentine writer Jorge Luis Borges behind the original cloisters, as well as a dormitory turned humanities library to complement Baldassare Longhena's original 17th-century science library. Across the Canale di San Marco, the continuing evolution of Venice's historic Arsenale (p123) shipyards has seen its medieval assembly-line sheds turned into fetching Biennale art galleries.

French billionaire art collector François Pinault hired Japanese minimalist architect Tadao Andō to repurpose two historic buildings into settings for his contemporary-art collection. Instead of undermining their originality, Andō's careful repurposing showcases the muscular strength of Giorgio Masari's 1749 neoclassical Palazzo Grassi (p63) in San Marco and Venice's late 17th-century Punta della Dogana (p80) customs houses in Dorsoduro. Around the corner from Punta della Dogana, Pritzker Prize–winning architect Renzo Piano reinvented the Magazzini del Sale as a showcase for the Fondazione Vedova (p81), an art foundation dedicated to abstract Venetian painter Emilio Vedova. Similar to Andō's approach, Renzo's conversion embraces the building's original essence, with historic roof trusses and brick walls integral elements of the modern makeover. Within this clear, uncluttered historical template, Piano added his respectful modern touches. The most unique of these is a conveyor system of 10 robotic arms, designed to rotate the gallery's artworks like a team of cyborg curators. Renzo's transformation is only fitting: Venice's salt monopoly was once its dearest treasure, but now its ideas are its greatest asset.

Culture and commerce coexist in Dutch architect Rem Koolhaas' redevelopment of the Fondaco dei Tedeschi (p72) (completed in 2016), steps away from the Rialto Bridge in San Marco. Once a base for German merchants, the revamped 16th-century *palazzo* now houses a department store with a publicly accessible rooftop, as well as dedicated public and cultural spaces. The highly publicised incorporation of noncommercial spaces into the project aimed to appease its opponents, who argued that the historical building's retail conversion undermined Venice's heritage.

The Arts

By the 13th century, Venice had already accomplished the impossible: building a glorious maritime empire on a shallow lagoon. But its dominance didn't last. Plague repeatedly decimated the city in the 14th century, new trade routes to the New World bypassed Venice and its tax collectors, and the Ottoman Empire dominated the Adriatic by the mid-15th century. Yet when Venice could no longer prevail by wealth or force, it triumphed on even loftier levels, with art, music, theatre and poetry.

Visual Arts

The sheer number of masterpieces packed into Venice might make you wonder if there's something in the water here, but the reason may be simpler: historically, Venice tended not to starve its artists. Multiyear commissions from wealthy private patrons, the city and the Church offered creatives a sense of security. Artists were granted extraordinary opportunities to produce new artwork without interference, with the city frequently declining to enforce the Inquisition's censorship edicts. Instead of dying young, destitute and out of favour, painters such as Titian and Giovanni Bellini survived into their 80s to produce late, great works. The side-by-side innovations of emerging and mature artists created schools of painting so distinct they still set Venice apart from the rest of Italy – and the world.

Early Venetian Painting

Once you've seen the mosaics at Basilica di San Marco (p52) and Basilica di Santa Maria Assunta (p150) in Torcello, you'll recognise key aspects of early Venetian painting: larger-than-life religious figures with wide eyes and serene expressions floating on gold backgrounds and hovering inches above Gothic thrones. Byzantine influence is clearly present in *Madonna and Child with Two Votaries,* painted c 1325 by Paolo Veneziano (c 1300–65) and on display at the Gallerie dell'Accademia (p75): like stage hands parting theatre curtains, two angels pull back the edges of a starry red cloak to reveal a regal Madonna, golden baby Jesus, and two tiny patrons.

By the early 15th century, Venetian painters were breaking with Byzantine convention. *Madonna with Child* (c 1455) by Jacopo Bellini (c 1400–70) in the Accademia is an image any modern parent might relate to: bright-eyed baby Jesus reaches one sandalled foot over the edge of the balcony, while a seemingly sleep-deprived Mary patiently pulls him away from the ledge. Padua's Andrea Mantegna (1431–1506) took Renaissance perspective to extremes, showing bystanders in his biblical scenes reacting to unfolding miracles and martyrdoms with shock, awe, anger and, even, inappropriate laughter.

Tuscan painter Gentile da Fabriano was in Venice as he was beginning his transition to Renaissance realism, and apparently influenced the young Murano-born painter Antonio Vivarini (c 1415–80), whose *Passion* polyptych in Ca' d'Oro (p111) shows tremendous pathos. Antonio's brother, Bartolomeo Vivarini (c 1432–99), created a delightful altarpiece

Winged lions carved onto Venetian facades symbolise St Mark, Venice's patron, but some served sinister functions. In the 1500s, the Consiglio dei Dieci established *bocca dei leoni* (lion's mouths) – stone lions' heads with slots for inserting anonymous denunciations of neighbours for crimes ranging from cursing to conspiracy.

Venetian Paintings that Changed Painting

....

Feast in the House of Levi (Veronese; Gallerie dell'Accademia)

....

Assunta (Titian; I Frari)

....

La tempesta (Giorgione; Gallerie dell'Accademia)

Madonna with Child Between Saints Catherine and Mary Magdalene (Giovanni Bellini; Gallerie dell'Accademia)

in I Frari (p94) showing a baby Jesus wriggling out of the arms of the Madonna, squarely seated on her marble Renaissance throne.

Venice's Red-Hot Renaissance

Jacopo Bellini's sons used a new medium that would revolutionise Venetian painting: oil paints. The 1500 *Miracle of the Cross at the Bridge of San Lorenzo* by Gentile Bellini (1429–1507) at the Accademia shows monks scrambling to retrieve a reliquary that had fallen into a canal during a procession, with crowds of bystanders stopped in their tracks in astonishment. Giovanni Bellini (c 1430–1516) takes an entirely different approach to his Accademia *Annunciation,* using luminous reds and oranges to focus attention on the solitary figure of the kneeling Madonna awed by an angel arriving in a swish of rumpled drapery.

From Venice's guild of painters emerged some of art history's greatest names, starting with Giovanni Bellini's apt pupils: Giorgione (1477–1510) and Titian (c 1488–1576). The two worked together on the frescoes that once covered the Fondaco dei Tedeschi (only a few fragments remain in the Palazzo Grimani), with teenage Titian following Giorgione's lead. Giorgione was a Renaissance man who wrote poetry and music, is credited with inventing the easel, and preferred to paint from inspiration without sketching out his subject first, as in his enigmatic, Leonardo da Vinci-style 1508 *La tempesta* (The Storm) at the Gallerie dell'Accademia.

When Giorgione died at 33, probably of the plague, Titian finished some of his works – but young Titian soon set himself apart with brushstrokes that brought his subjects to life, while taking on a life of their own. At Basilica di Santa Maria della Salute (p78), you'll notice Titian started out a measured, methodical painter in his 1510 *Saint Mark Ethroned with Saints.* After seeing Michelangelo's expressive *Last Judgment,* Titian let it rip: in his final 1576 *Pietà* he smeared paint onto canvas with his bare hands.

But even for a man of many masterpieces, Titian's 1518 altarpiece *Assunta* (The Assumption of the Virgin) at I Frari is nothing short of enigmatic, mysteriously lighting up the cavernous space with solar-like energy. Vittore Carpaccio (c 1460–1526) rivalled Titian's reds with his own sanguine hues – hence the dish of bloody beef cheekily named in his honour by Harry's Bar – but it was Titian's *Assunta* that cemented Venice's reputation for glowing, glorious hues.

Not Minding Their Manners: Venice's Mannerists

Although art history tends to insist on a division of labour between Venice and Florence – Venice had the colour, Florence the ideas – the Venetian School had plenty of ideas that repeatedly got it into trouble. Titian was a hard act to follow, but there's no denying the impact of Venice's Jacopo Robusti, aka Tintoretto (1518–94), and Paolo Cagliari from Verona, known as Paolo Veronese (1528–88).

A crash course in Tintoretto begins at Chiesa della Madonna dell'Orto (p111), his parish church and the serene brick backdrop for his action-packed 1546 *Last Judgment.* True-blue Venetian that he is, Tintoretto shows the final purge as a teal tidal wave, which lost souls are vainly trying to hold back. A dive-bombing angel swoops in to save one last person – a riveting image Tintoretto reprised on the upper floor of the Scuola Grande di San Rocco (p92). The artist spent some 15 years creating works for San Rocco, and his biblical scenes read like a graphic novel. Tintoretto sometimes used special effects to get his point across, enhancing his colours with a widely available local material: finely crushed glass.

TOP FIVE ARTISTS IN RESIDENCE

Albrecht Dürer (1471–1528) Dürer left his native Nuremberg for Venice in 1494, hoping to see the Venetian experiments in perspective and colour that were the talk of Europe. Giovanni Bellini took him under his wing, and once Dürer returned to Germany in 1495, he began his evolution from Gothic painter into Renaissance artist. When Dürer returned to Venice in 1505, he was feted as a visionary.

JMW Turner (1775–1851) Turner was drawn to Venice three times (in 1819, 1833 and 1840), fascinated by the former merchant empire that, like his native England, had once commanded the sea. His hazy portraits of the city are studies in light at different times of day; as he explained to art critic John Ruskin, 'atmosphere is my style'. Ruskin applauded the effort, but in London many critics loathed Turner's work.

James McNeill Whistler (1834–1903) The American painter arrived in Venice in 1879, bankrupt and exhausted after a failed libel case brought against John Ruskin. He rediscovered his verve and brush in prolific paintings of the lagoon city, returning to London in 1880 with a formidable portfolio that re-established his reputation.

John Singer Sargent (1856–1925) A lifelong admirer of Venice, the American visited at a young age and became a part-time resident from 1880 to 1913. His intimate knowledge of the city shows in his paintings, which capture new angles on familiar panoramas and illuminate neglected monuments.

Claude Monet (1840–1926) The French artist turned up in Venice in 1908, and immediately found impressionist inspiration in architecture that seemed to dissolve into lagoon mists and shimmering waters. Despite claiming that the city was too beautiful to paint, he set brush to 37 canvases during his short sojourn.

Veronese's colours have a luminosity entirely their own, earning him Palazzo Ducale (p55) commissions and room to run riot inside Chiesa di San Sebastiano (p79) – but his choice of subjects got him into trouble. When Veronese was commissioned to paint the last supper his masterpiece ended up looking suspiciously like a Venetian shindig, with apostles in Venetian dress mingling freely with Turkish merchants, Jewish guests, serving wenches, begging lapdogs and (most shocking of all) Protestant Germans. When the Inquisition demanded he change the painting, Veronese refused to remove the offending Germans and altered scarcely a stroke of paint, simply changing the title to *Feast in the House of Levi* (now hanging in the Gallerie dell'Accademia). In a victory for freedom of expression, Venice stood by the decision.

The next generation of Mannerists included Palma il Giovane (1544–1628), who finished Titian's *Pietá* after the master's death and fused Titian's early naturalism with Tintoretto's drama. Another Titian acolyte who adopted Tintoretto's dramatic lighting was Jacopo da Ponte from Bassano del Grappa, called Jacopo Bassano (1517–92). Bassano's work is so high in contrast and drama, at first glance you might wonder how black-velvet paintings wound up in the Gallerie dell'Accademia, Chiesa di San Giorgio Maggiore (p140) and Bassano del Grappa's Museo Civico.

Going for Baroque

By the 18th century, Venice had endured plague and seen its ambitions for world domination dashed – but the city repeatedly made light of its dire situation in tragicomic art. Pietro Longhi (1701–85) dispensed with lofty subject matter and painted wickedly witty Venetian social satires, while Giambattista Tiepolo (1696–1770) turned classical themes into a premise for dizzying ceilings with rococo sunbursts. Ca' Rezzonico (p79) is a showpiece for both their talents, with an entire salon of

Turbaned figures appear across Venice on the corners of Campo dei Mori, on diamond-encrusted jewels at Sigfrido Cipolato, and propping up I Frari funerary monuments. Misleadingly referred to as Mori (Moors), some represent Venetians from Greek Morea, others Turkish pirates, and others enslaved Africans who rowed merchant ships.

Longhi's drawing-room scenarios and Tiepolo's *trompe l'œil* ceiling masterpieces.

Instead of popes on thrones, portraitist Rosalba Carriera (1675–1757) captured her socialite sitters on snuffboxes, and painted in a medium she pioneered: pastels. Her portraits at Ca' Rezzonico walk a fine line between Tiepolo's flattery and Longhi's satire, revealing her sitters' every twinkle and wrinkle.

As the 18th-century party wound down, the Mannerists' brooding theatricality merged with Tiepolo's pastel beauty in works by Tiepolo's son, Giandomenico Tiepolo (1727–1804). His 1747–49 *Way of the Cross* in Chiesa di San Polo (p96) takes a dim view of humanity in light colours, illuminating the jeering faces of Jesus' tormentors. Giandomenico used a lighter touch working alongside his father on the frescoes at Villa Valmarana 'ai Nani' (p170) outside Vicenza, covering the walls with Chinese motifs, rural scenes and Carnevale characters.

The Vedutisti

Many Venetian artists turned their attention from the heavens to the local landscape in the 18th century, notably Giovanni Antonio Canal, aka Canaletto (1697–1768). He became the leading figure of the *vedutisti* (landscape artists) with minutely detailed *vedute* (views) of Venice that leave admiring viewers of his work with vicarious hand cramps. You might be struck by how closely his works resemble photographs – and, in fact, Canaletto created them with the aid of a forerunner to the photographic camera, the camera obscura. Light entered this instrument and reflected the image onto a sheet of glass, which Canaletto then traced. After he had the outlines down, he filled in exact details, from lagoon algae to hats on passers-by.

Vedute sold well to Venice visitors. Canaletto was backed by the English collector John Smith, who introduced the artist to such a vast English clientele that only a few of his paintings can be seen in the Veneto today, in Venice's Gallerie dell'Accademia and Ca' Rezzonico, and further afield in Vicenza's Palazzo Leoni Montanari (p169). Canaletto's nephew Bernardo Bellotto (1721–80) also adopted the camera obscura in his painting process, though his expressionistic landscapes use strong *chiaroscuro* (shadow and light contrasts). His paintings hang in the Accademia alongside works by Francesco Guardi (1712–93), whose impressionistic approach shows Venice's glories reflected in the lagoon. Among the last great *vedutisti* was Venetian impressionist Emma Ciardi (1879–1933), who captured Venetian mysteries unfolding amid shimmering early-morning mists in luminous landscapes at Ca' Rezzonico and Ca' Pesaro (p97).

Lucky Stiffs: Venetian Funerary Sculpture

Bookending Venice's accomplishments in painting are its sculpted marvels. The city kept its sculptors busy, with 200 churches needing altars and the fire-prone Palazzo Ducale requiring near-constant rebuilding for 300 years, not to mention the almost-endless chiselling of tombs for nobles with political careers cut short by age, plague and intrigue. The tomb of Doge Marco Corner in Zanipolo (p125) by Pisa's Nino Pisano (c 1310–68) is a sprawling wall monument with a massive, snoozing doge that somewhat exaggerated his career: Corner was doge for less than three years.

Venice's Pietro Lombardo (1435–1515) and his sons Tullio (1460–1532) and Antonio (c 1458–1516) sculpted heroic monuments to short-reigning doges: Nicolò Marcello (1473–74), Pietro Mocenigo (1474–76) and Andrea Vendramin (1476–78). This last gilded marble monument was

---

Top Venice Views Indoors

Miracle of the Relic of the True Cross on the Rialto Bridge (c 1494, Vittore Carpaccio; Gallerie dell'Accademia)

....

Procession on the Piazza San Marco (c 1496, Gentile Bellini; Gallerie dell'Accademia)

....

View of the Grand Canal from Ca' Balbi towards Rialto (1723–24, Canaletto; Ca' Rezzonico)

....

Piazza San Marco, Mass after the Victory (1918, Emma Ciardi; Museo Correr)

....

San Marco Basin with San Giorgio and Giudecca (1770–74, Francesco Guardi; Gallerie dell'Accademia)

probably completed under Tullio, who literally cut corners: he sculpted the figures in half relief, and chopped away part of Pisano's Corner tomb to make room for Vendramin. Tullio's strong suit was the ideal beauty of his faces.

The most prominent sculptor to emerge from the Veneto is Antonio Canova (1757–1822), whose pyramid tomb intended for Titian at I Frari would become his own funerary masterpiece. Mourners hang their heads and clutch one another, scarcely aware that their diaphanous garments are slipping off; even the great winged lion of St Mark is curled up in grief. Don't let his glistening Orpheus and Eurydice in Museo Correr (p62) fool you: Canova's seamless perfection in glistening marble was achieved through rough drafts modelled in gypsum, displayed at the Museo Canova (p174) near the hilltop town of Asolo.

Not Strictly Academic: Venetian Modernism

The arrival of Napoleon in 1797 was a disaster for Venice and its art. During his Kingdom of Italy (1805–14), churches were knocked down and artistic treasures were systematically plundered. Some works have been restored to Venice, including the bronze horses of Basilica di San Marco that arguably belong in İstanbul, given that Venice pilfered them from Constantinople. Yet even under 19th-century occupation, Venice remained a highlight of the Grand Tour, and painters who flocked to the city created memorable Venice cityscapes.

After joining the newly unified Italy in 1866, Venice's signature artistic contribution to the new nation was Francesco Hayez (1791–1882). The Venetian painter paid his dues with society portraits but is best remembered for Romanticism and frank sexuality, beginning with *Rinaldo and Armida* (1814), in the Gallerie dell'Accademia.

Never shy about self-promotion, Venice held its first Biennale in 1895 to reassert its role as global tastemaker and provide an essential corrective to the brutality of the Industrial Revolution. A garden pavilion showcased a self-promoting, studiously inoffensive take on Italian art – principally lovely ladies, pretty flowers, and lovely ladies wearing pretty flowers. Other nations were granted pavilions in 1907, but the Biennale retained strict control, and had a Picasso removed from the Spanish Pavilion in 1910 so as not to shock the public with modernity.

A backlash to Venetian conservatism arose from the ranks of painters experimenting in modern styles. Shows of young artists backed by the Duchess Felicita Bevilacqua La Masa found a permanent home in 1902, when the Duchess gifted Ca' Pesaro to the city as a modern-art museum. A leader of the Ca' Pesaro crowd was Gino Rossi (1884–1947), whose brilliant blues and potent symbolism bring to mind Gauguin, Matisse and the Fauvists, and whose later work shifted toward Cubism. Often called the Venetian van Gogh, Rossi spent many years in psychiatric institutions, where he died. Sculptor Arturo Martini (1889–1947) contributed works to Ca' Pesaro ranging from the rough-edged terracotta *Prostitute* (c 1913) to his radically streamlined 1919 gesso bust.

Future Perfect: From Futurism to Fluidity

In 1910, Filippo Tommaso Marinetti (1876–1944) threw packets of his manifesto from the Torre dell'Orologio promoting a new vision for the arts: futurism. In the days of the doge, Marinetti would have been accused of heresy for his declaration that Venice (a 'magnificent sore of the past') should be wiped out and replaced with a new industrial city. The futurists embraced industry and technology with their machine-inspired, streamlined look – a style that Mussolini co-opted in the 1930s for his vision of a monolithic, modern Italy. Futurism was conflated

Top for Modernism

Peggy Guggenheim Collection (Dorsoduro)

Ca' Pesaro (Santa Croce)

Fondazione Giorgio Cini (Isola di San Giorgio Maggiore)

Museo Fortuny (San Marco)

Top for Contemporary Art

La Biennale di Venezia (Castello)

Ca' Pesaro (Santa Croce)

Punta della Dogana (Dorsoduro)

Palazzo Grassi (San Marco)

Galleria Michela Rizzo (Giudecca)

with Mussolini's brutal imposition of artificial order until championed in Venice by a heroine of the avant-garde and refugee from the Nazis: American expat art collector Peggy Guggenheim, who recognised in futurism the fluidity and flux of modern life.

Artistic dissidents also opposed Mussolini's square-jawed aesthetics. Emilio Vedova (1919–2006) joined the Corrente movement of artists, which openly opposed Fascist trends in a magazine that the Fascists then shut down in 1940. After WWII, Vedova veered towards abstraction, and his larger works are now in regular robot-assisted rotation at the Magazzini del Sale (p81). Giovanni Pontini (1915–70) was a worker who painted as a hobby until 1947, when he discovered Kokoschka, van Gogh and Rouault, who inspired his empathetic paintings of fishermen, at the Peggy Guggenheim Collection (p77).

Venetian Giuseppe Santomaso (1907–90) painted his way out of constrictive Fascism with unbounded abstract landscapes. Rigidity and liquidity became the twin fascinations of Bologna-born and Venice-trained video artist Fabrizio Plessi (b 1940). His 1970s Arte povera (Poor Art) experiments in humble materials, while his multimedia installations feature Venice's essential medium: water.

Contemporary Art's Beating Heart

Although the attention-stealing Biennale has once again positioned Venice at the forefront of world art, local artists tend to be swamped by the international superstars. Venice's art schools, however, are flourishing and a selection of small, independent galleries continue to showcase local talent.

The island of Giudecca is the hub of a lively scene, which was recognised in 2019 when it was declared an 'art district'. Key venues include Giudecca 795 (p141), Galleria Michela Rizzo (p142) and **Spazio Punch** (Map p291; www.spaziopunch.com; Fondamenta San Bagio 800o, Giudecca; ◷hr vary; ⍾Palanca), the latter run by collage- and video-artist Lucia Veronesi. Other names to look out for include Mariateresa Sartori, Thomas Braida, Maria Morganti and Bulgarian-born Stefan Popdimitrov, who produces interesting multimedia works from his Castello studio-gallery.

Music

In its trade-empire heyday, La Serenissima had official musicians, including the distinguished directorship of Flemish composer Adrian Willaert (c 1490–1562) for 35 years at Capella Ducale. But when the city fell on hard times in the 17th to 18th centuries, it truly discovered its musical calling.

With shrinking trade revenues, the state took the quixotic step of underwriting musical education for orphan girls, and the investment yielded unfathomable returns. Among the *maestri* hired to conduct orphan orchestras was Antonio Vivaldi (1678–1741), whose 30-year tenure produced hundreds of concertos and popularised Venetian baroque music across Europe. Visitors spread word of extraordinary performances by orphan girls, and the city became a magnet for novelty-seeking moneyed socialites.

Modern visitors to Venice can still experience music performed, often on original 18th-century instruments, in the same venues as in Vivaldi's day – *palazzi* (mansions), churches, *scuole grandi* (confraternity houses) and *ospedaletti* (orphanages) such as La Pietà (p130), where Vivaldi worked.

Classical

Get ready to baroque-and-roll: Venetian classical musicians are leading a revival of 'early music' from medieval through to the Renaissance and baroque periods, with historically accurate arrangements played *con brio* (with verve) on period instruments. Venetian baroque was the rebel music of its day, openly defying edicts from Rome about which instruments could accompany sermons and what kinds of rhythms and melodies were suitable for moral edification. Venetians kept right on playing stringed instruments in churches, singing along to bawdy *opera buffa* and writing compositions that were both soulful and sensual.

Modern misconceptions about baroque being a polite soundtrack to wedding ceremonies are smashed by baroque 'early music' ensembles. Among Vivaldi's repertoire of some 500 concertos is his ever-popular *The Four Seasons,* instantly recognisable from hotel lobbies and ringtones – but all of those elemental flashes of brilliance seem sharper in the city of its birth.

Venetian venues make all the difference. The pleasure palace of Palazetto Bru Zane (p104) is now restored to its original function: concerts to flirt and swoon over, with winking approval from Sebastiano Ricci's frolicking, frescoed angels. Seek out programs featuring Venetian baroque composer Tomaso Albinoni (1671–1750/51), especially the exquisite *Sinfonie e concerti a 5.* For a more avant-garde take on classical music, look for works by Bruno Maderna (1920–73) or Luigi Nono (1924–90).

Opera

Today's televised talent searches can't compare to Venice's knack for discovering talents like Claudio Monteverdi (1567–1643), who was named the musical director of the Basilica di San Marco and went on to launch modern opera. Today, opera reverberates inside La Fenice (p63) and across town in concert halls and *palazzi* – but until 1637 you would have needed an invitation to hear it. Opera and most chamber music were the preserve of the nobility, performed in private salons. Then, in the 17th century, Venice threw open the doors of the first public opera houses. Between 1637 and 1700, some 358 operas were staged in 16 theatres to meet the musical demands of a population of 140,000.

Monteverdi wrote two standout operas, *Il ritorno di Ulisse in patria* (The Return of Ulysses) and *L'incoronazione di Poppea* (The Coronation of Poppaea), with an astonishing range of plot and subplot, strong characterisation and powerful music. Critical response couldn't have been better: he was buried with honours in I Frari. A singer at the Basilica di San Marco under Monteverdi, Francesco Cavalli (1602–76) became the outstanding 17th-century Italian opera composer, writing 42 operas. Baldassare Galuppi (1706–85) added musical hooks to *opera buffa* (comic opera) favourites like *Il filosofo di campagna* (The Country Philosopher), often working alongside with librettist Carlo Goldoni.

Literature

In a surprising 15th-century plot twist, shipping magnate Venice became a publishing empire. Johannes Gutenberg cranked out his first Bible with a movable-type press in 1455, and Venice became an early adopter of this cutting-edge technology, turning out the earliest printed Quran. Venetian printing presses were in operation by the 1470s, with lawyers settling copyright claims soon thereafter. Venetian publishers printed not just religious texts but histories, poetry, textbooks, plays, musical scores and manifestos.

THE ARTS LITERATURE

It's not all Vivaldi in Venice. The Venice Jazz Club features tribute nights year-round, and during July's Venice Jazz Festival, you may luck into a performance by Venetian saxophonist and composer Giannantonio De Vincenzo or Venetian trumpeter musicologist Massimo Donà.

Early Renaissance author Pietro Bembo (1470–1547) was a librarian, historian, diplomat and poet who expounded on the subject of platonic love and solidified Italian grammar in his *Rime* (Poems, 1530). Bembo collaborated with Aldo Manuzio on an invention that revolutionised reading and democratised learning: the Aldine Press, which introduced italics and paperbacks, including Dante's *La divina commedia* (The Divine Comedy). By 1500, nearly one in six books published in Europe was printed in Venice.

Poetry

Shakespeare has competition for technical prowess from the Veneto's Petrarch (aka Francesco Petrarca; 1304–74), who added wow to Italian woo with his eponymous sonnets. Writing in Italian and Latin, Petrarch applied a strict structure of rhythm (14 lines, with two quatrains to describe a desire and a sestet to attain it) and rhyme (no more than five rhymes per sonnet) to romance the idealised Laura. He might have tried chocolates instead: Laura never returned the sentiment.

Posthumously, Petrarch became idolised by Rilke, Byron, Mozart and Venice's *cortigiane oneste* (well-educated 'honest courtesans'). Tullia d'Aragona (1510–56) wrote sharp-witted Petrarchan sonnets that conquered men: noblemen divulged state secrets, kings risked their thrones to beg her hand in marriage, and much ink was spilled in panegyric praise of her hooked nose.

Written with wit and recited with passion, poetry might get you a free date with a high-end courtesan, killed, or elected in Venice. Leonardo Giustiniani (1388–1446) was a member of the Consiglio dei Dieci (Council of Ten) who spent time off from spying on his neighbours writing poetry in elegant Venetian-inflected Italian, including *Canzonette* (Songs) and *Strambotti* (Ditties). Giorgio Baffo (1694–1768) was a friend of Casanova's whose risqué odes to the posterior might have affected his political career elsewhere – but in Venice, he became a state senator. To experience his bawdy poetry, head to **Taverna da Baffo** (Map p278; ☑041 524 20 61; www.tavernadabaffo.com; Campiello Sant'Agostin 2346; ☺noon-11pm; ☎; ⛴San Tomà), where his ribald rhymes may be chanted by night's end.

One of Italy's greatest poets, Ugo Foscolo (1778–1827) studied in Padua and arrived in Venice as a teenager amid political upheavals. Young Foscolo threw in his literary lot with Napoleon in a 1797 ode to the general, hoping he would revive the Venetian Republic, and even joined the French army. But Napoleon considered Foscolo a dangerous mind, and the poet ended his days in exile in London.

Memoirs

Life on the lagoon has always been stranger than fiction, and Venetian memoirists were early bestsellers. Venice-born Marco Polo (c 1254–1324) captured his adventures across central Asia and China in memoirs entitled *Il milione* (Travels of Marco Polo; c 1299), as told to Rustichello da Pisa. The book achieved bestseller status even before the invention of the printing press, each volume copied by hand. Some details were apparently embellished along the way, but his tales of Kublai Khan's court remain riveting. In a more recent traveller's account, *Venezia, La città ritrovata* (Venice Revealed: An Intimate Portrait; 1998), Paolo Barbaro (1922–2014) captures his reverse culture shock upon returning to the lagoon city.

Memoirs with sex and scandal sold well in Venice. 'Honest courtesan' Veronica Franco (1546–91) kissed and told in her bestselling memoir, but for sheer *braggadocio* (boasting) it's hard to top the memoirs of Casanova (1725–98). Francesco Gritti (1740–1811) parodied the decadent Venetian aristocracy in vicious, delicious *Poesie in dialetto Veneziano*

Eighteenth-century Venetian *grande dame* Isabella Teotochi Albrizzi was practically wedded to her literary salon: when her husband received a post abroad, she got her marriage annulled to remain in Venice, and continue her discussions of poetry with the patronage of a new husband, her *cicisbeo* (manservant-lover) in devoted attendance.

In trying to describe the *Inferno* to contemporary readers c 1307, Dante compared it to Venice's Arsenale, with its stinking vats of tar, sparks flying from hammers and infernal clamour of 16,000 labourers working nonstop on its legendary ship-assembly lines.

VENICE'S BESTSELLING WOMEN WRITERS

At a time when women were scarcely in print elsewhere in Europe, Venetian women became prolific and bestselling authors in subjects ranging from mathematics to politics. Works from over 100 Venetian women authors from the 15th to 18th centuries remain in circulation today. Among the luminaries of their era:

Philosopher Isotta Nogarola (1418–66) The Verona-born teen prodigy corresponded with Renaissance philosophers and was widely published in Rome and Venice. An anonymous critic published attacks against her in 1439, claiming 'an eloquent woman is never chaste' and accusing her of incest. But she continued her correspondence with leading humanists and, with Venetian diplomat Ludovico Foscarini, published an influential early feminist tract: a 1453 dialogue asserting that since Eve and Adam were jointly responsible for expulsion from Paradise, women and men must be equals.

Musician and poet Gaspara Stampa (1523–54) A true Renaissance intellectual, Stampa was a renowned lute player, literary-salon organiser, and author of published Petrarchan sonnets openly dedicated to her many lovers. Historians debate her livelihood before she became a successful author; some claim she was a courtesan.

Writer Sara Copia Sullam (1592–1641) A leading Jewish intellectual of Venice's Accademia degli Incogniti literary salon, Sullam was admired for her poetry and spirited correspondence with a monk from Modena. A critic accused her of denying the immortality of the soul, a heresy punishable by death under the Inquisition. Sullam responded with a treatise on immortality written in two days; her manifesto became a bestseller. Sullam's writings remain in publication as key works of early modern Italian literature.

Dr Elena Lucrezia Cornaro Piscopia (1646–84) Another prodigy, Dr Piscopia became the first female university doctoral graduate in Europe in 1678 at the University of Padua, where a statue of her now stands. Her prolific contributions to the intellectual life of Venice are commemorated with a plaque outside Venice's city hall.

(Poetry in the Venetian Dialect) and satirised the Venetian fashion for memoirs with his exaggerated 'My Story: The Memoirs of Signor Tommasino Written by Him, a Narcotic Work by Dr Pifpuf'. Modern scandal, corruption and a cast of eccentric Venetians drive *The City of Falling Angels* by John Berendt (b 1939), an engrossing account of life in Venice following the fire that gutted La Fenice in 1996.

Modern Fiction

Venetian authors have remained at the forefront of modern Italian fiction. The enduring quality of Camillo Boito's 1883 short story 'Senso' (Sense), a twisted tale of love and betrayal in Austrian-occupied Venice, made it a prime subject for director Luchino Visconti in 1954. Mysterious Venice proved the ideal setting for Venice's resident expat American mystery novelist Donna Leon (b 1942), whose inspector Guido Brunetti uncovers the shadowy subcultures of Venice, from island fishing communities *(A Sea of Troubles)* to environmental protesters *(Through a Glass Darkly)*. But the pride of Venice's literary scene is Tiziano Scarpa (b 1963), who earned the 2009 Strega Prize, Italy's top literary honour, for *Stabat Mater,* the story of an orphaned Venetian girl learning to play violin under Antonio Vivaldi.

Venice's first movie role dates from the earliest days of cinema, as the subject of the 1897 short film *Panoramic View of Venice.* However, as Venice was complicated and expensive for location shooting, classics set in Venice, such as the Astaire-Rogers vehicle *Top Hat,* were shot in Hollywood backlots.

Film

Back in the 1980s, a Venice film archive found that the city had appeared in one form or another in 380,000 films – feature films, shorts, documentaries, and other works archived and screened at the city's

Always ready for action, Venice made appearances in *From Russia with Love* (1963), *Moonraker* (1979), *Indiana Jones and the Last Crusade* (1989), The *League of Extraordinary Gentlemen* (2003) and *Casino Royale* (2006), whose Grand Canal finale was shot in Venice with some help from CGI.

Casa del Cinema (p104). But Venice's photogenic looks have proved a mixed blessing. This city is too distinctive to fade into the background, so the city tends to upstage even the most photogenic co-stars (which only partly excuses 2010's *The Tourist*).

Since Casanova's escapades and a couple of Shakespearean dramas unfolded in Venice, the lagoon city was a natural choice of location for movie versions of these tales. In the Casanova category, two excellent accounts are Alexandre Volkoff's 1927 *Casanova* and *Fellini's Casanova* (1976), starring Donald Sutherland. Oliver Parker directed a 1995 version of *Othello*, but the definitive version remains Orson Welles' 1952 *Othello*, shot partly on location in Venice, but mostly in Morocco. Later adaptations of silver-screen classics haven't lived up to the original, including Michael Radford's 1994 *The Merchant of Venice* starring Al Pacino as Shylock, and Swedish director Lasse Hallström's 2005 *Casanova*, with a charmingly rakish Heath Ledger in the title role.

After WWII, Hollywood came to Venice in search of romance, and the city delivered as the backdrop for Katharine Hepburn's midlife Italian love affair in *Summertime* (1955). Gorgeous Venice set pieces compensated for some dubious singing in Woody Allen's musical romantic comedy *Everyone Says I Love You* (1996). But the most winsome Venetian romance is Silvio Soldini's *Bread and Tulips* (2000), a tale of an Italian housewife who restarts her life as a woman of mystery in Venice, trying to dodge the detective-novel-reading plumber hot on her trail.

More often than not, romance seems to go horribly wrong in films set in Venice. It turns to obsession in *Death in Venice*, Luchino Visconti's 1971 adaptation of the Thomas Mann novella, and again in *The Comfort of Strangers* (1990), featuring Natasha Richardson and Rupert Everett inexplicably following Christopher Walken into shadowy Venetian alleyways. A better adaptation of a lesser novel, *The Wings of the Dove* (1997) was based on the Henry James novel and mostly shot in the UK, though you can scarcely notice behind Helena Bonham Carter's hair. Venice also features in the 2008 film adaptation of Evelyn Waugh's *Brideshead Revisited,* starring Emma Thompson, Matthew Goode and Ben Whishaw.

Venice has done its best to shock movie-goers over the years, as with Nicolas Roeg's riveting *Don't Look Now* (1973) starring Julie Christie, Donald Sutherland, and Venice at its most ominous and depraved. *Dangerous Beauty* (1998) is raunchier but sillier, a missed opportunity to show 16th-century Venice through the eyes of a courtesan.

To see the latest big film to make a splash in Venice, don't miss the Venice International Film Festival (p21).

Theatre

Venice is an elaborate stage and, whenever you arrive, you're just in time for a show. Sit on any square, and the *commedia dell'arte* (featuring masked archetypes) and *opera buffa* commence, with stock characters improvising variations on familiar themes: graduating university students lurching towards another round of toasts, kids crying over gelato fallen into canals, neighbours hanging out laundry gossiping indiscreetly across the *calle* (lane). Once you've visited Venice, you'll have a whole new appreciation for its theatrical innovations.

Commedia dell'Arte

During Carnevale, *commedia dell'arte* conventions take over, and all of Venice acts out with masks, extravagant costumes and exaggerated gestures. It may seem fantastical today, but for centuries, this was Italy's dominant form of theatre. Scholars attribute some of Molière's running gags and Shakespeare's romantic plots to the influence of *commedia dell'arte* – although Shakespeare would have been shocked to note that in Italy, women's parts were typically played by women. But after a couple of centuries of *commedia dell'arte,* 18th-century Venice began to tire of bawdy slapstick. Sophisticated improvisations had been reduced to farce, robbing the theatre of its subversive zing.

Comedy & Opera Buffa

As the public tired of *commedia dell'arte,* Carlo Goldoni (1707–93), a former doctor's apprentice, occasional lawyer and whipsmart librettist, entered the scene offering some serious tragic opera. But of his 160 plays and 80 or so *libretti,* he remains best loved for *opera buffa,* unmasked social satires that remain ripe and delicious: battles of the sexes, self-important socialites getting their comeuppance, and the impossibility of pleasing one's boss.

Goldoni was light-hearted but by no means a lightweight; his comic genius and deft wordplay would permanently change Italian theatre. His *Pamela* (1750) was the first play to dispense with masks altogether, and his characters didn't fall into good or evil archetypes: everyone was flawed, often hilariously so. Some of his most winsome roles were reserved for women and *castrati* (male soprano countertenors), from his early 1735 adaptation of Apostolo Zeno's *Griselda* (based on Boccaccio's *Decameron,* with a score by Vivaldi) to his celebrated 1763 *Le donne vendicate* (Revenge of the Women). Princess Cecilia Mahony Giustiniani commissioned this latter work, in which two women show a preening chauvinist the error of his ways with light swordplay and lethal wordplay.

But one Venetian dramatist was not amused. Carlo Gozzi (1720–1806) believed that Goldoni's comedies of middle-class manners were prosaic, and staged a searing 1761 parody of Goldoni's work. Goldoni exiled himself to France in disgust, never to return to Venice. Gozzi went on to minor success with his fairy-tale scenarios, one of which would inspire the Puccini opera *Turandot.* But Gozzi's fantasias had little staying power, and eventually he turned to...comedy.

Meanwhile, Goldoni fell on hard times in France, after a pension granted to him by King Louis XVI was revoked by the Revolution. He died impoverished, though at his French colleagues' insistence, the French state granted his pension to his widow.

Theatre & Opera Today

Goldoni got the last laugh: while Gozzi's works are rarely staged, Goldoni regularly gets top billing along with Shakespeare at the city's principal theatre, Teatro Goldoni (p69). Its beautiful jewel-box interior is second only to the opera house, La Fenice, for opulence. The city's other main theatrical venue is La Fenice's offshoot, Teatro Malibran (p118). Avant-garde troupes and experimental theatres such as **Teatro Junghans** (Map p291; ✆041 241 19 74; www.accademiateatraleveneta.com; Campo Junghans 494b, Giudecca; prices vary; ♿; ⛴Redentore) and Laboratorio Occupato Morion (p136) also bring new plays, performance art and choreography to Venetian stages.

The Biennale Teatro (www.labiennale.org/en/theatre) is a showcase for experimental theatre, drawing on Venice's 400-year tradition of risk-taking performance. It's held over two weeks from late July in odd-numbered years.

The Fragile Lagoon

White ibis perch on rock outcroppings, piles of lagoon crab are hauled into the Pescaria (Fish Market), and waters change like mood rings from teal blue to oxidised silver: life on the lagoon is extraordinary, and extraordinarily fragile. When gazing across these waters to the distant Adriatic horizon, the lagoon appears to be an extension of the sea. But with its delicate balance of salty and fresh water, *barene* (mudbanks) and grassy marshes, the lagoon supports a unique aquaculture.

What is the Lagoon?

The lagoon is a 550-sq-km shallow dish, where ocean tides meet freshwater streams from alpine rivers. It's protected by a slender 50km arc of islands, which halt the Adriatic's advances. Between Punta Sabbioni and Chioggia, three *bocche di porto* (port entrances) allow the sea entry into the lagoon. When sirocco winds push ocean waves toward the Venetian gulf, *acque alte* (high tides) ensue. These seasonal tides help clear the lagoon of extra silt and maintain the balance of its waters.

The Venetian lagoon is the second-largest wetland in Europe and the largest in the Mediterranean Basin, and its highly productive ecosystem supports some 200,000 birds and unique lagoon species. Like all lagoons, it is a continually evolving environment, although through careful interventions, it is the only survivor of a system of estuarine lagoons that in Roman times extended from Ravenna to Trieste. In fact, the word *laguna* (lagoon) is Venetian.

Environmental & Human-Induced Challenges

Since the time of the Republic, human intervention has engineered the lagoon's survival against environmental forces. However, maintaining its delicate balance has become fraught with difficulty in the postindustrial era. In the 1920s, Marghera, at the southern end of the lagoon, was developed into an industrial zone centred on chemical plants and oil refineries. With few regulations, these factories released dioxins and heavy metals into the water, radically disturbing the delicate ecosystem. Although strict environmental laws put an end to the practice in the 1980s, the lagoon is still plagued by nonbiodegradable pollutants from this era, which contribute to phytoplankton and macroalgal blooms.

In addition, to facilitate the passage of modern tankers to Marghera, deep channels were dredged in the 1960s, the most damaging being the 12m-deep, 100m-wide Canale dei Petroli. The passage of boats through these channels has resulted in strong transverse currents across the lagoon. The currents flatten the *ghebbi* (capillary canals) and erode the sandbanks that have historically acted to dissipate the force of the tidal influx. In a 2006 report highlighting their destruction, Lidia Fersuoch, president of NGO Italia Nostra Venezia (www.italianostravenezia.org),

Since 1930 an estimated 20% of birdlife has disappeared, 80% of lagoon flora has gone, and lagoon-water transparency has dropped 60%.

THE TIDE IS HIGH

The alarm from 16 sirens throughout the city is a warning that *acqua alta* is expected to reach the city within two to four hours. Consult Venice's Centro Maree 48-hour tidal forecast at www.comune.venezia.it/maree for high-tide warnings between November and April. When alarms sound, it's not an emergency situation but a temporary tide that principally affects low-lying areas.

One even tone (up to 110cm above normal): barely warrants a pause in happy-hour conversation.

Two rising tones (up to 120cm): you might need *stivali di gomma* (rubber boots).

Three rising tones (around 130cm): check Centro Maree to see where *passarelle* (gangplank walkways) are in use.

Four rising tones (140cm and up): shops close early, everyone slides flood barriers across their doorsteps.

---

argued that the lagoon's sandbanks were 'in need of protection as much as the churches and palaces of the city'.

Well drilling by coastal industries in the 1960s and the lowering of the mainland water table has also caused the *caranto* (the layer of clay that forms the base of the lagoon) to subside, while the reduction in the lagoon's salt marshes from 255 sq km in the 17th century to 47 sq km by 2003 has allowed unobstructed wind to whip up large waves that further destabilise the lagoon bed. The effect of all this: a downward-eroding, sediment-exporting system that is slowly turning the lagoon into a marine bay and posing a critical danger to the city.

To add to this complex picture, global climate change is now being felt in the lagoon, with rising temperatures increasing levels of CO_2 in the water, causing acidification and anaerobic episodes – a factor that will be made worse if the lagoon is further isolated from the sea through the use of mobile flood barriers (MoSE). Furthermore, a recent bathymetry study of the lagoon bed by the Italian Institute for Marine Research (Ismar-Cnr) show significant erosion around MoSE's caissons and construction platforms, and accumulating sediment in canals washed in by the tides. So significant is the build-up of sediment in the Canal dei Petroli (7 million cu metres was excavated between 2004 and 2012) that in December 2018, PALAV, the regional authority responsible for the lagoon, approved the reinforcement of the canal's embankments with steel-sheet piling that Italia Nostra argues will cut the lagoon in two, and accelerate the process of subsidence.

Unesco has projected sea-level rises could be anywhere between 26cm and 100cm by the end of the 21st century. Venice itself can only survive a rise of 50cm.

Mobile Flood Barriers (MoSE)

The hot topic of the last three decades in Venice has been the mobile-flood-barrier project known as MoSE (Modulo Sperimentale Elettromeccanico; Experimental Electromechanical Module). These 78 inflatable barriers 30m high and 20m wide are intended to seal the three *bocche di porto* whenever the sea approaches dangerous levels. However, since its proposal in 1988 both the science and the management of the project have been dogged by controversy, culminating, in 2014, in the exposure of a corruption scandal in which the city mayor, the main contractor (Consorzio Venezia Nuova) and the government body responsible for the lagoon (Magistrato alle Acque) were implicated.

Despite an original completion date of 1995, MoSE remains a work in progress with constantly delayed completion dates, the latest being December 2021. In the meantime, costs have ballooned from €1.5 billion to €5.5 billion. The 2014 corruption scandal further undermined the project's credibility and even its supporters now concede that it offers only a temporary solution: it does nothing to address the issue of erosion, and if sea levels rise frequently enough above the 110cm barrier trigger, the gates may be closed so often as to compromise the entire lagoon.

Furthermore, tests of the barriers conducted in 2013 revealed significant problems. While the barriers were raised effectively, they could not be lowered due to a build-up of debris, which had to be cleared by divers. A 2017 report by the Ministry of Infrastructure pointed out issues with the degradation of critical hinge components and rust (because paintwork is more susceptible to corrosion than originally thought), while the operation of the gates at Treporti and Malamocco is hindered by the accumulation of mould, mussels and barnacles. More worryingly, subsidence beneath the caissons is distorting the position of the gates. Locals despair of the vast expense and everyone wonders where the €80 million per year required to maintain and manage the system will come from, if and when it ever becomes operational.

An unofficial referendum held in June 2017 asked Venetians whether or not large cruise ships should be banned entirely from the lagoon; 99% of those who voted (18,000 people) were in favour of a complete ban.

Every cruise ship pollutes as much as 14,000 cars. As of October 2016, the only limitations on cruise ships was restricting their fuel to maximum 1.5% sulphur (1500 times higher than the limits allowed on land).

No Grandi Navi (No Big Ships)

High waters aren't the only concern. Venice's foundations are taking a pounding as never before, with new stresses from wakes of speeding motorboats and mega cruise ships as well as pollution. When pollution and silt fill in shallow areas, algae takes over, threatening building foundations and choking out other marine life. The increase in the salt content of the lagoon also corrodes stone foundations and endangers unique lagoon aquaculture.

The spike in cruise ships entering the Bacino di San Marco (around 600 each year) has created new environmental threats. So severe is the concern, that Venice only narrowly avoided being placed on Unesco's Endangered Heritage Sites list in 2017 because it agreed to address issues of environmental degradation and over-tourism. Critics like Venice's No Grandi Navi (No Big Ships) committee also oppose cruise-ship entry for introducing pollution to the lagoon. ARPAV (www.arpa.veneto.it), the Veneto's regional agency for environmental protection has demonstrated that cruise ships are a major contributor to air pollution in Venice. The Veneto Cancer Institute says there is a statistically significant higher instance of lung cancers and bronchial problems in Venice and Mestre.

In response, the Port Authority maintains that the cruise-ship industry is a vital provider of local jobs and revenue, generating 3% to 4% of Venice's GDP, while Fincantieri, an Italian public company with a major construction yard in Marghera, employs 7700 people and is one of the biggest shipbuilding companies in the world.

In late 2017, the Comitatone (chaired by the transport minister) finally agreed to ban all cruise ships over 55,000 tons from St Mark's Basin. Instead, they will have to enter the lagoon at Malamocco, at the far end of the Lido, and dock on the mainland at Marghera. Ships weighing 55,000 to 96,000 tons will be allowed to continue along the Vittorio Emanuele canal to Venice's passenger terminal, while smaller vessels, less than 55,000 tons, can use the present route along the Giudecca Canal. The catch: these measures are only scheduled to come into effect in 2021, once a new port has been built in Marghera, and so far no environmental study has been conducted into the deepening of the Vittorio Emanuele canal, which may require the removal of toxic sludge.

Survival Guide

Transport

ARRIVING IN VENICE

Most people arrive in Venice by train, plane and, more controversially, cruise ship. There is a long-distance bus service to the city and it is also possible to drive to Venice, though you have to park at the western end then walk or take a *vaporetto* (small passenger ferry).

Flights, tours and rail tickets can be booked online at lonelyplanet.com/bookings.

Marco Polo Airport

Venice's main international airport, **Marco Polo Airport** (✈️flight information 041 260 92 60; www.veniceairport. it; Via Galileo Gallilei 30/1, Tessera), is located in Tessera, 12km east of Mestre.

Inside the terminal you'll find ticket offices for water taxis and Alilaguna water bus transfers, an ATM, currency exchange offices, a **left-luggage office** (first 6hr per item €6, thereafter per hr €0.30, bikes per 24hr €14; 🕐5am-9pm) and a Vènezia Unica **tourist office** (✆041 24 24; www.veneziaunica.it; Arrivals Hall, Marco Polo Airport; 🕐8.30am-7pm), where you can pick up pre-ordered travel cards and a map.

Alilaguna Airport Shuttle

Alilaguna (✆041 240 17 01; www.alilaguna.it; airport transfer one-way €15) operates three water shuttles that link the airport with various parts of Venice at a cost of €8 to Murano and €15 to all other landing stages. Passengers are permitted one suitcase and one piece of hand luggage. All further bags are charged at €3 per piece. Expect it to take 45 to 90 minutes to reach most destinations; it takes approximately 1¼ hours to reach Piazza San Marco. Lines include the following:

Linea Blu (Blue Line) Stops at Murano, Fondamente Nove, the Lido, San Marco, the Stazione Marittima and points in-between.

Linea Rossa (Red Line) Stops at Murano, the Lido, San Marco, Giudecca and the Stazione Marittima.

Linea Arancia (Orange Line) Stops at Fondamente Nove and Guglie in Cannaregio, Rialto and San Marco via the Grand Canal.

Bus

ACTV (Azienda del Consorzio Trasporti Veneziano;✆041 272 2111; http://actv.avmspa.it/ en) Runs bus 5 between Marco Polo Airport and Piazzale Roma (€8, 30 minutes, four per hour) with a limited number of stops en route. Alternatively, a bus+*vaporetto* ticket covering the bus journey and a one-way *vaporetto* trip within a total of 90 minutes costs €14.

ATVO (Map p281; ✆0421 59 46 71; www.atvo.it; Piazzale Roma 497g; 🕐6.40am-7.30pm; 🚌Piazzale Roma) Runs a direct bus service between the airport and **Piazzale Roma** (Map p281) (€8, 25 minutes, every 30 minutes from 8am to midnight). At Piazzale Roma you can pick up the ACTV *vaporetti* to reach locations around Venice.

Land Taxi

A taxi from the aiport to Piazzale Roma costs €40; the **taxi rank** (Map p281) is located by the **bus station** (Map p48). From there you can either hop on a *vaporetto* or pick up a **water taxi** (Map p281; Fondamente Cossetti) at the nearby Fondamente Cossetti.

Water Taxi

The dock for water transfers to the historic centre is a 10- to 15-minute walk from the arrivals hall, via a raised, indoor walkway accessed on the 1st floor of the terminal building. Luggage trolleys (requiring a €1 deposit) can be taken to the dock.

Private water taxis can be booked at the **Consorzio Motoscafi Venezia** (✆041 240 67 12; www.motoscafiven

ezia.it; ⊗9am-6pm Mon-Fri) or **Venezia Taxi** (⊘info 328 238 96 61; www.veneziataxi.it) desks in the arrivals hall, or directly at the dock. Private taxis cost from €110 for up to four passengers and all their luggage. Extra passengers (up to a limit of 12 or 16) carry a small surcharge.

If you don't have a large group, there is also the option of a **Venice Shuttle**. This is a shared water taxi and costs from €25 per person with a €6 surcharge for night-time arrivals. Seats should be booked online at www.venicelink.com. Boats seat a maximum of eight people and accommodate up to 10 bags. Those opting for a shared taxi should be aware that the service can wait for some time to fill up and has set drop-off points in Venice; only private transfers will take you directly to your hotel.

Treviso Airport

Ryanair and some other budget airlines use **Treviso Airport** (⊘0422 31 51 11; www.trevisoairport.it; Via Noalese 63), about 5km southwest of Treviso and a 26km, one-hour drive from Venice.

Bus

Barzi Bus Service (⊘0422 68 60 83; www.barziservice.com) The most direct service to Tronchetto in Venice (€12, 40 minutes, one or two per hour from 8.15am to 8.50pm) from where you can jump on the monorail to Piazzale Roma. Buy tickets on the bus or at the desk in the arrivals hall.

Azienda Trasporti Veneto Orientale (ATVO; ⊘0421 59 44; www.atvo.it) Offers a service to Mestre and Piazzale Roma in Venice (€12, one hour, one or two per hour from 8am to 9.55pm), but it takes a more circuitous route than Barzi Bus Service.

Land Taxi

Taxis from Treviso Airport to Venice cost €80.

Train

Mobilità di Marca (⊘call centre 840 011222; www.mobilitadimarca.it) is Treviso's urban bus operator. Line 6 connects Treviso Airport with Treviso train station (€1.30, 20 minutes, two to three an hour from 5.25am to 10.30pm), from where there are frequent services to Santa Lucia train station in Venice (€3.55, 30 to 40 minutes, half hourly).

Venezia Santa Lucia Train Station

Trains run frequently to Venice's **Santa Lucia train station** (www.veneziasantalucia.it; Fondamenta Santa Lucia) (appearing on signs as Ferrovia within Venice). The station has a **tourist office** (Map p282; ⊘041 24 24; www.veneziaunica.it; ⊗7am-9pm; 🖃Ferrovia) opposite platform 3 where you can obtain a map and buy *vaporetto* tickets, and a **left-luggage depot** (Left Luggage Office; ⊘041 78 55 31; Stazione Venezia Santa Lucia; ⊗6am-11pm) opposite platform 1.

Local trains linking Venice to the Veneto are frequent, reliable and remarkably inexpensive, including Padua (€4.35, 25 to 50 minutes, three to four per hour) and Verona (€9.23, 1¾ hours, three to four per hour). Expensive, high-speed Le Frecce trains also serve these Veneto destinations, but are a better option for longer journeys to Milan (from €28, 2½ hours) and Rome (from €50, 3¾ hours).

Train tickets can be purchased at self-serve ticketing machines in the station, online at www.trenitalia.it and www.raileurope.com or through travel agents. When buying train tickets, be sure

to specify Venezia Santa Lucia (VSL) for the station in central Venice, as opposed to Venezia Mestre on the mainland.

Validate your ticket in the orange machines on station platforms before boarding your train. Failure to do so can result in a hefty on-the-spot fine when the inspector checks tickets on the train.

Vaporetti (p247) connect Santa Lucia train station with all parts of Venice (€60 to the centre). There is also a handy water-taxi rank just out front if you are heavily laden.

Venezia Mestre Train Station

Venezia Mestre (www.veneziamestre.it; Piazzale Pietro Favretti) station is located on the mainland in Mestre directly across the channel from Venice. Trains, which take 10 to 12 minutes, and an ATVO shuttle bus connect the two stations.

Other services from the station include high-speed Le Frecce and Italo trains connecting Venice with Rome, Milan and Florence, as well as Eurocity trains to Munich.

Inside the station, you'll find a tourist information office, currency exchange and a **left-luggage depot** (Viale Stazione, Mestre; per piece 1st 5hr €6, next 6hr €0.90, thereafter per hr €0.40; ⊗8am-8pm).

Venezia Terminal Passeggeri

Cruise ships dock at Venice's main passenger terminal, **Venezia Terminal Passeggeri** (Map p48; ⊘041 240 30 00; www.vtp.it; Marittima Fabbricato 248), which is located at the western end of Santa Croce between the Isola del Tronchetto and Piazzale Roma.

The terminal is accessible by road but cars must be

CLIMATE CHANGE & TRAVEL

Every form of transport that relies on carbon-based fuel generates CO_2, the main cause of human-induced climate change. Modern travel is dependent on aeroplanes, which might use less fuel per kilometre per person than most cars but travel much greater distances. The altitude at which aircraft emit gases (including CO_2) and particles also contributes to their climate change impact. Many websites offer 'carbon calculators' that allow people to estimate the carbon emissions generated by their journey and, for those who wish to do so, to offset the impact of the greenhouse gases emitted with contributions to portfolios of climate-friendly initiatives throughout the world. Lonely Planet offsets the carbon footprint of all staff and author travel.

parked on the nearby Isola del Tronchetto. When in port, most big cruise ships provide their passengers with a complimentary shuttle bus or boat service into Venice.

Alilaguna Boat Shuttle

The Blue and Red Lines operated by **Alilaguna** (☑041 240 17 01; www.alilaguna.it; airport transfer one-way €15) connect the cruise terminal with San Marco (one-way €8, 15 minutes), the Lido (one-way €10, 45 minutes) and points in-between. The service also continues on to Marco Polo Airport (one-way €15, two hours).

Bus

A frequent, free shuttle bus connects the cruise terminal to Piazzale Roma. It runs every 15 to 20 minutes from Monday to Saturday during cruise season and whenever a big ship is in port.

Land & Water Taxis

Land taxis to the airport cost around €30 to €40. Or, they can ferry you and your luggage the brief 900m distance to Piazzale Roma (about €5) where you can meet airport buses.

A water taxi direct to your hotel in Venice will set you back around €90.

Monorail

The **People Mover Monorail** (www.avmspa.it; Piazzale Roma; per ride €1.50;

⊙7.10am-10.50pm Mon-Sat, 8.40am-8.50pm Sun) connects the cruise-ship terminal with Piazzale Roma. It takes less than two minutes and runs until 11pm.

Terminal San Basilio

Terminal San Basilio (Old Stazione Marittime; Fondamenta Zattere Al Ponte; 🚢San Basilio) is a small ferry terminal on the southern side of Dorsoduro, which serves high-speed **Venezia Lines** (☑041 847 09 03; www.venezialines.com; ⊙9am-5pm daily May-Sep, Mon-Fri Oct-Apr; 🚢San Basilio) boats from Croatia and Slovenia during the summer months.

Vaporetto

Vaporetto line 2 links Terminal San Basilio with Tronchetto, Piazzale Roma and San Zaccaria.

Terminal Fusina

Terminal Fusina (☑041 547 01 60; www.terminalfusina.it; Via Moranzani 79, Fusina) on the mainland, 12km south of Mestre, handles small ferries from Greece. Run by **Anek Lines Italia** (☑041 528 65 22; www.anekitalia.com; Via Dell 'Elettronica, Fusina) there are four services a week with boats docking at Igoumenitsa (dorm beds €150; 25½ hours) and Patras (dorm beds from €150; 32 hours).

Vaporetto

To reach Fusina from Venice take the Circolare Lineafusina *vaporetto* from Zattere (€8, 25 minutes, hourly) or Alberoni (€8, 35 minutes, every two hours) at the southern end of the Lido.

Car & Motorcycle

To get to Venice by car or motorcycle, take the often-congested Trieste–Turin A4, which passes through Mestre. From Mestre, take the 'Venezia' exit. Once over Ponte della Libertà from Mestre, cars must be left at a car park in Piazzale Roma or on the Isola del Tronchetto. Be warned: you'll pay a hefty price in parking fees, and traffic backs up at weekends.

Car Ferry

Car ferry 17 transports vehicles from Tronchetto to the Lido (vehicles up to 4m and motorcycles €13, not including the driver).

Parking

Prices in Venice start at €3.50 per hour and rise to €32 for five to 24 hours. At peak times, many car parks become completely full. However, you can book a parking place ahead of time at www.veneziaunica.it.

To avoid hassles (and to make the most of the cheaper car parks) consider parking in Mestre, and take the bus or train into Venice instead. Remember to take valuables out of your car.

For a range of parking options in Venice and Mestre, including prices and directions, head to http://avm.avmspa.it/en.

Garage Europa Mestre (☑041 95 92 02; www.garageeuropa-mestre.com; Corso del Popolo 55; per day €15; ◷8am-10pm) Has 300 spaces; ACTV bus 4 to/from Venice stops right outside the garage, or it's a 1.3km walk to the Mestre train station. It has the cheapest hourly rates.

Autoremissa Comunale (☑041 272 73 07; www.veneziaunica.it; Piazzale Roma 496; cars over/under 185cm per day €29/26; ◷24hr; ☒Piazzale Roma) Has 2152 spaces; the largest lot in Piazzale Roma. Discounts available with online reservations; free parking for people with disabilities for up to 12 hours.

Garage San Marco (☑041 523 22 13; www.garagesanmarco.it; Piazzale Roma 467f; per 24hr €32, overnight 5pm-4am €15; ◷24hr; ☒Piazzale Roma) Has 900 spaces; guests of certain hotels get discounts.

Parking Sant'Andrea (☑041 272 7304; www.avmspa.it; Piazzale Roma; per 2hr or less €7; ◷24hr) Has 100 spaces; best for short-term parking.

Interparking Venezia Tronchetto (☑041 520 75 55; www.veniceparking.it; Isola del Tronchetto; per 1/2/3/24hr

€3/6/11/21; ◷24hr; ☒Tronchetto) Has 3957 spaces; the largest lot with the cheapest 24-hour rate. *Vaporetti* connect directly with Piazza San Marco, while the People Mover monorail provides connections to Piazzale Roma and the cruise terminal.

GETTING AROUND

The city's main mode of public transport is the *vaporetto*. They are frequent and convenient but expensive, and they can get very full in peak season. Often, it is quicker to just walk to your destination. Cars and bikes are allowed on the Lido and Pellestrina. If you have cash to splash, gondolas and private water taxis are the most glamorous way to travel.

Vaporetto

ACTV (Azienda del Consorzio Trasporti Veneziano; ☑041 272 2111; http://actv.avmspa.it/en) runs all public transport in Venice, including waterborne services. Although the service is efficient and punctual, boats on main lines fill up and are prone to overcrowding during Carnevale and in peak season. One-way tickets cost €7.50.

Interisland ferry services to Murano, Torcello, the Lido and other lagoon islands are usually provided on larger *motonave*.

To plan itineraries, check schedules and buy tickets, download the useful *vaporetto* app daAaB (www.daaab.it). If you purchase tickets through the app, you can then scan your phone at the barriers in place of a ticket.

Tickets

Vènezia Unica (☑041 24 24; www.veneziaunica.it) is the main seller of public transport tickets, and you can purchase *vaporetti* tickets at booths at most landing stations. Free timetables and route maps are also available. Tickets and multiday passes can also be prepurchased online.

If you're going to be using the *vaporetto* frequently (more than three trips), instead of spending €7.50 for every one-way ticket, it is advisable to consider an ACTV Tourist Travel Card (p248) – a pass for unlimited travel within a set period beginning when you first validate your ticket at the yellow machine located at *vaporetto* stops. Swipe your card every time you board, even if you have already validated it upon your initial ride. If you're caught without a valid ticket, you'll be required to pay an on-the-spot fine of €59 (plus the €7.50 fare). No exceptions.

People aged six to 29 holding a Rolling Venice card (p252) can get a three-day ticket for €22 at tourist offices.

Routes

From Piazzale Roma or the train station, *vaporetto* 1 zigzags up the Grand Canal to San Marco and onward to the Lido. If you're not in a rush, it's a great introduction to Venice. *Vaporetto* 17 carries vehicles from Tronchetto, near Piazzale Roma, to the Lido.

Frequency varies greatly according to line and time of day. *Vaporetto* 1 runs every 10 minutes throughout most of the day, while lines

---

WAITING FOR YOUR SHIP TO COME IN

Vaporetto stops can be confusing, so check the signs at the landing dock to make sure you're at the right stop for the direction you want. At major stops like Ferrovia, Piazzale Roma, San Marco and Zattere, there are often two separate docks for the same *vaporetto* line, heading in opposite directions.

The cluster of stops near Piazza San Marco is especially tricky. If your boat doesn't stop right in front of Piazza San Marco, don't panic: it will probably stop at San Zaccaria, just past the Palazzo Ducale.

ACTV TOURIST TRAVEL CARD

The ACTV Tourist Travel Cards allow for unlimited travel on *vaporetti* (small passenger ferries) and Lido buses within the following time blocks:

24 hours €20
48 hours €30
72 hours €40
One week €60

such as the 4.1 and 4.2 only run every 20 minutes. Night services can be as much as one hour apart, and some lines stop running by around 9pm, so check timetables.

The key *vaporetto* lines and major stops are as follows:

No 1 Runs Piazzale Roma–Ferrovia–Grand Canal (all stops)–Lido and back (5am to 11.30pm, every 10 minutes from 7am to 10pm).

No 2 Circular line: runs San Zaccaria–Redentore–Zattere–Trochetto–Ferrovia–Rialto–Accademia–San Marco.

No 3/DM 'Diretto Murano' connects Piazzale Roma and the railway station to all five stops on Murano.

No 4.1 Circular line: runs Murano–Fondamente Nove–Ferrovia–Piazzale Roma–Redentore–San Zaccaria–Fondamente Nove–San Michele–Murano (6am to 10pm, every 20 minutes).

No 4.2 Circular line in reverse direction to No 4.1 (6.30am to 8.30pm, every 20 minutes).

No 5.1 & 5.2 Runs the same route, Lido–Fondamente Nove–Riva de Biasio–Ferrovia–Piazzale Roma–Zattere–San Zaccaria–Giardini–Lido, in opposite directions.

No 6 Circular line, limited stops, weekdays only: runs Piazzale Roma–Santa Marta–San Basilio–Zattere–Giardini–Sant'Elena–Lido.

No 8 Runs Giudecca–Zattere–Redentore–Giardini–Lido (May to early September only).

No 9 Runs Torcello–Burano and back (7am to 8.45pm, every 30 minutes).

No 11 A coordinated, hourly bus+*vaporetto* service from Lido to Pellestrina and Chioggia.

No 12 Runs Fondamente Nove–Murano–Mazzorbo–Burano–Torcello and back.

No 13 Runs Fondamente Nove–Murano–Vignole–Sant'Erasmo–Treporti and back.

No 16 Connects Fusina Terminal with Zattere.

No 17 Car ferry: runs Tronchetto–Lido and back.

No 18 Runs Murano–Sant'Erasmo–Lido and back (infrequent and summer only).

No 20 Runs San Zaccaria–San Servolo–San Lazzaro degli Armeni and back. In summer it also connects with the Lido.

N All-stops night circuit, including Giudecca, Grand Canal, San Marco, Piazzale Roma and the train station (11.30pm to 4am, every 40 minutes).

NMU (Notturno Murano) Night service from Fondamente Nove to Murano (all stops).

NLN (Notturno Laguna Nord) Infrequent night service between Fondamente Nove, Murano, Burano, Torcello and Treporti.

Gondola

A gondola ride offers a view of Venice that is anything but pedestrian. Official daytime rates are €80 for 40 minutes (€100 for 40 minutes from 7pm to 8pm), not including songs or tips. Additional time is charged in 20-minute increments (day/night €40/50). You may negotiate a price break in overcast weather or around noon. Agree on a price, time limit and singing in advance to avoid unexpected surcharges.

Gondolas cluster at *stazi* (stops) along the Grand Canal and near major monuments and tourist hotspots, but you can also book a pickup by calling **Ente Gondola** (☎041 528 50 75; www.gondola venezia.it).

Gondolas 4 All (Map p281;☎328 2431382; www.gondolas4all.com; Fondamente Cossetti; per 30min €80; ♿Piazzale Roma), supported by the Gondoliers Association, offers gondola rides to wheelchair users in a specially adapted gondola. Embarkation is from a wheelchair-accessible pier at Piazzale Roma.

Water Taxi

Licensed water taxis are a costly way to get around Venice, though they may prove handy when you're late for the opera or have lots of luggage. Fares can be metered or negotiated in advance. Official rates start at €15 plus €2 per minute, €5 extra if they're called to your hotel. There's a €10 surcharge for night trips (10pm to 6am), a €5 surcharge for additional luggage (more than five pieces) and a €10 surcharge for each extra passenger above the first four. Note: if you order a water taxi through your hotel or a travel agent, you will be subject to a surcharge. Tipping isn't required.

Make sure your water taxi has the yellow strip with the licence number displayed. There are official water-taxi ranks at the airport, outside the train station, in front of **Piazzale Roma** (Map p281; Fondamente Cossetti) and at Tronchetto.

Even if you're in a hurry, don't encourage your water-taxi driver to speed through Venice – this kicks up *moto-*

CHEAP THRILLS ON THE GRAND CANAL

A *traghetto* is the gondola service locals use to cross the Grand Canal between its widely spaced bridges. *Traghetti* rides cost just €2 for nonresidents and typically operate from 9am to 6pm, although some routes finish by noon. You'll find *traghetto* crossings at Campo San Marcuola, the Rialto Market, Riva del Vin, San Tomà, Ca' Rezzonico and beside the Gritti Palace, though note that service can be spotty at times at all crossings.

---

schiaffi (motorboat wakes) that expose Venice's ancient foundations to degradation and rot.

Boat

Aspiring sea captains can take on the lagoon (not the Grand Canal or canals in the historic centre) in a rented boat. You don't need a licence, but you will be taken on a test run to see if you can manoeuvre and park; and, if you're going out for a day, be sure to find out the location of the four boat-petrol stations around Venice.

Boat rentals are offered by **Brussa** (Map p282; ☑041 71 57 87; www.brussaisboat. it; Fondamenta Labia 331; 7m boat per hr/day incl fuel €43/196; ☺7.30am-5.30pm Mon-Fri, to 12.30pm Sat & Sun; ☒Ferrovia) in Cannaregio and **Venice Rental Services** (☑388 8888842; www.scooterrentvenice.com; Via Perasto 6b, Lido; bikes/e-bikes/scooters/cars/boats per day from €10/20/35/40/200; ☺9am-7pm; ☒Lido SME) on the Lido. Alternatively, for something more romantic hire a traditional San Pietro flat-bottomed boat with an electric engine from **CBV** (Classic Boats Venice; ☑041 523 67 20; www.classicboatsvenice.com; Isola della Certosa; 1/2/3/4/8hr rental €80/130/180/225/295; ☺9am-7pm Apr-Feb; ☒Certosa) ✔ on Murano.

Bicycle

Cycling is banned in central Venice. On the larger islands of Lido and Pellestrina, cycling is a pleasant way to get around or reach distant beaches. **Lido on Bike** (☑041 526 80 19; www.lidoonbike.it; Gran Viale Santa Maria Elisabetta 21b, Lido; bicycle rental per 90min/day €5/10; ☺9am-7pm summer; ☒Lido SME) and **Venice Rental Services** (☑388 8888842; www.scooterrentvenice.com; Via Perasto 6b, Lido; bikes/e-bikes/scooters/cars/boats per day from €10/20/35/40/200; ☺9am-7pm; ☒Lido SME) are both located near the *vaporetto* stop; ID is required for rental. On the Lido you'll also find an electronic, self-service bike-sharing scheme, **Bike Sharing Venezia** (☑800 655300; www.bicincitta.com; Lido; registration €20 incl €5 credit, per 1/2hr free/€1, additional hr €2; ☒Lido SME). To use it, register online.

To sort out a set of wheels for a Veneto day trip, contact **Veloce** (☑0586 40 42 04; www.rentalbikeitaly.com; touring/mountain/racing bicycle per day €20/25/35; ☺8am-8pm), which offers preloaded GPS units (€10), guided tours (€80 per person), advice in English on itineraries and local restaurants, and a handy drop-off and pickup service from train stations

and hotels. Bikes need to be prebooked.

Car & Motorcycle

Obviously you can't drive in Venice proper, but the Lido and Pellestrina allow cars, and they can be the most efficient way of seeing far-flung sites across the Veneto.

The car-rental companies **Avis** (☑041 523 73 77; www.avis.com; Piazzale Roma 496g; ☺8.30am-3.30pm Mon-Sat; ☒Piazzale Roma), **Europcar** (☑041 523 86 16; www.europcar.it; Piazzale Roma 496h; ☺8.20am-12.30pm & 2-6pm Mon-Fri, 8.30am-12.30pm Sat, 9am-noon Sun; ☒Piazzale Roma) and **Hertz** (☑041 528 40 91; www.hertz.it; Piazzale Roma 496f; ☺8.30am-12.30pm & 2.30-5.30pm Mon-Fri, 8.30am-12.30pm Sat; ☒Piazzale Roma) all have offices both on Piazzale Roma and at Marco Polo Airport. Several companies operate in or near Mestre train station as well.

Scooters are available for rent on the Lido at **Venice Rental Services** (☑388 8888842; www.scooterrentvenice.com; Via Perasto 6b, Lido; bikes/e-bikes/scooters/cars/boats per day from €10/20/35/40/200; ☺9am-7pm; ☒Lido SME). In other Veneto towns, bicycles rather than scooters are the preferred mode of transport.

Monorail

Venice's wheelchair-accessible **People Mover monorail** (www.avmspa.it; Piazzale Roma; per ride €1.50; ☺7.10am-10.50pm Mon-Sat, 8.40am-8.50pm Sun) connects the car parks on Tronchetto with the cruise-ship terminal and Piazzale Roma. Purchase tickets from the vending machines near the station.

Directory A–Z

Accessible Travel

With hundreds of bridges and endless stairs, Venice may not seem to be an easy destination for travellers with disabilities, but the city has made efforts in recent years to improve access. The city council now says that 70% of the centre is accessible to people with impaired mobility, with most of the main monuments and sites reachable by public transport. There's a useful article on how to enjoy Venice with a wheelchair, walkers or crutches at https://europe forvisitors.com/venice/arti cles/accessible_venice.htm.

If you have an obvious disability and/or appropriate ID, many museums and galleries offer free admission for yourself and a companion. Bear in mind that due to the historic (and protected) nature of the city, it is not always possible to access all areas of a site due to a lack of lifts and/or ramps.

Getting There & Around

The **Disabled Assistance Office** (Sala Blu; ☑800 906 060; Stazione Venezia Santa Lucia; ☉6.45am-9.30pm) is located at platform 4 in Venice's Santa Lucia train station.

Virtually all local buses, including those on the Lido, as well as those connecting Venice with the mainland, are wheelchair accessible. The monorail is also wheelchair accessible.

An 'Accessible Venice' map is available from the tourist office or online at **Vènezia Unica** (www.venezia unica.it). The map delimits the area around each water-bus stop that can be accessed without crossing a bridge.

Most *vaporetti* (small passenger ferries) have access for wheelchairs. *Vaporetto* lines 1 and 2, which serve the Grand Canal, have space for four wheelchairs. Lines 4.1/4.2 and 5.1/5.2 only have space for one wheelchair at a time. Line 12 to Murano, Burano and Torcello and the LN car ferry to the Lido are also wheelchair accessible.

Passengers with wheelchairs can buy single-fare tickets at the heavily-discounted rate of €1.50 from ACTV ticket booths and Hellovenezia offices. Each ticket is valid for 75 minutes, and a companion travels free.

Organise private, disability-adapted road transport and water taxis through **Sanitrans** (☑041 523 9977; www.sanitrans.net; Fondamenta Guglie (Fondamenta de Cannaregio) 1091/A; ⚓Guglie). They also supply walking aids.

Accessible Travel Agencies

Gondolas 4 All (Map p281; ☑328 2431382; www.gondolas 4all.com; Fondamente Cossetti; per 30min €80; ⚓Piazzale Roma) Manual (not electric) wheelchair users can now experience the city's iconic mode of transport. It's advisable to use the booking form on their Italian-language website.

L'Altra Venezia (www.laltra venezia.it; walking tours per hour €70, thematic tours from €200, boat tours from €400) Offers half- and full-day city and lagoon tours in specially adapted boats that can accommodate up to seven people (maximum four wheelchairs). Tours are proposed 'pilot only' or with a guide, and include lunch on-board or in local restaurants.

Rome & Italy (☑06 4425 8441; www.romeanditaly. com/tourism-for-disabled; Via Giuseppe Veronese 50; ☉9am-8pm) A mainstream travel agency with an accessible tourism arm that offers two, half-day customised tours

ACCESSIBLE TRAVEL TOP TIPS

➡ Plan your trip well ahead, including tours, guides and accommodation so you don't have to waste time after you've arrived.

➡ Consider hotel accommodation carefully. Some areas of the city are more accessible than others; also, check that the path to your hotel from the nearest *vaporetto* stop is free of bridges.

➡ Between October and March the city is subject to *acqua alta* (high tides) when parts of the city are prone to flooding. Avoid travelling during this period or check with your hotel about whether the surrounding area is affected. High tides can also make access to *vaporetto* stops problematic.

➡ Print off the 'Accessible Venice' map from the Vènezia Unica (p254) website.

➡ Buy a Travel Card (p248) or multiple, discounted 'disabled travel' tickets on arrival or, in advance, online.

➡ Consider engaging the services of an accredited tour guide from Best Venice Guides (p26), such as Luisella Romeo at See Venice (p26). They know the city and sights like the back of their hand and can put together fascinating itineraries adapted to your needs.

➡ Access to Venice's 11 civic and six state museums is free for persons with disabilities, plus one companion.

in Venice to the Doge's palace and Torcello island, accessible accommodation, and equipment and vehicle hire.

Accessible Italy (www.accessibleitaly.com) A San Marino–based nonprofit company that specialises in holiday services for people with disabilities, including equipment rental, adapted vehicle hire and arranging personal assistants. In Venice, it offers multiday individual, group and bespoke tours.

Sage Traveling (www.sagetraveling.com) A US-based accessible-travel agency offering tailor-made tours in Europe. Check out their website for a detailed access guide to Venice, which includes tips on how to use the *vaporetto* and water taxis, accessible walking and boating tours, and hotels.

Accessible Travel Online Resources

The **Venezia Unica** (www.veneziaunica.it/en/content/accessible-venice) accessibility page contains useful information, including how to get to the city, an accessible map, and information about accessible

gondola rides, public transport and wheelchair rental. The most-accessible tourist office is the one on **Piazza San Marco** (Map p274; ☎041 24 24; Piazza San Marco 71f; ⏰9am-7pm; 🚤San Marco).

Village for All (www.villageforall.net) Performs on-site audits of tourist facilities in Italy and San Marino. Most of the 70-plus facilities are accommodation providers, ranging from camping grounds to high-class hotels.

See Venice (www.seevenice.it) The blog of Venetian guide Luisella Romeo features a number of excellent road-tested itineraries. See www.seevenice.it/en/accessible-venice-tours-wheelchair and www.seevenice.it/en/more-tours-about-accessible-venice-wheelchair.

Download Lonely Planet's free *Accessible Travel* guides from http://lptravel.to/AccessibleTravel.

Discount Cards

The tourist information portal, Vènezia Unica, brings together a range of discount passes and services and

enables you to tailor them to your needs and prepurchase online. Services and passes on offer include the following:

➡ land and water transfers to the airport and cruise terminal

➡ ACTV Tourist Travel Cards

➡ museum and church passes

➡ select parking

➡ citywide wi-fi, and

➡ prepaid access to public toilets.

If purchasing online you need to print out your voucher displaying your reservation number (PNR) and carry it with you, then simply present it at the various attractions for admission or access.

To use public transport, however, you will need to obtain a free card (you will need your PNR code to do this), which is then 'loaded' with the credit you have purchased. You can do this at the ACTV ticket machines at **Marco Polo Airport** (☎flight information 041 260 92 60; www.veniceairport.it; Via Galileo Gallilei 30/1, Tessera), ticket desks at *vaporetto* stops and Vènezia Unica offices.

Chorus Pass

The association of Venetian churches offers a **Chorus Pass** (adult/student under 29 years €12/8) for single entry to 16 historic churches any time within one year (excluding I Frari). Otherwise, admission to these individual churches costs €3. Passes are for sale at church ticket booths; proceeds support city-wide restoration and maintenance of churches.

City Passes

Silver, Gold and Platinum city passes are available from Vènezia Unica. For keen sightseers with at least four to seven days on their hands, these are the most useful:

City Pass (adult/'junior' 6-29 years €39.90/29.90) Valid for seven days, offering entrance to the Doge's Palace, 12 civic museums and 16 Chorus churches. It also includes free admission to the casino.

San Marco City Pass (adult/reduced €28.90/21.90) A reduced version of the City Pass allowing entry to the Doge's Palace, four civic museums on Piazza San Marco, plus three churches on the Chorus Circuit.

Civic Museum Passes

The **Civic Museum Pass** (adult/reduced €24/18) is valid for six months and covers single entry to 11 civic museums, including Palazzo Ducale, Ca' Rezzonico, Ca' Pesaro, Palazzo Mocenigo, Museo Correr, the Museo del Vetro (Glass Museum) on Murano and the Museo del Merletto (Lace Museum) on Burano. Short-term visitors may prefer the **San Marco Pack** (adult/reduced €20/13), which covers four museums around Piazza San Marco (Palazzo Ducale, Museo Correr, Museo Archeologico Nazionale and Biblioteca Nazionale Marciana). Available from any civic museum, the tourist office and online at Vènezia Unica.

Other Combined Tickets

For art aficionados planning to visit Ca' d'Oro and Palazzo Grimani, consider the **combined ticket** (adult/18 to 25/under-18 years €10/4/free), valid for three months.

A combined adult/reduced ticket to the Palazzo Grassi and Punta della Dogana costs €18/15.

Both tickets can be purchased direct from the museums.

Rolling Venice Card

Visitors aged six to 29 years should pick up the €6 Rolling Venice card (from tourist offices and most ACTV public transport ticket points), entitling purchase of a 72-hour public transport pass (€22) and discounts on airport transfers, museums, monuments and cultural events.

ISIC

International Student Identity Cards (www.isic.org) can get you discounted admission prices at some sights but benefits are limited in Venice.

Electricity

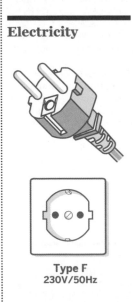

Type F
230V/50Hz

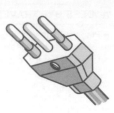

Type L
220V/50Hz

Emergency

Ambulance	☑118
Police	☑112
Venice area code	☑041

LGBT+ Travellers

Homosexuality is legal in Italy and generally accepted in Venice and the Veneto. ArciGay (www.arcigay.it), the national gay, lesbian, bisexual and transgender organisation, has information on the LGBT scene in Italy. The useful website www.gay.it (in Italian) lists gay and lesbian events across the country, but options in Venice are slim. Head to Padua for a wider range of gay-friendly nightlife and the nearest LGBT organisation, **ArciGay Tralaltro** (☑049 876 24 58; www.tralaltro.it; Corso Garibaldi 41; ☉6-9.30pm under-30s only, 9-11am Tue).

Medical Services

The standard of health care in Venice is generally good,

although the public system can be a little creaky at times. Some planning can save you trouble later. Bring medications in their original, clearly labelled containers. A signed and dated letter from your physician describing your medical conditions and medication, including generic names, is a good idea.

For emergency treatment, head straight to the *pronto soccorso* (casualty) section of a public hospital, where you can also get emergency dental treatment (carry your ID/passport and any relevant insurance card). Pharmacists can give you valuable advice and sell over-the-counter medication for minor illnesses.

Opening hours of medical services vary, though most are open 8am to 12.30pm and 4pm to 8pm Monday to Friday, and 9am to noon on Saturday. From 15 June to 15 September tourists can access an on-call doctor at 041 530 0874.

Comprehensive information on all health services in the city is provided at www.healthvenice.com.

Emergency Clinics

First Aid Point Piazza San Marco (First Aid Point; Procuratie Nuove 63/65, Piazza San Marco; ◷8am-8pm) Dedicated to tourists, this well-equipped first-aid point performs diagnostics and minor surgery, and issues drug prescriptions and referrals for further hospital treatment.

First Aid Point Piazzale Roma (First Aid Point; Piazzale Roma 496; ◷8am-8pm; ⬛Piazzale Roma) Offers similar services to the San Marco first-aid point, including minor surgeries and drug prescriptions.

Guardia Medica (☑041 238 56 00) This service of night-time call-out doctors in Venice operates from 8pm to 8am on weekdays and from 10am the day before a holiday (includ-

ing Sunday) until 8am the day after.

Ospedale dell'Angelo (☑041 965 71 11; www.ulss12.ve.it; Via Paccagnella 11, Mestre) Vast modern hospital on the mainland.

Ospedale SS Giovanni e Paolo (Map p48; ☑041 529 43 11; www.aulss3.veneto.it; Campo Zanipolo 6777; ⬛Ospedale) Venice's main hospital; provides emergency care and dental treatment. The entrance is on the water near the Ospedale *vaporetto* stop.

Money

ATMs are widely available and credit cards accepted at most hotels, B&Bs and shops. To change money you'll need to present your ID.

Tipping

➜ **Cafes and bars** Most Italians leave small change (€0.10 to €0.20 is fine).

➜ **Hotels** At least €2 per bag or night, for porter, maid or room service.

➜ **Restaurants** Tips of 10% are standard – though check to see that a tip isn't already added to your bill, or included in the flat *coperto* (cover) charge.

➜ **Transport** Tips may be given for gondolas and water-taxi service graciously provided, especially if singing is involved.

Opening Hours

The hours listed here are a general guide; individual establishments can vary. Also note that hours at shops, bars and restaurants can be somewhat flexible in Venice, as they are in the rest of Italy.

Banks 8.30am to 1.30pm and 3.30pm to 5.30pm Monday to Friday, though hours vary; some open Saturday mornings

Restaurants Noon to 2.30pm and 7pm to 10pm

Shops 10am to 1pm and 3.30pm to 7pm (or 4pm to 7.30pm) Monday to Saturday

Supermarkets 9am to 7.30pm Monday to Saturday

Public Holidays

For Venetians the main holiday periods are summer (July and especially August), the Christmas–New Year period and Easter. Restaurants, shops and most other activity also grind to a halt around Ferragosto (Feast of the Assumption; 15 August).

Capodanno/Anno Nuovo (New Year's Day) 1 January

Epifania/Befana (Epiphany) 6 January

Pasquetta/Lunedì dell'Angelo (Easter Monday) March/April

Giorno della Liberazione (Liberation Day) 25 April

Festa del Lavoro (Labour Day) 1 May

Festa della Repubblica (Republic Day) 2 June

Ferragosto (Feast of the Assumption) 15 August

Ognissanti (All Saints' Day) 1 November

Immaculata Concezione (Feast of the Immaculate Conception) 8 December

Natale (Christmas Day) 25 December

Festa di Santo Stefano (Boxing Day) 26 December

Safe Travel

➜ Mind your step on slippery canal banks and stone footbridges, especially after rains and *acque alte* (high tides).

➜ Venice is not childproof. Few canal banks and bridges have railings, and most Gothic palaces have pointy edges.

➜ You're very safe in Venice, even alone at night – but watch out for petty theft in and around Venice and Mestre train stations.

➜ Do not swim in the canals or even dangle your feet in them. Remember that roughly 30% of the city's sewage is still discharged into the canals.

Taxes & Refunds

If you're staying overnight within Venice, expect to pay €3.50 to €5 per night in tourist tax per person for up to five nights (additional nights are free). Children aged 10 to 15 receive a 50% discount. Children under 10 and hostels are exempt from the tax.

Value-added tax (VAT) of around 22% is added to purchases costing more than €155 in Italy.

Telephone

Italy's country code is 39. The city code for Venice is 041. The city code is an integral part of the number and must always be dialled. Toll-free (free-phone) numbers are known as *numeri verdi* and usually start with 800.

Time

Italy is one hour ahead of GMT/UTC during winter and two hours ahead during the daylight-saving period, which runs from the last Sunday in March to the last Sunday in October. Note that times are often listed using a 24-hour clock (ie 2pm is written as 14.00).

Toilets

➜ Most bars and cafes reserve the restroom for paying customers only.

➜ Look before you sit: even in women's bathrooms, some toilets don't have seats.

➜ Nineteen public toilets

BYLAWS & TOURIST TAXES

Booming tourism numbers have seen the attitudes of the long-suffering Venetian locals harden towards the behaviours of visitors that that they find disrespectful or inconvenient, which in turn has led to the city banning various activities. Some are obvious, such as littering, graffiti and posting bills, but others potentially less so. For instance, it is forbidden to sit and picnic in any of the squares or on the streets. Swimming in the canals is strictly forbidden, as is riding bikes or walking around shirtless or in swimwear in the centre of town. Irritating photo snappers can no longer clog city bridges, and stag and hen parties need to restrict their outdoor carousing to daytime and on the weekends. Store-bought alcohol can't be consumed on the streets between 8pm and 8am.

The authorities aren't joking about enforcement either. In 2019, two clueless German backpackers found this out the hard way when they were fined €950 and expelled from the city after lighting up a portable stove and making coffee just metres from the busy Rialto Bridge.

A new tourist tax has also come into force, targeting day-trippers (overnight stays already have a tax attached). The rates vary throughout the year but rise to €10 at the absolute peak times.

(€1.50) are scattered around Venice near tourist attractions (look for the 'WC Toilette' signs), and are usually open from 7am to 7pm (sometimes closing earlier in winter). All of them have facilities for people with disabilities. You can download a mobile app pinpointing their location from https://wctoilettevenezia.com.

Tourist Information

Vènezia Unica (📞041 24 24; www.veneziaunica.it) runs tourist information services in Venice. It provides information on sights, itineraries, transport, special events and exhibitions. Discount passes can be prebooked online.

Tourist Offices

Casa del Turismo (📞041 37 06 01; www.jesolo.it; Piazza Brescia 13, Jesolo; ⏰8.30am–

6.30pm Mon-Fri, 9am-6pm Sat & Sun; 🚌23a)

Marco Polo Airport Tourist Office (📞041 24 24; www.veneziaunica.it; Arrivals Hall, Marco Polo Airport; ⏰8.30am-7pm)

Piazzale Roma Garage ASM Tourist Office (Map p281; 📞041 24 24; www.veneziaunica.it; Garage ASM, L1, Piazzale Roma 496u; ⏰7am-8pm; 🚏Piazzale Roma)

Piazzale Roma Tourist Office (Map p281; 📞041 24 24; www.veneziaunica.it; ACTV office, Piazzale Roma; ⏰7am-8pm; 🚏Piazzale Roma Santa Chiara)

San Marco Tourist Office (Map p274; 📞041 24 24; www.veneziaunica.it; Piazza San Marco 71f; ⏰9am-7pm; 🚏San Marco)

Stazione Santa Lucia Tourist Office (Map p282; 📞041 24 24; www.veneziaunica.it; ⏰7am-9pm; 🚏Ferrovia)

Visas

Citizens of EU countries, Iceland, Norway and Switzerland do not need a visa to visit Italy. For more information, check the website of the Italian foreign ministry (www. esteri.it).

The standard tourist visa issued by Italian consulates is the Schengen visa, valid for up to 90 days. This visa is valid for travel in Italy and in several other European countries with which Italy has a reciprocal visa agreement (see www.eurovisa.info for the full list). These visas are not renewable inside Italy.

Women Travellers

Of the major travel destinations in Italy, Venice is among the safest for women, given the low rate of violent crime in Venice proper. Chief annoyances would be getting chatted up by other travellers in Piazza San Marco or on the Lido beaches, usually easily quashed with a *'Non mi interessa'* (I'm not interested), or an exasperated eye roll.

Language

Standard Italian is spoken throughout Italy, but regional dialects are an important part of identity in many areas, and this also goes for Venice. You'll no doubt hear some Venetian (also known as Venet) spoken or pick up on the local lilt that standard Italian is often spoken with. This said, you'll have no trouble being understood – and your efforts will be much appreciated – if you stick to standard Italian, which we've also used in this chapter.

Italian pronunciation is straightforward as most sounds are also found in English.

Note that ai is pronounced as in 'aisle', ay as in 'say', ow as in 'how', dz as the 'ds' in 'lids', and that r is a strong, rolled sound. Keep in mind that Italian consonants can have a stronger, emphatic pronunciation – if the consonant is written as a double letter, it should be pronounced a little stronger, eg *sonno son*·no (sleep) and *sono so*·no (I am). If you read our coloured pronunciation guides as if they were English (with the stressed syllables in italics), you'll be understood.

BASICS

Italian has two words for 'you' – use the polite form *Lei* lay if you're talking to strangers, officials or people older than you. With people familiar to you or younger than you, you can use the informal form *tu* too.

In Italian, all nouns and adjectives are either masculine or feminine, and so are the articles *il/la* eel/la (the) and *un/una* oon/oo·na (a) that go with the nouns.

WANT MORE?

For in-depth language information and handy phrases, check out Lonely Planet's *Italian phrasebook*. You'll find it at **shop. lonelyplanet.com**, or you can buy Lonely Planet's iPhone phrasebooks at the Apple App Store.

In this chapter the polite/informal and masculine/feminine options are included where necessary, separated with a slash and indicated with 'pol/inf' and 'm/f'.

Hello.	Buongiorno.	bwon·jor·no
Goodbye.	Arrivederci.	a·ree·ve·der·chee
Yes./No.	Sì./No.	see/no
Excuse me.	Mi scusi. (pol)	mee skoo·zee
	Scusami. (inf)	skoo·za·mee
Sorry.	Mi dispiace.	mee dees·pya·che
Please.	Per favore.	per fa·vo·re
Thank you.	Grazie.	gra·tsye
You're welcome.	Prego.	pre·go

How are you?
Come sta/stai? (pol/inf)   ko·me sta/stai

Fine. And you?
Bene. E Lei/tu? (pol/inf)   be·ne e lay/too

What's your name?
Come si chiama? pol   ko·me see kya·ma
Come ti chiami? inf   ko·me tee kya·mee

My name is ...
Mi chiamo ...   mee kya·mo ...

Do you speak English?
Parla/Parli   par·la/par·lee
inglese? (pol/inf)   een·gle·ze

I don't understand.
Non capisco.   non ka·pee·sko

ACCOMMODATION

I'd like to book a room, please.
Vorrei prenotare una   vo·ray pre·no·ta·re oo·na
camera, per favore.   ka·me·ra per fa·vo·re

Is breakfast included?
La colazione è   la ko·la·tsyo·ne e
compresa?   kom·pre·sa

How much is it per ...?	Quanto costa per ...?	kwan·to kos·ta per ...
night	una notte	oo·na no·te
person	persona	per·so·na

KEY PATTERNS

To get by in Italian, mix and match these simple patterns with words of your choice:

When's (the next flight)?
A che ora è
(il prossimo volo)?
a ke o·ra e
(eel pro·see·mo vo·lo)

Where's (the station)?
Dov'è (la stazione)?
do·ve (la sta·tsyo·ne)

I'm looking for (a hotel).
Sto cercando
(un albergo).
sto cher·kan·do
(oon al·ber·go)

Do you have (a map)?
Ha (una pianta)?
a (oo·na pyan·ta)

Is there (a toilet)?
C'è (un gabinetto)?
che (oon ga·bee·ne·to)

I'd like (a coffee).
Vorrei (un caffè).
vo·ray (oon ka·fe)

I'd like to (hire a car).
Vorrei (noleggiare
una macchina).
vo·ray (no·le·ja·re
oo·na ma·kee·na)

Can I (enter)?
Posso (entrare)?
po·so (en·tra·re)

Could you please (help me)?
Può (aiutarmi),
per favore?
pwo (a·yoo·tar·mee)
per fa·vo·re

Do I have to (book a seat)?
Devo (prenotare
un posto)?
de·vo (pre·no·ta·re
oon po·sto)

air-con	aria condizionata	a·rya kon·dee·tsyo·na·ta
bathroom	bagno	ba·nyo
campsite	campeggio	kam·pe·jo
double room	camera doppia con letto matrimoniale	ka·me·ra do·pya kon le·to ma·tree·mo·nya·le
guesthouse	pensione	pen·syo·ne
hotel	albergo	al·ber·go
single room	camera singola	ka·me·ra seen·go·la
youth hostel	ostello della gioventù	os·te·lo de·la jo·ven·too
window	finestra	fee·nes·tra

DIRECTIONS

Where's ...?
Dov'è ...?
do·ve ...

What's the address?
Qual è l'indirizzo?
kwa·le leen·dee·ree·tso

Could you please write it down?
Può scriverlo,
per favore?
pwo skree·ver·lo
per fa·vo·re

Can you show me (on the map)?
Può mostrarmi
(sulla pianta)?
pwo mos·trar·mee
(soo·la pyan·ta)

at the corner	all'angolo	a·lan·go·lo
behind	dietro	dye·tro
far	lontano	lon·ta·no
in front of	davanti a	da·van·tee a
left	a sinistra	a see·nee·stra
near	vicino	vee·chee·no
next to	accanto a	a·kan·to a
opposite	di fronte a	dee fron·te a
right	a destra	a de·stra
straight ahead	sempre diritto	sem·pre dee·ree·to

EATING & DRINKING

I'd like to reserve a table.
Vorrei prenotare
un tavolo.
vo·ray pre·no·ta·re
oon ta·vo·lo

What would you recommend?
Cosa mi consiglia?
ko·za mee kon·see·lya

What's in that dish?
Quali ingredienti
ci sono in
questo piatto?
kwa·li een·gre·dyen·tee
chee so·no een
kwe·sto pya·to

What's the local speciality?
Qual'è la specialità
di questa regione?
kwa·le la spe·cha·lee·ta
dee kwe·sta re·jo·ne

That was delicious!
Era squisito!
e·ra skwee·zee·to

Cheers!
Salute!
sa·loo·te

Please bring the bill.
Mi porta il conto,
per favore?
mee por·ta eel kon·to
per fa·vo·re

I don't eat ...	Non mangio ...	non man·jo ...
eggs	uova	wo·va
fish	pesce	pe·she
nuts	noci	no·chee
(red) meat	carne (rossa)	kar·ne (ro·sa)

Key Words

bar	locale	lo·ka·le
bottle	bottiglia	bo·tee·lya
breakfast	prima colazione	pree·ma ko·la·tsyo·ne
cafe	bar	bar
cold	freddo	fre·do
dinner	cena	che·na

drink list	lista delle bevande	lee·sta de·le be·van·de
fork	forchetta	for·ke·ta
glass	bicchiere	bee·kye·re
grocery store	alimentari	a·lee·men·ta·ree
hot	caldo	kal·do
knife	coltello	kol·te·lo
lunch	pranzo	pran·dzo
market	mercato	mer·ka·to
menu	menù	me·noo
plate	piatto	pya·to
restaurant	ristorante	ree·sto·ran·te
spicy	piccante	pee·kan·te
spoon	cucchiaio	koo·kya·yo
vegetarian (food)	vegetariano	ve·je·ta·rya·no
with	con	kon
without	senza	sen·tsa

Meat & Fish

beef	manzo	man·dzo
chicken	pollo	po·lo
duck	anatra	a·na·tra
fish	pesce	pe·she
herring	aringa	a·reen·ga
lamb	agnello	a·nye·lo
lobster	aragosta	a·ra·gos·ta
meat	carne	kar·ne
mussels	cozze	ko·tse
oysters	ostriche	o·stree·ke
pork	maiale	ma·ya·le
prawn	gambero	gam·be·ro
salmon	salmone	sal·mo·ne
scallops	capasante	ka·pa·san·te
seafood	frutti di mare	froo·tee dee ma·re
shrimp	gambero	gam·be·ro
squid	calamari	ka·la·ma·ree
trout	trota	tro·ta
tuna	tonno	to·no
turkey	tacchino	ta·kee·no
veal	vitello	vee·te·lo

Fruit & Vegetables

| apple | mela | me·la |
| beans | fagioli | fa·jo·lee |

cabbage	cavolo	ka·vo·lo
capsicum	peperone	pe·pe·ro·ne
carrot	carota	ka·ro·ta
cauliflower	cavolfiore	ka·vol·fyo·re
cucumber	cetriolo	che·tree·o·lo
fruit	frutta	froo·ta
grapes	uva	oo·va
lemon	limone	lee·mo·ne
lentils	lenticchie	len·tee·kye
mushroom	funghi	foon·gee
nuts	noci	no·chee
onions	cipolle	chee·po·le
orange	arancia	a·ran·cha
peach	pesca	pe·ska
peas	piselli	pee·ze·lee
pineapple	ananas	a·na·nas
plum	prugna	proo·nya
potatoes	patate	pa·ta·te
spinach	spinaci	spee·na·chee
tomatoes	pomodori	po·mo·do·ree
vegetables	verdura	ver·doo·ra

Other

bread	pane	pa·ne
butter	burro	boo·ro
cheese	formaggio	for·ma·jo
eggs	uova	wo·va
honey	miele	mye·le
ice	ghiaccio	gya·cho
jam	marmellata	mar·me·la·ta
noodles	pasta	pas·ta
oil	olio	o·lyo
pepper	pepe	pe·pe
rice	riso	ree·zo
salt	sale	sa·le

Numbers

1	uno	oo·no
2	due	doo·e
3	tre	tre
4	quattro	kwa·tro
5	cinque	cheen·kwe
6	sei	say
7	sette	se·te
8	otto	o·to
9	nove	no·ve
10	dieci	dye·chee
20	venti	ven·tee
30	trenta	tren·ta
40	quaranta	kwa·ran·ta
50	cinquanta	cheen·kwan·ta
60	sessanta	se·san·ta
70	settanta	se·tan·ta
80	ottanta	o·tan·ta
90	novanta	no·van·ta
100	cento	chen·to
1000	mille	mee·le

soup	minestra	mee·nes·tra
soy sauce	salsa di soia	sal·sa dee so·ya
sugar	zucchero	tsoo·ke·ro
vinegar	aceto	a·che·to

Drinks

beer	birra	bee·ra
coffee	caffè	ka·fe
(orange) juice	succo (d'arancia)	soo·ko (da·ran·cha)
milk	latte	la·te
red wine	vino rosso	vee·no ro·so
soft drink	bibita	bee·bee·ta
tea	tè	te
(mineral) water	acqua (minerale)	a·kwa (mee·ne·ra·le)
white wine	vino bianco	vee·no byan·ko

EMERGENCIES

Help!
Aiuto! a·yoo·to

Leave me alone!
Lasciami in pace! la·sha·mee een pa·che

I'm lost.
Mi sono perso/a. (m/f) mee so·no per·so/a

Call the police!
Chiami la polizia! kya·mee la po·lee·tsee·a

Call a doctor!
Chiami un medico! kya·mee oon me·dee·ko

Where are the toilets?
Dove sono i gabinetti? do·ve so·no ee ga·bee·ne·tee

I'm sick.
Mi sento male. mee sen·to ma·le

SHOPPING & SERVICES

I'd like to buy ...
Vorrei comprare ... vo·ray kom·pra·re ...

I'm just looking.
Sto solo guardando. sto so·lo gwar·dan·do

Can I look at it?
Posso dare un'occhiata? po·so da·re oo·no·kya·ta

How much is this?
Quanto costa questo? kwan·to kos·ta kwe·sto

It's too expensive.
È troppo caro/a. (m/f) e tro·po ka·ro/a

Can you lower the price?
Può farmi lo sconto? pwo far·mee lo skon·to

There's a mistake in the bill.
C'è un errore nel conto. che oo·ne·ro·re nel kon·to

ATM	bancomat	ban·ko·mat
post office	ufficio postale	oo·fee·cho pos·ta·le
tourist office	ufficio del turismo	oo·fee·cho del too·reez·mo

TIME & DATES

What time is it?	Che ora è?	ke o·ra e
It's one o'clock.	È l'una.	e loo·na
It's (two) o'clock.	Sono le (due).	so·no le (doo·e)
Half past (one).	(L'una) e mezza.	(loo·na) e me·dza

in the morning	di mattina	dee ma·tee·na
in the afternoon	di pomeriggio	dee po·me·ree·jo
in the evening	di sera	dee se·ra

yesterday	ieri	ye·ree
today	oggi	o·jee
tomorrow	domani	do·ma·nee

Monday	lunedì	loo·ne·dee
Tuesday	martedì	mar·te·dee
Wednesday	mercoledì	mer·ko·le·dee
Thursday	giovedì	jo·ve·dee
Friday	venerdì	ve·ner·dee
Saturday	sabato	sa·ba·to

Sunday	domenica	do·me·nee·ka
January	gennaio	je·na·yo
February	febbraio	fe·bra·yo
March	marzo	mar·tso
April	aprile	a·pree·le
May	maggio	ma·jo
June	giugno	joo·nyo
July	luglio	loo·lyo
August	agosto	a·gos·to
September	settembre	se·tem·bre
October	ottobre	o·to·bre
November	novembre	no·vem·bre
December	dicembre	dee·chem·bre

TRANSPORT

At what time does the ... leave/arrive?	A che ora parte/ arriva ...?	a ke o·ra par·te/ a·ree·va ...
boat	la nave	la na·ve
bus	l'autobus	low·to·boos
city ferry	il vaporetto	eel va·po·re·to
ferry	il traghetto	eel tra·ge·to
plane	l'aereo	la·e·re·o
train	il treno	eel tre·no

bus stop	fermata dell'autobus	fer·ma·ta del ow·to·boos
one-way	di sola andata	dee so·la an·da·ta
platform	binario	bee·na·ryo
return	di andata e ritorno	dee an·da·ta e ree·tor·no
ticket	biglietto	bee·lye·to
ticket office	biglietteria	bee·lye·te·ree·a
timetable	orario	o·ra·ryo
train station	stazione ferroviaria	sta·tsyo·ne fe·ro·vyar·ya

Does it stop at ...?
Si ferma a ...?   see fer·ma a ...

Please tell me when we get to ...
Mi dica per favore   mee dee·ka per fa·vo·re
quando arriviamo a ...   kwan·do a·ree·vya·mo a ...

I want to get off here.
Voglio scendere qui.   vo·lyo shen·de·re kwee

I'd like	Vorrei	vo·ray
to hire	noleggiare	no·le·ja·re
a/an ...	un/una ... (m/f)	oon/oo·na ...

bicycle	bicicletta (f)	bee·chee·kle·ta
car	macchina (f)	ma·kee·na
motorbike	moto (f)	mo·to
bicycle pump	pompa della bicicletta	pom·pa de·la bee·chee·kle·ta
helmet	casco	kas·ko
mechanic	meccanico	me·ka·nee·ko
petrol/gas	benzina	ben·dzee·na
service station	stazione di servizio	sta·tsyo·ne dee ser·vee·tsyo

Is this the road to ...?
Questa strada porta a ...? kwe·sta stra·da por·ta a ...

(How long) Can I park here?
(Per quanto tempo)   (per kwan·to tem·po)
Posso parcheggiare qui? po·so par·ke·ja·re kwee

I have a flat tyre.
Ho una gomma bucata. o oo·na go·ma boo·ka·ta

I've run out of petrol.
Ho esaurito la   o e·zow·ree·to la
benzina.   ben·dzee·na

VENETIAN BASICS

A few choice words in Venetian (or Venet, as it is also known) will endear you to your hosts, especially at happy hour. To keep up with the *bacaro* banter, try mixing them with your Italian:

Yes, sir!	Siorsi!
Oh, no!	Simènteve!
You bet!	Figuràrse!
How lucky!	Bénpo!
Perfect.	In bròca.
Welcome!	Benvegnù!
Cheers!	Sanacapàna!
Watch out!	Òcio!

cheap wine	brunbrùn
glass of wine	ombra (lit: a shade)
happy hour	giro di ombra (lit: round of shade)
to become Venetian	Venexianàrse
Venetian	venexiano/a (m/f)
you guys	voàltri

FOOD GLOSSARY

alla busara Venetian prawn sauce

anatra wild lagoon duck

baccala mantecato creamed cod

bigoli Venetian whole-wheat pasta

branzino sea bass

bruscandoli wild hop buds

canoce mantis prawn

capasanta/canastrelo large/small scallops

carpaccio finely sliced raw beef

castraure baby artichokes from St Erasmo Island

cicheti Venetian tapas

contorni vegetable dishes

crostini open-faced sandwiches

crudi Venetian sushi

curasan croissant

dolci sweets

dolci tipici venexiani typical Venetian sweets

fatto in casa house-made

fegato alla veneziana liver lightly pan-roasted in strips with browned onion and a splash of red wine

filetto di San Pietro fish with artichokes or *radicchio trevisano*

fritole sweet fritters

fritto misto e pattatine lightly fried lagoon seafood and potatoes

frittura seafood fry

gnochetti mini-gnocchi

granseola spider crab

krapfen doughnuts

latte di soia soy milk

lingue di suocere biscuit; 'mother-in-law's tongues'

macchiatone espresso liberally 'stained' with milk

margherite ripiene all'astice com sugo di pesce ravioli stuffed with lobster in fish sauce

moeche soft-shell crabs

moscardini baby octopus

mozzarella di bufala fresh buffalo-milk mozzarella

orechiette 'little ear' pasta

pan dei dogi 'doges' bread'; hazelnut-studded biscuits

panino sandwich

pastine pastry

peoci mussels

pizza margherita pizza with basil, mozzarella and tomato

pizzette mini-pizzas

polpette meatballs

radicchio trevisano feathery red radicchio

risotto di pesce fish risotto

saor Venice's tangy marinade

sarde sardines

sarde in saor sardines fried in tangy onion marinade with pine nuts and sultanas

senza limone without lemon

seppie squid

seppie in nero squid in its own ink

sfogio sole

sopressa Venetian soft salami

sopressa crostini soft salami on toast

sorbetto sorbet

spaghetti alla búsera spaghetti with shrimp sauce

surgelati frozen

tramezzini sandwiches on soft bread often with mayo-based condiments

verdure vegetables

zaletti cornmeal biscuits with sultanas

zuppa di pesce thick seafood soup

Behind the Scenes

SEND US YOUR FEEDBACK

We love to hear from travellers – your comments keep us on our toes and help make our books better. Our well-travelled team reads every word on what you loved or loathed about this book. Although we cannot reply individually to your submissions, we always guarantee that your feedback goes straight to the appropriate authors, in time for the next edition. Each person who sends us information is thanked in the next edition – the most useful submissions are rewarded with a selection of digital PDF chapters.

Visit **lonelyplanet.com/contact** to submit your updates and suggestions or to ask for help. Our award-winning website also features inspirational travel stories, news and discussions.

Note: We may edit, reproduce and incorporate your comments in Lonely Planet products such as guidebooks, websites and digital products, so let us know if you don't want your comments reproduced or your name acknowledged. For a copy of our privacy policy visit lonelyplanet.com/privacy.

WRITER THANKS

Peter Dragicevich

I still pinch myself that my work continues to allow me to spend time in such a magical city, and for that I have editor extraordinaire Anna Tyler to thank. Many thanks to Lonely Planet Local Jo-Ann Titmarsh for your good company and excellent advice on this assignment, and for the wealth of new listings that you had already uncovered. My eternal gratitude goes to my dear friend Bain Duigan, who accompanied me in spirit at least.

Paula Hardy

Mille grazie to all the creative and passionate people who shared their insights with me. In Venice: Luisella Romeo, Gioele and Heiby Romanelli, Emanuele dal Carlo, Valeria Duflot, Sebastian Fagarazzi, Fabio Carrera, Jo-Ann Titmarsh, Alice Braveri and Anat at the Comunità Ebraica di Venezia. And, thank you, Rob for sharing my love of the *bel paese*.

ACKNOWLEDGMENTS

Cover photograph: Gondola on the Rio dei Bareteri, David Erbetta/4Corners Images ©

Illustration pp60-61 by Javier Zarracina.

THIS BOOK

This 11th edition of Lonely Planet's *Venice & the Veneto* guidebook was researched and written by Peter Dragicevich and Paula Hardy. The 10th edition was written by Paula Hardy, Peter Dragicevich and Marc Di Duca, and the 9th edition by Cristian Bonetto and Paula Hardy.

This guidebook was produced by the following:

Destination Editor Anna Tyler

Senior Product Editor Elizabeth Jones

Regional Senior Cartographer Anthony Phelan

Product Editor Bruce Evans

Book Designers Brooke Giacomin, Jessica Rose

Assisting Editors Victoria Harrison, Helen Koehne, Jodie Martire, Charlotte Orr, Susan Paterson, Gabrielle Stefanos, Simon Williamson

Cartographer Hunor Csutoros

Cover Researcher Naomi Parker

Thanks to Alexandra Bruzzese, Gemma Graham, Martin Heng, Joe Revill, Sophia Seymour, Jo-Ann Titmarsh, Brana Vladisavljevic

Index

✖ EATING

Sights 000
Map Pages **000**
Photo Pages **000**

Venice Maps

Sights
- Beach
- Bird Sanctuary
- Buddhist
- Castle/Palace
- Christian
- Confucian
- Hindu
- Islamic
- Jain
- Jewish
- Monument
- Museum/Gallery/Historic Building
- Ruin
- Shinto
- Sikh
- Taoist
- Winery/Vineyard
- Zoo/Wildlife Sanctuary
- Other Sight

Activities, Courses & Tours
- Bodysurfing
- Diving
- Canoeing/Kayaking
- Course/Tour
- Sento Hot Baths/Onsen
- Skiing
- Snorkelling
- Surfing
- Swimming/Pool
- Walking
- Windsurfing
- Other Activity

Sleeping
- Sleeping
- Camping
- Hut/Shelter

Eating
- Eating

Drinking & Nightlife
- Drinking & Nightlife
- Cafe

Entertainment
- Entertainment

Shopping
- Shopping

Information
- Bank
- Embassy/Consulate
- Hospital/Medical
- Internet
- Police
- Post Office
- Telephone
- Toilet
- Tourist Information
- Other Information

Geographic
- Beach
- Gate
- Hut/Shelter
- Lighthouse
- Lookout
- Mountain/Volcano
- Oasis
- Park
- Pass
- Picnic Area
- Waterfall

Population
- Capital (National)
- Capital (State/Province)
- City/Large Town
- Town/Village

Transport
- Airport
- Border crossing
- Bus
- Cable car/Funicular
- Cycling
- Ferry
- Metro station
- Monorail
- Parking
- Petrol station
- S-Bahn/Subway station
- Taxi
- T-bane/Tunnelbana station
- Train station/Railway
- Tram
- U-Bahn/Underground station
- Other Transport

Routes
- Tollway
- Freeway
- Primary
- Secondary
- Tertiary
- Lane
- Unsealed road
- Road under construction
- Plaza/Mall
- Steps
- Tunnel
- Pedestrian overpass
- Walking Tour
- Walking Tour detour
- Path/Walking Trail

Boundaries
- International
- State/Province
- Disputed
- Regional/Suburb
- Marine Park
- Cliff
- Wall

Hydrography
- River, Creek
- Intermittent River
- Canal
- Water
- Dry/Salt/Intermittent Lake
- Reef

Areas
- Airport/Runway
- Beach/Desert
- Cemetery (Christian)
- Cemetery (Other)
- Glacier
- Mudflat
- Park/Forest
- Sight (Building)
- Sportsground
- Swamp/Mangrove

Note: Not all symbols displayed above appear on the maps in this book

MAP INDEX

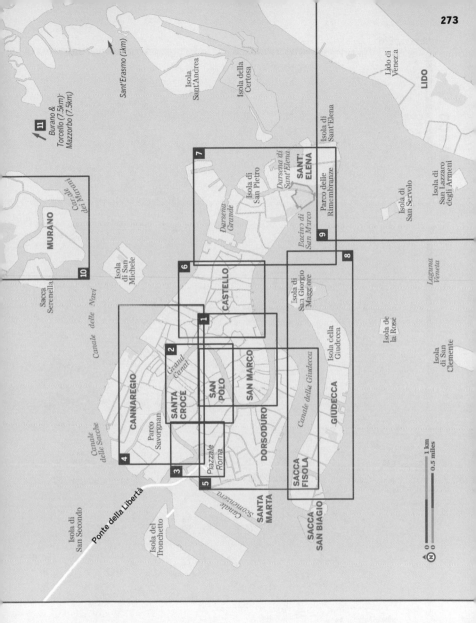

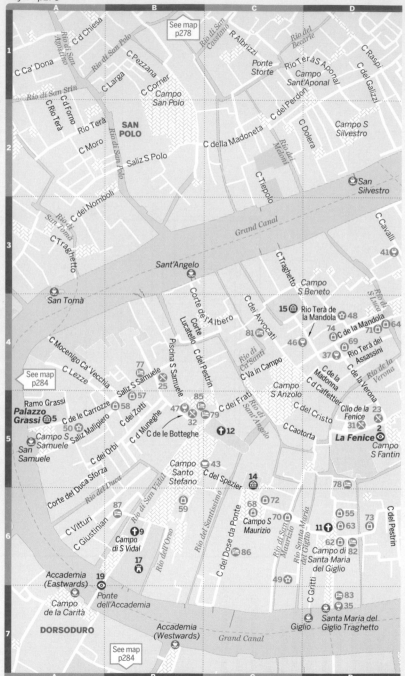

SAN MARCO

0   200 m
0   0.1 miles

See map p288

RIALTO

Campo San Giacomo di Rialto

Ruga dei Oresi

C de la Madonna

Ponte di Rialto

60

34

Corte del Tentor

33

C del Sturion

Riva del Vin

45

Rialto

Campo San Bartolomeo

29

30

C de la Bissa

Riva del Carbon

C Larga Mazzini

Via 2 Aprile

C Galeazza

C dei Stagneri

C del Carbon

C Bembo

56

Campo San Salvador

C del Lovo

8

Marzaria

C di Mezzo

67

Rio di S Lio

C Scaletta

Rio del Piombo

C de la Malvasia

Campo Santa Marina

C Pindemonte

C Carminati

CASTELLO

Campo San Lio

C d Vele

C d Nave

C d Volto

Fond dei Preti

C Saliz San Lio

C Mondo Novo

C d Fava

C de la Malvasia

Campo della Fava

Rio della Fava

C Sant'Antonio

Corte del Teatro

51

65

Piscina San Zulian

C Balbi

Campo della Guerra

C de la Guerra

C d Bande

See map p288

C Casseleria

C Loredan

36

Campo San Luca

C del Fabbri

C del Magazen

C d Monti

C d Balote

Ponte dei Baratteri

Marzaria S Zulian

76

Campo Manin

54

52

Goldoni

C d Gambaro

Rio dei Ferali

10

C dei Spechier

Ponte del Rimedio

C de le Locande

22

C dei Fuseri

C Ungheria

53

20

Rio Fuseri

24

C d Preti

80

28

88

61

Marzaria de l'Orologo

C Spadaria

C Larga San Marco

C di Canonica

SAN MARCO

Rio Tera de le Colonne

C S Gallo

C d Fabbri

C Fiubera

Corte Zorzi

Campo S Gallo

Rio Orseolo

Rio del Procurate

C del Cappello

21

40

27

Piazzetta dei Leoni

Ponte Capello

Basilica di San Marco

1

C del Frutarol

C del Bacareto

Frezzaria

C Venier

C Zorzi

C Frezzaria

Piscina di Frezzaria

Bacino Orseolo

16

Piazza San Marco

6

18

75

38

C del Carro

26

3

Museo Correr

39

Piazzetta San Marco

4

Palazzo Ducale

Ramo J Cte Contarina

Campo di San Moisè

66

7

C Larga de l'Ascension

C Vallaresso

Rio dei Giardinetti

Column of St Theodore

Lion of St Mark Column

C Veste

C del Cristo

C Larga XXII Marzo

C del Squero

Giardini Ex Reali

84

C Pedrochi

C del Traghetto

Corte Barozzi

13

C dei 13 Martiri

C Ridotto

42

44

San Marco Giardinetti

San Zaccaria (100m)

Salute

San Marco Vallaresso

Bacino di San Marco

Traghetto (Limited Hours)

Fond Dogana alla Salute

SAN MARCO *Map on p274*

SAN MARCO

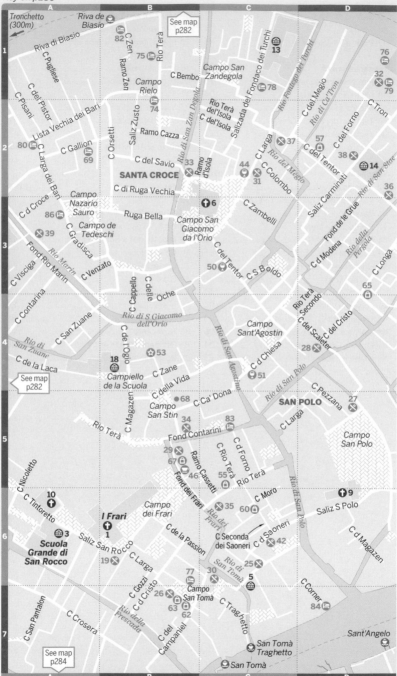

SAN POLO & SANTA CROCE

See map p282

See map p282

See map p284

Tronchetto (300m)

Riva de Biasio

Riva di Biasio

C Pugliese

C Pisani

C del Pistor

Lista Vechia dei Bari

80

C Larga dei Bari

C Gallion

69

C Orsetti

C Zen

Ramo Zen

82

75

Rio Terà

C Bembo

Campo San Zandegola

Campo Rielo

74

Saliz Zusto

Ramo Cazza

C del Savio

33

Ramo d'Isola

SANTA CROCE

C di Ruga Vechia

Rio Terà del'Isola

C del'Isola

Salizada del Fondaco dei Turchi

13

78

Campo Nazario Sauro

86

Ruga Bella

Campo San Giacomo da l'Orio

6

C d Croce

39

Campo de Tedeschi

C Gradisca

C Venzato

Fond Rio Marin

Rio Marin

C Visciga

C Contarina

C Contarina

C San Zuane

C Cappello

C delle Oche

Rio di S. Giacomo dell'Orio

50

C del Tentor

C S Boldo

C Zambelli

C d Modena

Fond de le Grue

Saliz Carminati

Rio della Pergola

C Longa

65

Rio di San Zuane

C de la Laca

C de l'Ogio

18

53

Campiello de la Scuola

C Magazen

C Zane

C della Vida

68

Campo Sant'Agostin

Rio di San Agostin

C d Chiesa

51

Rio Terà Secondo

C del Scaleter

C del Cristo

28

Rio di San Polo

SAN POLO

C Pezzana

27

Campo San Stin

34

83

Fond Contarini

Ramo Cassetti

Fond dei Frari

29

67

46

55

C Rio Terà

C d Forno

Rio Terà

C Larga

Rio Terà

Campo San Polo

C Nicoletto

C Tintoretto

10

3

Scuola Grande di San Rocco

Saliz San Rocco

I Frari

1

Campo dei Frari

C de la Passion

35

60

C Moro

C Seconda dei Saoneri

C d Saoneri

42

9

Saliz S Polo

C d Magazen

19

C Larga

77

30

25

Rio di San Tomà

5

C San Pantalon

C Gozzi

C d Cristo

26

63

62

Campo San Tomà

C del Campaniel

C Trag hetto

C Corner

84

San Tomà Traghetto

Sant'Angelo

C Crosera

Rio della Pescaria

San Tomà

76

32

79

C del Megio

C del Forno

C del Tenter

57

38

14

C Tron

C d Cà Tron

Rio del Megio

C Larga

37

C Colombo

44

31

36

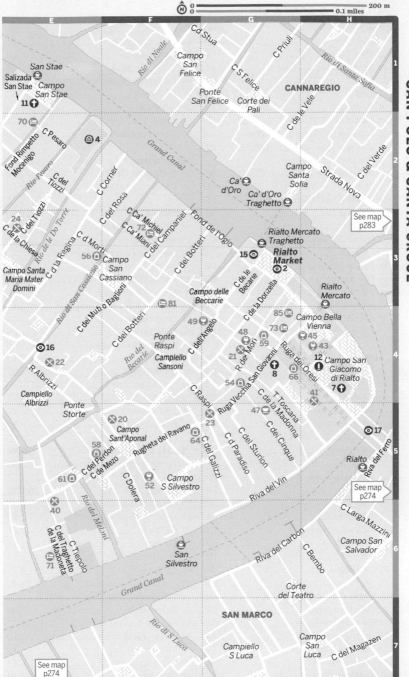

N 0 — 200 m
0 — 0.1 miles

Cd Stua
Campo San Felice
C S Felice
C Priuli
Rio di Santa Sofia
CANNAREGIO
San Stae
Salizada San Stae
Campo San Stae
11
70
C Pesaro
Fond Rimpetto Mocenigo
4
Rio di Node
Grand Canal
Ponte San Felice
Corte dei Pali
C de le Vele
C del Verde
Strada Nova
Campo Santa Sofia
Ca' d'Oro
Ca' d'Oro Traghetto
Rio Pesaro
C del Tiozzi
C Corner
C del Rosa
C Ca' Michiel
72
C Ca' Miani
C del Campaniel
Fond de l'Ogio
C dei Botteri
15
Rialto Mercato Traghetto
Rialto Market
2
24
C del Tiozzi
C de la Chiesa
C d la Regina
C de le Do Torre
C d Morti
56
Campo San Cassiano
Campo Santa Maria Mater Domini
Rio di San Cassiano
C dei Muti o Baglioni
C dei Botteri
81
Campo delle Beccarie
C de le Beccarie
C de la Donzella
Rialto Mercato
85
Campo Bella Vienna
49
C dell'Angelo
48
73
45
16
22
R Albrizzi
Rio del Beccarie
Ponte Raspi
Campiello Sansoni
21
R de Mori
59
43
12
Campo San Giacomo di Rialto
7
Campiello Albrizzi
Ponte Storte
C Raspi
54
8
66
Ruga dei Oresi
41
20
Campo Sant'Aponal
23
Ruga Vecchia San Giovanni
C de la Madona
47
T Toscana
17
58
Rugheta del Ravano
64
C del Galizzi
C d del Sturion
C dei Cinque
Rialto
Riva del Ferro
61
C del Perdon
C de Mezo
52
Campo S Silvestro
Riva del Vin
40
C Dolera
San Silvestro
Riva del Carbon
C Bembo
Campo San Salvador
71
C del Traghetto de la Madoneta
C del Tiepolo
Grand Canal
Corte del Teatro
Rio dei Meloni
Rio di S Luca
SAN MARCO
Campiello S Luca
Campo San Luca
C del Magazen

See map p283

See map p274

See map p274

SAN POLO & SANTA CROCE *Map on p278*

SAN POLO & SANTA CROCE

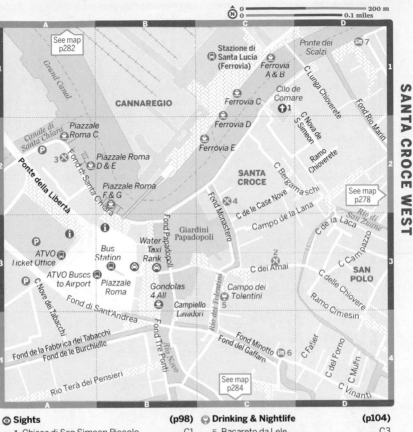

Sights (p98)
1 Chiesa di San Simeon Piccolo................C1

Eating (p101)
2 Al Bacco Felice...C3
3 Coop..A2
4 Zanze XVI..C2

Drinking & Nightlife (p104)
5 Bacareto da Lele......................................C3

Sleeping (p197)
6 Hotel Al Sole...C4
7 Hotel Canal Grande..................................D1

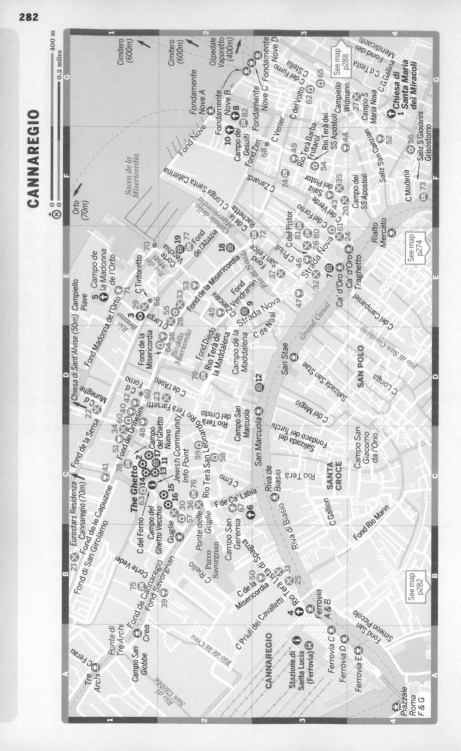

CANNAREGIO

CANNAREGIO

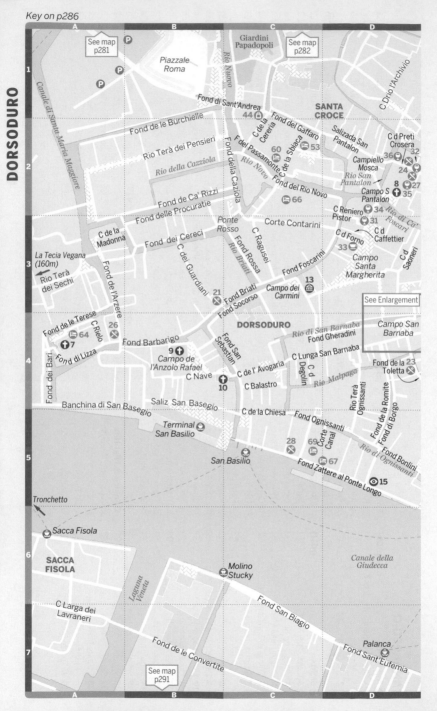

Key on p286

DORSODURO

See map p281

Piazzale Roma

Giardini Papadopoli

See map p282

SANTA CROCE

Fond di Sant'Andrea

Fond de le Burchielle

Rio Terà dei Pensieri

Rio della Cazziola

Fond della Caziola

Rio Novo

Fond del Gaffaro

C de la Cereria

F del Passamonte

C de la Sbiaca

Fond del Rio Novo

Salizada San Pantalon

C Drio l'Archivio

C d Preti Crosera

Campiello Mosca

Rio San Pantalon

Campo S Pantalon

Rio di Ca' Foscari

Fond de Ca' Rizzi

Fond delle Procuratie

C de la Madonna

Fond dei Cereci

Ponte Rosso

Corte Contarini

C Reniero Pistor

C d Forno

C d Caffettier

C d Saoneri

La Tecia Vegana (160m)

Rio Terà dei Sechi

Fond de l'Arzere

C del Guardiani

Rio Briati

Rio Rossa

C Ragusei

Fond Foscarini

Campo Santa Margherita

See Enlargement

Campo San Barnaba

Fond Briati

Fond Socorso

Campo dei Carmini

DORSODURO

Fond de le Terese

C Rielo

Fond Barbarigo

Fond San Sebastian

Rio di San Barnaba

Fond Gheradini

C Lunga San Barnaba

Fond de la Toletta

Fond dei Bari

Fond di Lizza

Campo de l'Anzolo Rafael

C Nave

C de l' Avogaria

C Balastro

C d Degolin

Rio Malpaga

Rio Terà Ognissanti

Fond de la Romite

Fond di Borgo

Banchina di San Basegio

Saliz San Basegio

C de la Chiesa

Fond Ognissanti

Terminal San Basilio

San Basilio

Corte Canal

Fond Zattere al Ponte Longo

Rio di Ognissanti

Fond Bonlini

Tronchetto

Sacca Fisola

SACCA FISOLA

C Larga dei Lavraneri

Laguna Veneta

Molino Stucky

Canale della Giudecca

Fond San Biagio

Fond de le Convertite

Palanca

Fond Sant'Eufemia

See map p291

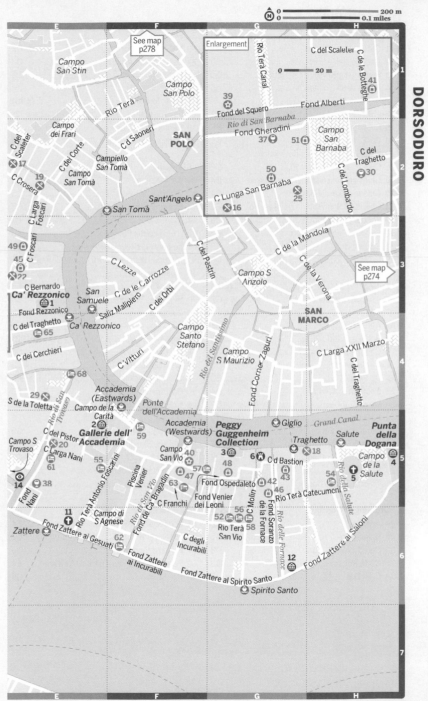

DORSODURO

N
0 — 200 m
0 — 0.1 miles

Campo San Stin

See map p278

Campo San Polo

Enlargement

Rio Terà Canal

C del Scaleter

C de le Botteghe

41

0 — 20 m

39

Fond del Squero

Fond Alberti

Rio Terà

Campo dei Frari

Rio di San Barnaba

Fond Gheradini

37 51

Campo San Barnaba

C del Traghetto

SAN POLO

C d Saoneri

C del Scaleter

C del Corte

Campiello San Tomà

Campo San Tomà

50

C Lunga San Barnaba

25

C del Lombardo

30

C Larga Foscari

19

17

C Crosera

San Tomà

Sant'Angelo

16

49

45

22

C Foscari

C Bernardo

C Lezze

C de la Carrozze

C del Pestrin

C de la Mandola

C de la Verona

See map p274

Ca' Rezzonico

1

Fond Rezzonico

San Samuele

C del Orbi

Campo S Anzolo

SAN MARCO

C del Traghetto

65

Ca' Rezzonico

Saliz Malipiero

Campo Santo Stefano

Rio del Santissimo

C Larga XXII Marzo

C dei Cerchieri

C Vitturi

Campo S Maurizio

Campo S Maurizio

Fond Corner Zaguri

C del Traghetto

68

Accademia (Eastwards)

29

S de la Toletta

Campo de la Carità

Ponte dell'Accademia

Accademia (Westwards)

Peggy Guggenheim Collection

Giglio

Grand Canal

Punta della Dogana

2

Gallerie dell' Accademia

59

3

6

C d Bastion

Traghetto

Salute

Campo S Trovaso

C del Pistor

20

Campo San Vio

40

57

47

48

18

54

Campo de la Salute

5

14

38

61

55

Piscina Venier

63

Fond Ospedaleto

42

43

46

5

Fond Nani

11

Campo di S Agnese

Fond Venier dei Leoni

C Molin

52

56

C degli Incurabili

Zattere

62

Fond Zattere ai Gesuati

Rio Terà San Vio

58

Rio Terà Catecumeni

Rio delle Fornace

Fond Zattere ai Saloni

Fond Zattere ai Incurabili

Fond Zattere al Spirito Santo

12

Fond Zattere al Saloni

Spirito Santo

CASTELLO *Map on p288*

CASTELLO

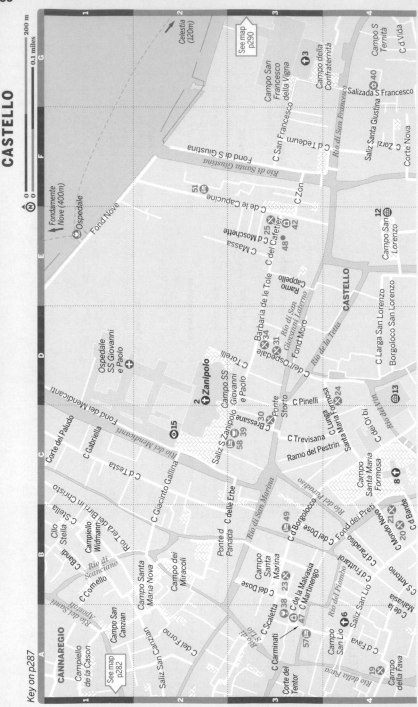

CANNAREGIO

CASTELLO

See map p290

See map p282

Celestia (120m)

Fondamente Nove (400m)

Campo S Ternità

C d Vida

Campo della Confraternita

Salizada S Francesco

Campo San Francesco della Vigna

Salizada S Giustina

Corte Nova

C Zorzi

C San Tedeum

C d Tedeum

Rio di San Francesco

Rio di Santa Giustina

Fond di S Giustina

C Zon

C de le Capucine

C Massa

C d Moschette

C del Cafetier

Ramo Cappello

Campo San Lorenzo

C Larga San Lorenzo

Borgoloco San Lorenzo

Barbaria de le Tole

Rio di San Giovanni Laterano

Fond Moro

C dell'Ospedale

Rio de la Tetta

C Pinelli

C dell'Ospedale

C Torelli

Ospedale SS Giovanni e Paolo

Campo SS Giovanni e Paolo

Ponte Storto

Bressana

Saliz S Zanipolo

Fond dei Mendicanti

Rio dei Mendicanti

Corte del Paludo

C Gabriella

C d Testa

Rio Tera del Birri in Cristo

C Stella

Cllo Stella

C Bandi

Campiello Widmann

Campo Santa Maria Nova

C Giacinto Gallina

C Cornello

Rio dei Santi Apostoli

Campiello de la Cason

Campo San Canzian

Saliz San Canzian

Campo dei Miracoli

C del Forno

Ponte d Paniada

C delle Erbe

Rio di San Marina

C Martinengo

Campo Santa Marina

C del Dose

C Scaletta

C de la Malvasia

C Carminati

Corte del Tentor

Rio di S Lio

Ramo del Pestrin

C Trevisana

C Lunga Santa Maria Formosa

Salizada Santa Maria Formosa

C del ORbi

Rio dell'Anzolo

Campo Santa Maria Formosa

Fond dei Preti

C del Paradiso

C d Frutariol

Rio del Piombo

C de la Malvasia

S Antonio

C Mondo Novo

C d Bande

Saliz San Lio

C d Fava

Campo San Lio

Rio del Fava

Campo della Fava

Rio del Piovan

Celestia

G 1 2 3 4
F
E
D
C
B
A

Points (numbered markers on map):
- 3
- 40
- 15
- 2 Zanipolo
- 12
- 13
- 51
- 25
- 48
- 42
- 34
- 31
- 24
- 30
- 58 39
- 8
- 49
- 21
- 20
- 38 23
- 47
- 6
- 57
- 19

200 m
0.1 miles

N

CASTELLO

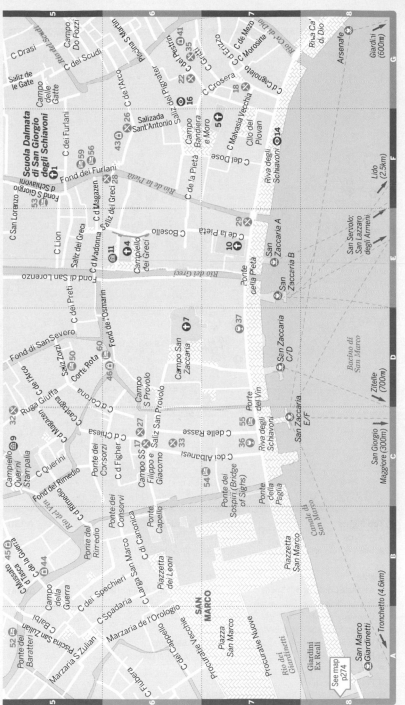

Scuola Dalmata di San Giorgio degli Schiavoni 1

Riva Ca' di Dio

Arsenale

Giardini (600m)

G

Lido (2.5km)

San Servolo; San Lazzaro degli Armeni

F

Riva degli Schiavoni

San Zaccaria A

San Zaccaria B

San Zaccaria

Zitelle (700m)

Bacino di San Marco

E

Campo San Zaccaria

San Zaccaria C/D

San Giorgio Maggiore (300m)

D

Canale di San Marco

Riva degli Schiavoni

San Zaccaria E/F

C

Ponte dei Sospiri (Bridge of Sighs)

Ponte della Paglia

Piazzetta San Marco

Tronchetto (4.6km)

B

Piazza San Marco

SAN MARCO

Procuratie Vecchie

Procuratie Nuove

Giardini Ex Reali

Rio dei Giardinetti

San Marco Giardinetti

See map p274

A

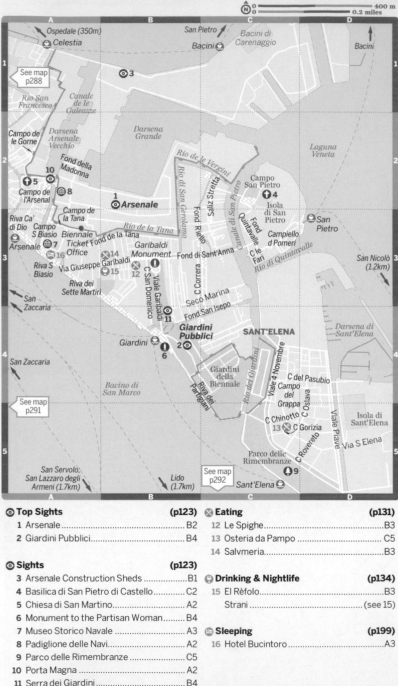

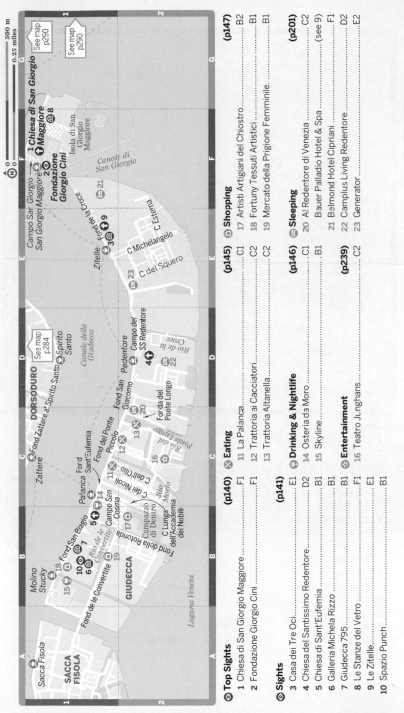

GIUDECCA

◎ **Top Sights** (p140)
1 Chiesa di San Giorgio Maggiore F1
2 Fondazione Giorgio Cini F1

◎ **Sights** (p141)
3 Casa dei Tre Oci E1
4 Chiesa del Santissimo Redentore D2
5 Chiesa di Sant'Eufemia B1
6 Galleria Michela Rizzo B1
7 Giudecca 795 .... B1
8 Le Stanze del Vetro F1
9 Le Zitelle E1
10 Spazio Punch B1

⊗ **Eating** (p145)
11 La Palanca C1
12 Trattoria ai Cacciatori C2
13 Trattoria Altanella C2

◉ **Drinking & Nightlife** (p146)
14 Osteria da Moro C1
15 Skyline B1

✪ **Entertainment** (p239)
16 Teatro Junghans C2

⊜ **Shopping** (p147)
17 Artisti Artigiani del Chiostro B2
18 Fortuny Tessuti Artistici B1
19 Mercato della Prigione Femminile B1

◉ **Sleeping** (p201)
20 Al Redentore di Venezia C2
  Bauer Palladio Hotel & Spa .... (see 9)
21 Belmond Hotel Cipriani F1
22 Camplus Living Redentore D2
23 Generator E2

LIDO VENEZIA

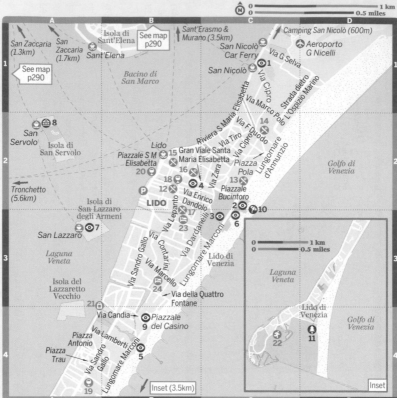

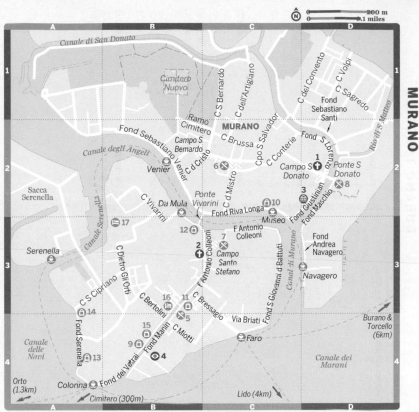

BURANO TORCELLO

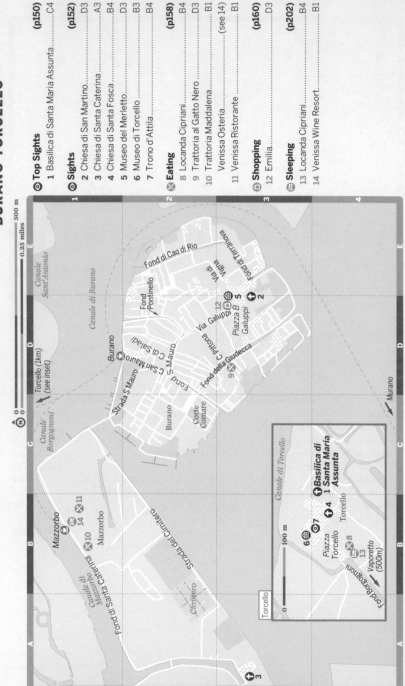

Our Story

A beat-up old car, a few dollars in the pocket and a sense of adventure. In 1972 that's all Tony and Maureen Wheeler needed for the trip of a lifetime – across Europe and Asia overland to Australia. It took several months, and at the end – broke but inspired – they sat at their kitchen table writing and stapling together their first travel guide, *Across Asia on the Cheap*. Within a week they'd sold 1500 copies. Lonely Planet was born.

Today, Lonely Planet has offices in Franklin, London, Melbourne, Oakland, Dublin, Beijing and Delhi, with more than 600 staff and writers. We share Tony's belief that 'a great guidebook should do three things: inform, educate and amuse'.

Our Writers

Peter Dragicevich
Dorsoduro; San Polo & Santa Croce; Giudecca, Lido & the Southern Islands; Murano, Burano & the Northern Islands

After a successful career in niche newspaper and magazine publishing, both in his native New Zealand and in Australia, Peter finally gave into Kiwi wanderlust, giving up staff jobs to chase his diverse roots around much of Europe. Over the last decade he's written dozens of guidebooks for Lonely Planet on an oddly disparate collection of countries, all of which he's come to love. He once again calls Auckland, New Zealand, his home – although his current nomadic existence means he's often elsewhere. Peter also wrote the History, Architecture and The Arts chapters.

Paula Hardy
San Marco; Castello; Cannaregio; Day Trips

Paula Hardy is an independent travel writer and editorial consultant, whose work for Lonely Planet and other flagship publications has taken her from nomadic camps in the Danakil Depression to Seychellois beach huts and the jewel-like bar at the Gritti Palace on the Grand Canal. Over two decades, she has authored more than 30 Lonely Planet guidebooks and spent five years as commissioning editor of Lonely Planet's bestselling Italian list. These days you'll find her hunting down new hotels, hip bars and up-and-coming artisans primarily in Milan, Venice and Marrakesh. Get in touch at www.paulahardy.com. Paula also wrote the Venice Today and The Fragile Lagoon chapters, as well as the Plan Your Trip and Survival Guide sections.

Published by Lonely Planet Global Limited
CRN 554153
11th edition – January 2020
ISBN 978 1 78701 414 5
© Lonely Planet 2020   Photographs © as indicated 2020
10 9 8 7 6 5 4 3 2 1
Printed in China